SPEECHES, CORRESPONDENCE
AND POLITICAL PAPERS OF

CARL SCHURZ

IN SIX VOLUMES

I am very truly yours

C. Schurz

SPEECHES, CORRESPONDENCE
AND POLITICAL PAPERS OF

CARL SCHURZ

SELECTED AND EDITED BY

FREDERIC BANCROFT

ON BEHALF OF
THE CARL SCHURZ MEMORIAL COMMITTEE

VOLUME I.
OCTOBER 20, 1852–NOVEMBER 26, 1870

G. P. PUTNAM'S SONS
NEW YORK   LONDON
The Knickerbocker Press
1913

17031

Jan.'39 Gift. O. G. Villard.

The Knickerbocker Press, New York

INTRODUCTION

Soon after its formation in 1906, the Carl Schurz Memorial Committee agreed that it could perform no greater service than to collect and publish the writings and public addresses of Mr. Schurz. That he, above all others, personified that extraordinary stream of German immigration which enriched the United States in the years immediately following the revolution of 1848, has been universally recognized. That he was an able, albeit modest general, a diplomat and statesman, a wise journalistic commentator upon political affairs and a public man whose utterances were of far-reaching importance in many a campaign, has also been widely appreciated. Few can, however, have had any true conception of the remarkable range of his interests, as evidenced by his correspondence, or of the extent and value of his public addresses. They form a vital contribution to the history of Carl Schurz's adopted country, beginning almost with the day upon which he set foot upon its shores. They are the more remarkable when it is considered how brief was the period in which Mr. Schurz—with the exception of Hamilton and Gallatin the greatest of the foreign-born statesmen of the country—actually held office. But Mr. Schurz needed no passing official authority to assure himself an audience or to lend vigor and weight to his utterances. Based on sound political principle and on unyielding loyalty to American institutions, his works must be his truest monument. They cannot fail to be of high value to all who would meet the political problems of the future by a study of the utterances of the past of those public men of unshaken courage, who knew no such thing as compromise on a principle, who never lost faith in American self-government; and particularly of one whose belief in liberty and democracy was as fresh and as ardent in his last years as in his youth when he risked his life to battle with absolutism.   It is to the memory of this faith and this courage, and in gratitude for a lifetime of unselfish and patriotic service, that these volumes are dedicated.

THE CARL SCHURZ MEMORIAL COMMITTEE.

By GEORGE McANENY,
     WILLIAM R. CORWINE,
     OSWALD GARRISON VILLARD, *Chairman*,
          the Sub-Committee on Publication.

EDITOR'S PREFACE

It is rare that a life so picturesque and varied as Carl Schurz's can be so fully traced in its own records. He carefully prepared everything that he said or wrote, if for publication, and he usually preserved a copy or the draft. It was also his habit to save the letters he received. At all periods of his life in America some member of his family —Mrs. Schurz for nearly a quarter of a century—supplemented and arranged the collections. This material forms more than the basis of the now extensive and important Schurz papers.

Of his personal letters Mr. Schurz rarely kept copies, unless they touched some public or private question of special importance. Thanks to the all but invariable kindness and generosity of his surviving friends or their heirs, copies of many hundreds of his private letters have been made and preserved. A volume containing twelve of the best of his early speeches, 1858–64, was published by Lippincott in 1865; but it has long been out of print and is hard to find except in the largest libraries.

It has been the aim of the Editor to select for the present work what will best illustrate Mr. Schurz's political career—his thoughts and acts as orator and reformer, diplomatist, Senator, Secretary of the Interior, and as publicist in the largest and best sense. Purely personal, journalistic and military matters have, as a rule, been excluded for lack of space or because not appropriate to the scope of these volumes. A few exceptions have been made for special and perhaps obvious reasons. They at least give occasional variety and color and afford a change from politics and reform. Especially for the period 1852–66, when the youthful Schurz was finding and cultivating fields for usefulness, biographical details were needed to supply the proper setting. These were all the more necessary as most of his manuscripts of that time were destroyed by fire. Happily, he had a large correspondence in German with relatives and intimate friends in which he described his aims and activities. Much of it has been published in Volume III of his *Lebenserinnerungen*, and translations from many of these letters have been made for this work by Miss Schurz and Miss Juessen, jointly.

Mr. Schurz's letters to Presidents and Presidential candidates from Lincoln to Roosevelt, both inclusive, and to others conspicuous in public affairs between 1857 and 1906, were numerous and often of great moment. Many answers he received were illuminating and instructive. As fully as circumstances would permit, this latter material also has been drawn upon for its inherent value and because it makes Mr. Schurz's letters more perspicuous. And the needs of the student and of the historian have been kept in mind. The historian rightly demands perfect frankness and the avoidance of all concealment. Nothing could be easier in the present case than to grant these, for in the life of Carl Schurz there was nothing to conceal.

In order to make the best use of the space, it has been found necessary not only to choose between documents but also to leave out unimportant sentences and paragraphs in the documents chosen. Where the choice had to be made between speeches of about equal value, the speech that is unprinted or less accessible has been preferred. Of the twelve speeches printed in the collection of 1865, four have been reprinted; and of the speeches in the Senate, room has been found for all having conspicuous historical value—numerous enough to supply the needs of all but a few special students. In most letters the salutations and the endings, such as "Dear Sir," "Very truly yours," "With thanks," etc., have been dropped out. *In all other cases, except in the translations* three dots indicate the omission of one or more sentences; when a paragraph of more than two or three sentences is omitted, the dots extend across the page. *For the translations from the German letters a special rule has been adopted.* As the passages chosen are rarely more than excerpts, taken from personal and private letters, they have been treated as such, and signs of omission have not often been used. Yet, in a few cases, dots have been inserted, lest the casual reader might otherwise assume that the excerpt was a whole letter.

In such works as James Madison's it may be very important to make the reproduction of the text literal, including abbreviations, misspellings, slips and errors of all sorts. But to do this in a collection of Webster's or Burke's or Gallatin's writings would be both injurious and absurd. As it is known, Carl Schurz, our American Burke, was one of the most careful and accurate of writers, and his mastery of English has perhaps never been and may never be surpassed by any German beginning to learn it after reaching manhood. Yet in what he wrote during the first twenty years of his life in the United States one occasionally meets with a construction, and especially the location of an adverb, that, if not German, is also not quite English. Although perhaps most readers would pass these unnoticed, the Editor feels that if he had undertaken to change them he would to that extent have favorably misrepresented what some persons might have considered essentially characteristic of the author.

In regard to spelling, to capitalization, to punctuation

best suited to bring out the intended meaning, and to slips of different kinds which have no special significance and may perhaps have been due to a careless copyist or printer long ago—in regard to these things only such liberties have been taken as the most conservative usage demands, for the sake of uniformity and to produce the desired effect.[1]

To the resolution not to depart from the rule of general thanks, one exception must be made. Dr. Herbert Putnam's intelligent and generous aid to students and scholars has made the Library of Congress the most attractive place in the world to persons engaged in literary or scientific work. The large resources of the Library have greatly facilitated the present task.

FREDERIC BANCROFT.

WASHINGTON, D. C., January, 1913.

[1] See p. 211 *n.*, *post.*, for more on this point and about special exceptions.

CONTENTS OF VOLUME I

Contents of Volume I XV

1865.

1867.

Contents of Volume I

THE WRITINGS OF CARL SCHURZ

The Writings of Carl Schurz

TO CHARLOTTE VOSS[1]

PHILADELPHIA, October 20, 1852.[2]

Doubtless you expected that I should be pleased with the United States. If Margarethe [Mrs. Schurz] occasionally has her little jests with me for thinking every shanty charming and heavenly, it is only because I am interested in every little thing that is characteristic. You know how she imagined this wild America would be. The facts quickly undeceived her. During the last few days of our voyage the monotonous sea became animated by the signs of distant land;[3] even the sky prepared us for new sights. The vast horizon, the deep transparent blue of the heavens and an unusually brilliant atmosphere announced the vicinity of land. At last one evening the purple hills of New Jersey appeared on the horizon. At night the brilliant illumination of light-houses surrounded us in a wide semicircle; and the rising sun, seeming to come up out of

[1] An intimate friend of Mrs. Schurz from girlhood and who a little later married Friedrich Althaus, Schurz's fellow-student at Bonn. Schurz had been in the United States only since Sept. 17, 1852. His arrival and early experiences are described in his *Reminiscences*, vol. ii., chap. i.

[2] Translated from the German. See Preface as to the translators and the translations.

[3] They came in a large sailing-vessel and the voyage occupied twenty-eight days.

1

a sea fringed with luxuriant trees and gleaming villas, called us on deck to enjoy the sights of the nearby shore. Indeed, the first view of the bay of New York was a great surprise. The water was alive with innumerable boats and ships of all kinds, crossing hither and thither in gay confusion; on the shore we saw the luxuriance of nature and the splendor of wealth; before our eyes was the mighty city bedecked with flags, and above us the brilliant American sky.

New York is as bustling as the most animated parts of London, yet it is very different. Life is much more cheerful, is free from the English monotony of physiognomy and morose taciturnity in the business transactions. Here the faces of all nationalities mingle, marked by their distinctive types, from the African negro to the native Indian. Here there is laughter and talk in a hundred different languages and manners. New York somewhat resembles Paris. Broadway, the principal street, has not the proud magnificence of Regent Street in London, but it approaches the rich elegance of the Parisian boulevards. In it gorgeous shops, restaurants and hotels stand in closely-built rows and an endless rumble of business traffic is concentrated. It is also the arena for the competition of feminine beauty and elegance. The side-streets are all the more quiet, with rows of trees planted on either side, and to a great extent built up with comfortable dwelling-houses. One day we drove out of the city streets to see the immediate neighborhood and we found the fields full of life, where streets were being laid out and already stately stone buildings stood near the original block-houses—strange juxtaposition of the old and the new. In a short time all these will be united within the continuously extending city limits.

From New York we went to Philadelphia. Philadelphia is more quiet than New York, but not at all quiet compared to any city on the continent. The placid, speculative Quakers founded this city and raised it to a high state of prosperity. It has not a proud metropolitan character like New York, nor the same aspiring element, nor adventurous recklessness of mercantile enterprise, but it has solid affluence and German industry. The aspect of the city would be more cheerful if the brick walls of the houses were covered with a coat of white paint, but in the better quarters a surprising luxury in the architecture is prevalent. All the door-steps, the bases of the windows and doors gleam in splendid white marble; often the ground floors, and not rarely the whole front of a house, are built of this dazzling stone. Independence Hall in Philadelphia is historically the most remarkable building of the Union. It is only a small court-house, insignificant and poor outside and inside and evidently not planned for so large a city. In its hall the Declaration of Independence of the United States was signed and from its windows it was proclaimed. Now the small building is living evidence of the insignificance of the North America of that time; and all around it is the populous city, a sign of its present increasing greatness. When the Declaration of Independence was signed—seventy years ago—Philadelphia had only five thousand inhabitants. Few things remain beside Independence Hall to remind us of that period.

We chanced to arrive during the municipal and State election; the campaign between the parties was nearing its end; only the final great efforts were to be made. In the streets we frequently met omnibuses filled with bands of music and drawn by gayly decorated horses. On all sides of the wagons were the names of the candidates, in enormous letters. Mass-meetings, attended by thousands, followed each other in quick succession. An American mass-meeting is a strange spectacle when compared with one of our popular meetings during the revolution. The American speaker is violent, aggressive, not rarely abusive. But respect for freedom of speech at a meeting is so great that a speaker is hardly ever interrupted, even if he says very foolish or exasperating things. Every one feels himself personally responsible for the order of the meeting and, if necessary, every one is a representative of the police. This characteristic trait contrasts strongly with the otherwise irrepressible exuberance of the American. Every one here feels the most complete independence.

This nation has a strange indifference to life, which manifests itself in its sports, its races, its wars and also in its daily life. Men who daily win their life anew in sustained effort give it up with reckless indifference. Nevertheless, there is the same personal safety as in Paris or London. There is much less stealing, and the stories of murder usually revolve around the question of " gentleman " or no " gentleman." An educated man lives as quietly as anywhere else, and to annoy a woman is considered a social crime. The cult of woman is almost enjoined by law; her social liberty is unlimited, she is mistress of herself. A woman can travel alone over the whole country and every gentleman must be ready to render her any service she may demand. Her privileges may sometimes be abused, but an admirable trait of the American character comes to the rescue. The abuse of the good does not prompt the American to abolish it. The abuse of liberty does not tempt him to curtail liberty. The American knows that liberty is the best means of education and that it is the highest guarantee for the Republic. We have not yet seen how a free people exercises its freedom. We have not seen in real life the practical application of the principles which we preach. Here all is spread before our gaze in a vast

tableau. There is only one shrill discord, and that is
slavery in the South. But of that later.

TO MALWIDA von MEYSENBUG[1]

[No date given; autumn or early winter of 1852.]

I have not yet seen much in America, but I have learned
much. I have never before lived in a democratic country
and been able to observe the conduct of a free people. I
confess without a blush that until now I had only a faint
conception of it. My political views have undergone a
kind of internal revolution since I began to read the book
that alone contains the truth—the book of reality. When
I now picture to myself the majority of the hot-headed
professional revolutionists that are fostered by emigration
or many of the strong-minded ladies of the educated class
with their sentimental ideas of democracy; when I imagine
them all transplanted in the conditions prevailing here,
and when I think how terribly they would harangue, the
former about the tone of the *bourgeoisie* and the machinations of the clericals and the latter about the wild lawless-
ness of the people, and how they would come to the
conclusion that, after all, their Eldorado is not realized
here—then, indeed, I begin to fear a little for the future
European Republic that must find its support in these two
elements. It is true, indeed, that the first sight of this
country fills one with dumb amazement. Here you see
the principle of individual freedom carried to its ultimate
consequences: voluntarily made laws treated with contempt; in another place you notice the crassest religious
fanaticism venting itself in brutal acts; on the one hand
you see the great mass of the laboring people in complete
freedom striving for emancipation, and by their side the

[1] Published in her *Memoiren einer Idealistin*, ii., 77–82. Translated
from the German.

speculative spirit of capital plunging into unheard of
enterprises; here is a party that calls itself Democratic
and is at the same time the mainstay of the institution of
slavery; there another party thunders against slavery but
bases all its arguments on the authority of the Bible
and mentally is incredibly abject in its dependence,—at
one time it displays an impetuous impulse for emancipation, while at another it has an active lust for oppression;
—all these in complete liberty, moving in a confused tu-
mult, one with the other, one by the side of the other. The
democrat just arrived from Europe, who has so far lived
in a world of ideas and has had no opportunity to see these
ideas put into actual, sound practice will ask himself,
hesitatingly, Is this, indeed, a free people? Is this a
real democracy? Is democracy a fact if it shelters under
one cloak such conflicting principles? Is this my ideal?
Thus he will doubtingly question himself, as he steps into
this new, really *new* world. He observes and reflects,
gradually casting aside, one after the other, the prejudices
with which Europe has burdened him and finally he will
arrive at the solution of the problem. Yes, this is humanity when it is free. Liberty breaks the chain of development. All strength, all weakness, all that is good, all
that is bad, is here in full view and in free activity.
The struggle of principles goes on unimpeded; outward
freedom shows us which enemies have to be overcome
before we can gain inner freedom. He who wishes liberty
must not be surprised if men do not appear better than
they are. Freedom is the only state in which it is possible
for men to learn to know themselves, in which they show
themselves as they really are. It is true, the ideal is not
necessarily evolved, but it would be an unhappy thought
to force the ideal in spite of humanity. Here they allow
the Jesuits to manage their own affairs; they are not
killed, they are not driven out, because democracy admits

the liberty of every creed as long as it does not impair the
civic liberty of others.   They are not opposed with the
weapon of official power but simply with that of public
opinion.   That is not only more democratic but also much
more effective, for if the struggle of public opinion with
mental subserviency is slow, it is only a sign that humanity
is not more mature.   This struggle has the advantage that
it continually keeps pace with the point of view of the
masses and for that reason its victories are less rapid, less
brilliant, but more enduring and more decisive.   So it is
here with everything.   The European revolutionist becomes impatient at this and would like to apply some
vigorous blows; but such is humanity that it does not
like to be beaten even into reason, and such is true democracy that it will be governed by the public mind not as it
ought to be but as it actually is.   It is my firm conviction
that the European revolutionists will drive the next
revolution into a reaction merely through their lust for
government, through their desire to improve things
quickly and positively.   Every glance into the political
life of America strengthens my convictions that the aim
of a revolution can be nothing else than to make room for
the will of the people—in other words, to break every
authority which has its organization in the life of the
state, and, as far as is possible, to overturn the barriers to
individual liberty.   The will of the people will have its
fling and indulge in all kinds of foolishness—but that is
its way; if you want to show it the way and then give it
liberty of action, it will, nevertheless, commit its own
follies.   Each one of these follies clears away something,
while the wisest thing that is done for the people accomplishes nothing until the popular judgment has progressed
far enough to be able to do it for itself.   Until then,
conditions must stand *à force de l'autorité*, or they will
totter.   But if they exist by the force of authority, then

democracy is in a bad way. Here in America you can every day see how slightly a people needs to be governed. In fact, the thing that is not named in Europe without a shudder, anarchy, exists here in full bloom. Here are governments but no rulers—governors, but they are clerks. All the great educational establishments, the churches, the great means of transportation etc., that are being organized here—almost all of these things owe their existence not to official authority but to the spontaneous co-operation of private individuals. One has glimpses here into the productivity of liberty. Here you see a gorgeously built church; a stock company founded it. There a university; a wealthy man left a large endowment, which is its main capital, and the university is almost entirely supported by subscription. In another place you see an orphan asylum of white marble; a rich citizen built it. And so it goes with an endless list of things. It is only here that you realize how superfluous governments are in many affairs in which, in Europe, they are considered entirely indispensable, and how the possibility of doing something inspires a desire to do it.

TO MRS. SCHURZ

WASHINGTON, D. C., March 15, 1854.[1]

In the first place let me tell you about the impressions of my trip. The journey from Philadelphia to Washington is rather monotonous, except the view of Chesapeake Bay, the crossing of several streams and the immediate vicinity of Washington. In approaching the city the attention is immediately arrested by some prominent objects, enormous marble buildings rising grandly above the smaller dwelling houses. Our first visit must,

[1] Translated from the German.

of course, be to the Capitol, the Federal palace of the United States, which contains the halls of Congress. The building is not entirely completed, but its proportions are noble in size and it is lavishly decorated with columns of white marble. Situated on a hill at the northern [southeastern] end of the city, it commands an unobstructed view of Washington and its environs. It is a strange-looking city. Imagine a broad street lined on both sides with hotels and shops, then wide stretches of open country and again streets interrupted by vacant lots; groups of houses scattered about in apparent disorder, with here and there a marble palace which contains one of the Government Departments. This strange jumble leaves the spectator in doubt whether all this grandeur is in a state of development or is already approaching decay. Opposite the Capitol, at the other end of the broad main street, which is about a mile and a half long, rises the White House, the residence of the President, beyond which the Potomac encircles the southern side of the city in a majestic sweep. Still beyond the river we see the hills of Virginia and on this side the hills of Maryland. That is the exterior, quite pleasing in its way. The life in the streets has a holiday character; there is very little business traffic, only enough to supply the wants of the government officials, the Members of Congress and visitors. This gives a city a marked physiognomy. The elegant toilets of the ladies add to the brilliance of the scene, and the gentlemen try to win their favor. Such is the out-of-door life.

An unusual sight adds to the gaiety of the spectacle: it is a delegation of Indians, come from the outer confines of civilization to discuss with the President a treaty about certain tracts of land. I saw them in all their wild splendor when I was going to the White House to-day. They wear moccasins and a kind of doe-skin leggins, decorated on both sides with gay feathers which make their legs resemble those of chickens with feathers extending down to their feet. They wrap themselves in blankets, generally blue. The most distinguished wear the skin of some wild animal, edged with red and trimmed with all sorts of metal balls, dangling down their back, so that at every step a sound like that of sleigh-bells, only not so loud, is produced. Their necks are encircled by strings of coral beads, but principally by necklaces of long, white bear claws—which look somewhat gruesome. Their ears are decorated, wherever they can find a space, with great earrings and a quantity of little glistening bits of metal and glass beads, as if they were edged with a shining fringe. Into their hair they plait all sorts of eagle and falcon feathers, arranged so that they partly stand erect and partly project on the side of the head. Their faces are gorgeously painted, mostly with bright red, particularly the part between the cheek bone and the ear. Some of them had added a fine, wide, bright-green stripe which encircled the whole face like whiskers. The two most prominent Indians had put an extra touch on the left side of their faces; it looked a little as if someone had dipped his hand in blacking and had then slapped their cheek. I need not add that they wore no "kid gloves." They are not of an imposingly vigorous stature, but they are well built. Their features are hard and deeply cut, the brow low and the skin a dirty reddish brown. Their speech consists, as far as I could hear it, of loud inarticulate sounds, and their conversation is accompanied by rapid gesticulation, almost like the conversation of deaf-mutes. So much for the wild Americans, now for the tame.

Yesterday I had bad luck in making calls, owing to the simple reason that the houses are not numbered and one has to spend much time in looking for them—often in vain. Yesterday I found only one of the persons to whom

I was recommended.   To-day I have been more fortunate.   I made the acquaintance of two Representatives
and one Senator and was well received.   It may be several
days before I penetrate into the higher spheres.   However,
I have learned much from the little I have seen and much
that does not please me.   Looking at things as an unprejudiced and disinterested spectator, this confusion
of schemes, interests, fears, personal considerations, ambitious plans and claims, manœuvres, mutual deceptions
etc.—one is involuntarily tempted not to venture further
into the turmoil.   However, within this sphere there are
great duties, noble tasks, momentous decisions, that rise
like columns from the dust in which the vermin crawl.
You learn here what good political institutions mean.
The country is being badly governed at this moment,
but, however it may be governed, incapable as the men
at the helm may be, things go well, nevertheless.

TO MRS. SCHURZ

WASHINGTON, Thursday, March 23, 1854.
Within the last few days I have met a number of Members of Congress and other extremely interesting political
and unpolitical persons.   I shall probably see the President
before the end of the week and am somewhat curious.
From all I hear about the conditions at the White House—
and that is not a little—the President presents the sorry
spectacle of an individual who has been placed at the helm
of a great republic without possessing the necessary strength
of character nor the equally necessary clearness of mind.
He has the unfortunate trait of wishing to please everybody and consequently he has displeased all.   He agrees
with every one who speaks to him and so says something
different to each one.   There has never been a President
in the White House who has to such a degree disappointed

all the good expectations centered on him, and consequently
no one who has so rapidly lost such enormous popularity.
This discouraging experience may prevent the people
from again electing such a person, from whom all things
are *hoped* because *nothing* is known.

Let me tell you a little more about my plans and activity here. It was my intention to urge upon the people I
came in contact with—especially if I should be able to reach
any member of the Cabinet—a certain course in their foreign policy. As far as the Members of Congress with
whom I have become acquainted are concerned, I have
had some success that was quite pleasing. My experience with the President and the Cabinet is, in a word,
that they have no foreign policy, neither have they a system
nor a fixed purpose. They regulate their foreign policy
entirely in accord with the tendency of public opinion
held by the political parties of the country. Their course
of action in foreign matters is based entirely upon the effect
to be made on the Nation, and therefore no consistency
nor fixed principles are to be expected of the Administration. It is in vain to-day to persuade the Administration
or to convince them of anything. The slightest deviation
of party tactics may upset to-morrow all the convictions
which have been laboriously built up to-day. I have,
therefore, come to the conclusion that there is only one
way of achieving anything and that is in the first place
to work upon public opinion and so to gain a real influence over the Government. Fortunately at this moment there is no great crisis looming up in Europe in
which America might be called upon to take part on the
side of freedom. This Administration would be too weak
to do anything of that kind.

I have already made real friends among the Members of
Congress. Shall I give you a glimpse into the future?
The other evening I sat with several of them and we talked

of European and American politics.   I took a lively part
in the conversation.   The next day one of them came to
me and said: "Sir, you have a fair opening before you.
You will have a future in this country.   I talked about
you with my friends and we came to the conclusion that,
if you settle in one of the new States, we will meet you
in a few years in this city, and then we shall listen to you
in the halls of Congress as you now listen to us."   These
remarks were so spontaneous, so unsolicited, that they
have given me courage.

I have made one other interesting acquaintance, a well-
known American poetess—Mrs. Sarah Bolton, who lives
in this house.   She is very simple, very entertaining and,
except for a little author's vanity, free from affectation.

Thursday evening, March 23, 1854.

I have just called upon a Senator who seems to be very
much interested in me, and to whom my ideas seem to
appeal.   He has invited me to breakfast to-morrow morning, where I am to meet some other persons.   I feel that I
might be able to do something worth while in this sphere,
if once I had become actively and officially a part of it.
I feel it more and more strongly as I become better acquainted with those who are influencing affairs.   Nature
has endowed me with a goodly capacity that only awaits
an opportunity to make itself useful, and I do not think I
am over-estimating my value when I say that I would
be second to very few here, not now, but in a few years.
When I come in touch with this atmosphere of political
activity, I feel the old fire of 1848 coursing in my veins
as fresh and young as ever.   I feel that the true vocation
of my life lies where my endeavor will reach out to universal problems.

Although the reaction in Europe has thrown me out of
my course, you may still see your husband coming to

his own. My courage promises much; and why should not success respond to my courage as it has done hitherto. It is true there are peculiar difficulties to overcome here, but difficulties diminish as you approach them and at last they shrink to the proportions of trifling matters.

Friday.

To-day I have met several Senators and have learned much. The hour has come when I am expected at General Shields's.[1]

TO GOTTFRIED KINKEL [2]

PHILADELPHIA, January 23, 1855.[3]

I quite understand your criticism of America. The present Administration, which took the helm under the most promising auspices, is what is called a total failure. The old parties are in a state of dissolution and the political atmosphere is impregnated with the odor of decay. Until this dissolution shall be accomplished and until there has been time for new developments to become fixed, there can be no thought of a decided policy. At this moment all is at loose ends. Confusion and intrigue reign. The Nebraska question, the tariff question, the homestead question, the naturalization question, the Pacific Railroad question, the Cuban question, the Sandwich Island question, the Nicaragua expedition—all these things are mixed up in a wild jumble and public opinion is unable to arrive at a sane conclusion. When Pierce went into office, public opinion forced him into the making of a new, strong

----

[1] One of the Senators from Ill.

[2] Schurz's favorite professor at Bonn, by whose liberal ideas and eloquence he was much influenced, and whose escape from Spandau he effected, etc. See 1 *Reminiscences*, passim.

[3] Translated from the German.

program of foreign policy.   He took a few steps in that
direction.   But hardly had the Cabinet been formed and
the other offices filled, before the corruption of the old
parties involved him in a lot of petty yet exhausting fights,
which a character like Jackson would have crushed with
prompt energy, but with which the weak Pierce was wholly
unable to cope.   He saw no other course than to seek refuge
in the Nebraska bill, which was the product of the unscrupulous ambition of Douglas; and immediately the
entire attention of the nation was diverted from foreign
politics and concentrated upon the slavery question.
Accordingly the Administration lost its natural program
and was at the mercy of all the evil influences which the
compromise of 1850 has cast about all the political parties.
The Nebraska bill burst the moral bonds, and the struggle
started again from the beginning.   Minds became agitated
and responsive to these influences.   This condition of
public sentiment was utilized by the native Americans
for the purpose of advancing their political interests.
This essentially weak, nativistic faction joined the majority which has its strongest basis in the Nebraska question.
Thus the Know-Nothings suddenly attained enormous
influence, which was all the more powerful because of the
fact that they conceal their true power beneath the veil
of a secret society.   While the anti-Nebraska movement
has carried away the entire North, and the admixture of
the nativistic spirit is perceptible in all these victories,
and is clouding the triumph of freedom, the slavery question and the foreign elements are the two points of view
from which all political matters are regarded at present—
and herein lies the confusion of the situation.   What is
favorable to the rights of the foreigners, is unfavorable
to slavery; and yet, not only are the rights of slavery to
be limited, but the influence of the foreigners is to be
destroyed as well.   That is the problem through which

the free-soil Know-Nothing must work his way. It is
certain that the nativistic movement will be wrecked on
this rock of inconsistency. But there is danger that the
anti-slavery movement will be weakened by it. Only
the South can be consistent in both questions, and unite
the strength of two formidable agitations. It will not be
long before the slave States become the headquarters of
the nativistic movement and there it will remain. This
will suffice to secure the rights of the foreign elements in
the North. I am convinced, moreover, that we have
nothing further to fear from the Know-Nothings, except
a weakening of the anti-slavery movement; this would be
all the more deplorable because that movement is already
so well under way.

The slavery question reveals itself in so many different
aspects to him who has recently come to America, that
he finds it difficult to work his way through the confusion
of considerations and interests, especially where the existence of the Union is involved. After studying all the
arguments I could find, with the exception of those in the
Bible, I have at length come to the final conclusion that,
whatever may be the considerations that demand compromise, there can be but one question of freedom, and
the faithful adherence to that principle is, on the whole,
more practical than it sometimes seems. It is not the
philanthropic side of the question which has brought me
to this conclusion, but the direct and indirect effect of the
system upon the whole Government of the United States,
the aristocratic character of Southern society, the de-
moralising influence of the slave-power upon the politicians of the North; the consequent partisanship of all
political ideas of justice and especially the influence upon
our foreign policy. When you ask me, "When will the
United States interfere practically in the interest of the
freedom of the peoples of the world?" I answer without

hesitation and with unquestioning conviction, "As soon
as the slaveholders have ceased to be a political power."
The slaveholder fears the propaganda of freedom, because
he does not know how far it may go. Even the mere
word of freedom has to him a dangerous and ambiguous
sound. For these reasons, I am decidedly opposed to
any extension of the domain of slavery, inclusive of the
annexation of Cuba. It is true that this annexation would
make the Creoles independent of Spain; but at the same
time, it would so much increase the menace to freedom
in the United States that the purchase would not be worth
the price. It would be splendid if the Spanish Government were to avail itself of the favorable moment and
establish the emancipation of the negro in Cuba; then,
Cuba would be welcome. It is deplorable that although
the anti-slavery party has many talented adherents, but
few understand practical politics. They do not know
that it is unwise to agitate violently unless there is an
immediate object in view. They forget that, at the
crucial moment, he predominates who has the reputation
of practising calm moderation. They usually consume
their best ammunition before the battle begins. Yet,
great things were won in the last campaign. Perhaps
in the year 1856 we shall completely succeed in breaking
up the country-gentry party. I can think of no happier
event for the politics of this country.

We have received news of peace in Europe to-day, which
will, I trust, not be corroborated. To conclude the war
by accepting the four points at issue would certainly be
a most disgraceful result. . . .

My wife and I send our greetings with unchanged
cordiality.

2

TO GOTTFRIED KINKEL

PHILADELPHIA, March 25, 1855.[1]

You seem to surmise that my visit to Europe means that I am returning there for good, and I see that many of my friends have the same idea. It is my intention that this visit shall be a mere interlude in my American life. As long as there is no upheaval of affairs in Europe it is my firm resolve to regard this country not as a transient or accidental abode, but as the field for my usefulness. I love America and I am vitally interested in the things about me—they no longer seem strange. I find that the question of liberty is in its essence the same everywhere, however different its form. Although I do not regard the public affairs of this country with the same devotion as those of our old home, it is not mere ambition nor eagerness for distinction that impels me to activity. My interest in the political contests of this country is so strong, so spontaneous, that I am profoundly stirred. More self-control is required for me to keep aloof than to participate in them. These are the years of my best strength. Shall I devote myself wholly to the struggle for existence while I have hopes that I may soon be independent in that respect? I venture to say that I am neither avaricious nor self-indulgent. If I now seek material prosperity, it is only that I may be free to follow my natural aspirations. Or shall I again subject myself to that dreary condition of waiting, which must undermine the strongest constitution when it is the only occupation? We have both tasted its bitterness; and I am burning with the desire to be employed with visible, tangible things and no longer to be bound to dreams and theories. I have a holy horror of the illusory fussiness which characterizes the life of the professional refugees. My devotion to the cause of the old Fatherland has not

[1] Translated from the German.

abated but my expectations have somewhat cooled; I
have only faint hopes for the next few years. Even if the
revolution should come sooner than I expect, I do not see
why I should not utilize the intervening time. I feel that
here I can accomplish something. I am convinced of it
when I consider the qualities of the men who are now
conspicuous. This inspires me, and even if the prospects
of success did not correspond with my natural impulses,
I should suddenly find that I had involuntarily entered
into the thick of the fight. In these circumstances, why
should I wish to return to Europe? I am happy that I
have a firm foothold and good opportunities.

After my return from Europe I expect to go to Wisconsin. I transferred some of my business interests there
when on my last trip to the West. The German element
is powerful in that State, the immigrants being so numerous, and they are striving for political recognition. They
only lack leaders that are not bound by the restraints of
money-getting. There is the place where I can find a sure,
gradually expanding field for my work without truckling
to the nativistic elements, and there, I hope, in time, to
gain influence that may also become useful to our cause.
It is my belief that the future interests of America and
Germany are closely interwoven. The two countries will
be natural allies as soon as a European upheaval takes
place. However different the two nations may be in character, they will have the same opponents, and that will
compel them to have a corresponding foreign policy.
American influence in Europe will be based on Germany,
and Germany's world-position will depend essentially on
the success of America. Germany is the only power in
Europe whose interests will not conflict with those of
America, and America is the only power in the civilized
world that would not be jealous of a strong, united Germany. They can both grow without being rivals, and it

will be to the interest of each to keep the adversaries of the other in check. Americans will realize this as soon as the Emperor of Austria and the King of Prussia need no longer be considered, and the Germans will become convinced of it as soon as they consider a national foreign policy.

————————

TO MRS. SCHURZ

WATERTOWN, [WIS.,] August 6, 1855.[1]

Life is extraordinarily cheap here. Mother does not use more than twelve or fourteen dollars a month for her housekeeping, and as soon as the crops in garden and fields are gathered, less will suffice.[2] When I go hunting I can often lay in a supply of game. Yesterday I went to the farm for a few hours and shot my first prairie chickens and snipe, a whole bagful, so that we have enough for two dinners. You can scarcely believe how rapidly this town is growing. Since I was here last, whole rows of three-story buildings have been built. Very soon the main street will have lost its character of a country town. You can judge of the enormous development by the fact that the census registered a population of eighty-five hundred, whereas in 1850 there were only one thousand inhabitants. This will show you how good my prospects are, and that we may indulge in hopes of a comfortable future.

I cannot deny that life here has many attractions for me. There are many persons who seek my acquaintance, and from the manner in which I am received I may conclude that I could easily attain prominence. I also believe that it is a very wholesome life, as I am obliged to walk on the farm, looking after things, and I intend to hunt and ride several times a week. The fatigue produced by

[1] Translated from the German.

[2] Schurz's parents, sisters and other relatives had recently come to the United States and had settled in Wis.

such violent exercise invigorates me. I think that you will find me well and strong and somewhat sun-burnt when you see me again.

I have planned to drive all the members of the family —including the babies, who are numerous—out to the farm for dinner some Sunday. I shall send for the farm wagon with the strong yoke of oxen and in that vehicle the whole clan can be transported. They put off buying horses until my return; so far, all the work has been done fairly well with oxen. You should see how on Sunday the farmers' families of the neighborhood are brought to church. The most elegant ladies in their feathers and furbelows sit with the greatest dignity in an ox-wagon; sometimes one yoke of oxen will draw a party of twenty-five in holiday attire. But there are also a number of fine turnouts here and some very good horses. I have seen many very gentle Indian ponies, which I should have liked to buy for you on the spot. While I am writing, a band of music is marching through the town in advance of a circus. At two o'clock this afternoon the first performance is to take place, and in the evening the second. As soon as the last spectators leave, the tents are taken down and hauled to the next place. All the farmers of the surrounding country are streaming into town and the whole fashionable world is assembled. Usually a troop of Indians on their ponies appear and are highly delighted with the performance of the circus riders. Lately a circus came with a band-wagon drawn by six elephants, which, of course, was a great occasion.

TO MRS. SCHURZ

WATERTOWN, Sept. 29, 1855.[1]

The whole week has been spent surveying the new farm.

[1] Translated from the German.

Now I have finished laying out the subdivisions and I shall begin to-morrow with the boundaries of the single lots. While I was employed in the surveying and before the land was put on the market, I had inquiries from many persons who wished to buy.

Day before yesterday, in the midst of these occupations, the news of the fall of Sebastopol reached me. You may imagine that I could no longer think of figures and that for the rest of the day my thoughts were roaming over the bloody battle-fields of the Crimea. The question, What will they do next? pursued me in a hundred different shapes, and when I took up the map and pictured to myself vividly the seat of war, I could not do otherwise than imagine myself for a few moments at the helm of affairs, deciding what I should do, were I there. Why must I sit here—a mere nonentity occupied with miserable plans for making money, although my head is full of ideas and the consciousness of inexhaustible strength—while out there momentous decisions are made and scoundrels and mediocrities crowd the world's stage? This miserably conducted war is conclusive evidence of how important it is that a storm should sweep over the earth and its wild tempestuous waves should bring new characters and talents to the surface. To be condemned to sit here and look on! To feed one's imagination on the stories of bygone times or the empty fantasies of possibilities in the future! And there is so much to do! It is fortunate for me, yes, for us both, that I possess such an inexhaustible gaiety of spirit; otherwise I should be consumed and I should break my head by running against obstructions that I know are insurmountable. Although it may seem foolish, you know that my happy fatalism keeps me up and has often been the source of resolutions and successes, and it is invaluable to me.

TO MRS. SCHURZ

WATERTOWN, Oct. 23, 1855.[1]

I might recently have been initiated into local politics. The State elections will be in November. The present governor, Barstow, who would like to be re-elected, is travelling about the State stumping for himself. He attended a large meeting here yesterday. A few days ago a delegation of citizens came to me, and asked if I would make the address of welcome to the governor and advocate his re-election. The present administration has been managing the finances of the State in such an unscrupulous way, and altogether their political principles are so entirely opposed to mine, especially in regard to National politics, that I declined their request and refused to support Barstow. By the way, I have frequently been asked if I would not take part in politics as soon as possible, and I am assured on all sides that I could be elected to the State assembly as soon as I should consent to be a candidate. So there is a possibility of our spending some months in Madison, the State capital, a year from this winter. I realize more and more what a wide field is open to me here and that, in a way, I need only grasp the opportunities presenting themselves in order to succeed. Many stimulating interests will come into our lives and variety and change will not be lacking.

TO GOTTFRIED KINKEL

WATERTOWN, Dec. 1, 1856.[2]

How often have I wished during recent months that you were here![3] There is a struggle going on in this country in which we should all take part—and, after

[1] Translated from the German. [2] Translated from the German.
[3] Kinkel was then living in London.

all, a spirited conflict for an idea gives true zest to life! The most contented person cannot deny that he has to suffer many deprivations here, but the consciousness of being able to do something worth while, of casting a thought, a deed, into the balance for the good of humanity, compensates me for everything. To have aims that lie outside ourselves and our immediate circle is a great thing and well worth the sacrifice.

The papers have probably kept you informed of the events that have occurred here during the last few months. Nothing more strange can be imagined than the attitude of the two parties since the campaign. The Democrats, although they have been victorious, are discouraged and depressed and full of dread of what may happen; the Republicans, though beaten, are full of the sense of power, full of assurance in consequence of the first results gained, and full of confidence for the future. Frémont has already been mentioned as a candidate for 1860 by a number of papers; the organization is everywhere preserved, and the agitation is continued as if nothing had happened. The spirit of the party is what might be called buoyant. It is rumored that Buchanan, moved by the imposing expression of opinion in the North, will do all in his power to keep slavery out of Kansas. He may secretly wish this result, but he will not be able to bring it about. He is not his own master. Because elected by a party that has its main strength in the South, he must follow Southern policies in order to preserve the party that is the only support of his Administration. He is placed between two factions of the Democratic party—the Southern and the Northern. They differ greatly in numbers, in character and in methods. The Southern faction knows what it wants and is ready at any moment to sacrifice the existence of the party to the interests of slavery. It is constantly trying to break the resistance of the Northern Democrats by threats of secession. The Northern faction is not so sure of itself; it has sacrificed the interests of the free North to the existence of the party and is accustomed to yield to the threats of secession and to the arrogance of the South. The first of these factions considers itself victorious; the other looks upon itself as beaten; the former is continually growing bolder in its demands; the other is afraid to submit unconditionally, but is too timid to refuse submission. Which one will be able to exert the greater influence on the impressionable character of Buchanan? If New York or Boston were the seat of the Federal Government, the Northern Democracy might have a chance, but in Washington the Southern element predominates. It is probable that Kansas will be forced into the Union as a slave State, unless part of the Northern Democrats in Kansas should become rebellious, or the fight in Kansas should develop into a revolutionary uprising on a large scale. In either case, I believe that Buchanan's Administration will be to the Democratic party what Fillmore's was to the Whig party—namely, the end.

From now on there can be only two parties in the Union: a Northern and a Southern party—an anti- and a pro-slavery party, and at the present moment the Democrats up here are only the outposts of the slave-power in the free States. At last the slavery issue has become the watchword of the day; the time for compromise has passed, and the last chance for a peaceful solution has come. The next four years will decide the fate of the United States; in both camps there is firm determination. We have on our side the spirit of the age, a great inspiring idea and superior ability. The South has unanimity and brutality. I am not sure that this fight can be decided without powder. I doubt it. However, should the force of arms be resorted to as a last measure, the result cannot be doubtful, for the material superiority of the North is immense.

Our victory in this State was gratifyingly brilliant. Wisconsin went for Frémont with fifteen thousand majority. Much persevering and devoted work was done and I honestly did my share. During my short activity I gained a relatively great influence and I shall soon have a voice in the affairs of Wisconsin. During the last four months I have been obliged to speak a great deal in public and I have made great progress. My voice and my limbs have become more supple, and I begin to understand the secret of the use of pathos. I have quite often succeeded in rousing my audience to the fire of enthusiasm, and I am no longer diffident when I wish to appeal to their sentiment. In short, I have gained courage as an orator, and I hope, should I enter the legislature next year, to be able to accomplish something. The foreign tongue no longer troubles me, and I even find that in many things English is more convenient and effective than German.

I am giving as much time as possible to the study of the law this winter, for I expect to begin my legal practice in March. The governor has appointed me a notary public, and I am also president of an insurance company. These things, together with the real-estate business and the matters that turn up accidentally, keep me sufficiently occupied. I also occasionally write political letters and articles; and if there is a vacancy in the city council and I become a member of it, I shall have only as much time for study as is absolutely necessary.

Our town is developing remarkably. We are going to have enormous railroad connections, which are already under construction, and in a few years the value of real estate will rise so much that we need no longer be anxious as to our financial situation.

December 17th.

My letter has been interrupted for two weeks, during which time I could not possibly finish it. In the
meantime honors and burdens have been heaped upon me,
and I have had little rest. We have succeeded in making our town the county-seat, and there are many
public enterprises connected with the change which will
have to be carried out—court-houses, administration
offices, school-houses, bridges etc. I have been appointed
commissioner of public improvements, a position which
is just now really the most important of all the municipal
offices. Although the building and improving will not
actually begin before the spring, there are many preparations to be made, and one of my principal duties will be
to obtain fifty thousand dollars on city bonds.

The sphere in which I now move and work is strangely
foreign to the preparations of my early youth, yet how
easily we adapt ourselves, if once we have tasted the joy
of effort—the joy of seeing things around us develop and
thrive. That is the peculiar charm of my present life,
which it is difficult to explain to those who have not experienced it. It is strange how quickly we here learn
without studying, and, after living in this atmosphere for
a time, how easily we are suddenly able to do things
which we never before paid attention to. And this gives
us a glimpse into the fruitfulness of political freedom.

I have lately taken up for my recreation T. Livii Pata-
vini *Historias*, and often you might have found me looking
up words in the dictionary like a dutiful schoolboy. I
have lost much of my classic knowledge, but I find after
reading a few pages that my Latin comes back to me with
a rush. I am expecting to receive Cicero's orations and
shall probably read them with greater appreciation than
at the gymnasium.

You may be surprised that I should turn again to the

Roman classics in the midst of the material activities of this Western life. This is due less to the fact that I do not wish to forget my Latin than that I believe one can learn from such authors much that has a bearing on American politics. . . .

TO FRIEDRICH ALTHAUS

WATERTOWN, February 6, 1857.[1]

If I did not know what an obstinate and incorrigible European you are, your last letter would have destroyed my doubts. When did you Europeans rise so high that you can superciliously regard a fight with brutality? When have you fought anything else? To be sure, you tell me: "The deeds of certain individuals in Kansas are, if possible, more barbarous than any atrocities of European despotism." How can you think so? The murders that have been perpetrated aside from skirmishes, are terrible enough, but they are very few in number. In view of the political principles of the Union, they were the most shocking things that demoralization could be capable of. But who that is familiar with the latest history of the two continents would compare them with the long list of legally sanctioned murders committed in Baden, Hungary, Lombardy, France, Naples etc., quite apart from the horrors that were perpetrated privately and praised publicly? It is true that the hated penal code of the slaveholding legislature of Kansas, is barbarous; but although these laws were systematically sinned against, where could the autocrat have been found that would have dared to brave public opinion in the United States to the extent of en-

[1] Translated from the German.

forcing even one of these laws? Of all those offenders
who were arrested for the violation of these laws, only a
few were sentenced, and of all that were sentenced none
were punished according to this code. Those laws were
stillborn. You say: "The victory of the slavery party
in the election of Buchanan has, indeed, brought America
to the very same level as continental Europe." Oddly
enough, this victory is due principally to recent European
immigrants. Apart from this, I have no more ardent
wish than that you might for a few months see our political life with your own eyes. Never has the anti-slavery
agitation been carried on with less disturbance and more
earnestness; any attempt to put the slightest check upon
the freedom of the press would be greeted with derisive
laughter. Even in the South the radicals carry their
heads high and show greater boldness than ever before.
Never has the work in Kansas, in favor of the free-State
cause, been more effective, and never were the chances for
success so favorable. The pro-slavery people are abandoning the territory in hordes because they have given up
the game; and the free-State people who are streaming
in already outnumber them eight to one. Even Pierce
is perplexed and would gladly give up the last resource of
the slavery party, the legislature of Kansas, if that were
possible. Only abolish the test oath, and Kansas is saved.
Meantime, there may be a lively skirmish, but the North
will not give up Kansas. And the improved conditions
came directly after the election of Buchanan. You
write: "Such occurrences as the attack upon Sumner
will be repeated frequently against the few who still retain
the courage to express their opinions in opposition to the
victorious party." Have you, by any chance, read extracts of the debate over the message of President Pierce?
When have the Free-Soilers shown themselves more fear-
less in their attacks and more cutting and unsparing in

their criticisms? Sumner's famous speech was mildness
and consideration itself compared with the things the
slaveholders have been made to hear since the 4th of
November. And how tame the latter have grown! The
arrogant speeches have become strangely rare and Preston
Brooks of South Carolina has died suddenly—of croup,
as the children of the world say; struck down by the hand
of God, say the pious Abolitionists, and that is also my
opinion. This change of conditions certainly is in strange
contrast with the results of the election, but its cause is
nevertheless to be sought in that result. The slaveholders never thought it possible for the North to be
united. Now the most zealous fire-eaters are unpleasantly
surprised by the overwhelming majorities won by Frémont
in the North, and they have subsided considerably. The
census of 1860 will show the enormous growth of Northern
preponderance since 1850, and that will "settle the
matter," as the saying is here. In a word, my friend, if
you compare the Free-Soil votes of 1852 with those of
1856, and contemplate the developments that followed the
election, you will find that the reaction in which we are
engaged is directed against slavery. A rebellion is preparing in the Democratic party, and possibly Buchanan
will be the gravestone of the country gentry, as Fillmore
is that of the Whig party. The fact is, there has never
been a more victorious defeat than that which the Republican party suffered last year, and never has a beaten
army gained so many advantages after a lost battle.
Since you have adapted yourselves to existing circumstances, you Europeans cannot imagine a party defeat
that is not followed by subjection. The victory of this
or that party does not cause the least change in the
usual routine of internal government. Federal politics
have not the slightest influence upon it, and you might
recently have read how the governors of different States

in their messages soundly criticized President Pierce
and pointed out the limitations of his functions, because
he had made slurring remarks about the people of the
different States. But enough of politics. . . .

TO HORACE RUBLEE[1]

JEFFERSON [WIS.], Nov. 11, 1857.

Our defeat is a disgrace to the name of Wisconsin. If
I were not personally concerned in it,[2] it would be no less
painful to me. It has ruined us morally and will have a
very bad effect upon those members of the party, whose
convictions are not so strong as to elevate them above
the demoralizing influence of a disaster. How, indeed, do
we stand? Beaten in consequence of our victories. If
every success leads us into the winter-quarters of Capua,
we shall always be defeated before being seriously attacked, and we shall never be able to keep the field in two
consecutive campaigns. We are now no better than the
French army after the battle of Rossbach.

At all events I want to have it understood that the
Germans who are with us have done their duty. They
have been at the polls almost to a man. But the result
will undoubtedly have a bad effect upon them. They
feel like young troops, who rush into the combat with
all the confidence of enthusiasm, and suddenly become
aware that the old guard refuse to fight, when it happens
to be dinner-time. It will be difficult to lead them on
again.

As for myself, I have got over it, as far as my personal
disappointment is concerned. I saw our defeat clearly
before me, when I learned the result in the main strongholds of Republicanism. Now, I feel like a man who has

---

[1] A Wis. journalist and one of the Republican managers in the State.
[2] Schurz had been the Republican candidate for lieutenant-governor.

done his duty and who is ready to do his duty again. And as things are, we ought to have a keen perception of our duty.

One thing would be exceedingly mortifying to me: if I should be obliged to let our Republican paper at Watertown go down. It has done good service and now we want it more than ever. Until now I have borne all the expenses myself, but, the campaign having exhausted my means completely, I can do so no longer. The party has to do something towards sustaining it. Is there no help at headquarters? There is hardly a place in the State where a German organ is more wanted than in Watertown, —and it is for the party to determine whether we shall put down arms entirely. It would be disgraceful to surrender our artillery while we can keep it. Have the kindness to let me know whether we can expect something in that respect from Madison. You must excuse me if I have presumed too much upon your kindness. I have not written to the State central committee because they have no means and will hardly be able to dispose of the business already heaped upon them.

I have to thank you most heartily for the promptness with which you have taken up my defense whenever I was attacked and for all the kind things you have said of me.

————————

TO HEINRICH MEYER[1]

WATERTOWN, Jan. 15, 1858.[2]

I am really glad that the abominable calendar year 1857 is closed at last. It was full of all sorts of ill luck. Think of it! I was forty-eight votes short in the election—45,005 against 45,053, and that owing to an obvious election fraud, but which can be proved only at

———————————————————————————————

[1] Mrs. Schurz's brother.   [2] Translated from the German.

considerable expense. I have no desire to incur that expense during these hard times. So I am contenting myself with the spurs I won in the campaign, where we were defeated because of the carelessness of our party.

So far as material conditions are concerned, I must admit that the money crisis weighs heavily upon us. The most disagreeable feature of the present state of affairs is the dreadful scarcity of money. It is impossible to convert anything into cash; consequently there is shortage everywhere. In the East, money is more plentiful and confidence is increasing and I hope that we shall soon feel the effect here. If this continues, the carpenter who wants to buy a leg of lamb of the butcher will soon pay for it with a table and take a chair as change.

TO GOTTFRIED KINKEL

MADISON, Feb. 15, 1858.[1]

My efforts and successes in the Frémont campaign of 1856 won more recognition than I had expected. On September 2d of last year, the Republican convention nominated me almost unanimously for lieutenant-governor, and since that time I have steadily advanced. Circumstances were very favorable. During the campaign, I made extensive trips throughout the State and my speeches were decidedly successful, especially those in English.

On the whole, I believe that my popularity has come too fast to be enduring. To the Americans, I was a unique type. A German who, as they declare, speaks English better than they do, and also has the advantage over their native politicians of possessing a passable knowledge of European conditions, naturally attracts their attention.

[1] Translated from the German. *17031*

Consequently I am more popular with the Americans than with the Germans, for some of these are envious. Otherwise, I have had little cause for complaint.

However events may develop in the near future, Buchanan's Administration will surely mark a turning-point in American politics and history. It has mercilessly revealed the logic of events and simplified the contest. However much the economic conditions demand the attention of the statesmen and the people, all things disappear before the overshadowing magnitude of the question of slavery, and all efforts to conceal it are of no avail. We watch the developments in Washington with greater suspense than fear and are ready to plunge into the fight. By the way, I am colonel of militia, and perhaps we shall have a little war, if need be.

WATERTOWN, Feb. 23, 1858.

I returned home yesterday and am looking forward to a week of rest. During that time, I shall think of other matters than politics. I am sending you one of my speeches, the only one of the last campaign that has been correctly reported. Upon this speech is based the greater part of my reputation in this country and with becoming modesty I herewith lay it at the feet of my master and instructor in the art. Portions of it have made the rounds of the American press and have been well received. I need hardly say that I prepared it carefully. I shall never become an extemporaneous speaker. I do well enough in debate, but to extemporize, that is, simply to trust to the inspiration of the moment, to make a great and beautiful speech, that will always be difficult. It would be invaluable; but I believe I lack the needed ready command of language. In this respect I envy you; for while study and practice do much, they do not make the master.

TO GERRIT SMITH

WATERTOWN, WIS., Sept. 14, 1858.

Your kind letter was to me a very agreeable surprise. I was almost sure that the ideas on true Americanism set forth in my speech would meet your approbation, but I had no right to expect so encouraging an applause. It seems to me, that the only way to fight the proscriptive tendencies of the misnamed Americanism successfully is by meeting it with an array of *positive* ideas. It will make a sensible Know-Nothing ashamed of himself.

It is impossible for me to accept your kind invitation to take part in the political campaign in New York, first, because I am not sufficiently conversant with New York politics, which do not appear to be quite so plain and simple as they ought to be, and secondly, because my business affairs do not permit my absence from here. The crisis has been rather hard on me, and although I would be happy to devote all my energies and my whole life to the propagation of ideas and principles which I consider just, yet I have to consider this now as a luxury which I cannot very extensively indulge in. I have, however, accepted an invitation of the Republican central committee of Illinois and shall spend a week there; besides this, I have to do a little work in my Congressional district. It would be impossible to devote any more time to political agitation this fall; I have to submit to the stern demands of life.

I understand your hostility to the Republican organization of the Eastern States perfectly well. I deplore with you the turn which things have taken and especially the course which the *Tribune* is following.[1] But I do not know whether I would have gone so far as you have, unless I considered the Republican party past redemption.

[1] See letter of Dec. 24, 1858, *post*.

I do not know what it is in New York, and I am not able to judge; but it is not so here. I believe that in the Western States that wing of the Republican party, which I might rather call the philosophical than the radical wing, will gradually obtain the control of the policy of that party. I think we shall be able to raise the standard of Republicanism gradually. We are now in one of those periods of reaction which are always unproductive. But that will pass away, I hope, before 1860. At all events, we shall struggle all we can to subdue the bargaining spirit which is gangrening all political organizations.

Permit me to say, sir, that there is no man in America for whom I entertain a deeper respect than for you.

TO FRIEDRICH ALTHAUS[1]

WATERTOWN, Nov. 5, 1858.[2]

For some time, I have again been swimming on the crest of the wave of public life, and as I have resolved to make my very best efforts to succeed, complete concentration is necessary. For several days, I have again enjoyed the comfort of my domestic life without interruption, and I beg of you to conclude from the fact that I write to you at once that I have waited for such a quiet moment to resume our correspondence.

We are still somewhat under the influence of the excitement of recent months. The anti-slavery party has made new and strenuous efforts in the political campaign of this year, and we are now literally resting on our laurels. In all the Northern States we have achieved an uninterrupted succession of the most brilliant victories this country has ever witnessed; we have stormed almost the

[1] Schurz's intimate fellow-student at Bonn.
[2] Translated from the German.

last citadels of our opponents, and even in Illinois, where it is uncertain whether Douglas has won or lost, there has been an emphatic protest against the Administration of Buchanan. If the Republican party is wise enough in its politics to hold the ground we have gained, we are sure of the Presidential election in the year 1860 and the political supremacy of the slave-power will be impossible.

If I mention to you the fact that my name has penetrated beyond the borders of Wisconsin and the Western States during the last fight, and that I have won a national reputation, I do not speak of this fact boastfully, but because I know that it will give you pleasure. A speech which I made in Chicago has been read from Maine to Minnesota; one million copies have been printed and distributed and the newspapers have given it boundless praise.[1] I am sending you a copy of it and also a copy of an academic address which I delivered last summer at Beloit College, one of the best institutions of this State and of the entire West.

There is soon to be a great change in our domestic life. We intend to settle in Milwaukee, but we shall not entirely break up our household here. Margarethe and the children will have a hired house in Milwaukee during the winter and will pass the summer here, in our pretty country home. The railway connections will make it possible for me to be here at least once a week, probably oftener, and so the interruption of our family life will not be too trying. I have assurances that promise me a good law practice, and my political reputation will naturally be a great help. I shall then dispose of my property here at the first favorable opportunity. At present, the prospects are not especially brilliant, as financial conditions in the West are only slowly recovering from the recent crisis. It

---

[1] "The Irrepressible Conflict," delivered in Chicago, Sept. 28, 1858. *Speeches* (1865), 9–37.

was terrible, and its lingering consequences are still very depressing. We have all suffered, and probably years will be required to remove the last traces of it. Only the lawyers are "doing well," as the phrase here is.

Some time ago, I was made a member of the board of regents of the University of Wisconsin. It is located in Madison, one of the most beautiful spots in the United States. It is, of course, not of the standard of German universities, but rather of that of the German "gymnasium," only more liberal and without the elementary classes. Yet the lecture system has been introduced into some courses. The instruction of modern languages is limited to German, French and English. There are excellent men among the professors; the conditions of college life are good and social relations are pleasant. How would such a position please you? If you were here, a mere suggestion from me would probably suffice.

TO J. F. POTTER[1]

MILWAUKEE, Dec. 24, 1858.

I must write you a few lines on a subject in which I feel a deep concern. Some time ago I received a very kind letter from Senator [Henry] Wilson, requesting me to send him a few copies of my Chicago and Milwaukee speeches. In answer to his letter I called his attention to the efforts which are being made to unite the whole opposition to the Administration on a common basis, and I availed myself of the opportunity to tell him frankly that in my opinion any sacrifice of principle, and especially an alliance with the American party, would certainly ruin us in all the Northwestern States. An article which appeared in the Washington *Republic* some time ago leads

[1] A Republican Representative from Wis.; previously a county judge.

me to believe that some Republican leaders think of uniting with the anti-Administration Democrats on a "popular
sovereignty" platform. How is this possible? Have we
been beaten at the last election? Are we too weak to
stand on our own feet? Or is not Douglas's "popular
sovereignty" to-day the same humbug it was two years
ago? How shall we stand before the people, if we now
adopt the very same principle in opposition to which our
party was originally organized? We are bound to conquer in 1860, if we stand to our colors and do not throw
away our chances by a tricky and inconsistent policy. I
know that you and I entertain the same views and feelings
about this subject. Will you be kind enough to keep me
advised of what is going on in Washington in this respect?
I think that every attempt to trade our principles away
should be met with a perfect hurricane in the newspapers.

There is another matter about which I want to speak
to you. My name has been mentioned in connection
with the nomination for governor. Several newspapers
have brought me forward and all our German Republican
papers have taken this thing up with great alacrity.
Then it went through the whole German Republican
press of the North, and my nomination was represented
as already made. This state of things embarrasses me
very much. If I had been consulted about it, before it
got into the newspapers, I would have stopped it, for the
reason that my name cannot be used in connection with
a nomination unless the thing is understood at all hands;
if, after it has been spoken of, adverse circumstances
should occur, which might induce the Republicans to
select somebody else, or should prevent me from accepting a nomination, it would hurt me in my political standing, and at the same time it would injure the Republican
party with the German population very much. Now,
what the feeling of the people of this State is, I do not

know and have taken no pains to ascertain. As for me,
I am wavering whether I shall let the thing go on or cut it
short by publicly declaring that I shall not be a candidate.
Allow me to consider you my confidential friend, to tell
you my thoughts and to ask your advice. To be governor
of this State, honorable as the position may be, is really
not the object of my ambition. My political standing
is such that I can do without any official station. The
thing has only one charm for me, and that is, that a success
of this kind would give me a powerful influence over the
German population of the Northern States, which would
tell in 1860. Beyond this the governorship has little
value for me personally.

Among the reasons which would induce me to decline a
nomination, the first is, that Harvey of Rock [county] is
likely to be a candidate before the convention. I owe
him much; he brought me forward for lieutenant-governor
last year, and he has always been a warm and consistent
friend of mine. I should not like to stand in the way of
his aspirations. Something is due to him, and I feel I
ought not to destroy his chances. The second reason is,
that I have not got the money for carrying on an electoral
contest, especially a hard one as this will be; and the
third is, that I cannot afford to suffer another defeat,
either before a convention or before the people. This,
however, I do not fear much, for I think I can carry the
State more easily than most others, provided no side
issues are brought up in the contest. At all events, a
nomination carried by a bare majority would not do for
me. If I cannot be nominated by a nearly unanimous
vote, I would prefer to withdraw altogether. But then
I have to do it at once, of my own free will, so that our
opponents have no right to say that I was but yielding
to outside pressure. I should not like to appear to be
obliged to do it. Meanwhile some Democratic papers

have commenced a bitter warfare on me.   Robinson of
the Green Bay *Advocate*, who expects to get the Democratic nomination, commenced to traduce me by attacking in the grossest and most sophistical manner my
Milwaukee speech, representing it as a libel on the people
of Wisconsin.   Another paper has started the story that
I was a minion and an agent of the king of Prussia and am
still in the pay of that Government, etc., and other Democratic organs have followed suit.   They endeavor to kill
me off before the nominations are made.   Well, all these
things cannot injure me, they will rather help me, but
they are in so far disagreeable to me, as they treat me as
a candidate while I am none.

Now, I want your advice, my dear Judge; tell me openly,
whether in your opinion I should put a stop to it by
declaring my intention not to be a candidate, or whether
I shall let the thing go on.

What effect had Douglas's decapitation on his Democratic friends?   My impression is, that he will not be
nominated by the Charleston Convention and that he
will gradually destroy his chances North and South by
carrying water on both shoulders.   Do you not think so?
But Douglas out of the way, and the victory will be ours
in 1860 unless we destroy ourselves by bad management.

How are you getting along personally?   I should be
very glad to hear from you at your earliest convenience.

TO EDWARD L. PIERCE[1]

MILWAUKEE, March 26, 1859.

Your favor of the 15th came duly to hand.   The action
of the legislature of Massachusetts on the suffrage question

[1] A young Massachusetts lawyer and reformer and, many years later,
biographer of Charles Sumner.

cannot but be a matter of deep regret to every true friend of the anti-slavery cause. A political party, which professes devotion to the rights of man in the abstract, and violates them in practice, will seldom possess and can never preserve the confidence of the people. I do not understand the logic of those who consider the right to vote a less inalienable right than the right to "life, liberty and the pursuit of happiness." That right is as essential to the exercise of self-government, as self-government is essential to the enjoyment of liberty. A repudiation of this doctrine would upset the whole theory on which the Republican party rests. The naturalization laws have set certain restrictions to the right of suffrage which were necessary in order to regulate its exercise. But to invent new restrictions beyond the limits of that necessity is certainly incompatible with the principles of those who adopt the Declaration of Independence as the basis of their political creed. There may have been abuses, but it is a ruinous policy to disregard fundamental principles when pressing abuses are to be corrected.

This is deeply felt by all those members of the Republican party who are directly concerned in it. The foreign-born Republicans were drawn to that party by the irresistible force of principle and nothing else. No wing of the party has worked more faithfully and disinterestedly. They did not aspire to position and preferment; but the only thing desired was to see the principles they loved faithfully carried out in practice. The friends of freedom could always count upon them as their truest confederates. They joined the Republican party in spite of the cry of Know-Nothingism, placing their trust in the power of principle over the souls of men and in the good faith of their political friends. Their labors did not remain unrewarded. Republicanism spread among the German population of the Northern States

with astonishing rapidity, and even in the South the
Germans stood everywhere in the vanguard of the
movement.

To no class of our population could the action of the
Massachusetts legislature be more mortifying than to
them. In the midst of successful exertions they saw
themselves suddenly betrayed and insulted, and the
predictions of their opponents, which they had so often
contradicted, partly verified; and that, too, by the legislature of a State which claims to stand first and foremost
in intelligence and progressive civilization. Do not
think, sir, that the effects of the action of your legislature
will be confined to the limits of your State. Massachusetts occupies a representative position, and the eyes
of the whole nation are naturally directed towards her.

It cannot be expected that the foreign-born Republicans, after this, should place implicit confidence in a
party that has given evidence of inconsistency and bad
faith, and that they should work with equal enthusiasm
as before; and I must confess, although I am no less
devoted to the anti-slavery cause than any other man in
this country, I can not blame them for it. If the people
of Massachusetts adopt the proposed amendments to the
constitution, the effect upon the political attitude of the
Western States will be a very serious one. In most of
the States west of the Alleghany Mountains, the Germans
hold the balance of power between the parties. The
Republican party would never have been able to carry
a single one of these States without their co-operation.
A change of a few thousand votes in Iowa, Wisconsin,
Illinois, Minnesota, Michigan and even Ohio might throw
those States into the hands of the pro-slavery party. And
as for Indiana, we cannot carry it without receiving large
accessions to the Republican ranks from the German
population. If the just indignation called forth by the

action ot your legislature be not allayed by a contrary
vote of the people, and if the intention (at present gaining
ground among the Germans) to leave the Republican
ranks *en masse* and to vote for independent candidates
be carried out, the Republicans may lose three or four
Western States in 1860, when the change of one may decide the result of the Presidential campaign. And then
the State of Massachusetts, that bulwark of anti-slavery
principles, would be responsible for the defeat of the
anti-slavery cause, and that, too, at a time when, without
this, success would have been almost certain.

Perhaps it would do the party good to learn that in
order to be victorious it must first be consistent and
true, and that without deserving success it will never
have any. Valuable as this experience may be, yet it
may be bought at too high a price.

I assure you, sir, that the drifting and scheming policy,
which was one of the characteristics of the old parties,
will never do for us. We can never conquer unless the
convictions and enthusiasm of the masses are on our side.
We cannot be ruled by the arts of secret diplomacy.
Every attempt to buy over former opponents by concessions of principle will result in the loss of a large number
of true and devoted friends. Expediency will always be
for us a dangerous stumbling-block. We must command
the esteem and confidence of the people in order to command their votes.

I repeat, sir, [the members of] the legislature of Massachusetts have taken a grave responsibility upon themselves. I wish the people would understand that the
question to be decided by their vote on the amendments
of the constitution is not, whether there shall be a little
more or a little less illegal voting in Massachusetts, but
whether the Republicans shall have the German vote and
all the Western States in 1860 or not.

I do not know, sir, whether this letter will bear publication; perhaps not the whole of it. But I assure you
that I have exaggerated nothing and that, much as I
would wish to see the evil consequences of that unfortunate affair averted, it would hardly be possible to accomplish it.

P. S.—I apprehend a publication of what I say about the
state of feeling among the Germans from *my* pen would
encourage the Democrats out here a little too much. I
would, therefore, recommend to you to use this letter
with some discrimination.

TO EDWARD L. PIERCE

MILWAUKEE, April 6, 1859.

Your favor of the 2nd inst. is received. I shall send
you all the papers you want as soon as I can hunt them
up. At the same time I shall write a few lines to the
committee who have honored me with an invitation to
the Jefferson festival.

Herewith I send you a copy of my speech on State-
rights delivered in our judicial campaign. Would it not
be a good thing to have it republished in a Massachusetts
paper and to state in a note that the foreigner who made
it would be disfranchised by your amendment if he
lived in your progressive and intelligent Commonwealth?
The fact is that I was naturalized and got my final
papers of citizenship not quite two years ago. It
would indeed be a telling illustration of the bearing of
the amendment.

If you should publish the speech, cut off the last paragraph about the "candidates."

TO MRS. SCHURZ

BOSTON, April 13, 1859.[1]

I arrived here in good season, having just time to dress for the [Jefferson birthday] banquet. My reception was genuinely enthusiastic and my reputation in New England is already established. I found that my speech on State-rights had already been widely circulated here and that I was expected with suspense and curiosity. They toasted gallant Wisconsin and me, and I was called on to respond. My little speech elicited hearty applause. Almost every sentence was greeted with a "Bravo!" and when I closed, the applause was prolonged. Then followed a general shaking of hands and hardly one of the speakers who followed concluded without a reference to "brave Wisconsin and her gallant champion." In short, the affair was a complete success. Governor Banks was not at the banquet. He was ailing, but I received an invitation to meet him at dinner to-morrow at the house of one of the most prominent men of the city. I have several days of strenuous work ahead of me, but I feel that I am in my element.

The great meeting is to be held at Faneuil Hall, on Monday, where I am to be given a grand reception. So far as the Know-Nothing amendments are concerned, the prospects are good. All sensible people are opposed to them, and I think Senator Wilson and other prominent Republican leaders will express their opinions boldly and fearlessly after I have made my speech. If we succeed in destroying that movement, our prospects for the future will be most excellent.

BOSTON, April 14, 1859.

I have just returned from the dinner of which I wrote you yesterday. We were the guests of Mr. Gardner

[1] Translated from the German.

Brewer, one of the richest men of Boston, and the dinner
was one of the most sumptuous affairs I ever attended.
When I return home, I will give you as much of the menu
as I can remember; it suffices to say to-day, that we sat
at table from six until ten o'clock and that, during all
this time, course after course and wine after wine were
served.   The company was not especially numerous,
but in quality it surpassed any I have yet seen in America.
Of men of letters, there were Longfellow, Whipple and
Holmes; of politicians, Governor Banks, Senator Wilson,
Burlingame, Allen, Adams (son of John Quincy Adams),
Andrew and a number of Congressmen.   I must describe
the conversation orally.   Longfellow and I had a long
talk about Germany, and we intend to continue it as soon
as I have leisure to accept his invitation to his home in
Cambridge.   On returning from the dinner, I found a lot
of cards, which will fill my time with social matters for
some days to come.   Have no fear that I shall overwork
here; if I am only left in peace long enough to think out
the details of my speech sufficiently before Monday!
This morning I was taken possession of immediately
and dragged through the town.   I was allowed only between three and four hours for writing.   Fortunately, it
is raining and I hope to be left to myself until dinner
to-morrow.   I live like Hannibal in Capua.   Luckily,
this sort of thing is not to continue long.   Have you
ever experienced how much a dinner can tire one?   I
am as tired out as if I had accomplished a vast amount
of labor, and I have, in fact, done great things at
table.   Oh, Boston is a wonderful city, too good to be
lived in!

April 15th, morning.

I am up early, gay as a lark and looking forward with
delight to the coming day and to the task which I have

to accomplish. The historical memories which are awakened here, in almost every street and public square, have put me into the same frame of mind in which I once, nine years ago, first wandered through the streets of Paris. The speech which I am writing is dominated by this feeling, and I am gladdened by the thought that you are to read the words which this enthusiasm has inspired. I believe that my hearers will be highly pleased and that I shall make a deep impression.

TRUE AMERICANISM[1]

MR. PRESIDENT AND GENTLEMEN:—A few days ago I stood on the cupola of your statehouse, and overlooked for the first time this venerable city and the country surrounding it. Then the streets, and hills, and waters around me began to teem with the life of historical recollections, recollections dear to all mankind, and a feeling of pride arose in my heart, and I said to myself, I, too, am an American citizen. There was Bunker Hill; there Charlestown, Lexington and Dorchester Heights not far off; there the harbor into which the British tea was sunk; there the place where the old liberty-tree stood; there John Hancock's house; there Benjamin Franklin's birthplace;—and now I stand in this grand old hall, which

[1] Speech delivered in Faneuil Hall, Boston, April 18, 1859. The legislature of Massachusetts had adopted an amendment to the constitution of the State, by which foreigners should not be permitted to vote until two years after they had become citizens of the United States. This amendment, generally known as the "two years' amendment," was soon to be voted upon by the people. It was one of the measures brought forth by the so-called "Know-Nothing" or "American" movement, which had met with surprising successes in many parts of the United States. It was against this spirit of proscription on account of birth, creed, or opinion, styling itself "Americanism," that the speaker directed his arguments.— From Mr. Schurz's introductory note, *Speeches* (1865), p. 51.

so often resounded with the noblest appeals that ever
thrilled American hearts, and where I am almost afraid
to hear the echo of my own feeble voice;—oh, sir, no man
that loves liberty, wherever he may have first seen the
light of day, can fail on this sacred spot to pay his tribute
to Americanism. And here, with all these glorious
memories crowding upon my heart, I will offer mine.
I, born in a foreign land, pay my tribute to Americanism?
Yes, for to me the word Americanism, *true* Americanism,
comprehends the noblest ideas which ever swelled a
human heart with noble pride.

It is one of the earliest recollections of my boyhood,
that one summer night our whole village was stirred up
by an uncommon occurrence. I say our village, for I
was born not far from that beautiful spot where the
Rhine rolls his green waters out of the wonderful gate of
the Seven Mountains, and then meanders with majestic
tranquillity through one of the most glorious valleys of
the world. That night our neighbors were pressing
around a few wagons covered with linen sheets and loaded
with household utensils and boxes and trunks to their
utmost capacity. One of our neighboring families was
moving far away across a great water, and it was said that
they would never again return. And I saw silent tears
trickling down weather-beaten cheeks, and the hands of
rough peasants firmly pressing each other, and some of
the men and women hardly able to speak when they
nodded to one another a last farewell. At last the train
started into motion, they gave three cheers for *America*,
and then in the first gray dawn of the morning I saw them
wending their way over the hill until they disappeared
in the shadow of the forest. And I heard many a man say,
how happy he would be if he could go with them to that
great and free country, where a man could be himself.

That was the first time that I heard of America, and

my childish imagination took possession of a land covered partly with majestic trees, partly with flowery prairies, immeasurable to the eye, and intersected with large rivers and broad lakes—a land where everybody could do what he thought best, and where nobody need be poor, because everybody was free.

And later, when I was old enough to read, and descriptions of this country and books on American history fell into my hands, the offspring of my imagination acquired the colors of reality, and I began to exercise my brain with the thought of what man might be and become when left perfectly free to himself. And still later, when ripening into manhood, I looked up from my school-books into the stir and bustle of the world, and the trumpet-tones of struggling humanity struck my ear and thrilled my heart, and I saw my nation shake her chains in order to burst them, and I heard a gigantic, universal shout for Liberty rising up to the skies; and at last, after having struggled manfully and drenched the earth of Fatherland with the blood of thousands of noble beings, I saw that nation crushed down again, not only by overwhelming armies, but by the dead weight of customs and institutions and notions and prejudices which past centuries had heaped upon them, and which a moment of enthusiasm, however sublime, could not destroy; then I consoled an almost despondent heart with the idea of a youthful people and of original institutions clearing the way for an untrammeled development of the ideal nature of man. Then I turned my eyes instinctively across the Atlantic Ocean, and America and Americanism, as I fancied them, appeared to me as the last depositories of the hopes of all true friends of humanity.

I say all this, not as though I indulged in the presumptuous delusion that my personal feelings and experience would be of any interest to you, but in order to show

you what America is to the thousands of thinking men
in the old world, who, disappointed in their fondest hopes
and depressed by the saddest experience, cling with their
last remnant of confidence in human nature, to the last
spot on earth where man is free to follow the road to
attainable perfection, and where, unbiased by the disastrous influence of traditional notions, customs and
institutions, he acts on his own responsibility.   They ask
themselves: Was it but a wild delusion when we thought
that man has the faculty to be free and to govern himself?
Have we been fighting, were we ready to die, for a mere
phantom, for a mere product of a morbid imagination?
This question downtrodden humanity cries out into the
world, and from this country it expects an answer.

As its advocate I speak to you.   I will speak of Americanism as the great representative of the reformatory age,
as the great champion of the dignity of human nature, as
the great repository of the last hopes of suffering mankind.
I will speak of the ideal mission of this country and of
this people.

You may tell me that these views are visionary, that
the destiny of this country is less exalted, that the American people are less great than I think they are or ought
to be.   I answer, ideals are like stars; you will not succeed
in touching them with your hands.   But like the sea-
faring man on the desert of waters, you choose them as
your guides, and following them you will reach your
destiny.   I invite you to ascend with me the watchtower
of history, overlooking the grand panorama of the development of human affairs, in which the American
Republic stands in so bold and prominent relief.

He who reviews the past of this country in connection
with the history of the world besides, cannot fail to
discover a wonderful coincidence of great events and
fortunate circumstances, which were destined to produce

everlasting results, unless recklessly thrown away by imbecile generations.

Look back with me four or five centuries. The dark period of the middle ages is drawing near its close. The accidental explosion of that mysterious black powder, discovered by an obscure German monk, is the first flash of lightning preluding that gigantic thunderstorm which is to shatter the edifice of feudal society to pieces. The invention of gunpowder strips the feudal lord of his prestige as a *warrior;* another discovery is to strip him of his prestige as a *man!* Gutenberg, another obscure German, invents the printing-press, and as gunpowder blows the castles of the small feudal tyrants into the air, so the formidable artillery of printed letters batters down the citadels of ignorance and superstition. Soul and body take up arms and prepare themselves for the great battle of the Reformation. Now the mighty volcano of the German mind bursts the crust of indolence which has covered it. Luther's triumphant thunder rattles against the holy see of Rome. The world is ablaze, all the elements of society are rising up in boiling commotion—two ages are battling against each other.

This is the time when the regeneration of the old world is to take place. But the old order of things, fortified in customs and prejudices and deeply-rooted institutions, does not surrender at the first blast of trumpets. The grand but fearful struggle of the reformatory movement plunges all Europe into endless confusion. The very wheel of progress seems to grind and crush one generation after another. The ideas which concerned the highest and most sacred relations of humanity seem at the same time to call into their service the basest and most violent passions of the human heart, and in all Europe the wars of great principles degenerate into wars of general devastation.

But, meanwhile, a new country has opened its boundless
fields to those great ideas, for the realization of which the
old world seems no longer to be wide enough. It is as
though the earth herself had taken part in the general
revolution, and had thrown up from her sea-covered womb
a new battle-ground for the spirit of the new era. That
is America. Not only the invention of gunpowder and
of the printing-press, but also the discovery of America,
inaugurates the modern age.

There is the new and immense continent. The most
restless and enterprising elements of European society
direct their looks towards it. First, the greediness of
the gold-hunting adventurer pounces upon the new conquest; but, his inordinate appetites being disappointed,
he gradually abandons the field to men in whose hearts
the future of the new world is sleeping, unborn.

While the coast of Virginia is settled by a motley immigration, led and ruled by men of ideas and enterprise,
the sturdiest champions of principle descend upon the
stony shores of New England. While the Southern
colonies are settled under the auspices of lordly merchants
and proprietaries, original democracy plants its stern
banner upon Plymouth Rock. Mercantile speculation,
aristocratic ambition and stern virtue that seeks freedom
and nothing but freedom, lead the most different classes
of people, different in origin, habits and persuasion, upon
the virgin soil, and entrust to them the task of realizing
the great principles of the age. Nor is this privilege
confined to one nationality alone. While the Anglo-
Saxon takes possession of New England, Virginia and
Pennsylvania, the Frenchman plants his colonies on the
soil of French Florida and the interior of the continent;
the Hollander locates New Netherlands on the banks of
the Hudson; the Swede, led there by the great mind of
Oxenstiern, occupies the banks of the Delaware; the

Spaniard maintains himself in peninsular Florida, and a
numerous immigration of Germans, who follow the call
of religious freedom, and of Irishmen, gradually flowing
in, scatters itself all over this vast extent of country.
Soon all the social and national elements of the civilized
world are represented in the new land. Every people,
every creed, every class of society has contributed its
share to that wonderful mixture out of which is to grow
the great nation of the new world. It is true, the Anglo-
Saxon establishes and maintains his ascendancy, but
without absolutely absorbing the other national elements.
They modify each other, and their peculiar characteristics
are to be blended together by the all-assimilating power
of freedom. This is the origin of the American nationality, which did not spring from one family, one tribe,
one country, but incorporates the vigorous elements of
all civilized nations on earth.

This fact is not without great importance. It is an
essential link in the chain of historical development.
The student of history cannot fail to notice that when new
periods of civilization break upon humanity, the people
of the earth cannot maintain their national relations.
New ideas are to be carried out by young nations. From
time to time, violent, irresistible hurricanes sweep over
the world, blowing the most different elements of the
human family together, which by mingling reinvigorate
each other, and the general confusion then becomes the
starting-point of a new period of progress   Nations which
have long subsisted exclusively on their own resources
will gradually lose their original vigor, and die the death
of decrepitude. But mankind becomes young again
by its different elements being shaken together, by race
crossing race and mind penetrating mind.

The oldest traditions of history speak of such great
revulsions and general migrations, and if we could but

lift the veil, which covers the remotest history of Asiatic
tribes, we should discover the first scenes and acts of the
drama, of which the downfall of the Roman Empire is a
portion. When that empire had exhausted its natural
vitality, the dark forests of the North poured forth a
barbarous but vigorous multitude, who trampled into
ruins the decrepit civilization of the Roman world, but
infused new blood into the veins of old Europe, grasping
the great ideas of Christianity with a bloody but firm
hand—and a new period of original progress sprang out
of the seeming devastation. The German element took
the helm of history. But, in the course of time, the
development of things arrived at a new turning-point.
The spirit of individualism took possession of the heart
of civilized humanity, and the reformatory movement of
the sixteenth century was its expression. But continental
Europe appeared unable to incorporate the new and
progressive ideas growing out of that spirit, in organic
political institutions. While the heart of Europe was
ravaged by a series of religious wars, the Anglo-Saxons
of England attempted what other nations seemed unable
to accomplish. But they also clung too fast to the traditions of past centuries; they failed in separating the
Church from the State, and did not realize the cosmopolitan tendency of the new principle. Then the time of a
new migration was at hand, and that migration rolled
its waves towards America. The old process repeated
itself under new forms, milder and more congenial to the
humane ideas it represented. It is now not a barbarous
multitude pouncing upon old and decrepit empires; not
a violent concussion of tribes accompanied by all the
horrors of general destruction; but we see the vigorous
elements of all nations, we see the Anglo-Saxon, the leader
in the practical movement, with his spirit of independence,
of daring enterprise and of indomitable perseverance;

the German, the original leader in the movement of ideas, with his spirit of inquiry and his quiet and thoughtful application; the Celt, with the impulsive vivacity of his race; the Frenchman, the Scandinavian, the Scot, the Hollander, the Spaniard and the Italian—all these peaceably congregating and mingling together on virgin soil, where the backwoodsman's hatchet is the only battle-axe of civilization; led together by the irresistible attraction of free and broad principles; undertaking to commence a new era in the history of the world, without first destroying the results of the progress of past periods; undertaking to found a new cosmopolitan nation without marching over the dead bodies of slain millions. Thus was founded the *great colony of free humanity*, which has not old England alone, but the *world*, for its mother-country.

This idea is, perhaps, not palatable to those who pride themselves on their unadulterated Anglo-Saxondom. To them I have to say that the destinies of men are often greater than men themselves, and that a good many are swerving from the path of glory by not obeying the true instincts of their nature, and by sacrificing their mission to one-sided pride.

The Anglo-Saxon may justly be proud of the growth and development of this country, and if he ascribes most of it to the undaunted spirit of his race, we may not accuse him of overweening self-glorification. He possesses, in an eminent degree, the enviable talent of acting when others only think; of promptly executing his own ideas, and of appropriating the ideas of other people to his own use. There is, perhaps, no other race that, at so early a day, would have founded the stern democracy of the Plymouth settlement; no other race that would have defied the trials and hardships of the original settler's life so victoriously. No other race, perhaps, possesses in so high a degree not only the daring spirit of independent enterprise, but at the same time the stubborn steadfastness necessary to the final execution of great designs. The Anglo-Saxon spirit has been the locomotive of progress; but do not forget, that this locomotive would be of little use to the world if it refused to draw its train over the iron highway and carry its valuable freight towards its destination; that train consists of the vigorous elements of all nations; that freight is the vital ideas of our age; that destination is universal freedom and the ideal development of man. That is the true greatness of the Anglo-Saxon race; that ought to be the source of Anglo-Saxon pride. I esteem the son who is proud of his father, if, at the same time, he is worthy of him.

Thus, I say, was founded the colony of free humanity on virgin soil. The youthful elements which constitute people of the new world cannot submit to rules which are not of their own making; they must throw off the fetters which bind them to an old decrepit order of things. They resolve to enter the great family of nations as an independent member. And in the colony of free humanity, whose mother-country is the world, they establish *the Republic of equal rights, where the title of manhood is the title to citizenship.* My friends, if I had a thousand tongues, and a voice strong as the thunder of heaven, they would not be sufficient to impress upon your minds forcibly enough the greatness of this idea, the overshadowing glory of this result. This was the dream of the truest friends of man from the beginning; for this the noblest blood of martyrs has been shed; for this has mankind waded through seas of blood and tears. There it is now; there it stands, the noble fabric in all the splendor of reality.

They speak of the greatness of the Roman Republic! Oh, sir, if I could call the proudest of Romans from his grave, I would take him by the hand and say to him,

Look at this picture, and at this! The greatness of thy
Roman Republic consisted in its despotic rule over the
world; the greatness of the American Republic consists
in the secured right of man to govern himself. The
dignity of the Roman citizen consisted in his exclusive
privileges; the dignity of the American citizen consists
in his holding the natural rights of his neighbor just as
sacred as his own. The Roman Republic recognized and
protected the *rights of the citizen*, at the same time dis-
regarding and leaving unprotected the *rights of man;*
Roman citizenship was founded upon monopoly, not
upon the claims of human nature. What the citizen of
Rome claimed for himself, he did not respect in others;
his own greatness was his only object; his own liberty,
as he regarded it, gave him the privilege to oppress his
fellow-beings. His democracy, instead of elevating mankind to his own level, trampled the rights of man into the
dust. The security of the Roman Republic, therefore,
consisted in the power of the sword; the security of the
American Republic rests in the equality of human rights!
The Roman Republic perished by the sword; the American
Republic will stand as long as the equality of human rights
remains inviolate. Which of the two Republics is the
greater—the Republic of the Roman, or the Republic of
man?

Sir, I wish the words of the Declaration of Independence
"that all men are created free and equal, and are endowed
with certain inalienable rights," were inscribed upon every
gate-post within the limits of this Republic. From this
principle the Revolutionary Fathers derived their claim
to independence; upon this they founded the institutions
of this country, and the whole structure was to be the
living incarnation of this idea. This principle contains
the programme of our political existence. It is the most
progressive, and at the same time the most conservative

one; the most progressive, for it takes even the lowliest
members of the human family out of their degradation,
and inspires them with the elevating consciousness of
equal human dignity; the most conservative, for it makes
a common cause of individual rights. From the equality
of rights springs identity of our highest interests; you
cannot subvert your neighbor's rights without striking
a dangerous blow at your own. And when the rights of
one cannot be infringed without finding a ready defense
in all others who defend their own rights in defending his,
then, and only then, are the rights of all safe against the
usurpations of governmental authority.

This general identity of interests is the only thing that
can guarantee the stability of democratic institutions.
Equality of rights, embodied in general self-government,
is the great moral element of true democracy; it is the
only reliable safety-valve in the machinery of modern
society. There is the solid foundation of our system of
government; there is our mission; there is our greatness;
there is our safety; there, and nowhere else! This is
true Americanism, and to this I pay the tribute of my
devotion.

Shall I point out to you the consequences of a deviation
from this principle? Look at the slave States. There
is a class of men who are deprived of their natural rights.
But this is not the only deplorable feature of that peculiar
organization of society. Equally deplorable is it, that
there is another class of men who keep the former in
subjection. That there are slaves is bad; but almost
worse is it, that there are masters. Are not the masters
freemen? No, sir! Where is their liberty of the press?
Where is their liberty of speech? Where is the man
among them who dares to advocate openly principles
not in strict accordance with the ruling system? They
speak of a republican form of government—they speak

of democracy, but the despotic spirit of slavery and
mastership combined pervades their whole political life
like a liquid poison.   They do not dare to be free, lest
the spirit of liberty become contagious.   The system of
slavery has enslaved them all, master as well as slave.
What is the cause of all this?   It is that you cannot deny
one class of society the full measure of their natural
rights without imposing restraints upon your own liberty.
If you want to be free, there is but one way: it is to
guarantee an equally full measure of liberty to all your
neighbors.   There is no other.

True, there are difficulties connected with an organization of society founded upon the basis of equal rights.
Nobody denies it.   A large number of those who come to
you from foreign lands are not as capable of taking part
in the administration of government as the man who was
fortunate enough to drink the milk of liberty in his cradle.
And certain religious denominations do, perhaps, nourish
principles which are hardly in accordance with the doctrines of true democracy.   There is a conglomeration
on this continent of heterogeneous elements; there is a
warfare of clashing interest and unruly aspirations; and,
with all this, our democratic system gives rights to the
ignorant and power to the inexperienced.   And the
billows of passion will lash the sides of the ship, and
the storm of party warfare will bend its masts, and
the pusillanimous will cry out—"Master, master, we
perish!"   But the genius of true democracy will arise
from his slumber, and rebuke the winds and the raging
of the water, and say unto them—"Where is your faith?"
Aye, where is the faith that led the Fathers of this Republic
to invite the weary and burdened of all nations to the
enjoyment of equal rights?   Where is that broad and
generous confidence in the efficiency of true democratic
institutions?   Has the present generation forgotten that

true democracy bears in itself the remedy for all the
difficulties that may grow out of it?

It is an old dodge of the advocates of despotism throughout the world, that the people who are not experienced
in self-government are not fit for the exercise of self-
government, and must first be educated under the rule
of a superior authority. But at the same time the advocates of despotism will never offer them an opportunity
to acquire experience in self-government, lest they suddenly become fit for its independent exercise. To this
treacherous sophistry the fathers of this republic opposed
the noble doctrine, that liberty is the best school for
liberty, and that self-government cannot be learned but
by practicing it. This, sir, is a truly American idea;
this is true Americanism, and to this I pay the tribute of
my devotion.

You object that some people do not understand their
own interests? There is nothing that, in the course of
time, will make a man better understand his interests
than the independent management of his own affairs on
his own responsibility. You object that people are
ignorant? There is no better schoolmaster in the world
than self-government, independently exercised. You
object that people have no just idea of their duties as
citizens? There is no other source from which they
can derive a just notion of their duties, than the enjoyment
of the rights from which they arise. You object that
people are misled by their religious prejudices, and by
the intrigues of the Roman hierarchy? Since when have
the enlightened citizens of this Republic lost their faith
in the final invincibility of truth? Since when have they
forgotten that if the Roman or any other church plants
the seed of superstition, liberty sows broadcast the seed
of enlightenment? Do they no longer believe in the
invincible spirit of inquiry, which characterizes the

reformatory age? If the struggle be fair, can the victory be doubtful? As to religious fanaticism, it will prosper under oppression; it will feed on persecution; it will grow strong by proscription; but it is powerless against genuine democracy. It may indulge in short-lived freaks of passion, or in wily intrigues, but it will die of itself, for its lungs are not adapted to breathe the atmosphere of liberty. It is like the shark of the sea: drag him into the air, and the monster will perhaps struggle fearfully and frighten timid people with the powerful blows of his tail, and the terrible array of his teeth, but leave him quietly to die and he will die. But engage with him in a hand-to-hand struggle even then, and the last of his convulsions may fatally punish your rash attempt. Against fanaticism genuine democracy wields an irresistible weapon—it is *Toleration*. Toleration will not strike down the fanatic, but it will quietly and gently disarm him. But fight fanaticism *with* fanaticism, and you will restore it to its own congenial element. It is like Antæus, who gained strength when touching his native earth.

Whoever reads the history of this country calmly and thoroughly, cannot but discover that religious liberty is slowly but steadily rooting out the elements of superstition, and even of prejudice. It has dissolved the war of sects, of which persecution was characteristic, into a contest of abstract opinions, which creates convictions without oppressing men. By recognizing perfect freedom of inquiry, it will engender among men of different belief that mutual respect of true convictions which makes inquiry earnest and discussion fair. It will recognize as supremely inviolable, what Roger Williams, one of the most luminous stars of the American sky, called the sanctity of conscience. Read your history, and add the thousands and thousands of Romanists and their offspring together, who, from the first establishment of the colonies,

gradually came to this country, and the sum will amount
to many millions; compare that number with the number
of Romanists who are now here, and you will find that
millions are missing. Where are they? You did not
kill them; you did not drive them away; they did not
perish as the victims of persecution. But where are
they? The peaceable working of the great principles
which called this Republic into existence, has gradually
and silently absorbed them. True Americanism, toleration, the equality of rights, has absorbed their prejudices,
and will peaceably absorb everything that is not consistent
with the victorious spirit of our institutions.

Oh, sir, there is a wonderful vitality in true democracy
founded upon the equality of rights. There is an inexhaustible power of resistance in that system of government, which makes the protection of individual rights a
matter of common interest. If preserved in its purity,
there is no warfare of opinions which can endanger it—
there is no conspiracy of despotic aspirations that can
destroy it. But if not preserved in its purity! There
are dangers which only blindness can not see, and which
only stubborn party prejudice will not see.

I have already called your attention to the despotic
tendency of the slaveholding system. I need not enlarge
upon it; I need not describe how the existence of slavery
in the South affected and demoralized even the political
life of the free States; how they attempted to press us,
you and me, into the posse of the slave-catcher by that
abominable act which, worse than the "alien and sedition
laws," still disgraces our statute-book; how the ruling
party, which has devoted itself to the service of that
despotic interest, shrinks from no violation of good faith,
from no adulteration of the constitutional compact,
from no encroachment upon natural right, from no
treacherous abandonment of fundamental principles. And

I do not hesitate to prophesy that, if the theories engendered by the institution of slavery be suffered to outgrow the equalizing tendency of true democracy, the American Republic will, at no distant day, crumble down under the burden of the laws and measures which the ruling interest will demand for its protection, and its name will be added to the sad catalogue of the broken hopes of humanity.

But the mischief does not come from that side alone; it is in things of small beginnings, but fearful in their growth. One of these is the propensity of men *to lose sight of fundamental principles, when passing abuses are to be corrected.*

Is it not wonderful how nations who have won their liberty by the severest struggles become so easily impatient of the small inconveniences and passing difficulties which are almost inseparably connected with the practical working of general self-government? How they so easily forget that rights may be abused, and yet remain inalienable rights? Europe has witnessed many an attempt for the establishment of democratic institutions; some of them were at first successful, and the people were free, but the abuses and inconveniences connected with liberty became at once apparent. Then the ruling classes of society, in order to get rid of the abuses, restricted liberty; they did, indeed, get rid of the abuses, but they got rid of liberty at the same time. You heard liberal governments there speak of protecting and regulating the liberty of the press; and, in order to prevent that liberty from being abused, they adopted measures, apparently harmless at first, which ultimately resulted in an absolute censorship. Would it be much better if we, recognizing the right of man to the exercise of self-government, should, in order to protect the purity of the ballot-box, restrict the right of suffrage?

Liberty, sir, is like a spirited housewife; she will have her whims, she will be somewhat unruly sometimes, and, like so many husbands, you cannot always have it all your own way. She may spoil your favorite dish sometimes; but will you, therefore, at once smash her china, break her kettles and shut her out from the kitchen? Let her practise, let her try again and again, and even when she makes a mistake, encourage her with a benignant smile, and your broth will be right after a while. But meddle with her concerns, tease her, bore her, and your little squabbles, spirited as she is, will ultimately result in a divorce. What then? It is one of Jefferson's wisest words that "he would much rather be exposed to the inconveniences arising from too much liberty, than to those arising from too small a degree of it." It is a matter of historical experience, that nothing that is wrong in principle can be right in practice. People are apt to delude themselves on that point; but the ultimate result will always prove the truth of the maxim. A violation of equal rights can never serve to maintain institutions which are founded upon equal rights. A contrary policy is not only pusillanimous and small, but it is senseless. It reminds me of the soldier who, for fear of being shot in battle, committed suicide on the march; or of the man who would cut off his foot, because he had a corn on his toe. It is that ridiculous policy of premature despair, which commences to throw the freight overboard when there is a suspicious cloud in the sky.

Another danger for the safety of our institutions, and perhaps the most formidable one, arises from the general propensity of political parties and public men to act on a policy of mere expediency, and to sacrifice principle to local and temporary success. And here, sir, let me address a solemn appeal to the consciences of those with whom I am proud to struggle side by side against human thraldom.

You hate kingcraft, and you would sacrifice your
fortunes and your lives in order to prevent its establishment on the soil of this Republic.   But let me tell you
that the rule of political parties which sacrifice principle
to expediency, is no less dangerous, no less disastrous,
no less aggressive, of no less despotic a nature, than the
rule of monarchs.   Do not indulge in the delusion, that
in order to make a government fair and liberal, the only
thing necessary is to make it elective.   When a political
party in power, however liberal their principles may be,
have once adopted the policy of knocking down their
opponents instead of voting them down, there is an end
of justice and equal rights.   The history of the world
shows no example of a more arbitrary despotism, than
that exercised by the party which ruled the National
Assembly of France in the bloodiest days of the great
French Revolution.   I will not discuss here what might
have been done, and what not, in those times of a fearful
crisis; but I will say that they tried to establish liberty
by means of despotism, and that in her gigantic struggle
against the united monarchs of Europe, revolutionary
France won the victory, but lost her liberty.

Remember the shout of indignation that went all over
the Northern States when we heard that the border
ruffians of Kansas had crowded the free-State men away
from the polls and had not allowed them to vote.   That
indignation was just, not only because the men thus
terrorized were free-State men and friends of liberty,
but because they were deprived of their right of suffrage,
and because the government of that territory was placed
on the basis of force, instead of equal rights.   Sir, if
ever the party of liberty should use their local predominance for the purpose of disarming their opponents instead
of convincing them, they will but follow the example set
by the ruffians of Kansas, although legislative enactments

may be a genteeler weapon than the revolver and bowie
knife. They may perhaps achieve some petty local
success, they may gain some small temporary advantage,
but they will help to introduce a system of action into
our politics which will gradually undermine the very
foundations upon which our republican edifice rests.
Of all the dangers and difficulties that beset us, there is
none more horrible than the hideous monster, whose
name is "Proscription for opinion's sake." I am an
anti-slavery man, and I have a right to my opinion in
South Carolina just as well as in Massachusetts. My
neighbor is a pro-slavery man; I may be sorry for it, but
I solemnly acknowledge his right to his opinion in Massachusetts as well as in South Carolina. You tell me,
that for my opinion they would mob me in South Carolina?
Sir, there is the difference between South Carolina and
Massachusetts. There is the difference between an anti-
slavery man, who is a freeman, and a slaveholder, who
is himself a slave.

Our present issues will pass away. The slavery
question will be settled, liberty will be triumphant and
other matters of difference will divide the political parties
of this country. What if we, in our struggle against
slavery, had removed the solid basis of equal rights, on
which such new matters of difference may be peaceably
settled? What if we had based the institutions of this
country upon a difference of rights between different
classes of people? What if, in destroying the generality
of natural rights, we had resolved them into privileges?
There is a thing which stands above the command of the
most ingenious of politicians: *it is the logic of things and
events*. It cannot be turned and twisted by artificial
arrangements and delusive settlements; it will go its own
way with the steady step of fate. It will force you, with
uncompromising severity, to choose between two social

organizations, one of which is founded upon privilege, and the other upon the doctrine of equal rights.

Force instead of right, privilege instead of equality, expediency instead of principle, being once the leading motives of your policy, you will have no power to stem the current. There will be new abuses to be corrected, new inconveniences to be remedied, new supposed dangers to be obviated, new equally exacting ends to be subserved, and your encroachments upon the natural rights of your opponents now, will be used as welcome precedents for the mutual oppression of parties then. Having once knowingly disregarded the doctrine of equal rights, the ruling parties will soon accustom themselves to consult only their interests where fundamental principles are at stake. Those who lead us into this channel will be like the sorcerer who knew the art of making a giant snake. And when he had made it, he forgot the charmword that would destroy it again. And the giant snake threw its horrid coils around him, and the unfortunate man was choked by the monster of his own creation.

On the evening of the 2d day of November, 1855, there stood on this very platform a man, known and loved by every true son of Massachusetts, who, unmoved by the whirlwind of proscriptive movement howling around him, spoke the following words:

It is proposed to attaint men for their religion, and also for their birth. If this object can prevail, vain are the triumphs of civil freedom in its many hard-fought fields; vain is that religious toleration which we all profess. The fires of Smithfield, the tortures of the inquisition, the proscription of the Non-conformists, may all be revived. Slowly among the struggling sects was evolved the great idea of the equality of all men before the law, without regard to religious belief; nor can any party now organize a proscription merely for religious (and I may add political) belief, without calling in question this unquestionable principle.

The man who said so was Charles Sumner. Then the day was not far off when suddenly the whole country was startled by the incredible news, that his noble head had drooped under the murderous blows of a Southern fanatic, and that his warm blood had covered the floor of the Senate Chamber, the noblest sprinkling that ever fertilized a barren soil. And now I tell you, when he lay on the lounge of the ante-chamber, his anxious friends busy around him, and his cowardly murderers slinking away like Cain—if at that solemn moment the first question addressed to his slowly returning senses had been: Shall those who support your dastardly assailants with their votes be deprived of their suffrage? he would have raised his bleeding head, and with the fire of indignation kindling in his dim eye, he would have answered: "No! In the name of my country, no! For the honor of Massachusetts, no! For the sake of the principles for which my blood is flowing, no! Let them kill me, but let the rights of man be safe!"

Sir, if you want to bestow a high praise upon a man, you are apt to say he is an old Roman. But I know a higher epithet of praise; it is—He is a true American! Aye, Charles Sumner is a true American; he is a representative of the truest Americanism, and to him I pay the tribute of my enthusiastic admiration.

Sir, I am coming to the close of my remarks. But I cannot refrain from alluding to a circumstance which concerns myself. I understand it has been said, that in speaking a few words on the principles of Jeffersonian democracy a few evenings since, I had attempted to interfere with the home affairs of this State, and to dictate to the Republicans their policy. Ah, sir, is there a man in Massachusetts, except he be a servant of the slave-power, who cannot hear me advocate the equal rights of man, without feeling serious pangs of conscience? Is there a son of this glorious old Commonwealth who cannot hear me draw logical conclusions from the Declaration of Independence—who cannot hear me speak of the natural right of man to the exercise of self-government, without feeling a blush fluttering upon his cheeks? If so, sir, I am sorry for him; it is his fault, not mine.

Interfere with your local matters! How could I? What influence could I, an humble stranger among you, exercise on the action of Massachusetts? But one thing I must tell you. It ought never to be forgotten that this old Commonwealth occupies a representative position. Her history is familiar to the nation; even South Carolina knows it. The nation is so accustomed to admire her glorious deed for freedom, that with this expectation their eyes are turned upon her. Massachusetts can do nothing in secret; Massachusetts can do nothing for herself alone; every one of her acts involves a hundredfold responsibility. What Massachusetts does is felt from the Atlantic to the Pacific. But Massachusetts need only be herself, in order to be great. This is her position among the free States, recognized by all. Can there be a more honorable one? Sons of Massachusetts, you may be proud of it. Do not forget that from her greatness you cannot separate your responsibility.

No, I will not meddle with your home concerns. I will however, say a word for the West. Strenuous advocate of individual rights and of local self-government as I am, if you ever hear of any movement in the West against the integrity of the fundamental principles underlying our system of government, I invite you, I entreat you, I conjure you, come one and all, and make our prairies resound and our forests shake, and our ears ring

and tingle, with your appeals for the equal rights of
man.

Sir, I was to speak on Republicanism at the West,
and so I did. This *is* Western Republicanism. These
are its principles, and I am proud to say its principles are
its policy. These are the ideas which have rallied around
the banner of liberty not only the natives of the soil, but
an innumerable host of Germans, Scandinavians, Scotch-
men, Frenchmen and a goodly number of Irishmen, also.
And here I tell you, those are mistaken who believe that
the Irish heart is devoid of those noble impulses which
will lead him to the side of justice, where he sees his own
rights respected and unendangered. Under this banner, all
the languages of civilized mankind are spoken, every creed
is protected, every right is sacred. There stands every
element of Western society, with enthusiasm for a great
cause, with confidence in each other, with honor to themselves. This is the banner floating over the glorious valley
which stretches from the western slope of the Alleghanies
to the Rocky Mountains—that Valley of Jehoshaphat
where the nations of the world assemble to celebrate the
resurrection of human freedom. The inscription on that
banner is not "Opposition to the Democratic party for
the sake of placing a new set of men into office"; for this
battle-cry of speculators our hearts have no response.
Nor is it "Restriction of slavery and restriction of the
right of suffrage," for this—believe my words, I entreat
you—this would be the signal of deserved, inevitable
and disgraceful defeat. But the inscription is "Liberty
and equal rights, common to all as the air of Heaven—
Liberty and equal rights, one and inseparable!"

With this banner we stand before the world. In this
sign—in this sign alone, and no other—there is victory.
And thus, sir, we mean to realize the great cosmopolitan
idea, upon which the existence of the American nation

rests.   Thus we mean to fulfill the great mission of true Americanism—thus we mean to answer the anxious question of down-trodden humanity—"Has *man* the faculty to be free and to govern himself?"   The answer is a triumphant "Aye," thundering into the ears of the despots of the old world that "a man is a man for all that"; proclaiming to the oppressed that they are held in subjection on false pretences; cheering the hearts of the despondent friends of man with consolation and renewed confidence.

This is true Americanism, clasping mankind to its great heart.   Under its banner we march; let the world follow.

TO EDWARD L. PIERCE

PRESCOTT HOUSE, NEW YORK, April 22, 1859.

Things are working well.   I had an interview with Greeley to-day, who will admonish the voters of Massachusetts to vote against the two years' amendment.   At the same time, an address to the citizens of Massachusetts, signed by the leading Republicans here, and urging your people in the same direction, will be published in the *Tribune*.   To-morrow I shall go to Auburn in order to get Seward to write to his friends in Massachusetts to the same effect.   Thurlow Weed, I think, will make his voice heard in the Albany *Evening Journal*.   A German Republican editor of this place will furnish you some more protests and articles of Democratic papers.   This morning I wrote another letter to General Wilson.   Tell him that Greeley will back him strongly as soon as he comes out. Urge him on, urge him on! there is no time to be lost. I shall try to see the editor of the *Evening Post* to-morrow, in order to start him in the same direction.

It seems to me, if there were besides you half a dozen

men who are determined that this thing *must* be voted
down, it would be voted down. Give Wilson no rest
until he has written the letter and see to it that it be a
strong one. No milk and water! Let nothing be done
by halves.

Next Tuesday I intend to be at Milwaukee. If you
should receive any letters for me, please send them to
that place. And, believe me, I shall be always very happy
to hear from you. I am sorry that we have not more
opportunities to work side by side. But who knows?

Attend to Wilson, and get that letter out of him as soon
as possible. Give him no rest.

TO EDWARD L. PIERCE

MILWAUKEE, April 30, 1859.

I arrived here safely and in good condition a few days
ago, and found that while I was gone and the Know-Nothing
papers of Massachusetts abused me for having worked
against the two-year amendment, the Democratic papers of
Wisconsin abused me to their hearts' content for having associated with the Know-Nothings of Massachusetts. While
I am censured there for having meddled with your local
concerns, I am censured here for not having done so, and
Democracy is found in fraternal embrace with Know-
Nothingism. This is exhilarating and I think I am at the
present moment one of the best abused men in the country.
The Republican papers, of course, stand by me most vigorously, and so I find it not very difficult to weather the
storm. I have written out my Worcester speech almost
literally as I delivered it, and it will appear in a Milwaukee
paper next Monday. I will send you a copy. The report
of the Worcester *Spy* is very defective; perhaps you can
use my own report there. You would do me a favor by

writing a correspondence [letter] to the Milwaukee *Sentinel* about the effect of my speeches and the manner in which they were understood there.

Where is General [Henry] Wilson's letter? I fear it will come too late, if it does come at all. The press almost unanimously sets him down as an opponent of the amendment, and he cannot back out. Why does he hold back? He can gain only by a straightforward and manly course. Do all you can to make him step forward boldly.

The West stands on tiptoe; the eyes of the people are fixed on Massachusetts and her action one way or the other will have an immense influence. The matter is being discussed here with the greatest interest and the excitement is increasing every day.

The responsibility of Massachusetts is awful, and I have no words strong enough to make you comprehend its full extent. Will the Republicans be patriotic enough to sacrifice their little prejudices to the welfare of our great cause? Will they at last learn that our principles cannot be victorious unless they are clear, pure and consistent?—that by trades and bargains we are bound to lose our honor and the victory at the same time? I read Massachusetts papers as often as I can get hold of one. They are almost silent on the subject. I understand that your great article has appeared in the Worcester *Spy*. How does it work? Has it acquired a sufficient circulation? I wish I could instil my zeal and activity into every true Republican heart. Where so much depends on a single vote, every man who has a just notion of his duty ought to stand by his gun.

Would it not be good now to publish the letter I wrote you some time ago, in full or the principal part of it? I do not care whether it compromises me here or not. The result in Massachusetts is of far greater importance. This, however, I leave to your judgment.

My dear friend, I was very happy to make the acquaintance of one Massachusetts Yankee whom I found thoroughly sound and above prejudice; that man is Edward L. Pierce and I shall be glad to take him by the hand again. Just while I am writing these lines Cogswell hands me the Worcester *Spy* containing your article. It is great and cannot fail to have its effect. Work is the great principle; "impossibility" ought not to be in our dictionary. I wish every voter would read your article.

Let me hear from you again; I should be glad to know how the thing works, and, please, do not fail to notify me of the result as soon as the vote is taken.

TO EDWARD L. PIERCE

MILWAUKEE, May 12, 1859.

Your letter of the 5th is received and the result has proved the correctness of your predictions. General Wilson sent me a copy of his second letter; it is straightforward and manly and he will have his reward. I am informed that Governor Banks through his appointees worked for the amendment. Is this true? If it is, he will have music by the whole Western band and find out very soon that such wholesale deceptions cannot be practised now-a-days.

Well, "the deed is done"; now we have to look out for the consequences. The effect on the Republican party in the Western States will be very serious. I am afraid we shall lose this State next fall. There is a great deal of excitement about it. The Democrats are having a regular jubilee over it, and I am most fiercely abused by their principal organs. You have no idea how the whole thing will embarrass me, unless proper measures are taken to put the responsibility for the measure where it belongs.

There is in my opinion but one way to set the Republican party right before the people: it is to organize a straight Republican party in Massachusetts, and now is the time to do it.   No doubt the Democrats will make the repeal of the two years' amendment the issue in your next State campaign.   This will place the Republicans of Massachusetts in a very bad position unless they take a similar ground.   Banks and the whole American wing of the party will certainly not do it, and there is a very good opportunity for rallying the true and liberal elements of the party.   You might get up a separate organization, call a convention and nominate a State ticket of your own and go into the canvass with a right hearty good-will. You will probably be beaten, but what of it?   You keep up your organization, elect a straight Republican delegation to the National Convention next year and I think you will be admitted there in preference to the American-Republican delegates.   I have no doubt the whole West will stand by you throughout the whole operation.   You may rely upon this.   In this way we can crush the Know-Nothing movement and render all demoralizing alliances and amalgamations impossible.   The issue will be plainly placed before the Republican party in its national capacity and I have no doubt the decision will be in our favor.   Do you not think Wilson might be prevailed upon to put himself at the head of such a movement?   I have no doubt Sumner will go into it.   I shall write to Wilson about it.

This operation may seem bold, but it is safe.   It requires only promptness and decision.   The question arises, Are we in danger to lose [of losing] Massachusetts in the next Presidential election if the American-Republican delegation be rejected by the National Convention?   I think not, if you act with vigor and determination.   You must commence your operations in time.   Suppose you

call some fifty or sixty earnest men together without delay
and put the ball in motion at once, commence building up
an organization and be ready for an open fight next fall,
—do you not think you can make a considerable show of
strength? The Republicans of all the States outside of
Massachusetts would applaud your movement, and the
best and most energetic elements of the anti-slavery
party will be with you.

If you see Wilson, give him my best regards and tell
him that I thank him from my heart for the noble letters
he has written.

TO J. F. POTTER

MILWAUKEE, Aug. 12, 1859.

My dear Friend: I hoped to see you here some time last
week, but, being disappointed in that respect, I have to
write you a few lines. The note of the *Atlas*, which I had
endorsed, was extended for sixty days, and the matter
settled for the present in that way. I have given them a
further endorsement so as to keep them running until
the campaign commences. The party will then have to
take care of the concern, if necessary.

Did you hear from Doolittle?[1] I understand he is not
inclined to do anything in regard to [the] gubernatorial
contest. This is a disappointment to me. I thought
that his advice, joined to yours, would carry a great weight
with it in the convention. I shall follow your advice not
to withdraw at present. The general impression is that
my chances are improving as the convention approaches,
but I am, of course, the last man to judge. I feel that
my being a candidate before the convention is a dangerous
experiment, but there is no backing out at present. I
must rely on the energetic support of my friends. I hope

[1] James R. Doolittle, U. S. Senator.

you will be a delegate to the convention.   Do so by all
means.   Did you write to Washburn and will he be there?

I think the best way to manage things would be to have
a kind of informal consultation, a committee of the whole,
before the vote is taken, and to discuss matters there.
I saw Randall yesterday and had a talk with him and
several of his friends.   He thinks he can get the nomination, but he seems to be a little troubled about the election.
There is one thing that puzzles them very much.   Their
opinion is, that a ticket can hardly be successful without
there being a German on it; now if he should be nominated
they would have to find some new man (for I have declared definitely that I shall accept no nomination under
him).   Who shall be that man?   And suppose we find
one, where is the place for that man?   There is, I think,
no German in the State suited for the position of lieutenant-
governor.   They might think of the treasury, but can
they discard Hastings?   There is no German Republican,
as far as I know, who would be fit for attorney-general.
Where, then, find the man, and if the man can be found,
where the place for that man?   There Randall's friends
are at a deadlock and they know it.   I think that this
matter if calmly explained in an informal meeting of the
delegates before the opening of the convention might
decide the contest.   I should not wonder if this very
difficulty should induce Randall to decline.

At all events I should be very glad to have you go to the
convention as a delegate.   If consistent, let me know what
I may expect of Doolittle and Washburn.   Doolittle's influence would be very valuable.   I do not like the idea of
writing to him myself.   Randall's friends boast of being
sure of the whole delegation from Walworth.   Is that so?

When shall I have the pleasure of seeing you here?[1]

[1] The following letter throws an interesting sidelight on the youthful
Schurz:

DOUGLAS AND POPULAR SOVEREIGNTY[1]

Gentlemen:—When great political or social problems, difficult to solve and impossible to put aside, are pressing upon the popular mind, it is a common thing to see a variety of theories springing up which purport to be unfailing reme-

---

RACINE, Sept. 10, 1859.

Dear Judge [Potter]: I hoped to meet you at Milwaukee, but did not. I am going to try and raise $100 in Kenosha and $100 in Racine towards the amount, $750, for which our friend, Mr. Schurz, is liable as endorser for the German Republican papers. I said to one friend that I thought Mr. Durkee would pay fifty dollars, Washburn fifty, you fifty, and I fifty, making two hundred dollars of the amount. Now whatever course the German Republicans may pursue in this election makes no difference to me and should make no difference with our friends in this matter. But now is the time for the true and wise friends of Col. Schurz to take care of him, and not allow him to be sacrificed. He is a man of noble impulses, and of the highest order of genius. But like men of that character he needs some men of strong practical good sense to act for him at this juncture, which is perhaps the crisis of his life as well as the crisis in our Republican battle so far as Wisconsin is concerned. The people, if the German Republicans should, as some anticipate, bolt Randall, will place these two facts in juxtaposition, and no explanations will ever separate them. The German Republicans urged Mr. Schurz's nomination for governor. The convention by a large majority nominated Randall for governor and unanimously tendered any other office on the ticket to Mr. Schurz, which he declined. The German Republicans bolted the nomination of Randall, and the inference, whether right or wrong, will be irreparably drawn in the popular mind that the Germans bolted because a German was not nominated for governor. It will not remove the inference to say they would accept Hanchett or somebody else. Nothing could do so much to rekindle into a flame all the elements of American Know-Nothingism among our people, and Mr. Schurz, our most eloquent and gifted orator, would be crushed between the upper and nether millstone, between German Know-Nothingism and American Know-Nothingism, and our Republican party at once divided by the element which I had hoped was forever laid aside. Dear Judge, will you see that our good Republican friends in your neighborhood raise say one hundred dollars towards paying off his liability by endorsement? Please remember us kindly to Mrs. P. I remain ever devotedly yours,

J. R. DOOLITTLE.

If you do not come and see me, write me.

[1] Speech delivered in Springfield, Mass., Jan. 4, 1860.

dies and to effect a speedy cure.   Men who look only
at the surface of things will, like bad physicians, pretend
to remove the disease itself by palliating its most violent
symptoms, and will astonish the world by their inventive
ingenuity, no less than by their amusing assurance.   But
a close scrutiny will, in most cases, show that the remedies
offered are but new forms of old mistakes.

Of all the expedients which have been invented for the
settlement of the slavery question, Mr. Douglas's doctrine
of popular sovereignty is certainly the most remarkable,
not only by the apparent novelty of the thing, but by the
pompous assurance with which it was offered to the nation
as a perfect and radical cure.   Formerly compromises
were made between the two conflicting systems of labor
by separating them by geographical lines.   These compromises did indeed produce intervals of comparative
repose, but the war commenced again with renewed
acrimony, as soon as a new bone of contention presented
itself.   The system of compromises as a whole proved a
failure.   Mr. Douglas's doctrine of popular sovereignty
proposed to bring the two antagonistic elements into
immediate contact and to let them struggle hand to hand
for the supremacy on the same ground.   In this manner,
he predicted, the slavery question would settle itself in
the smooth way of ordinary business.   He seemed to be
confident of success; but hardly is his doctrine, in the
shape of a law for the organization of territories, put upon
the statute-book, when the struggle grows fiercer than
ever, and the difficulties ripen into a crisis.   This does
not disturb him.   He sends forth manifesto upon manifesto, and even during the State campaign of last fall, he
mounts the rostrum in Ohio in order to show what he
can do, and like a second Constantine he points his finger
at the great principle of popular sovereignty, and says to
his followers: In this sign you will conquer.   But the

tendency of events appeared unwilling to yield to his
prophecy. There seemed to be no charm in his command;
there was certainly no victory in his sign. He had hardly
defined his doctrine more elaborately than ever before,
when his friends were routed everywhere, and even his
great party is on the point of falling to pieces. The failure
is magnificently complete.

There certainly was something in his theories that
captivated the masses. I do not speak of those who
joined their political fortunes to his, because they saw in
him a man who some day might be able to scatter favors
and plunder around him. But there were a great many
who, seduced by the plausible sound of the words "popular sovereignty," meant to have found there some middle
ground, on which the rights of free labor might be protected and secured without exasperating those interested
in slave labor. They really did think that two conflicting organizations of society, which are incompatible
by the nature of things, might be made compatible by
legislative enactments. But this delusion vanished.
No sooner was the theory put to a practical test, than
the construction of the Nebraska bill became no less a
matter of fierce dispute than the construction of the
Constitution had been before. Is this pro-slavery, or is
it anti-slavery? it was asked. The South found in it the
right to plant slave labor in the territories unconditionally,
and the North found in it the right to drive slavery out
of them. Each section of the country endeavored to
appropriate the results of the Nebraska bill to itself, and
the same measure, which was to transfer the struggle
from the halls of Congress into the territories, transferred
it from the territories back into Congress, and there the
Northern and Southern versions of the Nebraska bill
fight each other with the same fury with which the Southern and Northern versions of the Constitution have

6

fought each other before. What does the Constitution
mean in regard to slavery? That question remains to
be settled. What does the Nebraska bill mean? This
question depends upon the settlement of the former.

Of all men, Mr. Douglas ought to be the first to know
what the true intent and meaning of the Nebraska bill
and the principle of popular sovereignty are. He is said
to be a statesman, and it is to be presumed that his measure
rests upon a positive idea; for all true statesmanship is
founded upon positive ideas.

In order to find out Mr. Douglas's own definition of his
own "great principle," we are obliged to pick up the most
lucid of his statements, as we find them scattered about
in numerous speeches and manifestoes. After multifarious
cruisings upon the sea of platforms and arguments, Mr.
Douglas has at last landed at the following point: "A
slave," says he, in his famous *Harper's Magazine* article,
"a slave, within the meaning of the Constitution, is a
person held to service or labor in one State 'under the laws
thereof'—not under the Constitution of the United States,
or under the laws thereof, nor by virtue of any federal
authority whatever, but under the laws of the particular
State where such service or labor may be due." This is
clear, and with his eyes firmly fixed upon the people of
the North, he goes on:

If, as Mr. Buchanan asserts, slavery exists in the territories by virtue of the Constitution of the United States,
then it becomes the imperative duty of Congress, to the
performance of which every member is bound by his conscience and his oath, and from which no consideration of
policy or expediency can release him, to provide by law such
adequate and complete protection as is essential to the enjoyment of an important right secured by the Constitution;
in one word, to enact a general slave code for the territories.

But Mr. Douglas is not satisfied with this. In order

to strengthen his assumption, and to annihilate Mr. Buchanan's construction of the Nebraska bill still more, he proceeds:

The Constitution being uniform everywhere within the dominions of the United States, being the supreme law of the land, anything in the constitutions or laws of any of the States to the contrary notwithstanding—why does not slavery exist in Pennsylvania just as well as in Kansas or in South Carolina, by virtue of the same Constitution, since Pennsylvania is subordinate to the Constitution in the same manner and to the same extent as South Carolina and Kansas?

Just so. Mr. Douglas having been so positive, he cannot deny us the privilege of making a few logical deductions from his own premises. We expect him to proceed in the following manner: "Since a slave is held under the laws of a State, and not under the Constitution or the laws of the United States, slavery exists only by virtue of local law," or, as the Court of Appeals of Kentucky expressed it, "the right to hold a slave exists only by positive law of a municipal character and has no foundation in the law of nature or the unwritten and common law." If slavery cannot exist except by virtue of local law of a municipal character, it follows as an irresistible consequence, that a slaveholder cannot hold a slave as property in a territory where there is no local law of a municipal character establishing that right of property. And, further, the right to hold a slave having no foundation in the law of nature or the unwritten and common law, we are forced to the conclusion, that a slave, brought by his owner upon the soil of a territory before the territorial legislature has enacted laws establishing slavery, becomes of necessity free, for there is no local law of a municipal character under which he can be held as a slave.

This principle is recognized by the decisions of several Southern courts. Having gone so far (and, indeed, I cannot see how a logical mind can escape these conclusions from Mr. Douglas's own premises), Mr. Douglas would be obliged to define his popular sovereignty to be the right of the people of a territory, represented in the territorial legislature, to admit slavery by positive enactment, if they see fit, but it being well understood that a slaveholder has not the least shadow of a right to take his slave property into the territory before such positive legislation has been had. This definition would have at least the merit of logical consistency.

But what does Mr. Douglas say? "Slavery," so he tells us in his *Harper's Magazine* article, "being the creature of local legislation and not of the Constitution of the United States, it follows that the Constitution does not establish slavery in the territories, beyond the power of the people to control it by law." What? The Constitution does not establish slavery in the territories beyond a certain something! What does that mean? If slavery is the creature of local law, how can the Constitution by its own force permit slavery to go into a territory at all?

Here is a dark mystery, a pitfall, and we may well take care not to fall into the trap of some sophistry. Why does he not speak of the admission of slavery by positive enactment? Why not even of the power of the people to exclude it by law? We look in vain for light in *Harper's Magazine*—(and is it indeed true what Judge Black intimates, that the article is one of the obscurest documents by which ever a politician attempted to befog his followers) but we may gather Mr. Douglas's real opinion from another manifesto preceding this. In his New Orleans speech, delivered after his recent success in Illinois, he defined his position, in substance, as follows: "The

Democracy of Illinois hold that a slaveholder has the same
right to take his slave property into a territory as any
other man has to take his horse or his merchandise."

What? Slavery is the creature of local law, and yet
a slaveholder has a right to take his slave property into
a territory before any local law has given him that right?
A slave does not become free when voluntarily brought
by his owner upon the soil of a territory where no positive
local law establishing slavery exists? How is this possible?
How can even the elastic mind of a Democratic candidate
for the Presidency unite these contradictory assumptions?
And yet there it stands, and nothing that Mr. Douglas
ever said can be more unequivocal in its meaning. And
here again we may claim the privilege of drawing a few
logical deductions from Mr. Douglas's own premises.
If, as Mr. Douglas distinctly and emphatically tells us,
a slaveholder has a right to take his slave as property
into a territory and to hold him there as property, before
any legislation on that point is had, from what source
does that right arise? Not from the law of nature—for
the right to hold a slave is "unfounded in the law of
nature and in the unwritten and common law," and even
Mr. Douglas, little as he may care about nature and her
laws, will hardly dare to assert that the system of slave
labor is the natural and normal condition of society. It
must then spring from positive law. But from what kind
of positive law? Not from any positive law of a local and
municipal character, for there is none such in the territory
so far. Where is its source then? There is but one kind of
positive law to which the territories are subject, before any
local legislation has been had, and that is the Constitution
of the United States. If, therefore, Mr. Douglas asserts,
as he does, that a slaveholder has a right to take his slave
as property into a territory, he must at the same time
admit that, in the absence of local legislation positively

establishing slavery, the Constitution of the United
States, the only valid law existing there, is the source of
that right. What else does Mr. Buchanan assert, but
that slavery exists in the territories by virtue of the
Federal Constitution? Where is, then, the point of
difference between Mr. Buchanan and Mr. Douglas?
Why all this pomp and circumstance of glorious war?
Whence these fierce battles between the Montecchi and
Capuletti of the democratic camp? Are ye not brothers?

But Mr. Douglas is a statesman—so they are all, all
statesmen—and pretends that the Constitution does not
establish slavery in the territories, "beyond the power
of the people to control it by law." What does that mean?
It means that the people of a territory shall have the
power to embarrass the slaveholder in the enjoyment of
his right by "unfriendly legislation." "The right to
hold slaves," says he, in another place, "is a worthless
right, unless protected by appropriate police regulations.
If the people of a territory do not want slavery, they have
but to withhold all protection and all friendly legislation."
Indeed, a most ingenious expedient.

But alas! Here is one of those cases where the abstract
admission of a right is of decisive importance. Suppose,
for argument's sake, a slave might escape from his owner
in a territory, without being in actual danger of recapture,
would that in any way affect the constitutional right of
the slaveholder to the possession and enjoyment of his
property? I have already quoted Mr. Douglas's own
answer to this question. "If," says he, "slavery exists
in the territories by virtue of the Constitution" (that
is, if a slaveholder has a right to introduce his "slave
property" where there is no other law but the Constitution) "then it becomes the imperative duty of Congress,
to the performance of which every member is bound by
his oath and conscience, and from which no consideration

of policy or expediency can release him, to provide by
law such adequate and complete protection as is essential
to the enjoyment of that important right."

And Mr. Douglas, after having emphatically admitted
the right of property in a slave, where that right can
spring from no other law but the Constitution, then
dares to speak of unfriendly legislation? Where is his
conscience? Where is his oath? Where is his honor?

But Mr. Douglas says more: "The Constitution being
the supreme law of the land in the States as well as in
the territories, then slavery exists in Pennsylvania just
as well as in Kansas and in South Carolina, and the irrepressible conflict is there?" Aye, the irrepressible conflict
is there, not only between the two antagonistic systems
of labor, but between Mr. Douglas's own theories; not
only in the States and territories, but in Mr. Douglas's
own head. Whatever ambiguous expressions Mr. Douglas may invent, the dilemma stares him in the face (and
here I put myself on his grounds): either slavery is excluded from the territories so long as it is not admitted
by a special act of territorial legislation; or, if a slaveholder
has the right to introduce his slave property there before
such legislation is had, he can possess that right by virtue
of no other but the only law existing there, the Constitution of the United States. Either slavery has no rights
in the territories except those springing from positive
law of a local or municipal character, or, according to
Judge Douglas's own admission, the Southern construction
of the Constitution and of the principle of popular sovereignty is the only legitimate one: that the Constitution
by its own force carries slavery wherever it is the supreme
law of the land, that Congress is obliged to enact a slave
code for its protection, and that popular sovereignty means
the power of the people to vote *for* slavery but by no
means against it. There is no escape from this dilemma.

Which side will Mr. Douglas take? Will he be bold
enough to say that slavery, being the creature of local
law only, is excluded from the territories in the absence
of positive law establishing it, or will he be honest enough
to concede that, according to his own proposition in his
New Orleans speech, slavery exists in the territories by
virtue of the Federal Constitution? He will neither be
bold enough to do the first, nor honest enough to do the
second; he will be just bold and honest enough to do
neither. He is in the position of that Democratic candidate for Congress in the West, who, when asked, "Are you
a Buchanan or Douglas man?" answered, "I am." If
you ask Mr. Douglas: "Do you hold that slavery is the
creature of local law, or that a slaveholder has the right
to introduce his slave property where there is no local
law?" he will answer, "I do."

Such is Mr. Douglas's doctrine of popular sovereignty.
But after having given you Mr. Douglas's own definitions in his own words, I see you are puzzled all the more,
and you ask me again: "What is it?" I will tell you
what judgment will be passed upon it by future historians,
who may find it worth while to describe this impotent
attempt to dally and trifle with the logic of things. They
will say: "It was the dodge of a man who was well
aware that, in order to be elected President of the United
States, the vote of a few Northern States must be added
to the united vote of the South. Knowing by experience
that the Democratic road to the White House leads
through the slaveholding States, he broke down the last
geographical barrier to the extension of slavery. So he
meant to secure the South. But in conceding undisputed
sway to the slaveholding interests, he saw that he was
losing his foothold in the Northern States necessary to
his election; he availed himself of the irresistible pressure
of the free-State movement in Kansas, and opposed the

Lecompton Constitution. So he saved his Senatorship in Illinois, as the champion of free labor. But the South frowned, and immediately after his victory he went into slaveholding States and admitted in his speeches that slavery may go into the territories without a special act of territorial legislation. Believing the South satisfied, and seeing his chances in the North endangered, he wrote his *Harper's Magazine* essay, assuming that slavery can exist only by virtue of local law. The South frowning again, he endeavored to make his peace with the slave-holders by declaring that he would submit to the Charles-ton Convention, and instructing his nearest friends in the House to vote for the Administration candidate for the Speakership. So he endeavored to catch both sections of the Union successively in the trap of a double-faced sophistry. He tried to please them both in trying to cheat them both. But he placed himself between the logic of liberty on one, and logic of slavery on the other side. He put the sword of logic into the hands of his opponents, and tried to defend himself with the empty scabbard of 'unfriendly legislation.' Unfriendly legis-lation, which in one case would have been unnecessary, in the other unconstitutional—the invention of a mind without logic and of a heart without sympathies; recog-nized on all sides as a mere subterfuge, behind which the moral cowardice of a Presidential candidate entrenched itself."

Such will be the verdict of future historians. They will indulge in curious speculations about the times when such doctrines could be passed off as sound statesmanship —a statesmanship indeed, the prototype of which may be found, not in Plutarch, but in Aristophanes—but they will be slow to believe that there were people dull enough to be deceived by it.

Leaving aside the stern repudiation which Mr. Douglas's

popular sovereignty has received at the hands of the people at the last State elections all over the Union, it is a characteristic sign of the times that even one of his political friends, an anti-Lecompton Democrat, recently went so far as to declare on the floor of Congress that he would not vote for Mr. Douglas if nominated by the Charleston Convention, unless a clear and unequivocal construction were affixed to the re-affirmation of the Cincinnati platform. A wise precaution, indeed! But whatever construction might be given to the Cincinnati platform, what will that gentleman do with the double-faced platform which Mr. Douglas has laid down for himself? What will the abstract pledge of a convention be worth to him, if Mr. Douglas's principles pledge him to nothing? What will he do with a man who, when pressed to take an unequivocal position, is always ready to sneak behind a superior authority, declaring that "these are questions to be settled by the courts"?

Mr. Douglas's position is certainly a very perplexing one. On one side he is ostracised by the Administration Democracy for his illogical and unconstitutional doctrine, that the legislature of a territory has control over slavery; and on the other hand one of his nearest friends, Mr. Morris, of Illinois, in his recent speech on the President's message, denounces the doctrine that slave property may be carried into the territories, just like other property, as an atrocious "abomination." Was Mr. Morris not aware that this "abomination" is the identical doctrine advocated by Mr. Douglas in his New Orleans speech? Let Mr. Morris examine the record of Judge Douglas, and he will find out that whatever abominations Mr. Buchanan may bring forward in his message, he advocates none that is not a direct logical consequence of Mr. Douglas's own admissions.

I see the time coming when many of those who rallied

around Douglas's colors because they believed in his principles, will, from his most devoted friends, become his most indignant accusers. They are already unwittingly denouncing his doctrines, even while trying to defend him; they will not be sparing in direct denunciations as soon as they discover how badly they have been deceived and how ignominiously they were to be sold. We might, indeed, feel tempted to pity him, if we had not to reserve that generous emotion of our hearts for those who are wrong by mistake and unfortunate without guilt.

Mr. Douglas's ambiguous position, which makes it possible for him to cheat either the North or the South, without adding a new inconsistency to those already committed, makes it at the same time necessary for him to put his double-faced theories upon an historical basis, which relieves him of the necessity of expressing a moral conviction on the matter of slavery either way. To say that slavery is right, would certainly displease the North; to say that slavery is wrong, would inevitably destroy him at the South. In order to dodge this dangerous dilemma, he finds it expedient to construe the history of this country so as to show that this question of right or wrong in regard to slavery had nothing whatever to do with the fundamental principles upon which the American Republic was founded. Dealing with slavery only as a matter of fact, and treating the natural rights of man and the relation between slavery and republican institutions as a matter of complete indifference, he is bound to demonstrate, that slavery never was seriously deemed inconsistent with liberty, and that the black never was seriously supposed to possess any rights which the white man was bound to respect.

But here he encounters the Declaration of Independence laying down the fundamental principles upon which the Republic was to develop itself; he encounters the ordinance

of 1787, the practical application of those principles;
both historical facts, as stern and stubborn as they are
sublime.   But as Mr. Douglas had no logic to guide him
in his theories, so he had no conscience to restrain him in
his historical constructions.   To interpret the Declaration of Independence according to the evident meaning
of its words would certainly displease the South; to call
it a self-evident lie would certainly shock the moral sensi-
bilities of the North.   So he recognizes it as a venerable
document, but makes the language, which is so dear to
the hearts of the North, express a meaning which coincides
with the ideas of the South.

We have appreciated his exploits as a logician; let
us follow him in his historical discoveries.

Let your imagination carry you back to the year 1776.
You stand in the hall of the old colonial courthouse of
Philadelphia.   Through the open door you see the Continental Congress assembled; the moment of a great decision is drawing near.   Look at the earnest faces of the
men assembled there, and consider what you may expect
of them.   The philosophy of the eighteenth century counts
many of them among its truest adepts.   They heartily
welcomed in their scattered towns and plantations the new
ideas brought forth by that sudden progress of humanity,
and, meditating them in the dreamy solitude of virgin
nature, they had enlarged the compass of their thoughts
and peopled their imaginations with lofty ideals.   A
classical education (for most of them are by no means
illiterate men) has put all the treasures of historical knowledge at their disposal, and enabled them to apply the
experience of past centuries to the new problem they
attempt to solve.   See others there of a simple but strong
cast of mind, whom common sense would call its truest
representatives.   Wont to grapple with the dangers and
difficulties of an early settler's life, or, if inhabitants of

young uprising cities, wont to carry quick projects into
speedy execution, they have become regardless of obstacles
and used to strenuous activity. The constant necessity
to help themselves has developed their mental independence; and, inured to political strife by the continual defense
of their colonial self-government, they have at last become familiar with the idea of introducing into practical
existence the principles which their vigorous minds have
quietly built up into a theory.

The first little impulses to the general upheaving of the
popular spirit—the tea tax, the stamp act—drop into insignificance; they are almost forgotten; the revolutionary
spirit has risen far above them. It disdains to justify
itself with petty pleadings; it spurns diplomatic equivocation; it places the claim to independence upon the broad
basis of eternal rights, as self-evident as the sun, as
broad as the world, as common as the air of heaven. The
struggle of the colonies against the usurping government
of Great Britain has risen to the proud dimensions of a
struggle of *man* for liberty and equality. Behold, five
men are advancing towards the table of the president.
First, Thomas Jefferson, whose philosophical spirit grasps
the generality of things and events; then Benjamin
Franklin, the great apostle of common sense, the clear
wisdom of real life beaming in his serene eye; then the
undaunted John Adams, and two others. Now Jefferson
reads the Declaration of Independence, and loudly proclaims the fundamental principle upon which it rests:
"All men are created free and equal!" It is said history
tells you what it meant. The scepter of royalty is flung
back across the ocean; the prerogatives of nobility are
trodden into the dust; every man a king, every man a
baron; in seven of the original colonies the shackles of
the black men struck off; almost everywhere the way
prepared for gradual emancipation. "No recognition

of the right of property in man!" says Madison. "Let slavery be abolished by law!" says Washington. Not only the supremacy of old England is to be shaken off, but a new organization of society is to be built up on the basis of liberty and equality. That is the Declaration of Independence! That is the American Revolution! All men free and equal! Not even the broad desert of the Atlantic ocean stops the triumphant shout. Behold, the nations of the old world are rushing to arms. Bastiles are blown into the dust, as by the trumpets of Jericho, and, like a pillar of fire by night and a pillar of cloud by day, the great watchword of the American Revolution shows forever the way to struggling humanity. All men are created free and equal! Whence the supernatural power in these seven words?

Turn your eyes away from the sublime spectacle of 1776, from that glorious galaxy of men whose hearts were large enough for all mankind, and let me recall you to the sober year of 1857. There is Springfield, the capital of Illinois, one of those States which owe their greatness to an ordinance originally framed by the same man whose hand wrote the Declaration of Independence. In the hall of the assembly there stands Mr. Douglas, who initiates an eager crowd into the mysteries of "popular sovereignty." He will tell you what it meant, when the men of 1776 said that "all men are created free and equal." He says:

No man can vindicate the character, the motives and the conduct of the signers of the Declaration of Independence, except upon the hypothesis that they referred to the white race alone, and not to the African, when they declared all men to have been created free and equal—that they were speaking of British subjects on this continent being free and equal to British subjects born and residing in Great Britain— that they were entitled to the same inalienable rights, and among them were enumerated life, liberty and the pursuit of happiness. The Declaration of Independence was adopted merely for the purpose of justifying the colonists in the eyes of the civilized world in withdrawing their allegiance from the British crown and dissolving their connection with the mother country.

What? Is that all? Is that little heap of quicksand the whole substructure on which a new organization of society was to be built? The whole foundation upon which the proud and ponderous edifice of the United States rests? They did, then, *not* mean *all* men, when they said all men. They intended, perhaps, even to disfranchise those free blacks who, in five of the original thirteen colonies, enjoyed the right of voting. They meant but the white race. Oh no! by no means the *whole* white race; not the Germans, not the French, not the Scandinavians; they meant but British subjects: "British subjects on this continent being equal to British subjects born and residing on the other side of the great water!"

There is your Declaration of Independence, a diplomatic dodge, adopted merely for the purpose of excusing the rebellious colonies in the eyes of civilized mankind. There is your Declaration of Independence, no longer the sacred code of the rights of man, but a hypocritical piece of special pleading, drawn up by a batch of artful pettifoggers, who, when speaking of the rights of man, meant but the privileges of a set of aristocratic slaveholders, but styled it "the rights of man," in order to throw dust into the eyes of the world, and to inveigle noble-hearted fools into lending them aid and assistance. These are your boasted revolutionary sires, no longer heroes and sages, but accomplished humbuggers and hypocrites, who said one thing and meant another; who passed counterfeit sentiments as genuine, and obtained arms and money and assistance and sympathy on false pretenses! There is your great American Revolution, no longer the great champion of universal principles, but a mean Yankee trick—a wooden nutmeg—the most impudent imposition ever practised upon the whole world!

This is the way Mr. Douglas wants you to read and to understand the proudest pages of American history! That is the kind of history with which he finds it necessary to prop his mongrel doctrine of popular sovereignty! That is what he calls vindicating the character and the motives and the conduct of the signers of the Declaration of Independence! Thus he did not blush to slander Jefferson, who, when speaking of the country, meant the world, and, when speaking of his fellow citizens, meant mankind; and Franklin, in whose clear head theory and practice were the same, and who, having declared "all men to be created free and equal," became the first president of the first great abolition society; and John Adams, the representative of that State which abolished slavery within its limits with one great stroke of legislation; and Washington, who declared it to be "his fondest wish to see slavery abolished by law," and affixed to the Declaration of Independence the broad signature of his heroic sword; and Madison, who deemed it "absurd to admit the idea of property in man"; and the framers of the Constitution, who took care not to disgrace that instrument with the word "slavery," and before adopting it finally, blotted out from the extradition clause the word "servitude," *avowedly, because it signified the condition of a slave,* and substituted the word "service," *avowedly, because it signified the condition of a freeman.* Thus Mr. Douglas dares to speak of all those true men who, after having proclaimed their principles in the Declaration, endeavored to introduce them into practical life in almost every State in the way of *gradual emancipation!* That they have failed in this, is it a fault of theirs? It shows not that they were less great and sincere, but that subsequent generations were hardly worthy of so noble an ancestry! There is Mr. Douglas's version of your history. He despairs of converting you without slandering your fathers. His present doctrines cannot thrive unless planted in a calumny on the past. *He* vindicate the signers of the Declaration of Independence! Indeed, they need it sadly. I see the illustrious committee of five arise from their graves—at their head Thomas Jefferson, his lips curled with the smile of contempt, and I hear him say to Mr. Douglas: "Sir, you may abuse us as much as you please, but have the goodness to spare us with your vindications of our character and motives."

It is a common thing for men of a coarse cast of mind so to lose themselves in the mean pursuit of selfish ends as to become insensible to the grand and sublime. Measuring every character and every event in history by the low standard of their own individualities, applying to everything the narrow rule of their own motive, incapable of grasping broad and generous ideas, they will belittle everything they cannot deny, and drag down every struggle of principles to the sordid arena of aspiring selfishness or of small competing interests. Eighteen hundred years ago, there were men who saw nothing in incipient Christianity but a mere wrangle between Jewish theologians, got up by a carpenter's boy, and carried on by a few crazy fishermen. Three hundred years ago, there were men who saw in the great reformatory movement of the sixteenth century, not the emancipation of the individual conscience, but a mere fuss kicked up by a German monk who wanted to get married. Two hundred years ago, there were men who saw in Hampden's refusal to pay the ship-money, not a bold vindication of constitutional liberty, but the crazy antics of a man who was mean

7

enough to quarrel about a few shillings. And, now, there are men who see in the Declaration of Independence and in the American Revolution, not the reorganization of human society upon the basis of liberty and equality, but a dodge of some English colonists who were unwilling to pay their taxes.

But the dignity of great characters and the glory of great events find their vindication in the consciences of the people. It is vain for demagogism to raise its short arms against the truth of history. The Declaration of Independence stands there. No candid man ever read it without seeing and feeling that every word of it was dictated by deep and earnest thought, and that every sentence of it bears the stamp of philosophical generality. It is the summing up of the results of the philosophical development of the age; it is the practical embodiment of the progressive ideas which, very far from being confined to the narrow limits of the English colonies, pervaded the very atmosphere of all civilized countries. That code of human rights has grown on the very summit of civilization, not in the miry soil of a South Carolina cotton-field. He must have a dull mind or a disordered brain, who misunderstands its principles; but he must have the heart of a villain, who knowingly misrepresents them.

Mr. Douglas's ambition might have been satisfied with this ignominious exploit. But the necessities of the popular sovereignty doctrine do not stop there. After having tried to explain away the fundamental principles underlying this Republic, which are hostile to slavery and its extension, Mr. Douglas finds it exceedingly inconvenient to encounter facts which prove, beyond doubt, that these principles, from a mere theoretical existence, rose to practical realization. Popular sovereignty, which is at war with the doctrines of the Declaration of Inde-

pendence, demands the slaughter of the ordinance of 1787,
and Mr. Douglas is up to the task. He does not stop at
trifles. And here we must return to the *Harper's Magazine* manifesto. He leads us through a century of colonial
history in order to show that the people of the colonies
claimed the right to legislate on the subject of slavery.
And, remarkably enough, all the instances quoted show a
uniform tendency adverse to the peculiar institution.
Mr. Douglas then proceeds to discover the germs of his
popular sovereignty doctrine in the first Congressional
legislation concerning the territories. I will not undertake to criticise that singular historical essay, although
some of its statements are such as to make the freshmen of
our colleges smile. The "statesman" Douglas does not
seem to be aware that the ability to read history ought to
precede the attempt to write it. He leads us back to the
Congress of 1784. Mr. Jefferson and his colleagues have
just executed the deed of cession of the Northwestern
territory, and the same Mr. Jefferson, as chairman of a
committee, then submits "a plan for the temporary
government of the territories ceded or to be ceded by the
individual States to the United States." Mr. Douglas
proceeds to describe how the territorial governments
were to be organized, what rights and powers were put
into the hands of the people and how they were to be
exercised; and after having demonstrated that the term
"new States" meant the same thing which is now designated by "territories," he comes to the conclusion that the
spirit pervading that plan was in exact consonance with
his doctrine of "popular sovereignty." Mr. Douglas ostentatiously calls this "the Jeffersonian plan." "It was,"
says he, "the first plan of government for the territories
ever adopted in the United States. It was drawn by the
author of the Declaration of Independence, and revised
and adopted by those who shaped the issues which pro-

duced the Revolution, and formed the foundations upon
which our whole system of American government rests."
But Mr. Douglas skips rather nimbly over the significant
fact, that the same "author of the Declaration of Independence" put into that plan a proviso, *excluding slavery
from the territories*. Was that a mere accident? Mr.
Jefferson showed thereby conclusively that, in his opinion,
the exclusion of slavery by Congressional legislation was
by no means inconsistent with the spirit of "popular
sovereignty" which Mr. Douglas discovers in the plan of
1784, but this does not disturb Mr. Douglas. "The fifth
article," says he, "relating to the prohibition of slavery,
having been rejected by Congress, never became a part
of the Jeffersonian plan of government for the territories,
as adopted April 23, 1784."

Although with a large numerical majority in its favor
(16 to 7), this article did, indeed, fail to obtain a constitutional majority, the vote of New Jersey not being
counted in consequence of there being but one delegate
from that State present; yet it had been drawn up by
Mr. Jefferson, introduced by Mr. Jefferson and sustained by Mr. Jefferson's vote. Nevertheless, Mr. Douglas persists in calling a plan, from which the peculiar
Jeffersonian feature had been struck out, the "Jeffersonian plan." This, indeed, is the play of Hamlet with
the character of Hamlet omitted. "This charter compact," proceeds Mr. Douglas, "with its fundamental
conditions which were unalterable without joint consent
of the people interested in them, as well as of the United
States, then stood upon the statute book unrepealed and
irrepealable, when on the 14th day of May, 1787, the
federal convention met at Philadelphia." Does Mr.
Douglas not know that on the 16th of March, 1785, a
proposition was introduced in Congress by Rufus King,
to exclude slavery from the States described in the resolve

of April 23, 1784, and to make this provision part of the
compact established by that resolve? Does he not know
that this provision, restoring the Jeffersonian feature to
the "Jeffersonian plan," was committed by the vote of
eight States against four? Does he not know that the
plan of 1784 never went into practical operation, but was
expressly set aside by Congress in 1787? Does he not
know that the ordinance of 1787 was the first legislative
act ever practically organizing a territory of the United
States, and that one of its most prominent features was
the proviso excluding slavery from all the territories then
in possession of the United States?

Mr. Douglas's historical recollections of the ordinance
of 1787 seem to be very indistinct. Indeed, he deems it
only worthy of an occasional, passing, almost contemp-
tuous notice. He speaks of it as "the ordinance of the
12th of July, 1787, which was passed by the remnant of
the Congress of the Confederation, sitting in New York,
while its most eminent members were at Philadelphia,
as delegates to the Federal Convention." For three quarters of a century people were in the habit of thinking that
the ordinance of 1787 was an act of the highest order of
importance, but we now learn that it was a rather indifferent affair, passed on an indifferent occasion by an
exceedingly indifferent set of fellows, while the plan of
1784, a mere abstract program completely overruled by
subsequent legislation, is represented as the true glory
of the age. How is this? The reason is obvious.

Mr. Douglas belongs to that class of historians who
dwell upon those facts which suit their convenience, and
unceremoniously drop the rest. I once heard of a Jesuit
college where they used a text-book of history, in which
the French Revolution was never mentioned, while the
Emperor Napoleon figured there only as modest Marquis
Bonaparte, who held a commission under Louis XVII,

and fought great battles for the glory of the Catholic
Church. So it is with Mr. Douglas and the history of
our country. He ignores the universal principles of the
Declaration of Independence, and represents the great
founders of the Republic as merely paving the way for
his "great principles," while a few village politicians
get up an abusive ordinance, adverse to the general
tendency of things. But as those Jesuits never could
prevent their students from peeping out of their college
windows into the wide world, where they perceived a very
different state of things, so Mr. Douglas cannot prevent
us from travelling out of the yellow covers of *Harper's
Magazine* into the open records of history, where we find
Mr. Jefferson's anti-slavery clause, although accidentally
lost in 1784, strenuously insisted upon by the leading
spirits of the Republic, incorporated in the great act of
1787, solemnly reaffirmed by the first Congress under the
Constitution, and firmly maintained even against the
petition of the people of one of the territories. This is
the true "Jeffersonian plan," the plan which Jefferson
framed, voted for and which was carried out in his spirit;
not that mangled report of 1784, which Mr. Douglas wants
us to take as the foundation of all territorial government,
because an historical accident happens to coincide with
his schemes.

That true Jeffersonian plan rested, indeed, on the
principle of popular sovereignty, but it will be conceded
that Mr. Jefferson's great principle was as widely different
from that of Mr. Douglas as the ordinance of 1787 is
different from the Nebraska bill. While Jefferson's
notion of popular sovereignty sprang from the idea that
man has certain inalienable rights which the majority
shall not encroach upon, Mr. Douglas's doctrine rests
upon the idea that the highest development of liberty
consists in the right of one class of men to hold another

class of men as slaves, if they see fit to do so.   While Mr.
Jefferson excluded slavery from the territories, *in order
to make room for true popular sovereignty*, Mr. Douglas
invents his false popular sovereignty in order to make room
for slavery.   The ordinance of 1787, the true "Jeffersonian plan," was indeed no mere accident, no mere occasional
act of legislation.   It sprang from the idea, as Madison
expressed it, "that republican institutions would become
a fallacy where slavery existed," and in order to guarantee
republican institutions to the territories, they excluded
slavery.

The ordinance of 1787 was the logical offspring of the
principles upon which your independence and your Constitution are founded; it is the practical application of the
Declaration of Independence to the government of the
territories.   Its very existence sets completely at nought
Mr. Douglas's doctrine and historical construction, and
the dwarfish hand of the demagogue tries in vain to tear
this bright page out of your annals.   The ordinance of
1787 stands written on the very gateposts of the Northwestern States; written on every grain field that waves in
the breeze, on every factory that dots the course of their
rushing waters, on every cottage that harbors thrifty
freemen; written in every heart that rejoices over the
blessings of liberty.   There it stands in characters of light.
Only a blind man cannot see; only a fool can misunder-
stand it; only a knave can wilfully misinterpret it.

Such is Mr. Douglas's principle of popular sovereignty
in its logical and historical aspect; apparently adopting
the doctrine that slavery is the creature of local law only,
and fighting against a Congressional slave code, but, on
the other hand, admitting the very principle on which
protection to slave property becomes a logical necessity;
and again assuming the ground, that slave property may
be introduced where there is no local law, but explaining

away the logical consequences of that doctrine by the
transparent sophistry of unfriendly legislation; dragging
the proudest exploits of American statesmanship into the
dust, emasculating the Declaration of Independence because incompatible with its principles; setting aside the
ordinance of 1787 because that stern fact is a conclusive
historical argument against it; a Jesuitical piece of
equivocation and double-dealing; unable to stand before
the criticism of a logical mind, because it is a mixture of
glaring contradictions; *unable to stop the war of principle
and interests, because it is at war with itself.*

It is true, its principal champion worked hard to cover
with bullying boisterousness the moral cowardice from
which it sprang, but in vain.   He mistakes the motive-
power which shapes the actions of free nations.   Having
no *moral* convictions of his own to stand upon, he could
never address himself *to the moral sense of the people.*
Having no moral convictions of his own!   This is a grave
charge, but I know what I say.   I respect true convictions
wherever I find them.   Among the fire-eaters of the South
there are men who speak of the moral basis of slavery, and
believe in it; who speak of the blessings of servitude and
believe in it; who assert that slavery is right, and believe it.
Atrocious as their errors may be, and deeply as I deplore
them, yet I respect their convictions as soon as I find them
to be such.   But look into the record of the champion of
"popular sovereignty"; scan it from syllable to syllable,
and then tell me, you Douglasites of the South, do you find
one word there indicating a moral conviction that slavery
is right?   And you Douglasites of the North, who are in the
habit of telling us that you are the true anti-slavery men,
and that popular sovereignty will surely work the overthrow of the institution—did your master ever utter a
similar sentiment?   Do you find in his record one word of
sympathy with the downtrodden and degraded?   One

spark of the humane philosophy of our age?   One syllable
in vindication of the outraged dignity of human nature?
One word which might indicate a moral conviction that
slavery is *wrong?*   Not one!

But one thing he does tell you: "*I do not care whether
slavery be voted up or down.*"   There is then a human
heart that does not care!   Sir, look over this broad land,
where the struggle has raged for years and years; and
across the two oceans, around the globe, to the point
where the far West meets the far East; over the teeming
countries where the cradle of mankind stood; and over
the workshops of civilization in Europe, and over those
mysterious regions under the tropical sun, which have not
emerged yet from the night of barbarism into the daylight
of civilized life,—and then tell me how many hearts
you find that do not tremble with mortal anguish or
exultant joy as the scales of human freedom or human
bondage go up or down?   Look over the history of the
world, from the time when infant mankind felt in its
heart the first throbbings of aspiring dignity, down to
our days, when the rights of man have at last found a bold
and powerful champion in a great and mighty Republic;
where is the page that is not blotted with blood and
tears shed in that all-absorbing struggle; where a chapter
which does not tell a tale of jubilant triumph or heart-
breaking distress, as the scales of freedom or slavery went
up or down? But to-day, in the midst of the nineteenth
century, in a Republic whose program was laid down
in the Declaration of Independence, there comes a man to
you, and tells you with cynical coolness that he does not
care! And *because* he does not care, he claims the confidence of his countrymen and the highest honors of the
Republic! *Because* he does not care, he pretends to be
the representative statesman of the age!

Sir, I always thought that he can be no true statesman

whose ideas and conceptions are not founded upon profound moral convictions of right and wrong. What, then, shall we say of him who boastingly parades his indifference as a virtue? May we not drop the discussion about his statesmanship, and ask, What is he worth as a man? Yes, he mistakes the motive power which shapes the events of history. I find that in the life of free nations mere legal disquisitions never turned the tide of events, and mere constitutional constructions never determined the tendency of an age. The logic of things goes its steady way, immovable to eloquence and deaf to argument. It shapes and changes laws and constitutions according to its immutable rules, and those adverse to it will prove no effectual obstruction to its onward march. In times of great conflicts, the promptings and dictates of the human conscience are more potent than all the inventive ingenuity of the human brain. The conscience of a free people, when once fairly ruling the action of the masses, will never fail to make new laws, when those existing are contrary to its tendency, or it will put its own construction upon those that are there. Your disquisitions and plausibilities may be used as weapons and stratagems in a fencing match of contending parties, but powerless as they are before the conscience of man, posterity will remember them only as mere secondary incidents of a battle of great principles, in which the strongest motive powers of human nature were the true combatants.

There is the slavery question; not a mere occasional quarrel between the two sections of country, divided by a geographical line; not a mere contest between two economic interests for the preponderance; not a mere wrangle between two political parties for power and spoils; but the great struggle between two antagonistic systems of social organization; between advancing civilization and retreating barbarism; between the human conscience and a burning wrong. In vain will our impotent mock giants endeavor to make the test-question of our age turn on a ridiculous logical quibble, or a paltry legal technicality; in vain will they invent small dodges and call them "great principles"; in vain will they attempt to drag down the all-absorbing contest to the level of a mere pothouse quarrel between two rival candidates for a Presidential nomination. The wheel of progressing events will crush them to atoms, as it has crushed so many abnormities, and a future generation will perhaps read on Mr. Douglas's tombstone the inscription: "Here lies the queer sort of a statesman, who, when the great battle of slavery was fought, pretended to say that he did not care whether slavery be voted up or down."

But as long as the moral vitality of this nation is not entirely exhausted, Mr. Douglas and men like him will in vain endeavor to reduce the people to that disgusting state of moral indifference which he himself is not ashamed to boast of. I solemnly protest that the American people are not to be measured by Mr. Douglas's self-made moral standard. However degraded some of our politicians may be, the progress of the struggle will show that the popular conscience is still alive, and that the people DO CARE.

TO J. F. POTTER

COLUMBUS, O., March 17, 1860.

My dear Friend: I have just taken a survey of the State of Indiana; a hard State, but I think we can carry it if proper exertions are used. There is a strong Fillmore element there, which is now just what it was in 1856, and I am assured by reliable men that it will be exceedingly difficult to unite that element with the Republican party. The Bates movement is dead in that State:

it has worked only mischief and nothing else. All true Republicans seem to have turned their backs from [on] it. From what I have seen there I am led to believe that we can turn about ten thousand German votes that were formerly Democratic,—perhaps a great many more. That, it seems to me, is the only way to carry the State. There is a very strong demand there for the German translation of my Springfield speech; the Indiana members ought to send a good supply to the southern districts of their State. I have tried to establish a system of correspondence all over the State, and I think that after the National Convention we shall get the machine in good working order. Please let me know what the feeling in regard to the Presidential candidates is in Congressional circles. Seward seems to be gaining everywhere. It will require much hard work to carry Indiana and Illinois for him, but still I think it can be done.

.   .   .   .

TO MRS. SCHURZ

MILWAUKEE, March 2, 1860.[1]

Last evening I returned from the State convention. With great enthusiasm and without a dissenting vote, I was placed at the head of the State delegation [to go to the Republican National Convention at Chicago]; and to-morrow I shall send you my short speech of acceptance. A. D. Smith was very badly beaten and Scott Sloan was nominated as chief justice. So far all is well.

Now for something more serious. Last evening Booth was again arrested by the United States marshal on account of his opposition to the fugitive-slave law. This case brings the question of State-rights to an issue. We

[1] Translated from the German.

shall now have the final decision of the great contest between the State of Wisconsin and the United States Supreme Court. It is really dreadful that that rascal Booth is involved in this case and that the great cause has to bear the burden of his sins. But the principles that must be maintained are of so lofty a nature that all other considerations vanish. The supreme court of Wisconsin will be requested next Wednesday to issue a writ of habeas corpus, and in about two weeks the great argument for the support of this case will have to be made. I have been chosen to make that argument and have agreed to do so when my other matters shall have been attended to. I leave here to-morrow to meet my appointments. It is still undecided when the supreme court will take up the matter; the extent of my journey will depend upon this. If it should become very urgent, I should not go to Philadelphia, as that would necessitate my giving up all my appointments. It imposes a lot of work upon me, but it is most profitable.

This is my birthday. Thirty-one years old! I have grown rapidly without growing old. I am still young in strength, ambition and affection. The serious side of life has, indeed, taken a firmer hold of me, but I am as hale as I was ten years ago.

CHICAGO, March 5, 1860.

I have never seen such political excitement as that which at present makes Chicago seem to stand on its head. Douglas or anti-Douglas is the battle-cry. I arrived Saturday and that evening spoke at two meetings: first, at the German Theatre, where our fellow-countrymen were so crowded together that an apple could not have fallen between them, and many hundred more stood outside in vain trying to get in; and then at the American meeting, in Metropolitan Hall, where at least four thousand persons were packed like sardines, while fully two thousand more filled the streets and listened to several speakers. My reception at the American meeting was tremendously—indescribably enthusiastic. The audience fairly trembled with excitement.

The Republican headquarters is crowded from early morning until late at night and is a continuous mass-meeting. "Long John" [Wentworth] commands like a field-marshal and everything seems to proceed in military fashion. It is really ludicrous to see how even the most quiet persons have lost their senses. The Democrats are also making the most strenuous efforts, but it is generally believed that the Republicans will carry Chicago by their old majority.

SOUTH BEND, INDIANA, March 9, 1860.

Since I wrote you from Jacksonville, I have had hardly a moment's rest. I was actually unable to find a half-hour's leisure. Our German brothers in Terre Haute and Evansville thought so much of me that they would scarcely allow me to go to bed; and before I was sound asleep, I was wakened by their serenade. This week has really been a hard one and I have been compelled to make great efforts. I have passed three nights on the train, and only one of these in a sleeper. I arrived here a half hour ago (it 's now 10 A.M.), and now, at last, I am to have a day to myself. This life on the train is abominable; for breakfast indescribable beefsteak, tough as tanned leather, warmed-up potatoes and saleratus "biscuits" that smell like green soap. Ditto at noon, ditto at night; then the lecture and the same answers to the same compliments, and finally to bed, quite worn out; and the next morning I am on the train again. I am heartily tired of this now and am delighted at the prospect of soon being at home.

The political situation is excellent here. You have doubtless already heard of the surprisingly great success at Chicago. That is a severe blow for Douglas, perhaps the most severe one he could have received under the circumstances. There is great delight over the result among the Republicans. The news was greeted with joyful salutes almost everywhere. I believe that this Republican victory completely destroys Douglas's prospects for the nomination at Charleston. In my opinion, they were never very good, but a Democratic victory in the Chicago election would have given him new prestige. Here in Indiana things look better than I had supposed. The German vote is coming over to our side with increasing numbers, and I have little doubt that we will carry Indiana in the election. My Springfield speech has been very widely read here in the West. In Indiana alone three or four editions have been printed. It has been in almost everybody's hands. Indiana is the only State in which strong sympathy for Bates has been perceptible; elsewhere he is not mentioned. Seward is evidently gaining. If Douglas is not nominated in Charleston, I consider it most probable that Seward will get the nomination in Chicago. If Douglas is nominated, Lincoln will probably be the man for our side. I should be very well satisfied with either.

TO J. F. POTTER

MILWAUKEE, April 12, 1860.

You have learned the result of our judicial election. To be defeated is bad; but to see Republicans rejoice over it is worse. I did, indeed, expect that Sloan would be elected by a small majority, but I must confess Dixon's sweep does not surprise me very much. Sloan has been defeated by his own friends, or rather the friends of the

State-rights cause. The fire-eaters of our party (and you know there are such, who are always apt to undo by over-doing) threatened to bolt unless Sloan would make a public statement of his views on the State-rights question. Shortly after the convention, while I was travelling in Indiana, I wrote Sloan that there was some difficulty in Milwaukee and Racine, probably instigated by A. D. Smith and his particular friends, and that he, probably, would be called upon to write a letter for publication. I told him that I would consider it very improper for a candidate for a judicial office to make a public statement of his views on matters which might come up to him for adjudication; but if it was necessary that something should be done, I advised him to write private letters to some prominent Republicans, enabling them to endorse him as a State-rights man, without publishing the letters. When I got home, the first thing that met my eye was a letter from Sloan stating that my advice had come too late, and that he had yielded to the urgent demands of the State-rights men. He had, indeed, showed himself to be driven into doing a very weak thing and doing it in a very weak manner too. You have probably seen Sloan's letter to his "dear brother" in Janesville. That letter has cost him over two thousand votes, for it made even State-rights men doubt of the good sense of their candidate. So there was no fire, no enthusiasm, no alacrity in the fight on our side, while Dixon's friends were active and working in all parts of the State. Recent developments show that the farm-mortgage interest went in for Dixon, while, during the campaign, Sloan had to bear the odium of it. In short, there was foul play, discontent, disaffection, treachery everywhere; men who had worked to get Sloan nominated and voted for him in the convention, turned right against him as soon as his letter appeared, and our opponents found in the apparent make-up of the thing

a new ground to place their batteries upon. Thus the
thing was done. Meanwhile we have to rally for a new
battle. The Democrats are no stronger than they were
before, and, whatever may have happened, the State is
sure for the Chicago nominee by an increased majority.

You have heard of our municipal election here. We
have made large inroads upon the Democracy, and if our
Republicans had believed in the possibility of victory,
victory would have been ours. The whole work was done
by a few young men. The old stagers did not move. I
venture to predict that, if Douglas is not nominated at
Charleston and the Chicago Convention gives us a good
Republican candidate, Milwaukee will give us a majority
next fall, and the Second ward will be the Republican
banner ward of the city. Seward stock is rising in the
West. Bates may have gained a little by his letter, but
he will not get the foreign vote. I think that Seward
stands the best chance, but, if he should fail to get the
nomination, Lincoln's and Wade's prospects are the next
best.

Give my best regards to Washburn and Doolittle. I
shall reply to their letters as soon as I can find time.
You have won golden opinions by your defense of the
freedom of debate. Lovejoy and yourself did nobly.
Your two or three sentences and determined action were
better than a long and eloquent speech.

As to your running for Congress again next fall I think
you will hardly escape the nomination and we shall re-
elect you as a matter of course. How they feel in the
rural districts I do not know, but I suppose it is all the
same way. It would be difficult to unite upon any other
man, and now, more than ever before, we want Representatives who stand their ground.

8

TO J. R. DOOLITTLE

MILWAUKEE, April 12, 1860.

My dear Friend: Since yesterday the Republicans of this city are in a state of great excitement about Potter. The telegraph has not informed us yet whether he has accepted the challenge or not.[1] We expect further news about noon. We all feel deeply anxious. God grant that all goes well. Whatever the result may be, do me the favor to send me all the particulars you can gather.

You have learned of the result of the judicial election in this State. Yesterday I wrote a letter to Potter about this very matter, and I think he will show it to you—if he survives. This morning the official returns are coming in, and Dixon's majorities are coming down so wonderfully that there is still some hope of Sloan's election.

In your kind letter of March 13th you speak of the candidates for the Presidency. As to Wade I agree with you perfectly. I have a kind of fondness for the brave old Roundhead, but I think Lincoln will be stronger in the Convention. If Pennsylvania and New Jersey should unite upon Wade, that would alter the case. But as things now are it looks as though Seward would go into the Convention with nearly a majority of the delegates.

The day of division is drawing near now and I hope you will be kind enough to keep me advised of what is going on in high circles.

Excuse this short and hasty letter. I feel so anxious about our brave friend Potter that I can hardly think of anything else. But I must not forget to congratulate

---

[1] Roger A. Pryor, then a Representative from Va., challenged Potter to a duel on account of personal differences of opinion in discussing slavery in the House. Potter accepted and named bowie-knives. This caused much excitement and merriment in the North and indignation in the South. Although the duel never came off, Potter quickly became a popular hero among anti-slavery men.

you upon your excellent speech on State-rights. It is a grand vindication of the doctrine.

TO J. F. POTTER

MILWAUKEE, April 17, 1860.

Your constituency have come to the conclusion that you are "a devil of a fellow." Indeed, this impression seems to be quite general in this region. People threw up their hats when the news came that you had driven Pryor to the wall. Republicans congratulated each other and Democrats swore they would vote for you the next time. The question whether you will be renominated and reëlected seems to be settled. All those that had any aspirations that way will have to hang up their harps. You will be renominated, if I understand the temper of the people, not only on account of your availability, but of your unavoidability. Your fate is sealed. You have done the right thing at the right time and in the right place. I felt terribly anxious about you when I learned that you were challenged. I knew that you would show them your teeth, but I did not know that you would show it in so emphatic a way, that could not be but successful. This was even better than declining to fight. You will see the effect of your course next fall. That is all I can say.

For two days the papers had Sloan elected by a small majority. But since yesterday Dixon is ahead again, very little indeed, but in all probability sufficiently to elect him. Almost any Republican might have defeated him. This is a lesson which we are not likely to forget soon.

TO ABRAHAM LINCOLN

WATERTOWN, WIS., May 22, 1860.

As a man of honor and faithful to the wishes of my constituents, I stood by Governor Seward for the nomination. If I am able I shall do the work of a hundred men for Abraham Lincoln's election. I congratulate you upon having received at the hands of the Republican party so high an acknowledgment of your merits; I congratulate the party on so strong and unobjectionable a candidate; and the country upon the prospects of an able, high-toned and pure administration. I feel some delicacy in telling you this, for I do not belong to those worshippers of success whose hearts and minds are readily turned by the changing breezes of fortune. But I deem it my duty to establish between us that confidence which must exist between the head of the party and those who are to fight in the front ranks—and, so let me assure you, that after I have done my duty in paying a debt of honor to the old chieftain of the anti-slavery movement, there is no feeling of disappointment left in my heart, and I shall carry into this struggle all the zeal and ardor and enthusiasm of which my nature is capable. The same disinterested motives that led me and my friends to support Governor Seward in the Convention, will animate and urge us on in our work for you, and wherever my voice is heard and my influence extends you may count upon hosts of true and devoted friends.

Now let us turn to things of practical moment. I was elected a member of the National Central Committee and, as a matter of course, the "foreign department," if it may so be called, fell to my special charge. The plan I wish to carry out is as follows: I intend to get up a complete list of all the Germans, Norwegians, Hollanders, etc., who can serve our cause in the way of public speaking and to make regular contracts with them. I would then send them in little squads into those States in which the principal work is to be done, have them stump township after township in regular succession as the exigencies of the case may demand, and as soon as they get through with their work in that particular State, have them relieved by another party and sent off into another State. In this way we can carry on the agitation in a regular and systematic way, keep the work going without interruption, and concentrate our forces where it may seem most desirable. I would, of course, go to all the principal points and do the heavy work myself. In order to carry out this system of canvassing the doubtful States efficiently, it will be necessary for me to take a survey of the whole ground first, to make my arrangements in detail with the different State central committees, to organize local committees and clubs where there are none, and to establish a complete system of correspondence. In 1856, piles of money and much work were spent for no purpose, because it was done at random and without plan and direction. The plan I propose will, in my opinion, be the cheapest and most efficient. It seems to me that much work is to be done, especially in Indiana and Pennsylvania, before the Democrats nominate a candidate. The field is all our own for four weeks, and we ought not to neglect the opportunity of committing people before they receive an impulse from the other side. This work will of course occupy all my time from now till election day, and I am now endeavoring to arrange my private affairs so as to be able to devote myself exclusively to it. I intended to start this matter in a meeting of the National Committee before we left Chicago, but people were in such a hurry that nothing could be done. You are undoubtedly now in active correspondence with the principal managers of the party and I wish you would direct their attention to it. By a canvass of this systematic kind I have no doubt we can at least double the foreign Republican vote in the Northern States and may secure Indiana, Pennsylvania and New York beyond peradventure.

In the first and second week of June I shall in all probability go down to Pennsylvania and open my campaign there. If I can get ready by that time I shall make a leading campaign speech (I hope at least it will become a leading one) on your doctrine of the "irrepressible conflict" on account of which the Democratic papers are already attacking you. If you should wish this or that topic to be brought prominently into the foreground, please let me know. I wish to consult you about several matters before I start out, but I do not know whether I shall have an opportunity to see you.

Let me again press the above plan upon your attention. Time is precious and not a day ought to be lost before the Baltimore Convention comes off. I would not have troubled you with this matter, but our friends are scattered all over the country, and you are now the natural centre towards which everything converges and from which everything radiates. I shall address a circular to the members of the National Committee as soon as I find time to write it.

We shall have ratification meetings all over this State during this and next week, and you may be sure that Wisconsin will give a good report of herself.

FROM ABRAHAM LINCOLN

SPRINGFIELD, ILLS., June 18, 1860.

Yours of May 22nd was duly received; and now, on a careful re-perusal of it, I am much mortified that I did not attend to it an [at] once. I fear I have no sufficient apology. I received it with multitudes of others, glanced over it too hastily to properly appreciate its importance, laid it by, and it passed from my mind, till Governor Koerner mentioned it to-day. In a general bringing up of my correspondence, I perhaps should have reached it to-day.

The main object of the letter—time—so far as it depended on *me*, is lost. I hope you have gone forward on your plan without my advice. To me it appears an excellent plan; and I have no sufficient experience to suggest any improvement of it. I think it would be desirable to have the opinion of the National Committee upon it, if it can be obtained without too much loss of time.

And now, upon this bad beginning, you must not determine to write me no more; for I promise you that no letter of yours to me shall ever again be neglected.

I beg you to be assured that your having supported Governor Seward, in preference to myself, in the Convention, is not even remembered by me for any practical purpose, or the slightest unpleasant feeling. I go not back of the Convention to make distinctions among its members; and, to the extent of our limited acquaintance, no man stands nearer my heart than yourself.

Very truly your friend,

A. LINCOLN.

TO MRS. SCHURZ

ALTON, July 25, 1860.[1]

I was with Lincoln yesterday. He is the same kindly old fellow, quite as unpretentious and ingenuous as ever. The reception committee had reserved quarters for me at the hotel, and Lincoln was one of the first to knock at my door. He wears a linen sack-coat and a hat of doubtful age, but his appearance is neat and cleanly. We talked in my room nearly two hours. I was lying on my bed

[1] Translated from the German.

resting, when he came, and he insisted on my remaining so. He talked of the Presidential election with as much placid, cheerful frankness as if he were discussing the potato crop. He told me of all the letters and visits with which he was flooded, and said that he was not answering those asking for office and the like. "Men like you," he added, "who have real merit and do the work, are always too proud to ask for anything; those who do nothing are always the most clamorous for office, and very often get it, because it is the only way to get rid of them. But if I am elected, they will find a tough customer to deal with, and you may depend upon it that I shall know how to distinguish deserving men from the drones."

"All right, old Abe!" thought I.

In the evening I took supper with Lincoln. The Madam was very nicely dressed up and is already quite skillful in handling her fan. She chats fairly well and will adapt herself to the White House cleverly enough. Lincoln's boys are typical Western youngsters. One of them insisted on going about barefooted. After supper, to which a number of "leading men" had been invited, we lit our cigars and chatted. At eight o'clock the Wideawakes came to escort me to my mass-meeting in the capitol. I have never seen so large a torch-light procession. Lincoln insisted on accompanying us, although he had not appeared in public since his nomination. He declared that he must once hear "that tremendous speaker." And so the Wideawakes surrounded "Old Abe" and me; thus arm in arm we marched to the capitol. The cheering was tremendous. My German speech was about the best I ever made. Then I spoke in English, and tried to do specially well. Lincoln sat directly in front of me all evening, watched every movement and applauded with tremendous enthusiasm. When I had finished, he came to me and shook hands and said: "You

are an awful fellow! I understand your power now!"
He presented me with a copy of his debate with Douglas,
and he and Mrs. Lincoln impressed upon me that, on my
next visit, I must be sure to bring you and we must be
their guests.

I left Springfield this morning at five and arrived here
at eight, well and cheerful and as ready for debate as ever.

BELLEVILLE, July 29, 1860.

It was my intention to write you yesterday, but you
have no idea of the commotion in which I live. I have
scarcely a moment to myself. With great effort and
difficulty, I have succeeded in finishing two-thirds of my
St. Louis speech and hope to be able to write the remainder
to-morrow, Sunday; but I am compelled to close my door
to all comers. It is to be the greatest speech of my life,
and I know you will not be angry with me if my letters
are somewhat shorter that my speech may be still better.
I am utilizing every free moment for work.

There is to be a great demonstration here to-day; the
entire town is decorated with flags and garlands. Hecker
will be here and speak at the same meeting. The enthusiasm is at fever-heat. I have been in all respects highly
successful. The Germans are coming to our side by hundreds and thousands. If things go everywhere as they did
in Egypt,[1] where there were scarcely any Republican
votes cast in 1856, Lincoln's election is inevitable.

Good Heavens! The cannon are thundering again,
the drums are rumbling, the marshals are dashing by my
window. Four and thirty maidens, clad in white, are
waiting. Here's the committee coming for me. Good-bye!

[1] The colloquial name for southern Illinois.

THE DOOM OF SLAVERY[1]

MR. PRESIDENT AND GENTLEMEN:—To deny the existence of an evil they do not mean to remedy, to ascribe to paltry causes the origin of great problems they do not mean to solve, to charge those who define the nature of an existing difficulty with having originated it—these are expedients which the opponents of reformatory movements have resorted to since mankind has a history. An appeal to ignorance or timidity is their last hope, when all resources of logic and argument are exhausted. The old comedy is repeated again and again.

The assertions that the great contest between free and slave labor has no foundation in fact, that the origin of the slavery controversy is to be found in the fanaticism of a few Northern abolitionists, and that those who speak of an "irrepressible conflict" are to be made responsible for its existence—these form the argumentative staple of those who possess either not sagacity enough to discern or not courage enough to state facts as they are.

In investigating the causes of the great struggle which has for years kept the minds of the people in constant uneasiness and excitement, I shall endeavor to act with the most perfect fairness. I will not indulge in any denunciations. I shall impeach the motives of no one. I shall not appeal to prejudice or passion. I invite you to pass in review the actual state of things with calmness and impartiality.

[1] A speech delivered in Verandah Hall, St. Louis, Mo., August 1, 1860. by invitation of the emancipationists of that city. The Presidential campaign had begun, and there was much popular excitement. Anti-slavery sentiment was strong in St. Louis, but still weak in the interior of the State. The speaker especially desired to help the emancipationists elect their Congressional candidates; he also availed himself of the opportunity to make a direct appeal to slaveholders.—From Schurz's introductory note, *Speeches*, 121.

It is one of the best traits of human nature that we form our first opinions on matters of general interest from our innate sense of right and wrong. Our moral impressions, the dictates of our consciences, the generous impulses of our hearts, are the sources from which our first convictions spring. But custom, material interest, and our natural inclination to acquiesce in that which *is*, whether right or wrong, that *vis inertiæ* which has brought so much suffering upon humanity, are apt to overrule the native instincts of our moral nature. They are sicklied o'er by the pale cast of calculation; the freshness of their impelling power is lost, and questions essentially moral are imperceptibly changed into questions of material interest, national economy, or political power.

The people of the South have evidently gone through that process in regard to the institution of slavery; they have become accustomed to identify its existence with the existence of Southern society, while even a large majority of the people of the North were rather inclined to silence their moral objections to it, and to acquiesce, until its immediate interference with matters of general interest gave a new impulse to their native antipathy. Although I am not ashamed to confess, that the moral merits of the question would alone have been more than sufficient to make me an anti-slavery man, yet I will confine myself to a discussion of its practical effects, in order to make myself intelligible even to those who do not sympathize with me. This is the first time that I have had the honor to address a meeting in a slave State, and even now I owe the privilege of expressing my opinions freely and without restraint to the circumstance that, although in a slave State, I stand upon the soil of a free city, and under the generous protection of free men. Must I call "a privilege" what ought to be universally respected as the sacred birthright of every American citizen?

Ask any slaveholder who may be present in this vast assembly whether he does not deem it wrong and unjustifiable that I, an anti-slavery man, should be permitted to give a public expression of my views in a slave State; whether he would not be in favor of silencing me by whatever means within his reach; whether I should not be silenced at once in a strong slaveholding community? I do not mean to blame him for it. Let us give him a fair hearing. The slaveholder will state his political views substantially, as follows:

"On the point of astronomy or chemistry or medicine you may entertain whatever opinion you please; but we cannot permit you to discuss the relation between master and servant, as it exists here in the slave State, for in doing so you would endanger our safety and undermine our social system. Our condition is such that the slightest movement of insubordination, once started, is apt to grow with uncontrollable rapidity; we have, therefore, to guard against everything that may start it; we cannot allow free discussion of the subject; we have to remove from our midst every incendiary element; we cannot be expected to tolerate opinions of persons among us that are opposed to the ruling order of things. Whenever a mischievous attempt is made, we are obliged to repress it with such energy and severity as to strike terror into the hearts of those who might be capable of repeating the attempt. Our condition requires the promptest action, and when, in cases of imminent danger, the regular process of the courts is too slow or uncertain, we are obliged to resort to lynch-law in order to supply its deficiencies.

"Moreover, we must adapt our rules and customs of government to the peculiar wants of our social organization. In order to be safe, we must intrust the government, in its general administration as well as in its details, to those who, by their own interests, are bound to be the natural guardians of the system. Hence our safety requires that the political power in our States should be put into the hands of the slaveholders; and where we have no law to that effect, custom upholds the rule.

"In order to put the political ascendency of those who are most interested in the preservation of slavery upon a solid basis, we must put down everything that would produce and foster independent aspirations among the other classes of society. It would not only be insane to educate the slaves, but highly dangerous to extend to the great mass of poor white non-slaveholders the means of education; for in doing so we might raise an element to influence and power whose interests are not identical with those of the slaveholder. This is our policy of self-preservation, and we are bound to enforce it."

Sir, I mean to be just to the slaveholders, and, strange as it may sound, as to the propriety of their policy, I agree with them. Having identified their social existence with the existence of slavery, they cannot act otherwise.

It is necessity that urges them on. It is true that slavery is an inflammable element. A stray spark of thought or hope may cause a terrible conflagration. The torch of free speech and free press, which gives light to the house of liberty, is very apt to set on fire the house of slavery. What is more natural than that the torch should be extinguished, where there is such an abundance of explosive material?

It is true that in a slaveholding community the strictest subordination must be enforced, that the maintenance of established order requires the most rigorous, preventive and repressive measures, which will not always allow a strict observance of the rules of legal process; it is equally true that the making and the execution of the laws can be safely intrusted only to those who, by their position, are bound to the ruling interest; true, that popular education is dangerous to the exclusive rule of an exclusive class; true, that men must be kept stupid to be kept obedient. What is more consistent, therefore, than that the fundamental liberties should be disregarded whenever they become dangerous; that the safeguards of human rights in the administration of justice should be set aside whenever the emergency calls for prompt and energetic action; that the masses should be left uneducated, in order to give the slaveholding oligarchy an undisputed sway? In one word, that the rights, the liberties and the security of the individual should have to yield to the paramount consideration of the safety of the ruling interest? All this is true; and accepting the premises, all these necessities exist. You seem startled at this proposition and ask, What is the institution that demands for its protection such measures? The slave States are by no means original in this respect. Look at the kingdom of Naples, where the ruling power is governed by similar exclusive interests and acts on the same instinct of self-preservation; does it not resort to the same means? You tell me that the principles underlying our system of government are very different from those of the kingdom of Naples, and that the means of protection I spoke of run contrary to the spirit of our institutions. Indeed, so it seems to be. What does that prove? Simply this: That a social institution which is in antagonism with the principles of democratic government, cannot be maintained and protected by means which are in accordance with those principles; and, on the other hand, that a social institution that cannot be protected by means that are in accordance with the democratic principles of our government, must essentially be in antagonism to those principles. It proves that the people in the slaveholding States, although pretending to be free men, are, by the necessities arising from their condition, the slaves of slavery. That is all.

But I am told that the slave States are sovereign, and may shape and govern their home concerns according to their own notions, subject only to the Constitution of the United States. Granted. But the necessities of slavery do not stop there. The slave States are members of a federal family, and as the King of Naples in his foreign policy is governed by his peculiar interests, so is the policy of the slave States in our federal affairs governed by their peculiar necessities.

I hear much said of the aggressive spirit of the slave power, but I am inclined to acquit it of that charge, for all its apparently aggressive attempts are no less dictated by the instinct of self-preservation than are the most striking features of its home policy.

Let us listen to the slaveholder again. He says: "What will become of the security of our slave property, if inside of this Union a slave may finally escape from the hands of his master, by simply crossing the line of his State? But the fanatical anti-slavery spirit prevailing in the free States will avail itself of every facility the common legal process affords, as the trial by jury and the writ of habeas corpus, to aid the fugitive in his escape. We are, therefore, obliged to demand such legislation at the hands of the general government as will remove these obstacles thrown in the way of the recapture of our property, and oblige the citizens, by law, to assist us in the re-apprehension of the fugitive." So the trial by jury and the writ of habeas corpus will have to yield, and the good old common-law principle, that in all cases concerning life and property the presumption be in favor of liberty, goes by the board. This may seem rather hard, but is it not eminently consistent?

The necessities of slavery do not stop there. Let us hear how the slaveholder proceeds. "In order to obtain such legislation from our national councils, it is necessary that the prejudices against slavery existing in the free States be disarmed. It is impossible that the slave interest deem itself secure as long as a violent agitation is kept up against it, which continually troubles us at home, and exercises upon the national legislature an influence hostile to slavery. We are, therefore, obliged to demand that measures be taken to stop that agitation." Nothing more natural than that. The right of petition, held sacred even by some despotic governments, must be curtailed. Post-office regulations must prevent the dissemination of anti-slavery sentiments by the newspapers. Even in the free States willing instruments are found, who urge the adoption of measures tending to suppress the very discussion of this question. Laws are advocated in Congress (and that "champion of free labor" Douglas, takes the lead), making it a criminal offense to organize associations hostile to slavery, and empowering the general government to suppress them by means of a centralized police. This may seem somewhat tyrannical, but is it not eminently consistent?

But in order to succeed in this, slavery needs a controlling power in the general government. It cannot expect to persuade us, so it must try to subdue and rule us. Hear the slaveholder: "It is impossible that we should consider our interests safe in this Union, unless the political equilibrium between the free and the slave States be restored. If the free States are permitted to increase and the slave States stand still, we shall be completely at the mercy of a hostile majority. We are, therefore, obliged to demand accessions of territory out of which new slave States can be formed, so as to increase our representation in Congress, and to restore the equilibrium of power." Nothing more sensible. The acquisition of foreign countries, such as Cuba and the northern States of Mexico, is demanded; and, if they cannot be

obtained by fair purchase and diplomatic transaction, war
must be resorted to; and, if the majority of the people are
not inclined to go to war, our international relations must
be disturbed by filibustering expeditions, precipitating,
if possible, this country into wars, thus forcing the peaceable or cheating the enthusiastic into subserviency to the
plans of the slave power. You may call this piracy, disgracing us in the eyes of the civilized world. But can you
deny that slavery needs power, and that it cannot obtain
that power except by extension?

So, pressed by its necessities, it lays its hand upon our
national territories. Time-honored compacts, hemming
in slavery, must be abrogated. The Constitution must
be so construed as to give slavery unlimited sway over
our national domain. Hence your Nebraska bills and
Dred Scott decisions and slave-code platforms. You may
call that atrocious, but can you deny its consistency?

"But," adds the slaveholder, "of what use to us is the
abstract right to go with our slave property into the territories, if you pass laws which attract to the territories a
class of population that will crowd out slavery; if you
attract to them the foreign immigrant by granting to him
the immediate enjoyment of political rights; if you allure
the paupers from all parts of the globe by your preëmption
laws and homestead bills? We want the negro in the
territories. You give us the foreign immigrant. Slavery
cannot exist except with the system of large farms, and
your homestead bills establish the system of small farms,
with which free labor is inseparably connected. We are,
therefore, obliged to demand that all such mischievous projects be abandoned." Nothing more plausible.
Hence the right of the laboring man to acquire property
in the soil by his labor is denied; your homestead bills
voted down; the blight of oppressive speculation fastened
on your virgin soil, and attempts are made to deprive the

9

foreign immigrant in the territories of the immediate
enjoyment of political rights, which in the primitive state
of social organization are essential to his existence. All
this in order to give slavery a chance to obtain possession
of our national domain. This may seem rather hard.
But can you deny that slavery for its own protection needs
power in the general government; and that it cannot
obtain that power except by increased representation;
and that it cannot increase its representation except by
conquest and extension over the territories; and that with
this policy all measures are incompatible, which bid fair
to place the territories into the hands of free labor?

This is not all. Listen to the slaveholder once more:
"Our States," he tells us, "are essentially agricultural,
producing States. We have but little commerce, and still
less manufacturing industry. All legislation tending principally to benefit the commercial and manufacturing interests is, therefore, to our immediate prejudice. It will
oblige us to contribute to the growth and prosperity of the
free States at our expense, and consequently turn the
balance of political power still more against us. We are,
therefore, obliged to demand that all attempts by Federal legislation to promote the industrial interest be
given up." Nothing more logical. The system of slave
labor has never permitted them to recognize and develop
the harmony of agricultural, commercial and industrial
pursuits. What is more natural than that they should
seek to give the peculiar economic interest in which their
superiority consists, the preponderance in our economic
policy? Hence their unrelenting opposition to all legislation tending to develop the peculiar resources of the
free States.

Here let us pause. Is there nothing strange or surprising in all this? You may call it madness, but there
is method in this madness. The slave power is im-

pelled by the irresistible power of necessity. It cannot exist unless it rules, and it cannot rule unless it keeps down its opponents. All its demands and acts are in strict harmony with its interests and attributes; they are the natural growth of its existence. I repeat, I am willing to acquit it of the charge of wilful aggression; I am willing to concede that it struggles for self-preservation. But now the momentous question arises: How do the means which seem indispensable to the self-preservation of slavery agree with the existence and interests of free labor society?

Sir, if Mr. Hammond of South Carolina, or Mr. Brown of Mississippi, had listened to me, would they not have been obliged to give me credit for having stated their case fairly? Now, listen to me while I state our own.

Cast your eyes over that great beehive called the free States. See by the railroad and the telegraphic wire every village, almost every backwoods cottage, drawn within the immediate reach of progressive civilization. Look over our grain fields, but lately a lonesome wilderness, where machinery is almost superseding the labor of the human hand; over our workshops, whose aspect is almost daily changed by the magic touch of inventive genius; over our fleets of merchant vessels, numerous enough to make the whole world tributary to our prosperity; look upon our society, where by popular education and the continual change of condition the dividing lines between ranks and classes are almost obliterated; look upon our sytem of public instruction, which places even the lowliest child of the people upon the high road of progressive advancement; upon our rapid growth and expansive prosperity, which is indeed subject to reverses and checks, but contains such a wonderful fertility of resources, that every check is a mere incentive to new enterprise, every reverse but a mere opportunity for the development of new powers.

To what do we owe all this? First and foremost, to that perfect freedom of inquiry, which acknowledges no rules but those of logic, no limits but those that bound the faculties of the human mind. Its magic consists in its universality. To it we owe the harmony of our progressive movement in all its endless ramifications. No single science, no single practical pursuit exists in our day independently of all other sciences, all other practical pursuits. This is the age of the solidarity of progress. Set a limit to the freedom of inquiry in one direction and you destroy the harmony of its propelling action. Give us the Roman inquisition, which forbids Galileo Galilei to think that the earth moves around the sun, and he has to interrupt and give up the splendid train of his discoveries and their influence upon all other branches of science is lost; he has to give it up, or he must fight the inquisition. Let the slave power or any other political or economic interest tell us that we must think and say and invent and discover nothing which is against its demands, and we must interrupt and give up the harmony of our progressive development, or fight the tyrannical pretension, whatever shape it may assume.

Believing, as we do, that the moral and ideal development of man is the true aim and end of human society, we must preserve in their efficiency the means which serve that end. In order to secure to the freedom of inquiry its full productive power, we must surround it with all the safeguards which political institutions afford. As we cannot set a limit to the activity of our minds, so we cannot muzzle our mouths or fetter the press with a censorship. We cannot arrest or restrain the discussion of the question, What system of labor or what organization of society promotes best the moral and intellectual development of

man. We cannot deprive a single individual of the
privileges which protect him in the free exercise of his
faculties and the enjoyment of his right, so long as these
faculties are not employed to the detriment of the rights
and liberties of others. Our organization of society
resting upon equal rights, we find our security in a general
system of popular education which fits all for an intelligent
exercise of those rights. This is the home policy of free
society. This policy in our Federal affairs must necessarily correspond. Deeming free and intelligent labor
the only safe basis of society, it is our duty to expand its
blessings over all the territory within our reach; seeing
our own prosperity advanced by the prosperity of our
neighbors, we must endeavor to plant upon our borders
a system of labor which answers in that respect. So we
recognize the right of the laboring man to the soil he
cultivates, and shield him against oppressive speculation.
Seeing in the harmonious development of all branches of
labor a source of progress and power, we must adopt a
policy which draws to light the resources of the land,
gives work to our workshops and security to our commerce.
These are the principles and views governing our policy.

Slaveholders, look at this picture and at this. Can
the difference escape your observation? You may say,
as many have said, that there is, indeed, a difference of
principle, but not necessarily an antagonism of interests.
Look again.

Your social system is founded upon forced labor, ours
upon free labor. Slave labor cannot exist together with
freedom of inquiry, and so you demand the restriction of
that freedom; free labor cannot exist without it, and so
we maintain its inviolability. Slave labor demands the
setting aside of the safeguards of individual liberty, for
the purpose of upholding subordination and protecting
slave property; free labor demands their preservation as

essential and indispensable to its existence and progressive development. Slavery demands extension by an aggressive foreign policy; free labor demands an honorable peace and friendly intercourse with the world abroad for its commerce, and a peaceable and undisturbed development of our resources at home for its agriculture and industry. Slavery demands extension over national territories for the purpose of gaining political power. Free labor demands the national domain for workingmen, for the purpose of spreading the blessings of liberty and civilization. Slavery, therefore, opposes all measures tending to secure the soil to the actual laborer; free labor, therefore, recognizes the right of the settler to the soil, and demands measures protecting him against the pressure of speculation. Slavery demands the absolute ascendency of the planting interest in our economic policy; free labor demands legislation tending to develop all the resources of the land, and to harmonize the agricultural, commercial and industrial interests. Slavery demands the control of the general government for its special protection and the promotion of its peculiar interests; free labor demands that the general government be administered for the purpose of securing to all the blessings of liberty, and for the promotion of the general welfare. Slavery demands the recognition of its divine right; free labor recognizes no divine right but that of the liberty of all men.

With one word, slavery demands, for its protection and perpetuation, a system of policy which is utterly incompatible with the principles upon which the organization of free-labor society rests. There is the antagonism. That is the essence of the "irrepressible conflict." It is a conflict of principles underlying interests, always the same, whether appearing as a moral, economic, or political question. Mr. Douglas boasted that he could repress it

with police measures; he might as well try to fetter the
winds with a rope. The South means to repress it with
decisions of the Supreme Court; they might as well, like
Xerxes, try to subdue the waves of the ocean by throwing
chains into the water.

The conflict of constitutional constructions is, indeed,
a mere incident of the great struggle, a mere symptom of
the crisis. Long before the slavery question in the form
of an abstract constitutional controversy agitated the
public mind, the conflict of interests raged in our national
councils. What mattered it that the struggle about the
encouragement of home industry and internal improvements was not ostensibly carried on under the form of
pro- and anti-slavery? What mattered it that your new-
fangled constitutional doctrines were not yet invented,
when slavery tried to expand by the annexation of foreign
countries; that no Dred Scott decision was yet cooked up,
when the right of petition was curtailed, when attempts
were made to arrest the discussion of the slavery question
all over the Union, and when the trial by jury and the
writ of habeas corpus were overridden by the fugitive-
slave law? And even lately, when the slave power, with
one gigantic grasp, attempted to seize the whole of our
national domain, what else was and is your new constitutional doctrine but an ill-disguised attempt to clothe a
long-cherished design with the color of law?

Read your history with an impartial eye, and you will
find that the construction of the Constitution always shaped
itself according to the prevailing moral impulses or the
predominance of the material over political interests.
The logic of our minds is but too apt to follow in the track
of our sympathies and aspirations. It was when the
South had control of the government that acts were passed
for the raising of duties on imports, for the creation of a
national bank, and in aid of the American shipping interest.

It was under the lead of the South that the systems of internal improvements and of the protection of home industry were inaugurated; it was the South, no less than the North, that insisted upon and exercised the power of Congress to exclude slavery from the territories. So long as these measures seemed to agree with the predominant interest there seemed to be no question about their constitutionality. Even Mr. Calhoun himself said in one of his most celebrated speeches, delivered in the session of 1815–16, "that it was the duty of the Government, as a means of defense, to encourage the domestic industry of the country." But as soon as it was found out that this policy redounded more to the benefit of free labor than that of the unenterprising South, then the same men who had inaugurated it worked its overthrow, on the plea that it was at war with the principles of the Constitution. The constitutionality of the ordinance of 1787 was never questioned as long as the prevailing sentiment in the South ran against the perpetuation of slavery. The Missouri compromise was held as sacred and inviolable as the Constitution itself, so long as it served to introduce slave States into the Union; but no sooner, by virtue of its provisions, were free territories to be organized, than its unconstitutionality was discovered.

The predominance of interests determines the construction of the Constitution. So it was and it will ever be. Only those who remained true to the original program of the Fathers remained true to the original construction. Decide the contest of principles underlying interests, and the conflict of constitutional constructions will settle itself. This may seem a dangerous political theory. It is not an article of my creed, not a matter of principles, but a matter of experience; not a doctrine, but a fact.

Thus the all-pervading antagonism stands before us, gigantic in its dimensions, growing every day in the awful

proportions of its problems, involving the character of
our institutions; involving our relations with the world
abroad; involving our peace, our rights, our liberties at
home; involving our growth and prosperity; involving
our moral and political existence as a nation.

How short-sighted, how childish, are those who find
its origin in artificial agitation! As though we could produce a tempest by blowing our noses, or cause an earth-
quake by stamping our puny feet upon the ground. But
how to solve, how to decide it? Let us pass in review our
political parties and the remedies they propose. There
we encounter the so-called Union party, with Bell and
Everett, who tell us the best way to settle the controversy
is to ignore it.

"Ignore it! Ignore it, when attempts are made to
plunge the country into war and disgrace, for the purpose
of slavery extension! Ignore it, when slavery and free
labor wage their fierce war about the possession of the
national domain! Ignore it, when the liberties of speech
and of the press are attacked! Ignore it, when the actual
settler claims the virgin soil, and the slaveholding capitalists claim it also! Ignore it, when the planting interest
seeks to establish and maintain its exclusive supremacy
in our economic policy! Ignore it, indeed! Ignore
the fire that consumes the corner posts of your house!
Ignore the storm that breaks the rudder and tears to
tatters the sails of your ship! Conjure the revolted elements with a meek Mount Vernon lecture! Pour upon
the furious waves the placid oil of a quotation from Washington's farewell address!

It is true they tell us that they will enforce the laws and
the Constitution well enough! But what laws? Those
that free labor demands or those that slavery gives us?
What Constitution? That of Washington and Madison,
or that of Slidell, Douglas and Taney?

The conflict stands there with the stubborn brutal force of reality. However severely it may disturb the nerves of timid gentlemen, there it stands and speaks the hard, stern language of fact. I understand well that great problems and responsibilities should be approached with care and caution. But times like these demand the firm action of men who know what they will, and will do it; not that eunuch policy which, conscious of its own unproductiveness, invites us blandly to settle down into the imbecile contentment of general impotency. They cannot ignore the conflict if they would, but have not nerve enough to decide it if they could.

The next party that claims our attention is the so-called Democracy. As it is my object to discuss the practical, not the constitutional merits of the problem before us, I might pass over the divisions existing in that organization. In fact, the point that separates Mr. Douglas from Mr. Breckenridge is but a mere quibble, a mere matter of etiquette. Mr. Douglas is unwilling to admit in words what he has a hundred times admitted in fact—for, can you tell me what practical difference in the world there is between direct and indirect intervention by Congress in favor of slavery and that kind of non-intervention by Congress which merely consists in making room for direct intervention by the Supreme Court? And besides, in nearly all practical measures of policy, Mr. Douglas is regularly to be found on the side of the extreme South. Like that great statesman of yours (I beg your pardon, gentlemen, for alluding to him in decent political company) he always votes against measures for the encouragement of home industry, perhaps because he does not understand them. He is one of the firmest supporters of the ascendency of the planters' interests in our economic questions, and, as to the extension of slavery by conquest and annexation, the wildest fillibusters may always count upon his tenderest sympathies.

So I say I might have ignored him, if he had not succeeded in creating the most deafening of noises with the hollowest of drums.

He proposes to repress the "irrepressible conflict" with what he emphatically styles "his great principle." At first he defined it as "self-government of the people in the territories"; but it soon became apparent that under his great principle the people of the territories were governed by anybody but *self*, and he called it "popular sovereignty." It soon turned out that this kind of sovereignty was not very popular after all, and he called it "non-intervention." Methinks something will intervene pretty soon and he will strain his imagination for another name, if it be worth while at all to christen a thing which never had any tangible existence.

But if we may believe him, his "great principle," and nothing but his "great principle," will settle the "irrepressible conflict," and restore peace and harmony to the nation; and save the Union.

Let us judge the merits of the great principle by its results. Has it secured to the inhabitants of the territories the right of self-government? Never were the people of a territory subject to a despotism more arbitrary and to violence more lawless and atrocious than were the people of Kansas after the enactment of the Nebraska bill. Has it removed the slavery question from the halls of Congress? The fight has never raged with greater fierceness, and Congress hardly ever came so near debating with bowie knives and revolvers, as about the questions raised by the Nebraska bill. Has it established safe and uniform rules for the construction of the Constitution? It has set aside the construction put upon the Constitution by those who framed it; and for the rest, let Mr. Douglas give you his opinion on the Dred Scott decision. Has it given peace and harmony to the country by repressing the "irrepressible conflict"? Alas! poor great principle! this harangue of peace and harmony inflamed the "irrepressible conflict" even inside the Democratic party, and rent into two sections an organization that claimed the exclusive privilege of nationality.

These were its immediate results. It is true, Mr. Douglas accuses his adversaries of having created the disturbance. Certainly, if the whole American nation had bowed their heads in silent obedience before Mr. Douglas's mandate, there would have been no strife. Mr. Slidell, Mr. Buchanan and Mr. Breckenridge may say the same; so may the Emperor of Austria, and the King of Naples. Such men are apt to be disturbed by opponents, and Mr. Douglas need not be surprised if he has a few!

The true source of the difficulty was this: The Kansas-Nebraska bill was thrown, as an ambiguous, illogical measure, between two antagonistic interests, each of which construed it for its own advantage. It brought the contesting forces together, face to face, without offering a clear ground upon which to settle the conflict. Thus it quickened and intensified the struggle, instead of allaying it. Hence its total failure as a harmonizing measure.

What, then, is the positive result? As to its practical importance in the conflict between free and slave labor, Mr. Douglas himself enlightens us as follows:

Has the South been excluded from all the territory acquired from Mexico? What says the bill from the House of Representatives now on your table, repealing the slave-code in New Mexico established by the people themselves? It is part of the history of the country that under this doctrine of non-intervention, this doctrine that you delight to call squatter sovereignty, the people of New Mexico have introduced and

protected slavery in the whole of that territory.   Under this
doctrine they have converted a tract of free territory into
slave territory, more than five times the size of the State of
New York.   Under this doctrine slavery has been extended
from the Rio Grande to the Gulf of California, and from the
line of the Republic of Mexico, not only up to 36° 30′ but up
to 38°—giving you a degree and a half more territory than
you ever claimed.   In 1848 and 1849 and 1850 you only asked
to have the line of 36° 30′.   The Nashville Convention fixed
that as its ultimatum.   I offered it in the Senate in August,
1848, and it was adopted here but rejected in the House of
Representatives.   You asked only up to 36° 30′, and non-intervention has given you up to 38°—a degree and a half more
than you asked; and yet you say that this is a sacrifice of
Southern rights.

These are the fruits of this principle which the Senator
from Mississippi regards as hostile to the rights of the South.
Where did you ever get any more fruits that were more palatable to your taste or more refreshing to your strength?
What other inch of free territory has been converted into
slave territory on the American continent since the Revolution, except in New Mexico and Arizona under the principle
of non-intervention affirmed at Charleston?   If it is true that
this principle of non-intervention has conferred upon you all
that immense territory; has protected slavery in that comparatively Northern and cold region where you did not expect it to go, cannot you trust the same principle farther
South when you come to acquire additional territory from
Mexico?   If it be true that this principle of non-intervention
has given to slavery all New Mexico, which was surrounded
on nearly every side by free territory, will not the same principle protect you in the northern States of Mexico, when
they are acquired, since they are now surrounded by slave
territory?

Indeed! This, then, is the practical solution of the
difficulty which Mr. Douglas proposes: The "great prin-

ciple of non-intervention" which, according to his own
testimony, strengthens slavery by increasing the number
of slave States and their representation and power in
the general government; to which is to be added the
annexation of Cuba and the northern States of Mexico,
out of which an additional number of slave States is to
be carved.   But his Northern friends say that he is the
champion of free labor—and they are honorable men.

Oh! what a deep-seated, overweening confidence Mr.
Douglas, when he made this statement, must have had
in the unfathomable, desperate, incorrigible stupidity
of those Northern Democrats who support him for the
purpose of baffling and punishing the fire-eaters of the
South.   Good, innocent souls, do they not see that by
supporting Mr. Douglas's policy which throws into the lap
of slavery territory after territory, they will strengthen
and render more overbearing the very same slave power
they mean to baffle and punish?   Do they not see that
they were preparing a lash for their own backs?   It is
true, when they feel it—and they deserve to feel it—they
may console themselves that it is a whip of their own
manufacture.

At last we arrive at the program of the slave power
in its open and undisguised form, of which Mr. Breckenridge is the representative and Mr. Douglas the servant,
although he does not wear its livery except on occasions
of state.

This program is as follows: The agitation of the
slavery question, North and South, is to be arrested; the
fugitive-slave law, in its present form, is to be strictly
carried out, and all State legislation impeding its execution
to be repealed; the constitutional right of slavery to
occupy the territories of the United States and to be protected there is to be acknowledged; all measures tending
to impede the ingress of slavery and its establishment in

the territories, are to be abandoned; the opposition to the conquest and annexation of foreign countries, out of which more slave States can be formed, is to be given up; the economic policy of the planting interest, to the exclusion of the encouragement of home industry, is to become the ruling policy of the country.

This is the Southern solution of the "irrepressible conflict."

This program possesses at least the merit of logic—the logic of slavery and despotism against the logic of free labor and liberty. The issue is plainly made up. Free labor is summoned to submit to the measures which slavery deems necessary for its perpetuation. We are called upon to adapt our laws and systems of policy, and the whole development of our social organization, to the necessities and interests of slavery. We are summoned to surrender. Let us for a moment judge the people of the free States by the meanest criterion we can think of; let us apply a supposition to them, which, if applied to ourselves, we would consider an insult.

If the people of the free States were so devoid of moral sense as not to distinguish between right and wrong; so devoid of generous impulses as not to sympathize with the downtrodden and the degraded, so devoid of manly pride as to be naturally inclined to submit to everybody who is impudent enough to assume the command; tell me, even in this worst, this most disgusting of all contingencies, could free labor quietly submit to the demands of the slave power so long as it has a just appreciation of its own interests? If we cared, neither for other people's rights nor for our own dignity, can we submit as long as we care for our own pockets? Surrender the privilege of discussing our social problems without restraint! Be narrowed down to a given circle of ideas, which we shall not transgress! Do we not owe our growth, prosperity and power to that freedom of inquiry which is the source of all progress and improvement? Surrender the national territories to slavery! Do we not owe our growth and prosperity to the successful labor of our neighbors just as well as our own? Shall we consent to be surrounded and hemmed in with thriftless communities, whose institutions retard their growth and thereby retard our own? Abandon all laws like the homestead bill, tending to establish free labor on our national domain! Shall we thus give up the rights of labor, and destroy the inheritance of our children? Give up our opposition to the extension of slavery by the conquest of foreign countries! Shall we squander the blood of our sons and the marrow of the land in destructive wars, for the profit of the enemies of free labor, while it is a peaceful development to which we owe our power in the world? Adopt the exclusive economic policy of the planting interest! Shall our mineral wealth sleep undeveloped in the soil? Shall our water-powers run idle, and the bustle of our factories cease? Shall the immense laboring force in our increasing population be deprived of the advantage of a harmonious development of all the branches of human labor? Shall we give up our industrial and commercial independence of the world abroad?

And what price do they offer to pay us for all our sacrifices, if we submit? Why, slavery can then be preserved! How can we hesitate? Impossible! It cannot be thought of! Even the most debased and submissive of our doughfaces cannot submit to it as soon as the matter comes to a practical test; and, therefore, the success of the Southern program will never bring about a final decision of the conflict. Suppose we were beaten in the present electoral contest, would that decide the conflict of interests forever? No! Thanks to the nobler impulses of human nature, our consciences would not let us sleep; thanks to the good sense of the people, their progressive interests would not suffer them to give up the struggle. The power of resistance, the elasticity of free society, cannot be exhausted by one, cannot be annihilated by a hundred defeats. Why? Because it receives new impulses, new inspirations from every day's work; it marches on in harmony with the spirit of the age.

There is but one way of settling the "irrepressible conflict." It is not by resisting the spirit of the times, and by trying to neutralize its impelling power, for you attempt that in vain; but it is by neutralizing the obstacles which have thrown themselves in the path. There is no other. The irrepressible conflict will rage with unabated fury until our social and political development is harmonized with the irrepressible tendency of the age.

That is the solution which the Republicans propose. Their program is simple and consistent:—

Protection of our natural and constitutional rights.

Non-interference with the social and political institutions existing by the legislation of States. Exclusion of slavery from the national territories; they must be free because they are national.

Promotion and expansion of free labor by the homestead bill and the encouragement of home industry.

Will this effect a settlement of the conflict? Let the Fathers of this Republic answer the question, and I will give you the Southern construction of their policy. In a debate which occurred in the Senate of the United States, on the 23d of January, Mr. Mason of Virginia, said:

Now, as far as concerns our ancestry, I am satisfied of this— they were not abolitionists. On the contrary, I believe this was their opinion—their prejudice was aimed against the foreign slave-trade, the African slave-trade; and their belief was that, cutting that off, slavery would die out of itself, without any act of abolition. I attempted at one time to show by the recorded opinions of Mr. Madison, that the famous ordinance of 1787, so far as it prohibited slavery in the territory northwest of the Ohio River, was aimed at the African slave-trade, and at that alone; the idea being that if they would restrict the area into which slaves would be introduced from abroad, they would, to that extent, prevent the importation of slaves; and that, when it was altogether prevented, the condition of slavery would die out of itself; but they were not abolitionists, far less within the meaning and spirit of the abolitionists of the present day.

Well, I am willing to accept this as it stands, and Mr. Mason may certainly be considered good Southern authority. I will not stop to investigate the depth and extent of the anti-slavery sentiments of such men as Franklin, who was father of an abolitionist society, and of Washington, who expressed his desire "to see slavery abolished by law"; I am satisfied with Mr. Mason's admission.

This, then, is what the Fathers intended to effect: to bring about a state of things by which slavery would die out of itself. What else do we want? "You mean, then," I am asked, "to adopt a policy which will work the peaceable and gradual extinction of slavery?" And I answer, "Yes; for if we do not, we shall have to submit to a policy which will work the gradual extinction of liberty." There is the dilemma. Our answer is understood. If Washington, Madison and Jefferson were abolitionists, we are; Mr. Mason says they were not; well, then, we are not, for our policy has been theirs, and theirs has become ours.

Will this policy effect a solution of the conflict? It will; because it will harmonize our social and political development with the tendency of our age, by neutralizing the obstacles that stand in its way.

But I am told that these obstacles refuse to be neutralized. They will resist. Resist by what? By dissolving the Union! This specter has so long haunted the imaginations of timid people that it is time at last to anatomize the frightful apparition.

They threaten to dissolve the Union. Why? First, because we do not stop the agitation of the slavery question. It is true, we do discuss every social problem that presents itself to our consideration; we agitate it, and we do not mean to stop. And, therefore, slaveholders, you will dissolve the Union? Do you think we shall make haste to stop the agitation, to muzzle our mouths and our press after you have dissolved it? United as we are with you at present, we certainly are not devoid of fraternal sympathy; but let the acrimonious feelings arising from a divorce embitter our relations, will not the agitation, which annoys you now, be a hundred times more dangerous to you then?

Secondly, you threaten to dissolve the Union because we do not show sufficient alacrity in the catching of fugitive slaves. True, we are not much inclined to perform for the slaveholder a menial, dirty service, which he would hardly stoop to do for himself. And, therefore, you will dissolve the Union! Do you not see that, while now, indeed, a great many slaves escape, the North would, after a dissolution, scorn to surrender a single one? Would not what is now the Canada line be removed right to the banks of the Ohio?

Thirdly, you threaten the dissolution of the Union because we do not mean to surrender the territories to slavery! True, we mean to use every constitutional means within our reach to save them to free labor. And, therefore, you will dissolve the Union! Do you think that after a dissolution we shall courteously invite slavery to make itself comfortable on our national domain? As things are now, "champions of free labor," such as Douglas, may occasionally offer you a chance to acquire for slavery a territory "five times as large as the State of New

York," but will that be possible after the Union is dissolved? Mark well what position the North will take, if, by a revolutionary act against our national government, you should attempt to cut loose from the Union. The territories are the property of the Union as such; those who in a revolutionary way desert the Union, give up their right to the property of the Union. That property, the territories, will remain where the Union remains, and the slave-power would do well first to consider how much blood it can spare, before it attempts to strip the Union of a single square foot of ground. Thus, while according to Judge Douglas, you now have a chance to acquire slave territory by the operation of his "great principle," that chance will be entirely gone as soon as by a secession you give up the least shadow of a right to the property of the Union.

Lastly, you threaten to dissolve the Union, because the North refuses to submit to the exclusive economic policy of the planting interests. You want to establish the commercial and industrial independence of the slaveholding States. For years you have held Southern conventions and passed resolutions to that effect. You resolved not to purchase any longer the products of Northern industrial labor, but to build your own factories; not to carry on your exporting and importing trade any longer by Northern ships, but to establish steamship lines and commercial connections of your own. Well enough. Why did you not do it, after having resolved it? Was it want of money? You have an abundance of it. Was it want of determination? Your resolutions displayed the fiercest zeal. What was it, then? And, indeed, the failure is magnificently complete. Senator Mason's homespun coat, sewn with Yankee thread and needle, adorned with Yankee buttons, hangs in the closet, a lone star in solitary splendor. After trying to establish a large shoe factory for the South,

you came after awhile to the irresistible conclusion that
you must wear Massachusetts shoes and boots or go
barefooted. And even your Norfolk steamships are not
launched yet from the dry-docks of Southern imagination.
How is this? I will tell you. The very same institution
for the protection and perpetuation of which you want
to establish your commercial and industrial independence,
is incompatible with commercial and industrial labor and
enterprise.

For this there are several excellent reasons. First, that
class of your society which rules and wants to perpetuate
its rule, does not consist of workingmen. The inspiration
of regular activity is foreign to their minds. Living upon
the forced labor of others, they find their pride in being
gentlemen of leisure. But it requires men of a superior
organization to make leisure productive; men of the
ordinary stamp, who have too much leisure for doing
something, will in most cases do nothing. But it requires
active labor to make us understand and appreciate labor;
and we must understand and appreciate labor in order to
be able to direct labor. Hence, the slaveholders cannot
take the lead in such a commercial and industrial movement without changing the nature of their condition.
But you may object, that they can at least encourage
commerce and industry, and leave the execution of their
plans and wishes to others. Indeed! But you must not
forget that in modern times the most active and enterprising class of society, as soon as it becomes numerous,
will inevitably become the ruling class. How can, therefore, the slaveholders do as you say, without undermining
the foundation of their own ascendency! But it is just
that ascendency which they mean not to weaken, but to
fortify. Do not bring forward this city of St. Louis as
proof to the contrary. Your commerce and your industry
are, indeed, largely developed, although Missouri is a slave

State; but do you not see that in the same measure as they rise, the ascendency of the slave-power disappears? Thus this has become a free city on slave soil.

But this is not all. Not only are the slaveholders, as a class, unfit to direct the commercial and industrial movement, but their system of labor is unfit to carry it out. Commerce and industry, in order to become independent, need intelligent labor. In the North, every laborer thinks, and is required to think. In the South the laborer is forbidden to think, lest he think too much, for thought engenders aspirations. With us, progress and enterprise derive their main support, their strongest impulses, from the intellectual development of the laboring classes. We do not dread the aspirations arising from it; it is the source of our prosperity, and, at the same time, of our safety. Our laboring man must be a freeman, in order to be what he ought to be—an intelligent laborer. Therefore, we educate him for liberty by our system of public instruction. In the South, the intellectual development of the laboring classes necessary for intelligent labor would create aspirations dangerous to your domestic institutions. Your laboring man must be a brute in order to remain what you want him to be—a slave. Therefore, you withhold from him all means of intellectual development. Among our farms and workshops there stands an institution from which our system of labor derives its inspirations—that is, our schoolhouse, where our free laborers are educated. On your plantation-fields there stands another institution, from which your system of labor derives its inspirations; and that is your schoolhouse, where your slaves are flogged. And you speak of establishing the commercial and industrial independence of the slaveholding States! Do you not see that, in order to do this, you must adapt your system of labor to that purpose by making the laborer intelligent,

respectable, and at the same time aspiring? But if by
making the laborer intelligent, respectable, and aspiring,
you attempt to force industrial enterprise, in a large
measure, upon the slave States, do you not see that your
system of slave labor must yield? To foster commerce
and industry in the slave States, for the purpose of protecting slavery! Would it not be like letting the sunlight
into a room which you want to keep dark? Hence, the
slave States can never become commercially and industrially independent as long as they remain slave States.
They will always be obliged to buy from others, and others
will do their carrying-trade. At present they do their
business with friends, who are united with them by the
bonds of the Union. They speak of dissolving that
Union; then, as now, they will be obliged to transact the
same business with us, their nearest neighbors; for if they
could do otherwise, they would have done so long ago.
Would they prefer by the dissolution of the Union to make
enemies of those on whom they will always be commercially and industrially dependent?

Thus, you see, the dissolution of the Union would in
all points of dispute defeat the very objects for which the
South might feel inclined to attempt it. It would effect
just the contrary of what it was intended for, and, indeed,
if there is a party that can logically and consistently
advocate the dissolution of the Union, it is the party of
extreme abolitionists who desire to extinguish slavery
and to punish the South by a sudden and violent crisis.
But as to the slave States, as long as they have sense enough
to understand their interests and to appreciate their
situation, they may thank their good fortune if they are
suffered to stay in the Union with confederates who
are, indeed, not willing to sacrifice their own principles
and interests to slavery, but by the radiating influence
of their own growth and energy will at least draw the

Southern States also upon the road of progressive development.

But we are told that the people of the slave States are a warlike race, and that they will gain by force what we are unwilling peacefully to concede. War! What a charm there is in that word for a people of colonels and generals! Well, since that old German monk invented that significant black powder, which blew the strongholds of feudalism into the air, war falls more and more under the head of the mathematical sciences. Don Quixote who, undoubtedly, would have been a hero in the ninth century, would certainly be the most egregious fool in the nineteenth. I have nothing to say about the bravery of the Southern people; for aught I care they may be braver than they pretend to be; but I invite them candidly to open their eyes like sensible men.

I will not compare the resources of the South, in men and money, with those of the North, although statistical statements would demonstrate the overwhelming superiority of the latter. We can afford to be liberal and, for argument's sake, admit that the South will equal the North in numbers; and, if they insist upon it, excel us in martial spirit. But it requires very little knowledge of military matters to understand that, aside from numbers, equipment, courage and discipline, the strength of an army consists in its ability to concentrate its forces, at all times, upon the decisive point. Providence is on the side of the big battalions, said Napoleon. That means not that victory will always be with the most numerous army, but with that which is always able to appear in strength where the decisive blow is to be struck. An army that is always scattered over a large surface is, properly speaking, no army at all. Even by a much less numerous but concentrated enemy, it will be beaten in detail, division after division; it is defeated before having lost a man. This is plain.

Keep in mind that the South thinks of going to war for the benefit and protection of slavery. But slavery is not merely an abstract principle; slavery consists materially in the individual slaves—in so-and-so many millions of human chattels scattered over so-and-so many thousands of square miles. In order to protect slavery, it is essential that the individual slaveholders be protected in the possession of their individual slaves.

I say, therefore, that slavery cannot be protected in general without being protected in detail. But how can you protect it in detail? By guarding fifteen hundred miles of Northern frontier and two thousand miles of seacoast against an enemy who is perfectly free in his movements, and, aided by an extensive railroad system, always able to concentrate his forces wherever he pleases? It is impossible; the dullest understanding sees it. It may be said that it will not be necessary; indeed, for the free States it would not; they may, in order to concentrate their forces, expose their territory, for the damage done by an invasion is easily repaired. The retreating invader cannot carry the liberties of the invaded country away with him. Not so with slavery. A Northern anti-slavery army or even a small flying corps invading a slaveholding State would, perhaps not at once systematically liberate the slaves, but at all events it would not squander much time and health in catching the runaways. The probability, therefore, is that wherever a Northern army appears, the slaves will disappear, and so much of slavery with them—at least for the time being. Invade a free State, and the restoration of liberty, after the attack is repulsed, requires only the presence of freemen. But the restoration of slavery will require capital; that capital consisted principally in the slaves;

the slaves have run away, and with them the capital necessary for the restoration of slavery.

The slave States, therefore, cannot expose their territory without leaving unprotected the institution for the protection of which the war was undertaken. They have to cover thousands and thousands of vulnerable points, for every plantation is an open wound, every negro cabin a sore. Every border or seaboard slave State will need her own soldiers, and more too, for the protection of her own slaves; and where then would be the material for the concentrated army?

Besides, the slave States harbor a dangerous enemy within their own boundaries, and that is slavery itself. Imagine them at war with anti-slavery people whom they have exasperated by their own hostility. What will be the effect upon the slaves? The question is not whether the North will instigate a slave rebellion, for I suppose they will not; the question is, whether they can prevent it, and I think they cannot. But the anticipation of a negro insurrection (and the heated imagination of the slaveholder will discover symptoms of a rebellious spirit in every trifle) may again paralyze the whole South. Do you remember the effect of John Brown's attempt? The severest blow he struck at the slave-power was not that he disturbed a town and killed several citizens, but that he revealed the weakness of the whole South. Let Governor Wise of Virginia carry out his threatened invasion of the free States, not with twenty-three, but with twenty-three hundred followers at his heels—what will be the result? As long as they behave themselves we shall let them alone; but as soon as they create any disturbance they will be put into the station-house; and the next day we shall read in the newspapers of some Northern city, among the reports of the police-court: "Henry A. Wise and others, for dis-

orderly conduct, fined $5." Or, if he has made an attempt
on any man's life, or against our institutions, he will most
certainly find a Northern jury proud enough to acquit
him on the ground of incorrigible mental derangement.
Our pictorial prints will have material for caricatures
for two issues, and a burst of laughter will ring to the
skies from Maine to California. And there is the end
of it. But behold John Brown with twenty-three men
raising a row at Harper's Ferry; the whole South frantic
with terror; the whole State of Virginia in arms; troops
marching and countermarching, as if the battle of Auster-
litz were to be fought over again; innocent cows shot as
bloodthirsty invaders, and even the evening song of the
peaceful whippoorwills mistaken for the battle cry of rebellion. And those are the men who will expose themselves
to the chances of a pro-slavery war with an anti-slavery
people! Will they not look upon every captain as a John
Brown, and every sergeant and private as a Coppoc or a
Stevens? They will hardly have men enough to quiet
their fears at home. What will they have to oppose to
the enemy? If they want to protect slavery then, every
township will want its home regiment, every plantation
its garrison. No sooner will a movement of concentration
be attempted, than the merest panic may undo and frus-
trate it. Themistocles might say that Greece was on his
ships; a French general might say that the Republic was
in his camps; but slavery will be neither on the ships nor
in the camp; it will be spread defenseless over thousands
of square miles. This will be their situation: either they
concentrate their forces, and slavery will be exposed
wherever the army is not; or they do not concentrate
them, and their army will be everywhere, but in fact
nowhere. They want war? Let them try it! They will
try it but once. And thus it turns out that the very
same thing that would be the cause of the war, would at

the same time be indefensible by war. The same institution that wants protection will at the same time disable its protectors. Yes, slavery, which can no longer be defended with arguments, cannot be defended with arms.

There is your dissolution of the Union for the perpetuation of slavery. The Southern States cannot reasonably desire it, for it would defeat the very objects for which it would be undertaken; they cannot reasonably attempt it, for slavery would lie helpless at the feet of the North. Slavery, which may die a slow, gradual death in the Union, will certainly die an instantaneous and violent death if they attempt to break out of the Union. What then will the South do in case of a Republican victory? I answer that question with another one, What *can* the South do in case of a Republican victory? Will there be a disturbance? If they know their own interests, the people of the South themselves will have to put it down. Will they submit? Not to Northern dictation, but to their own good sense. They have considered us their enemies as long as they ruled us; they will find out that we are their friends as soon as we cease to be their subjects. They have dreamed so long of the blessings of slavery; they will open their eyes again to the blessings of liberty. They will discover that they are not conquered, but liberated. Will slavery die out? As surely as freedom will *not* die out.

Slaveholders of America, I appeal to you. Are you really in earnest when you speak of perpetuating slavery? Shall it never cease? Never? Stop and consider where you are and in what day you live.

This is the nineteenth century. Never since mankind has a recollection of times gone by, has the human mind disclosed such wonderful powers. The hidden forces of nature we have torn from their mysterious concealment and yoked them into the harness of usefulness; they carry our thoughts over slender wires to distant nations; they draw our wagons over the highways of trade; they pull the gigantic oars of our ships; they set in motion the iron fingers of our machinery; they will soon plow our fields and gather our crops. The labor of the brain has exalted to a mere bridling and controlling of natural forces the labor of the hand; and you think you can perpetuate a system which reduces man, however degraded, yet capable of development, to the level of a soulless machine?

This is the world of the nineteenth century. The last remnants of feudalism in the old world are fast disappearing. The Czar of Russia, in the fulness of imperial power, is forced to yield to the irresistible march of human progress, and abolishes serfdom. Even the Sultan of Turkey can no longer maintain the barbarous customs of the Moslem against the pressure of the century, and slavery disappears. And you, citizens of a Republic, you think you can arrest the wheel of progress with your Dred Scott decisions and Democratic platforms?

Look around you and see how lonesome you are in this wide world of ours. As far as modern civilization throws its rays, what people, what class of society is there like you? Cry out into the world your "wild and guilty fantasy" of property in man, and every echo responds with a cry of horror or contempt; every breeze, from whatever point of the compass it may come, brings you a verdict of condemnation. There is no human heart that sympathizes with your cause, unless it sympathizes with the cause of despotism in every form. There is no human voice to cheer you on in your struggle; there is no human eye that has a tear for your reverses; no link of sympathy between the common cause of the great human brotherhood and you. You hear of emancipation in Russia and wish it to fail. You hear of Italy rising, and fear the spirit of liberty may become contagious. Where all mankind rejoices, you tremble. Where all mankind loves, you hate. Where all mankind curses, you sympathize.

And in this appalling solitude you stand alone against a hopeful world, alone against a great century, fighting your hopeless fight—hopeless, hopeless as the struggle of the Indians against the onward march of civilization. Exhaust all the devices which the inventive genius of despotism may suggest, and yet how can you resist? In every little village schoolhouse, the little children who learn to read and write are plotting against you; in every laboratory of science, in every machine shop, the human mind is working the destruction of your idol. You cannot make an attempt to keep pace with the general progress of mankind, without plotting against yourselves. Every steam whistle, every puffing locomotive, is sounding the shriek of liberty into your ears. From the noblest instincts of our hearts down to sordid greediness of gain, every impulse of human nature is engaged in this universal conspiracy. How can you resist? Where are your friends in the North? Your ever-ready supporters are scattered to the winds as by enchantment, never to unite again. Hear them trying to save their own fortunes, swear with treacherous eagerness that they have nothing in common with you. And your opponents? Your boasts have lost their charm, your threats have lost their terrors, upon them. The attempt is idle to cloak the sores of Lazarus with the lion skin of Hercules. We know you. Every one of your boasts is understood as a disguised moan of weakness—every shout of defiance as a disguised cry for mercy. We will no longer be imposed upon. Do not deceive yourselves. This means not only the destruction of a party—this means the defeat of a cause. Be shrewder than the shrewdest, braver than the bravest—it is all in vain; your cause is doomed.

And in the face of all this you insist upon hugging,

with dogged stubbornness, your fatal infatuation? Why not manfully swing round into the grand march of progressive humanity? You say it cannot be done to-day. Can it be done to-morrow? Will it be easier twenty, fifty years hence, when the fearful increase of the negro population will have aggravated the evils of slavery a hundredfold, and with it the difficulties of its extinction? Did you ever think of this? The final crisis, unless prevented by timely reform, will come with the inexorable certainty of fate, the more terrible the longer it is delayed. Will you content yourself with the criminal words, "after me the deluge"? Is that the inheritance you mean to leave to coming generations—an inheritance of disgrace, crime, blood, destruction? Hear me, slaveholders of America! If you have no sense for the right of the black, no appreciation of your own interests, I entreat, I implore you, have at least pity on your children!

I hear the silly objection that your sense of honor forbids you to desert your cause. Sense of honor! Imagine a future generation standing around the tombstone of the bravest of you, and reading the inscription: "Here lies a gallant man who fought and died for the cause—of human slavery." What will the verdict be? His very progeny will disown him, and exclaim, "He must have been either a knave or a fool!" There is not one of you who, if he could rise from the dead a century hence, would not gladly exchange his epitaph for that of the meanest of those who were hung at Charlestown.

Is it, then, so dishonorable to give up the errors of yesterday for the truths of to-day?—to prevent future disasters by timely reforms? Since when has it ceased to be the highest glory to sacrifice one's prejudices and momentary advantages upon the altar of the common weal? But those who seek their glory in stubbornly resisting what is glorious, must find their end in inglorious misery.

I turn to you, Republicans of Missouri. Your countrymen owe you a debt of admiration and gratitude to which my poor voice can give but a feeble expression. You have undertaken the noble task of showing the people of the North that the slaveholding States themselves contain the elements of regeneration; and of demonstrating to the South how that regeneration can be effected. You have inspired the wavering masses with confidence in the practicability of our ideas. To the North you have given encouragment; to the South you have set an example. Let me entreat you not to underrate your noble vocation. Struggle on, brave men! The anxious wishes of millions are hovering around you. Struggle on, until the banner of emancipation is planted upon the capitol of your State, and one of the proudest chapters of our history will read: "Missouri led the van and the nation followed!"

TO MRS. SCHURZ

PHILADELPHIA, Sept. 24, 1860.[1]

On the 28th and 29th I have appointments in Indiana. We have now reached the crisis of the campaign. I have had a succession of triumphs and my exertions have been almost superhuman. Only a few days more of work—a short effort in Pennsylvania and Indiana—and the battle will be decided according to the outcome of the State elections in these States on October 9th. It would be wicked of me to save my strength so near the goal. I am standing in the thickest of the fight. Every day I feel that I speak better and my powers grow with the heat of the struggle. The old "Pennsylvania Dutch" follow me like little children, although they can only half understand me. The Democrats are furious, and wherever I

[1] Translated from the German.

have spoken they telegraph like mad in all directions for German speakers to neutralize the effect of my speeches. But it is quite in vain. The Democratic newspapers attack and abuse me wildly, with the result that even German Democrats become angry and everybody's curiosity is aroused. Consequently all my meetings are crowded and I drive everything before me. The newspapers are discussing me almost as much as if I were a Presidential candidate. My printed speeches are flooding the country in hundreds of thousands and are more and more in demand.[1]

I am feeling better than ever in this turmoil. It seems as if victory could not fail us—and, by Jove! I have done my share towards it.

You were anxious about my success in New York. You might have known that the inspiring enthusiasm of the moment would sustain me.

On October 18th I shall speak to the Germans. I shall work out a speech for that occasion in which I shall do my best and shall try to excel everything I have done before.[2]

---

[1] A letter of February 23, 1860, to Mrs. Schurz contained these sentences: "Naturally countless copies of my Douglas speech have been distributed all about, and it has had excellent effect. I hear that it is being published in pamphlet form in a number of places. Lincoln writes that he is envious. In Madison, the greenhorns in the legislature stared at me in open-eyed wonder."

[2] Although these opinions of a still youthful orator were expressed only to his enthusiastic and sympathetic wife, they were far from being exaggerations. The following quotations from letters from campaign managers in five different States, speak for themselves:

Horace Rublee, Madison, Wis., Oct. 12, 1859: "Can the State central committee now announce some appointments for you in this State? No other man can do as much for the Republican cause at certain points as you."

J. W. Tillman, Detroit, Aug. 27, 1860: "Our German friends in different localities are very desirous of seeing and hearing you. Can you give us from five to ten days for which we would gladly give you *twenty-five dollars per day*. Your expenses would be little or nothing."

T. H. Ford, Mansfield, Ohio, Sept. 12, 1860: "A very general and

FORT WAYNE, Sept. 28, 1860.

I have generally been obliged to travel at night and to steal the necessary sleep in the daytime, and I have always been so surrounded that I could scarcely catch my breath. On Wednesday I was at Harrisburg, where I met the three Blairs and Preston King at Senator Cameron's. Preston King is at the head of our document committee and tells me that my New York speech[1] is a tremendous success and is more in demand than any other document.

On Thursday we had a great demonstration in Pittsburg, the largest and most brilliant I have seen. There must have been between seventy thousand and one hundred thousand persons present. In the evening I spoke in a crowded hall. Last night I left there and arrived here at 3 o'clock this afternoon. . . .

Unfortunately what I feared has really happened. I

---

earnest desire [exists] among our people to see and hear you and we comply with that wish as well as the instructions of our central county committee by earnestly requesting you to be present with us as one of the speakers of the occasion. The Germans (who are numerous in our small city) need the truth through the medium of their native language. We know of no one in the nation, whom they as well as ourselves would be more delighted to welcome among us than yourself."

Richard F. Gaggin, Erie, Pa., Sept. 13, 1860: "Besides this, we are well satisfied that above all other men in the party, you could influence a large vote in favor of our cause which is at present wavering between Douglas and Lincoln. We are making accessions almost every day from the other side and our German friends tell us that some of their acquaintances are yet undecided but say to them—'Wait until we hear Carl Schurz.' P.S. I have just heard that Douglas has agreed to be here on the 24th. Now, do give us an antidote to such a dose as that."

A. H. Conner, Indianapolis, Sept. 18, 1860: "We are doing considerable work amongst our German friends, but find no one capable of wielding so great an influence as yourself, and hope you will come to Indiana as soon as possible. I cannot write you the particulars of the canvass further than to say, Come and help us by all means; one week's work from you is worth more than all the German help we have in the State."

[1] "The Bill of Indictment," delivered at Cooper Union, N. Y. City, Sept. 13, 1860, Speeches, 162–221.

shall not be able to go home on Sunday. A delegation
came to me in Pittsburg to assure me that my appearance
in Erie might make a difference of five hundred votes,
which might decide the result of the October election.
Should that be true, and I should not go, and the October
election should be lost by a small majority—how I should
reproach myself! So I have decided to go.

TO HORACE RUBLEE

BUFFALO, Oct. 14, 1860.

I received your letter only a few minutes before I left
Milwaukee, and my appointments were then already made.
I should like to go to Green Bay, but I calculated that in
filling an appointment there I would lose two valuable days,
which I might make very good use of. The appointments
I fixed upon are the following:

Oct. 24   Oak Creek, afternoon.
    Milwaukee, evening.
" 25   Oshkosh.
" 26   Mayville, Dodge county, afternoon or evening.
" 27   West Bend, Washington county, afternoon, so
    that I can get to Milwaukee before Sunday.
" 29   Manitowoc, provided there is a boat leaving
    Milwaukee on Sunday evening.
" 30   Sheboygan.
" 31   Newburg, Ozaukee county.
Nov. 1   Wauwatosa, afternoon.
    Watertown, evening.

The remaining three days I shall speak in Milwaukee
county in the afternoon and at different places in the
city in the evening. I find that Potter's district is by no
means as safe as is generally supposed, and it will require
considerable labor to give him as large a majority as he
ought to have. Besides, we will do our best to carry

Milwaukee county, where the battlefield of the first district will be.   The appointments are as many as I can fill and will exhaust my vocal powers to the last gasp.   But no matter.

As to expenses, etc., I think it will be by no means extravagant if I ask $15 a day while I am in the field, Oct. 24th inclusive to Nov. 6th.   I wish I could offer my services gratis and foot the bills in addition, but unfortunately "les jours des fêtes sont passés"—I am not so situated as to be able to do so.

I am sorry I am obliged to disappoint James Howe. There is no man in Wisconsin whom I would rather endeavor to please, but time is so scarce and the necessities of the campaign so urgent that it could not be done.

TO MRS. SCHURZ

MILWAUKEE, Nov. 14, 1860.[1]

You have no idea how I am swamped with letters from office-seekers asking me to appeal to Lincoln in their behalf.   I intend to have printed a circular answer to send to the unfortunates.   The secession movements in the South are still continuing and it is not improbable that we shall have stormy times.   The probability is, however, that the inevitable reaction, which even the South will feel before the inauguration of Lincoln, will check the disturbance.   These are very momentous times. Every day may bring new decisions—but I long for rest. Rest and family! is inscribed on my banner.

I must make a speech to-morrow, but have not yet completed it.   I still lack the stirring peroration, and though I am perfectly well, my mind is tired.

[1] Translated from the German.

TO J. F. POTTER

PHILADELPHIA, Nov. 30, 1860.

I expected to see you at Milwaukee before your departure for Washington, but was disappointed. Well, the crisis is upon us, and it depends upon the attitude of the Republicans to make its result final and decisive. If the North now remains firm, the slave-power is done for. We have to choose between a short and violent crisis and a long, exhausting and dangerous one. Common prudence seems to dictate that we should meet the issue boldly, take the bull by the horns, meet treason when and where it is committed, and put it down by all the means which manifest destiny has put into our hands. My dear Potter, if slavery in its present form and strength exists in this Republic ten years hence, the Republican party will be responsible for it. We have got them at last; do not let them escape once more. If no compromise had been made in 1833, we should never again have heard of the disunion cry. Let not that mistake be repeated. The future of the country, the repose of the nation, depends on our firmness.

Now a few words about a matter of personal interest. You remember that on that memorable night when we went to the town of Oak Creek in the dark, you requested me to make you the depositary of my wishes as to the position I would desire to occupy under the Republican Administration. I will now do so without reserve. It is generally supposed, and perhaps not without some reason, that Mr. Lincoln will offer me some appointment or other, and when I passed through Chicago a few days ago, several gentlemen, who acted as though they were in the confidence of Mr. Lincoln, requested me to let them know as soon as possible, what position would most gratify me. I did not feel like doing so on the spot, because I wanted to consult you about the matter. I shall, of course, not ask or petition for anything, and do not wish that the Administration should offer me anything unless they feel like it. But if they do feel like it, it would be an unpleasant thing if they offered me anything which I should not feel warranted in accepting. First, I should like to be in a place where I can do something; I do not want a sinecure. Secondly, as I am generally looked upon as the representative of the German element, I consider it due to those I do represent that I should not take an inferior place. I am told that the matter has been extensively talked about among leading politicians, and the prevailing opinion was that I should be sent abroad. If so, I should want a place where I can turn my knowledge of men and things to account. To be sent to Germany would in many respects gratify my feelings most, but it might bring up questions of etiquette unpleasant to the Administration, and if there is anything I would religiously endeavor to avoid, it is to embarrass the government by anything arising from my peculiar position. Prussia and Austria are, therefore, out of the question.

Europe is now in a dissolving state, politically, and now, as old governments are decaying and new ones springing up, now is the time for this Government to take advantage of this general confusion. Therefore we want men of general knowledge of persons and things and of energy and activity. There are two fields of action in which most can be accomplished. The one is France. The mission to Paris is of so prominent a nature that the custom to send an old, deserving man there seems to be a very just and proper one. I have, therefore, not the impudence to claim anything like that. My aspirations do not run away with my sense of propriety. The other field of action is Italy, and I think there is the place for me, provided it be raised to a first-class mission, which will undoubtedly be the case. I feel that my turn of mind, my education and my knowledge of things fit me for the place, and that circumstances fit the place for me. This is not only my own opinion, but I know it is shared by many of our leading men. I should, therefore, be very much gratified if the Administration, supposing they intend to offer me anything, would offer me the mission to Turin.

I understand (Colfax, whom I met here told me so) Burlingame is an aspirant for the same position. I should be sorry to rival him, but, to tell the truth, I really do think, without overestimating my powers, I am better fitted for it than he is. But if he gets it and I remain at home, I shall not shed any tears. Now, friend Potter, I wish you to understand that I have communicated this to you at your own request. I do not intend to make any application myself, nor do I desire to have anybody act as my agent in the matter. I will not embarrass Mr. Lincoln by any demands, nor by declining any offer, unacceptable to myself, which he perhaps might feel inclined to make. But if the matter should become a subject of conversation at Washington among such men as are likely to be in Mr. Lincoln's confidence, you will then be able to speak knowingly about my feelings about it. You may, if you see fit, communicate this confidentially to Doolittle. Trumbull knows probably more about Mr. Lincoln's intentions than any other man in Washington, and you or Doolittle may easily ascertain from him what Mr. Lincoln means to do.

I repeat that I shall be perfectly satisfied if the Administration offers me nothing, but if they do want to send me abroad, I wish they would give me timely notice of it, so that I may make the necessary preparations in the way of collecting information, etc. If I do go, I wish to go as the best-informed man who ever represented this

Government abroad. Colfax talked to me about this matter and he, spontaneously, struck the same track.

Give Doolittle my regards and tell him that I agree exactly with the views he expressed in his letter to the Milwaukee celebration meeting. I should like to spend a few days at Washington this winter, but I shall hardly be able to do so. My time is all taken up by a variety of engagements. . . .

TO MRS. SCHURZ

BOSTON, Dec. 17, 1860.[1]

Yesterday I wrote a letter to Lincoln explaining my views about present political conditions and intimating that I should never submit to a compromise, and should leave the party the moment it abandoned its principles. I must confess that I have complete confidence in Lincoln's honesty as well as in his courage; but it might be possible for the present Congress to tie his hands with resolutions of a compromise. I wish I were a member of the Senate, if for only three days; I would sing them a new song. It seems probable that the general confusion in Washington will prevent the passing of compromise resolutions; but perhaps the party standards will be lowered, and Lincoln may be compelled to submit.

I have been reflecting on the question for two days, and I shall not yield. I am still hoping for the best. I am in very active correspondence with Washington and am prodding our men to the best of my ability.

TO J. F. POTTER

BOSTON, Dec. 17, 1860.

I have just read the papers of to-day and must write you

[1] Translated from the German.

a line before I start for my lecture appointment.   I see
by the telegraphic news that Mr. Corwin has submitted
resolutions yielding the liberty of the territories, yielding
our principles in regard to the fugitive-slave law and to
the admission of slave States, yielding everything we have
been contending for.   It is incredible, and yet it is not
impossible.   But is it true that a majority of the Republicans in that committee, as is stated, can assent to such
propositions?   Is it possible that they can trample
under foot everything that is dear to their constituents?
I cannot, cannot believe it.   One thing is sure.   As soon
as these resolutions, or anything like them, are adopted,
the Republican party has ceased to exist.   I have been
travelling all over Pennsylvania, New York, and New
England lately, and outside of the large commercial cities
I have not found one single Republican who did not scorn
the idea of receding from a single principle laid down in
the Chicago platform.

The public sentiment, even among so-called conservative men, is rapidly settling in favor of a prompt and
vigorous execution of the laws as against the seceders,
and every man in Congress who bends his knee now is
sealing his political death-warrant.

I cannot help flattering myself with the idea that even
Mr. Corwin cannot be in earnest with these resolutions,
that they are introduced merely for the purpose of gaining
time.   But even in that case, their very introduction is an
act of degradation, a slur upon the moral sense of the people.

The policy of the true and firm Republicans, in my
opinion, is this: Let our men in the committee offer
amendment upon amendment; let them discuss every
proposition at length, make speech upon speech, motion
upon motion, so as to prevent the committee from making
an early report.   Then let them get up as many minority
reports as possible, and as soon as they are submitted to

the House, discuss them at length, every one of them, amend them again, and in this way drag along the discussion so as to prevent the House from coming to a final vote before the 4th of March. Everything is gained if Congress does not close and compromise Mr. Lincoln's Administration beforehand. Everything is lost if the moral power of the Republican party is frittered away before Lincoln goes into office.

Press this policy upon the attention of our friends and let the voice of the people be heard in the halls of Congress. I have thought of writing a speech on the crisis if I could get somebody to deliver it in Congress. But I think that is impossible.

I thank you for the information you have given me in regard to the Sardinian mission. But I confess I am so completely preoccupied with the dangers threatening our cause that I cannot think of anything that regards myself. I would willingly sacrifice reputation, prospects and everything if I could but for a few weeks infuse my spirit into the Republican members of Congress. I should have profoundly deplored a defeat at the Presidential election, but I would rather have been beaten then than see the party commit suicide now.

My dear friend, now is the time for the true friends of freedom to act with circumspection, promptness and energy; the prospects of the anti-slavery cause for the next twenty years are at stake.

Please do me the favor to give me your views about the present state of things as soon as possible. I am morbidly anxious to learn what is going on behind the curtain. . . .

TO J. P. SANDERSON

BOSTON, Dec. 22, 1860.

Your favor of Dec. 22d is in my hands. I should go down

to New York at once to call upon Mr. Hutchins if my lecturing appointments in this neighborhood did not make it impossible for me to do so. I shall, however, address him a note and try to go to New York City on Jan. 5th. Meanwhile I return you my sincerest thanks for the pains you have taken on my behalf.

I do not see, why I should not "find it consistent with my views of propriety" to give you the facts in regard to McClure's statements. When the campaign commenced, it was generally supposed that my services were needed, and I considered it my duty to devote all my time to the work before us. I did so from the very day the National Convention adjourned down to the day of the election. My correspondence and my active participation in the contest swallowed up every minute of my time, and I had to let my private affairs, disordered as they were, take care of themselves. The demands made upon me were enormous and I did my best to satisfy them. The chairman of the National Committee wrote me that I should consider myself in the service of the Committee. I wrote Governor Morgan a letter stating that it would be hard for me to devote all my time to the canvass without some remuneration, being in straitened circumstances, partly in consequence of sacrifices made for the party; and some time afterwards I addressed a note to Mr. Goodrich, the financial manager of the National Committee, making the same statement, but adding that, if nothing were done, I should try to do my work anyhow the best way I could. Situated as I was, embarrassed, with a family to support, obliged to neglect my business and private affairs, I think I had a right to demand something, and it was my duty to do so. Well, I went through the campaign, travelled over 21,000 miles from the adjournment of the National Convention to the sixth of November, delivered I do not know how many speeches, and now I will tell you what I received: From the National Committee, $500; from Indiana, $500; from Pennsylvania, not $800 but $600; and, aside from that, here and there small amounts for extra expenses incurred, the whole amounting to a little over $1800. My railroad fare alone throughout the campaign amounted to about $800. Counting the incidental wear and tear and occasional expenses as hotel-bills, etc., the money I received was just sufficient to keep myself at work and my family alive during the five months that I was active. Certain it is, that I could not pay off a single dollar I owed and had to depend upon the longanimity of my creditors as far as my private obligations are concerned. From what I learned during the campaign, there was hardly a speaker at work outside of his own State who did not receive more pay, on the whole, than I did. The consequence is that, instead of being able to rest as I ought to have done after the campaign, I have to start out again, in order to make, outside of my business, some money.

TO J. F. POTTER

BOSTON, MASS., Dec. 24, 1860.

I thank you for your letter of the 20th inst. The description you give of the condition of things is rather gloomy, but if I may judge from the telegraphic reports in to-day's papers, the force of circumstances will whip our weak brethren into line. The Crittenden resolutions voted down in the Senate committee, Lincoln standing on the Chicago platform as firm as an oak, the fire-eaters fluttering, the effect of Ben. Wade's speech upon friends and opponents,—all these are things which cannot fail to encourage even the most timid. We are looking with the intensest anxiety for the report of the Committee of

Thirty-three. As soon as that is made, then we shall have arrived at the decisive crisis, which will put the mettle and generalship of the Republicans in Congress to the test.

Now, I think, has the time come when they can abandon their awkward, miserable, demoralizing, defensive position. If the reports, for I think there will be more than one, are such as to remove all danger of the passage of a compromise, then let it be acted upon with promptness. But if there is any such danger, it will be necessary to shift the discussion upon a new field, so as to push the matter into the background.

For this there are two splendid opportunities. It is more than probable that Buchanan has been and is now playing into the hands of the seceders. If any facts can be ascertained which will give a substantial foundation to this suspicion, he is undoubtedly liable to impeachment. From what the newspapers tell us I have no doubt you can make a strong case of it. There is the point from which the Republicans can start a new aggressive movement. Whether the impeachment can be carried on or not, I care little; a vigorous and prompt movement in that direction will monopolize the attention of Congress and of the people. It will place our opponents on the defensive and the Republicans into a new commanding position, with the advantage all on their side. It will operate irresistibly upon the imaginations of the people, and cannot fail to drown the cry for a compromise. But let the movement be pressed with the utmost energy and determination. I know it requires boldness and backbone, but I should wonder, indeed, if times like these did not call into action latent powers and unconscious forces.

Another matter I want to call your attention to is this: The opinion is gaining ground, and I must confess I share it, that the revolutionists will attempt to take possession

of Washington City and to prevent Mr. Lincoln's inauguration.   I am led to believe by many things that there is
such a plan entertained by the most desperate of Southern
fire-eaters.   The more the chances of the original secession
movement decrease, the more will a plan like that come
into prominence as their last resort.   But, however vague
and indefinite the rumors in circulation may be, the matter
ought to be brought up before Congress, be it in the shape
of a resolution calling upon the Administration to provide
for such an emergency, or whatever other form.   Whether
such a resolution can be carried, or, if carried, will have
any effect upon the Executive, is a matter of indifference.
The introduction of this subject and the discussion it will
necessarily draw out, will at all events serve two great
objects: First, it will divert the attention of Congress
from the plans of compromise and concentrate it upon
subjects of practical importance.   Two subjects like
this and the impeachment, if well managed, will inevitably
kill all concession schemes, however plausible.   But the
most important effect the discussion of this last point will
have, is to draw the attention of the people of the North
upon a danger which, at present, seems to be too little
thought of.

A few days ago I addressed a letter to Governor Morgan
as chairman of the National Committee, requesting him
to send a circular to the different State committees and
to invite them to make preparations for an escort of honor
to the President on the 4th of March.   As soon as the
matter is broached in Congress, we may go one step further.   The governors of the States may then proceed to
arm and organize their militia for the emergency, and
demand appropriations from their legislatures for that
purpose.   It may be said that the danger exists only in
our imagination.   I tell you, it does not; I am almost
certain the attempt will be made if we are not prepared

to meet it.   It will probably not be made if we are on the
spot with a force sufficient to make its success impossible.
But I deem it absolutely necessary that the emergency
should be provided for.   I have a plan in my head, on
which these preparations can be made; and as soon as
the thing is brought into prominence by a movement in
Congress I mean to write to the different Republican
governors about it.

These are the two points I wish to bring to your notice.
I deem it of the highest importance that the Republicans
should drop their defensive attitude and resume the
aggressive with resolution and vigor.   Action, action is
the great secret of success, and if ever a time called for it,
it is now.   I do not understand the men who, when the
decision of one of the vital questions of the age is within
their grasp, stand there chicken-hearted and cast about
for small contemptible expedients.   What right had they
to demand the votes of the people, if, at the aspect of the
first difficulty they find in their path, they are ready to
throw away the victory gained by those votes?   Let
them know that the people want to have an end of it,
and an end of them too, if they should wantonly fritter
away what is the fruit of an arduous and earnest struggle
of many years.   Let them know that the stock exchange
does not rule the popular heart, and shall not rule those
who are commissioned to represent the feelings of the
popular heart.

The change of public opinion in favor of vigorous and
decisive action is most encouraging.   Even timid men
want no longer to hear of a timid policy, and our Republican compromisers, if they should succeed in bartering
away our principles and our honor, will have to face a
storm of popular indignation, which in the delusions of
their puny statesmanship they do not dream of.

I am distressed to find myself tied down to this tame

lecturing business, to be obliged to devote my time and energies to the poorest of all occupations—making money —while the time ripens for great decisions. I feel as though I could do something in Washington—but then I cannot help it. I have to pay my tribute to the necessities of life.

I shall write that speech on the crisis as soon as the report of the Thirty-three is out and distinct propositions are before the people. And then I shall let you know of it.

One word about personal matters. I received a letter from Doolittle (who, by the way, deserves the thanks of every true Republican for the firm stand he took in the Senate committee), asking me whether I wanted the Sardinian mission; in my reply I repeated in substance what I had written you about it. The matter seems to have been talked of in Senatorial circles. I am informed that George P. Marsh of Vermont and Jay Morris are pushing for the same position. Now let me say, however much an offer of that kind on the part of the Administration would gratify me, I do not want to engage in a scramble of aspirants. If the Government means to tender me anything, let it be a spontaneous offer. To ask for an office is, in my opinion, to pay too high a price for it. I shall not do that myself, nor do I wish to have others do it for me. I will tell you why I am somewhat scrupulous on that point. If I ask for a place, I lose part of my independence; if I merely accept what is spontaneously offered, I am bound by no obligation; and I must confess my independence in political life is worth more to me than all the favors which a government can shower upon a man.

Let me hear from you again and keep me well posted. Every letter from Washington will be considered a great favor.

TO MRS. SCHURZ

BOSTON, Dec. 24, 1860.[1]

Yesterday and to-day I rested, to-morrow work begins again. I can tell you with great joy, that the danger of a Republican surrender to Southern demands has decreased more than ever. Lincoln himself stands firm as an oak, and his determination has communicated itself to the timid members of the party. The letters which I receive from Washington (and my correspondence with my friends who are there is most lively) have been full of encouraging news during the last few days. The bravery of our people seems to grow in the same measure in which the embarrassment of our adversaries increases. I have used all the time I could spare to feed the fire vigorously, and nearly every day I send my views and suggestions regarding the steps to be taken.

It seems probable that the matter will go well in Congress. But one thing has become almost certain. There will be a fight between the North and the South. How long it will continue will depend upon the determination with which it is carried on, that is to say, the greater the vigor of the North in handling the matter, the shorter will be the crisis. Then men of firmness and resources will come to the front, and it would not be strange if I were then called into service.

I shall probably not enter the ranks again, but it is quite possible that I shall be active in the preparations for this struggle, in the organization etc. As soon as the matter has reached the crucial point, I shall send to the different Republican governors a plan of organization which I recently worked out.

We live in a great age and we should not be less great than the demands which this age makes upon us. Unless

---

[1] Translated from the German.

12

all signs deceive me, the end of the political slave-power
is close at hand.   The Republican party has only to
understand its strength, in order to accomplish at a
blow one of the greatest reforms of our day.   Why cannot
I be in Congress now?   I could say things there that
would make our timid brothers' heads swim.   However,
I am not as far removed from Congress as people think.
I am at this moment busy with a speech which is to be
delivered in Congress by one of the Representatives.   Is
that not amusing?   Even though I cannot be there myself
my speeches are making themselves heard there.   I have
already discovered traces of the effects of the letters which
I have sent to Washington.

Dec. 27, 1860.

The secessionists are attempting to draw Virginia and
Maryland into the movement.   If they succeed, their next
step will be to take possession of the city of Washington,
which lies wedged in between Virginia and Maryland.
As this will be done while Buchanan is still in office, or on
the fourth of March, if the step is taken at all, military
measures will have to be resorted to, not only that the
policy of the next Administration may be carried out,
but also, meantime, in order to make sure of Lincoln's
coming into office at all.   In my opinion, the whole
disturbance can be prevented if the Northern States will
arm themselves as soon as possible and show their readi-
ness to fight for the preservation of the Union.

Such preparations and a demonstration of such a determination seem to me to be the only way in which the
Southern desperadoes can be frightened out of their scheme.
They assume that the Northerners will not fight.   In this
they are mistaken.   The fighting spirit of the people is
growing with the increasing boldness of our Representatives at Washington.   In whatever way the struggle may

break out, I am certain that it will be short. I shall write to Lincoln to-day to submit to him the outlines of a plan for the arming of the free States.

You see what matters I am brooding over most. I confess that often, while I am delivering a lecture, my thoughts wander to questions quite foreign to the subject of my discourse. That makes the "lecture business" repulsive to me. But what is the use? I must earn money and there is no way but to grind away at work. I want nothing more than to be in Washington, if only for a few days, but that's impossible.

The owners of the *Atlantic Monthly* sent for me the other day. I went to see them and they requested me to write for their magazine, at the rate of five dollars to eight dollars per page. That will be a good thing when I am finally able to work quietly again. . . . They advised me not to publish my speeches, for there is no sale for books at present.

SPRINGFIELD, Feb. 10, 1861 (evening).

I have just left Lincoln with whom I spent the whole afternoon and a part of the evening. We canvassed everything that was of common interest and were mutually very cordial. Suddenly bringing our conversation to a halt, he said: "I will give you a mark of confidence which I have given no other man." Then he locked the door and read to me the draft of his inaugural address. After we had discussed it point by point, he said: "Now you know better than any man in this country how I stand, and you may be sure that I shall never betray my principles and my friends." (Don't mention this reading of the inaugural.) As I was leaving him after this long conversation, in which he explained his opinions and plans with the greatest frankness, I told him that I should ask his Administration for a few offices for my friends. He answered: "You write to me and you may be sure that I shall attend to everything you may ask for; and as for your own case, which you have not spoken of to me, I shall never forget you." Others tell me that he himself has spoken of sending me to Sardinia.

WASHINGTON, March 4, 1861.

It was literally impossible to write Saturday or yesterday. People crowded about me so that I was scarcely able to move. And this morning I can barely steal a few moments; so forgive me if I am brief.

The great day has come; the city is quiet; the soldiers ready; a countless mass of Republicans from different States throng the streets. Probably there will be no disturbance. The preparations made by the Government are excellent.

TO PRESIDENT LINCOLN

NEW YORK, May 19, 1861.

I have just received your kind letter of the 16th instant. You will meanwhile have seen a captain of the 7th New York, one of the German regiments. The brigade is formed by the State board and consists of the 7th, 8th and 20th, all German regiments, and Ellsworth's Zouaves. The field-officers of the three German regiments have resolved to vote for me, unanimously, at the brigade election, and have addressed a letter to Colonel Ellsworth, informing him of their desire. All this is probably known to you. Yesterday, Major-General Dix, commanding the First Division, of which the Second Brigade forms a part, informed us, that the election will be put off ten days, according to the militia laws of this

State; but the field-officers desiring to have the brigade organized at once, he intimated that this could be done, provided the four regiments were unanimous in their choice. The whole matter, according to this, depends on Colonel Ellsworth. If he will signify his acquiescence in the choice of the three regiments, either by telegram or letter to General Dix, it will facilitate matters very much. It is very important that the brigade be organized *without delay;* I shall then be able to take hold of matters officially and get the regiments ready for field service *as a brigade* in a very short time. The best way to dispose of this red-tape business, which rests like an incubus upon the military matters of this State, would be, if you would telegraph to General Dix yourself to have the thing done at once. There will then be no unnecessary delay.

As to the disposition to be made of the brigade I know I express the sentiment of the three regiments here in saying that they would be glad to be sent where there will be the first chance to do something, be it at Washington or Fortress Monroe, provided the brigade, the three regiments and Colonel Ellsworth, remain together. As far as Fortress Monroe is concerned, the difficulty about the rank seems to be removed by General Butler's promotion.

I should be glad to have some authority from you in another matter. At Hoboken, there is a battery of German artillery, all old artillerymen, fully equipped and ready for service. Major Hexamer, commanding the same, called upon me and wanted to be attached to my brigade. His battery consists of six beautiful six-pounders and will be one of the most efficient in the army. Will you have the kindness to authorise me to bring them along as part of the brigade? If so, a telegram to myself and one to the governor of New Jersey would set the thing in motion.

You would oblige me very much by advising General Dix and myself by telegraph of your desires in the matter above referred to.

To this the following informal answer was made:

If it will make no confusion, let all the German regiments be of those going to Fort Monroe. This will only, at most, transfer, and not change, the proportions going there and coming here.

May 27, 1861.

LINCOLN.

TO ADOLPH MEYER[1]

PARIS, July 3, 1861.[2]

We are busy with the purchase of equipments here. The preparations for court-life are most unpleasant, and I am not able to imagine myself as "Excellency." We have learned our first lesson regarding the required uniforms and court-costumes here. My head is quite confused by all these gold embroideries, brocades and laces, and, in addition to this, the whole stupid monkey-comedy is so expensive that my salary of $12,000 seems very petty to me for the first twelve months. Here, it appears, democratic simplicity has reached its limits. I left America hoping that a Minister of the United States would be allowed to conduct himself as sensibly abroad as at home. But here, I am told that the court regulations are relentless. If one wishes to have diplomatic influence, one must participate in the masquerade as gracefully as possible. I must wear a uniform and my wife must wear a court train. And to think of spending so much money, only to look as absurdly as others! But as many a wise man has already said, "Man is an adaptable creature," even to the extent of seeming foolish to himself.

[1] Mrs. Schurz's brother.   [2] Translated from the German.

TO N. B. JUDD, UNITED STATES MINISTER TO PRUSSIA

MADRID, Aug. 27, 1861.

These lines may show you that I am still alive and well, although not half as proud of our fighting brethren in the United States as I was when we met at New York. These are indeed dark days for American pride, but if the war brings about the final destruction of the slavery-system, as it bids fair to do, the price we are paying is not too heavy. I am homesick and wish I had never taken this mission. It is easier work to fight in America than to disguise our defeats in Europe. But let us hope for brighter days.

This letter is written for an object. You can do me a great service if you are willing, of which I have no doubt. I have considerable property interests in the city of Hamburg which want looking after.[1] For this purpose it is exceedingly desirable that I should spend a few days there some time this fall. In order to get there I have to pass through Prussia, unless I take the circuitous route by London. You are probably aware that in consequence of my connection with the revolutionary trouble of '48 and '49 my relations with the Prussian Government are not of the most friendly nature. Some time ago the King of Prussia granted an amnesty to the political offenders of that period, but whether its provisions apply to my case I do not know.

Now I would not undertake to set my foot upon Prussian soil without having previously come to some understanding with that Government, and in no case would I avail myself of the privileges of my present position for the purpose of giving offense in that way. I would not even go to Hamburg by way of London if my presence there could be disagreeable to Prussia. In my present

[1] This referred to property of Mrs. Schurz, coming from her father.

situation as Minister of the United States I can not very well afford to treat with that Government myself or to appear as a supplicant before it.   But I think you might, if you should deem it consistent to do so, ask the Secretary of Foreign Affairs in an unofficial and informal way whether the Government would have any objection to my crossing the Prussian territory on my way from Belgium to Hamburg.   I have hardly any doubt that motives of international courtesy will induce them to grant the request.

You may assure them on your (and my) word as a gentleman, that the voyage will be undertaken for none but purposes of a strictly private nature; that for a number of years, in fact since my emigration to the United States, I have been in no connection whatever with the political affairs or parties of Germany, and that, while on Prussian soil, I shall conform myself to whatever restrictions the Government may reasonably impose upon me.   Of course, if such restrictions should be incompatible with my character and position, I would then rather give up the project.   It is hardly necessary that, aside from these statements, I should give you any further assurances of the perfect loyalty of my intentions.

You would greatly oblige me by conducting this affair in as quiet and private a manner as possible.   I am so tired of seeing my name in the newspapers as to studiously avoid everything that might draw public attention upon me.

This is the service I wish you to do me, if you can. My wife and children are at present at a water-cure establishment near Hamburg and I desire to take them back with me to Madrid.   This is a dull place, and if our affairs did not keep me busy, the ennui would kill me. I have no doubt you like Berlin, the German Athens.

TO SECRETARY SEWARD

LEGATION OF THE UNITED STATES,
SAN ILDEFONSO, Sept. 14, 1861.

Permit me to address you upon a question which indeed does not seem to have any immediate bearing upon the pending negotiations between the United States and Spain, but the decision of which may in the course of time do more to determine our standing in Europe than all our diplomatic operations.

When the civil war broke out in America it became at once apparent, that not only the commercial and manufacturing interests depending upon a regular supply of cotton, but also the anti-democratic sentiments of governments and political parties would be either openly or secretly arrayed against us. While the former accused the Federal authorities of having, by precipitate action and an unconciliatory spirit, brought ruin upon them, the latter saw in the war a final and conclusive failure of democratic institutions and found in our increasing embarrassments an inexhaustible source of argument in their favor. This enmity to our cause may have been disguised in various manners, but it was natural; and being natural it will only await a favorable opportunity for manifesting itself in open action. Sound statesmanship must have foreseen this and cannot be deluded by appearances to the contrary.

For reasons equally natural it might have been expected that the liberal instincts, the philanthropic impulses of European nations would have embraced our cause with warmth and enthusiasm, and that public opinion, determined by the popular sentiment, would have been powerful enough to restrain or divert the action of Governments.

Since my arrival in Europe I have carefully watched the fluctuations of public opinion, as they manifested themselves in the press and in private correspondence and conversation, and in stating the results of that observation I do not speak of Spain alone, but of France, England and Germany as well.

It is my conviction, and I consider it a duty to communicate to you, that the sympathies of the liberal masses in Europe are not as unconditionally in our favor as might be desired, and that, unless the war end soon or something be done to give our cause a stronger foothold in the popular heart, they will, in the end, not be decided and powerful enough to control the actions of those Governments whose goodwill or neutrality is to us of the greatest importance.

When the struggle about the slavery question in the United States assumed the form of an armed conflict, it was generally supposed in Europe, that the destruction of slavery was to be the avowed object of the policy of the Government, and that the war would in fact be nothing else than a grand uprising of the popular conscience in favor of a great humanitarian principle. If this opinion had been confirmed by the evidence of facts, the attitude of Europe, as determined by popular sentiment, could not have been doubtful a single moment. But it was remarked, not without a feeling of surprise and disappointment, that the Federal Government, in its public declarations, cautiously avoided the mentioning of the slavery question as the cause and origin of the conflict; that its acts, at the beginning of the war at least, were marked by a strikingly scrupulous respect for the sanctity of slave-property, and that the ultimate extinction of an institution so hateful to the European mind was most emphatically denied to be one of the objects of the war. I do not mean to question the wisdom of the Government under circumstances so difficult and perplexing, but I am bearing witness to the effect its attitude produced upon public opinion in Europe. While the impression gained ground that the war, as waged by the Federal Government, far from being a war of principle, was merely a war of policy, it was at the same time discovered that, from this point of view, much might be said in favor of the South. It is exceedingly difficult to make Europeans understand, not only why the free and prosperous North should fight merely for the privilege of being reassociated with the imperious and troublesome slave States, but also why the principle, by virtue of which a population sufficiently strong for establishing and maintaining an independent national existence possessing the right to have a government and institutions of its own choice, should be repudiated in America, while it is almost universally recognized in monarchical Europe.   I have had to discuss this point with men whose sympathies were most sincerely on our side, and all my Constitutional arguments failed to convince them that such a right can be consistently denied, unless our cause was based upon principles of a higher nature.   I know that journalists who in their papers work for us to the best of their ability, are secretly troubled with serious scruples on that point.   The agents of the South, whose footprints are frequently visible in the public press, are availing themselves of this state of things with great adroitness.   While they carefully abstain from alluding to the rights of slavery, they speak of free-trade and cotton to the merchant and the manufacturer, and of the right of self-government to the liberal.   They keep it well before the people that the same means of repression which are of so baneful a memory to most European nations—the suspension of the writ of habeas corpus, arbitrary imprisonment, the confiscation of newspapers, the use of armed force—are now found necessary to prop the Federal Government; and that the latter, in its effort to crush the independent spirit of eight millions of people, is with rapid strides approaching the line which separates democratic government from the attributes of arbitrary despotism. The incidents of the war, so unfavorable to our arms, could not fail to give weight and color to these representations.

It seems as if people of the North had set up pretensions, which they had neither the courage nor the power to sustain; and the failure of our first military operations was attributed by many to a lack of moral force in our cause. It cannot be denied that many, who earnestly sympathized with us at the beginning, were gradually led to doubt the possibility of subduing a people who are fighting for an independent national existence and whose all is staked upon the issue of the struggle.

And if opinions like these could gain ground among our natural friends, what have we to expect of those who secretly desire a permanent disruption of the Union? I do not know what assurances may have been given to the Government, but whatever they may be I am sanguine enough to suppose, that those Powers, which would find a vindication of their principles in the destruction of the American Republic, or whose commercial and manufacturing interests would be saved from incalculable embarrassments by a speedy termination of hostilities, will always adhere to their policy of neutrality, if the chances of the war should much longer appear doubtful. They may hesitate awhile, but it is in the very nature of things that they will soon think of acting as their interests command them to act.

Nor will they be at a loss to find arguments plausible enough to justify them in the eyes of the public. They will say, that the Confederate States have, on principle, a right to a separate national existence; that undeniable events have demonstrated the impossibility of reducing the South by force of arms; that it is their duty as Governments to protect the commercial and manufacturing

interests of their subjects from utter ruin by putting an
end to the useless strife, either by way of diplomatic
intercession or by aiding the party to which their interests
are most closely attached, and that therefore the recommendation of the Southern Confederacy and the breaking
up of our blockade, as a first step in that direction, have
become an urgent necessity. They may even represent
it as an act of humanity and kindness to the people of
the United States, to contribute to the conclusion of a
strife which they think as useless as it is destructive.

And what will the Federal Government have to oppose
to this plausible reasoning? A rupture of relations, which
undoubtedly would be more disagreeable to us than to
them? Fleets and armies, which so far have been hardly
able to close some Southern ports and to protect the
President from capture in his capital? The resentment
of the American people, which has ceased to be formidable? There are in my opinion but two ways in which
the overwhelming perplexities can be averted which a
rupture with foreign Powers, added to our troubles at
home, would inevitably bring upon us. The one consists
in great and decisive military successes speedily accomplished, and the other in such measures and manifestations
on the part of the Government as will place the war
against the rebellious slave States upon a higher moral
basis and thereby give us the control of public opinion in
Europe. Whether we have any reason to expect the
first I am, at so great a distance, unable to see; but it
would, if we may judge by the experience of the past,
appear at least very doubtful. As to the second I consider its effect certain, and here my statements, the results of my observation, stand above the level of mere
conjecture.

While in the same measure as the struggle in the United
States appeared as a mere political war on the part of the

North, we lost caste in the eyes of those who were our
natural friends, in the same measure as the conflict assumes the character of an anti-slavery war, even our
opponents are compelled to do us justice.   Of this I have
the most striking illustrations before me. No sooner
had the act of Congress, liberating the slaves of rebel
masters, and the instructions issued to military commanders, relative to the reception of fugitives, become known
in Europe, than the indifference of the liberal masses gave
room to new hopes and good wishes for our cause.   These
acts are constantly paraded by our friends as indications
of the general tendency of the war, and in this they find
a ready excuse for the restraints temporarily placed upon
civil rights and liberties; and even our opponents, after
having for some time professed doubt as to the truth-
fulness of the news, are at last compelled to concede, that
the ultimate extinction of slavery would indeed be a
most desirable object to be accomplished.   But at the
same time the emphatic desire is added [sic] by the first,
that such measures ought to assume a more general scope,
while the second, pretending that they proceed from our
necessities and not from principle, predict they never will.
All these opinions are to be traced in numberless and
striking manifestations of the public press.

It is my profound conviction that, as soon as the war
becomes distinctly one for and against slavery, public
opinion will be so strongly, so overwhelmingly in our
favor, that in spite of commercial interests or secret spites
no European Government will dare to place itself, by declaration or act, upon the side of a universally condemned
institution.   Our enemies know that well, and we may
learn from them.   While their agents carefully conceal
from the eyes of Europeans their only weak point, their
attachment to slavery, ought we to aid them in hiding
with equal care our only strong point, our opposition

to slavery? While they, well knowing how repugnant slavery is to the European way of feeling, do all to make Europeans forget that they fight for it, ought we, who are equally well acquainted with European sentiment, abstain from making Europeans remember that we fight against it? In not availing ourselves of our advantages, we relieve the enemy of the odium attached to his cause. It is, therefore, my opinion that every step done [taken] by the Government towards the abolition of slavery is, as to our standing in Europe, equal to a victory in the field. I do not know how this advice may agree with the home-policy of the Government. But however bold it may seem, I am so sincerely convinced of its correctness, as far as our foreign policy is concerned, that I do not hesitate to place it upon the records of the State Department.

FROM SECRETARY SEWARD

DEPARTMENT OF STATE,
WASHINGTON, Oct. 10, 1861.

Your despatch of September 14th, No. 18, has been received.

I have read carefully the views concerning our domestic policy which you have submitted. Of the propriety of your submitting them there can be no question, especially when they are presented with reference to the public sentiment of Europe and the possible action of the Governments of that continent.

It would, however, be altogether inconvenient, and it might be in some degree hazardous for me to engage in explanations of domestic policy in a correspondence which, for all practical purposes, is to be regarded as involving only the foreign relations of the country. Moreover, the policy on which an Administration charged with the duty of maintaining itself and preserving the Union shall conduct a civil war, must be confined always to the existing condition of political forces and to the public sentiment of the whole country.

I am not surprised when you inform me that sympathies with the United States regarded as a nation struggling to maintain its integrity against the assaults of faction are less active in Europe than they might or ought to be in view of the benefits which the Republic has already conferred and the still greater benefits which it promises to confer on mankind.

Nations like individuals are too much wrapped up in their own interests and ambitions to be deeply concerned by accidents or reverses which befall other nations.

I can well enough conceive also that the United States in the first emergency might excite more fervent sympathies abroad by avowing a purpose not merely or even chiefly to maintain and preserve their existing Constitutional organizations, but to modify and change it so as to extirpate at once an institution which is obnoxious to the enlightened censure of mankind.

But, on the other hand, it is never to be forgotten that although the sympathy of other nations is eminently desirable, yet foreign sympathy or even foreign favor never did and never can create or maintain any state; while in every state that has the capacity to live, the love of national life is and always must be the most energetic principle which can be invoked to preserve it from suicidal indulgence of fear of faction as well as from destruction by foreign violence.

For my own part, it seems to me very clear that there is no nation on earth whose fortunes, immediate and remote, would not be the worse for the dissolution of the American Union.   If that consideration shall not be sufficient to save us from unjust intervention by any foreign state or states in our domestic troubles, then that intervention must come as a natural incident in our unnatural domestic strife, and I entertain no fears that we shall not be able to maintain ourselves against all who shall combine against us.

If it were profitable I might reply to your point that our case suffers abroad because we do not win victories so fast as impatient friends could wish.   But I have no time for such discussions in the midst of daily duties and cares.   It must suffice to say that rebellion if at all successful, matures fast, acts by surprise, with vehement energy, and wins considerable successes in the beginning. Government gathers its forces more slowly and may well be content if it maintains itself until the revolutionary passion submits to the inevitable law of reaction. Especially must this be so in a federative republican government like our own. While you who have gone abroad are hearing apprehensions of the failure of the Government on all sides, there is not one citizen who has remained at home who is not more confident in the stability of this Union now than he was on the day of your departure upon your mission. This confidence is not built on enthusiasm, but on knowledge of the true state of the conflict, and the exercise of calm and dispassionate reflection.

TO PRESIDENT LINCOLN

LEGATION OF THE UNITED STATES,
MADRID, Nov. 11, 1861.

When I was sent to Spain I received the instruction to use my best efforts to prevent the recognition of the Southern Confederacy and to place the relations between this country and the United States upon a satisfactory footing. I was well aware of the importance of this task, and upon my arrival here I found that it was not altogether an easy one. Spain had indeed defined her policy with regard to our domestic troubles in a manner which won your approval. But the irritation caused by our protest against the annexation of Dominica and the efforts of my predecessor, who had most zealously served the interests of the rebellion before openly joining it, had produced a state of feeling here which under unfavorable circumstances would have led to disagreeable results. The symptoms of a decided and widely spread hostility were alarming. In struggling against these difficulties I have used all the means which my position placed at my disposal and which corresponded with the justice of our

13

cause and the loyalty of my intentions.   I endeavored to
arrest the insulting invectives of the press, which threatened to control public opinion; to place the United States
.in a just light before the Government and the people;
to secure to the American Republic that respect to which
she is entitled, and finally to make the Spanish Government, as much as possible, forget that there is any question
of difficulty between us.   In this I succeeded beyond my
expectations, and I may say that at present the relations,
not only between my legation and the Spanish Government, but also between the two countries, are under the
influence of mutual good-will.   It is my sincere conviction
that they will remain so, if the action of your Government
and of Congress be in harmony with the policy which I
deemed it my duty to follow and which I thought would
best meet your views.

I believe, therefore, that the task which fell to my lot
is so far accomplished.   New questions and discussions
may indeed turn up, but the principal obstacles to a
friendly correspondence being removed, the easy duties
of this legation will hardly render the constant presence
of a Plenipotentiary indispensable, especially as we possess
a Secretary who joins a large diplomatic experience to a
high order of ability, who has always been regarded by
me less as a subordinate than as a co-laborer, and who,
as I know, justly enjoys the full confidence of the Secretary
of State.

Good feeling being thus restored and secured, it seems
that my future activity here, for some time at least, will
be limited more or less to quiet observation and the enjoyment of a comfortable and distinguished position.   While
I find myself in this manner condemned to elegant leisure,
which in times like these is to me rather oppressive than
agreeable, I see the struggle in the United States becoming
more critical with every day that passes—without decisive

results. From what I learn I cannot persuade myself, that the sanguine hopes expressed by many are justified in reality. The crisis certainly calls for the best efforts and the highest degree of decision and activity on the part of every patriotic citizen. Under these circumstances it is exceedingly difficult for me to spend my time in comparative idleness or easy pursuits,—especially as in the course of things the state of our foreign relations will chiefly depend upon events at home. It is no mere impatience which makes me slight the advantages of my position here, but grave doubts arising from my view of the ensemble of our affairs; and to have these doubts solved one way or the other is for me a matter not of convenience or curiosity but of conscience.

I beg you therefore to grant me leave to return to the United States for a time to be limited according to the exigencies of the public service. If you should find it inconsistent with your views of propriety to do so, I shall feel myself forced, although to my great regret, to offer you my resignation. The feeling of duty which urges me to write this letter, obliges me also to place myself frankly into this alternative. While I sincerely hope that you will find it possible to give me permission to return without severing my connection with your Government, I shall under all circumstances consider it an act of friendship on your part if, by the steamer whose departure will next follow the arrival of this letter, you will send me an answer which will enable me to return in whatever manner it may be.

TO CHARLES SUMNER

MADRID, Nov. 14, 1861.

My dear Friend: First let me thank you for the glorious speech you have delivered before the Massachusetts convention. I agree with you on every point and expect shortly to fight by your side.

Mr. Perry[1] has shown me the letter he mailed to you on the 11th inst. It does honor to his heart. Since he has advised you of what I have done and asked you to take an interest in this matter, I think it due you that you should know all. I have no doubt the President will show you the letter I addressed to him. These lines will furnish you the commentary.

Looking at the ensemble of our affairs, the state of the case seems to me utterly desperate; and what makes matters worse, a large majority of the people and the Government seem to indulge in the most unwarrantable delusions as to the means by which the rebellion can be overcome. Suppose our armies to be numerous and good, our resources to be ample, the spirit of the people to be most enthusiastic; suppose even we win victories in the field—and yet all these things are not sufficient to over-balance the immense advantage of the defensive position of the Confederates. Six or eight months ago it might have been possible to bring about a reaction in the South by a rapid succession of victories. That is now out of the question. The Union feeling in the seceding States is not only paralyzed but I fear almost exterminated. For a year they have practically maintained their independence; they not only love it but are already accustomed to it. We are already regarded as foreign enemies, even by many of those who originally did not desire the dissolution of the Union. Our Government has shown itself unable to protect the Unionists of the South; nothing more natural than that they should consider themselves released of their obligation towards that Government; a few determined spirits always excepted, but they stand

[1] Horatio J. Perry, secretary of Legation at Madrid.

alone. Every day that passes without decisive results
consolidates secession in itself. We must make up our
minds to conquer the South as we would conquer a foreign
country;—a thing so much more difficult as this is not a
war of armies but of the people, where the advantages
are all on the side of the defensive. The idea of starving
them out is utterly absurd. Their resources are inferior
but better used; besides, standing on the defensive, they
have them near at hand. To annihilate their armies and
to beat the rebellious spirit thoroughly out of them will,
it seems to me, in the ordinary way of warfare, require
more time than our own resources will permit us to
spend upon it,—and perhaps also more military strength
than we possess. Thus the war bids fair to assume the
character of the Carlist war in Spain; that is to say,
thoroughly exhaust and demoralize the country and
finally leave the advantage with the defensive,—*unless*
we avail ourselves of the only thing which is sure to settle
the business quickly and definitely. *We must* proclaim
the emancipation of the slaves. You know well that my
opinions in relation to slavery are sufficiently decided.
And yet, in point of principle, I would not be anxious
to see the emancipation measure adopted so suddenly, for
I think slavery will perish at all events in consequence of
this struggle. But if we want to save the Union it seems
to me utterly indispensable to avail ourselves of this most
powerful weapon *without delay*.

What I hear from the United States leads me to believe
that the Administration is strongly opposed to this policy.
I have some reason to suspect that some of its members
still hope for a change of public opinion, a spontaneous
reaction in the South. If the war is to be conducted
upon such ideas, I fear thousands of lives and hundreds
of millions will be spent in vain. Our victories, if indeed
we should be lucky enough to achieve any, will be useless

butcheries and neither the gallantry of our armies nor the enthusiasm of the people will be able to save us. This being my view of things, it is impossible for me to sit still, eat diplomatic dinners, repose upon distinguished consideration and wait for news from America. I, too, feel some responsibility in what is going on there. After having contributed my share to the election of Mr. Lincoln, it is incompatible with my way of thinking to enjoy the comforts and luxuries of a distinguished position while the country is on the road to wreck and ruin. It is my duty to stand or fall with our cause. My present intention is this. I shall return to the United States under all circumstances. If on a careful survey of the state of things at home I find my impressions confirmed, I shall help you and our friends who think as we do, in urging Mr. Lincoln on to decisive measures; and if that be found impossible, work upon public opinion in every way possible so as to force the Administration into the right course.

I was about to offer my resignation pure and simple to the President, when Mr. Perry made an effort to dissuade me from that step. He thinks that a change in this legation will prejudice our interests here, and in this he is probably right. The American Legation in Spain was never more respected than at this moment. I had to overcome all kinds of prejudices when I arrived here; but by patient labor and discreet conduct I have conquered them all and succeeded to turn the very things which seemed to be against me, to account. I have proposed a conciliatory course throughout and thus, without concealing my principles, gained the confidence of the Spanish Government and of the leading statesmen. Thus my influence is firmly established here. A change in the legation would be received with regret, and perhaps even with distrust at the present moment. If I should receive

leave of absence for a limited time, the service would
hardly suffer. Mr. Perry would as chargé d'affaires
steadily follow the course I have adopted. He is a man
of great diplomatic ability, prudent and very well versed
in Spanish affairs. This is the principal reason why I
modified my original intention and presented to the
Government the alternative of giving me a leave of
absence or accepting my resignation. Another reason
is that a resignation pure and simple for political grounds
might be looked upon as a demonstration against the
Administration, and I do not deem it desirable that I
should be placed into an antagonistic position as long as
it can be avoided.

While under these circumstances it would seem the
wiser course for the Government to give me a leave of
absence, I shall also receive my letter of recall with gratitude. I shall never cling to the advantages of an official
position, which might hinder me in following the dictates
of my conscience. If you feel like doing anything for me,
urge the Government to enable me at once to return, by
immediately granting either leave or recall. By this you
will greatly oblige me.

Please regard this letter as a confidential one as far as
the exposition of my views on home affairs and my
intention is concerned. As I shall have to explain these
matters to the Government immediately after my arrival
in the United States you will readily understand why I
should not like to be anticipated. In case my resignation
be accepted my enemies may possibly try to create the
impression that I was forced to offer it by the difficulties
of my diplomatic position or something of that kind. My
defense in that respect, if any should be necessary, I
must entrust to my friends.

Permit me a word to you as chairman of the Committee on Foreign Relations. If it can possibly be done,

put off the action of the Senate on any other matters with which Spain is concerned until my arrival at Washington. I may be able to give you useful information.

Will you have the kindness to give me your views on the state of affairs at home in reply to this letter? If you write soon and send your letter by the State Department it will reach me before my departure, and I should feel greatly indebted to you.

TO SECRETARY SEWARD

LEGATION OF THE UNITED STATES,
MADRID, Nov. 16, 1861.

Sir: The English papers which went to America by last mail have probably already informed you that, instead of General Serrano, General Prim has been placed at the head of the Spanish expedition to Mexico. As soon as the appointment was determined upon, I endeavored to inform myself of the causes and the significance of this change of program and will give you the result of my investigations.

General Prim is a very important man in this kingdom. He occupies a high position and sustains it with considerable talent. As a military leader he excels by his address and the brilliancy of his exploits. His popularity is as great with the people as his prestige is in the army. His instincts are liberal, and the political opinions he professes identify him with the *Progressista* party. He is generous and frank, and his character is somewhat of the romantic turn. But he is supposed to be very impressionable and apt to shape his course according to circumstances. His elevation to the position of a grandee of Spain is said to have had some influence upon his way of thinking, as it certainly had upon his social relations. In his private

life he is magnificent in the extreme, princely in his
expenditures, careless in the administration of his affairs,
apt to run recklessly into debt and almost always sadly
in want of money. A few years ago he married a Mexican
lady of great wealth, spent her available means in a
marvellously short time and is now overburdened with
enormous pecuniary liabilities. These are his elements
of strength and of weakness. I have been thus minute
in the description of the man, because his character may
determine the nature of his operations in Mexico.

His appointment to the leadership of the expedition
is differently explained. I had a conversation with the
Chief of the *Progressista* party, Mr. Olozaga, who thought
that England had made certain concessions to Spain in
stipulating the program of action of the three powers
on the express condition that General Prim be placed at
the head of the enterprise—because Prim had made a
very strong speech in the Spanish Senate against the
Clerical rule in Mexico some two years ago and would now
be likely not to favor the intrigues of the party he then
had so emphatically denounced. This, however, plausible as it may seem, was not confirmed by what Sir John
Crampton subsequently told me. The latter professes
to be entirely ignorant of such an arrangement and thinks
that Lord John Russell knows probably very little of
General Prim and his political opinions. It is likely
that French influence has had more to do with General
Prim's appointment. He is known to be a great favorite
at the Tuileries and in intimate relations with the French
Ambassador here.

Another explanation of this event was given me by one
of the principal leaders of the *Moderado* party. Prim,
he said, was so overwhelmed with financial embarrassments that something had to be done for him or he would
do something for himself. The Government feared that

Prim, pressed by his necessities, might some day place himself at the head of a few regiments, issue a *pronunciamiento*, call the people to arms and upset the Cabinet and the dynasty together. Prim was not only capable of doing such things, but his popularity furnished him also the means for doing them. The Government, therefore, in order to get rid of a very dangerous man, had placed him at the head of an expedition which would remove him from the country and at the same time give him an opportunity for filling his pockets. This somewhat uncharitable explanation, although coming from an opponent of General Prim and undoubtedly colored a little by party feeling, may be not quite unfounded as far as the views of the Government are concerned; for it is currently believed that Spanish generals are somewhat unsafe persons when out of funds. It is by no means unlikely that the Government, after having undertaken the Mexican expedition in order to relieve itself of a political embarrassment, should have seen itself forced, in order to relieve itself of another embarrassment, to place the same expedition under the control of a man whom it is exceedingly difficult to govern.

Last night I had a long conversation with General Prim himself. He expressed himself with that frankness which is one of his characteristic qualities, and I will give you the substance of what he said. He assured me that he would use all his power to insure to the Mexican people full liberty in arranging their own affairs. He considered it absurd to think of the establishment of a monarchy in Mexico; all the traditions of the people were republican and he was sure there were but few Mexicans who seriously thought of introducing monarchical institutions. He knew well that the misfortunes and the demoralization of the Mexican people were largely owing to the influence of the clergy, and this conviction would not be

without influence upon his actions. He would endeavor
to secure to the Mexican people a fair opportunity to
express their will at the ballot-box and then with his whole
power sustain the Government of their choice, whatever
party might carry the day. As between Miramon and
Juarez, he was in favor of Juarez, and he believed that
at a fair election a majority of the people would be on
Juarez's side.

I remarked that, according to Mr. Calderon's statements, the three powers were not in favor of calling a
constitutional convention or taking a vote of the people.
The General seemed surprised and gave me clearly to
understand that he did not care very much what the
Government might think of it, and that, as he was the
political as well as the military head of the expedition,
he would act as he thought best. He had been a liberal
all his life and would be as true to his principles in Mexico
as he had been in Spain; he would not have accepted the
command of the expedition, if he were not permitted to
play a generous and disinterested part in the business.

I thought it proper to inform the General of the offer
of mediation, made by the United States through me to
the Spanish Government, and explained to him the views
expressed by you in your despatch on that subject. I
informed him further, that the United States had undoubtedly great influence with the Juarez Government,
and that, if our good offices were accepted now or at a
subsequent stage of the proceedings, great complications
might be avoided and all difficulties settled in an amicable
manner; I had made that suggestion to Mr. Calderon but
received no satisfactory answer.

The General replied that nothing would afford him
greater pleasure than to operate in good understanding
with the United States; the great American Republic
had his hearty sympathy; he loved her institutions and

esteemed her people, and if her Government would do anything to bring about a satisfactory solution of the difficulties under which Mexico now was laboring, he would meet it with a corresponding spirit. It was his object to do what might be best for the liberty and independence of the Mexican people, and he would be obliged to me if I would inform my Government of what he had said.

Permit me a few remarks as a commentary to this conversation. I have taken pains to obtain the most reliable information about General Prim's character and views, and according to the opinion I have thus formed, I am convinced that he was perfectly sincere in what he said at the time when he said it. But he is versatile and changeable and, therefore, not absolutely to be relied upon. But about two things there is no doubt: first, his impulses are thoroughly liberal and he will act accordingly unless biased by his material interests; and, second, he feels his power and importance, does not entertain a very high regard for the present Government and is naturally inclined to act as he pleases. He is not inaccessible to flattery, feels proud of having a great political task assigned to him, will please himself in the part of a great pacificator and restorer of the liberty and independence of an unfortunate nation and will by no means be disinclined to listen to overtures made to him directly by the Government of a great and powerful country. He is not quite unknown to the Mexicans. He has spent some time in Mexico and has, by his wife, great property interests there and extensive family connections.

What I wrote to you in my despatch No. 22, the receipt of which, to my surprise, has not yet been acknowledged, is confirmed by information subsequently obtained. The demonstrations in favor of the Spanish flag made by one of the insurgent generals in Mexico seem to indicate

what influences are at work there. As to the candidates
for the Mexican throne, whose merits and chances are
canvassed at Court, there seems to be a discrepancy of
opinion. Don Sebastian was most freely spoken of while
the Court was at La Granja; but a few days ago one of
the Government journals stated that the Mexican throne
would be occupied not by a Spanish prince, but by a prince
who would marry a Spanish princess. It would seem
that the aspirations of this Court have not received the
anticipated encouragement from the Governments of
France and England, and it is possible that the Queen is
endeavoring to reconcile discordant interests by some
family alliance. She is said to be in search of a throne for
her daughter, the Infanta Isabel, and this circumstance
has probably given rise to the mysterious statement of
the above-mentioned journal.

But the wishes of the Court will probably be considered
as of secondary importance by General Prim, especially
if the right influences be brought to bear upon him. With
regard to the manner in which this might be accomplished
I beg leave to offer a suggestion. Mr. Corwin will probably be confined by his duties to the City of Mexico, at
a large distance from that part of the country which,
at the beginning of operations at least, will be the principal
field of action. The United States will, as you have
informed me, send a little squadron to the Mexican
waters for the purpose of watching the proceedings of
the three Powers. Would it not be possible to attach to
that squadron a diplomatic agent? I have no doubt,
if you select a person of ability, sufficient knowledge of
human nature, good social qualities and conversational
powers, who speaks Spanish or French fluently, and
instruct him to attach himself to the person of General
Prim, he will not remain without influence upon the
course of events. General Prim informs me that he

intended to visit the United States after his Mexican campaign, and it is very probable that he will endeavor to make himself agreeable to the American people.

TO PRESIDENT LINCOLN

PHILADELPHIA, May 16, 1862.

. . .[1] Yesterday's papers brought the news of General Hunter's proclamation freeing the slaves in his department. I am convinced it must and will come to this all over the cotton States during the summer, and a month or two hence a proclamation like Hunter's would be looked upon as the most natural thing in the world. At the present moment it is perhaps a little premature. The thing might have been practically done without being ostensibly proclaimed. At the same time I am persuaded the people will readily acquiesce if you see fit to sustain Hunter in his act; and then the Administration must take its position with firmness and determination. Your personal influence upon public opinion is immense; you are perhaps not aware of the whole extent of your moral power. Thus, if you should see fit to justify and sustain the act as one commanded by local military necessity, there will not be a murmur against it a fortnight hence.

But if you should feel obliged to modify Hunter's proclamation, I would entreat you to consider this: As our armies proceed farther South the force of circumstances will drive us into measures which were not in the original program, but which necessity will oblige you to adopt. It seems to me of the greatest importance that the Government make no public declaration of policy which might be likely to embarrass it in the future. In fact you can hardly tell at the present moment how far you will have

[1] Two sentences about where he was stopping.

to go six weeks hence. The best policy would be to avoid public declarations altogether. The arming of negroes and the liberation of those slaves who offer us aid and assistance are things which must and will inevitably be done; in fact they are being done, and it would perhaps be best boldly to tell the whole truth and to acknowledge the necessity—all of which is respectfully submitted.

In regard to my own affairs permit me to repeat what I said at our last interview; I shall receive with gratitude your orders whatever they may be, especially if you should find it possible to end this suspense without much further loss of time.

P. S. To-day I have heard Hunter's proclamation quite extensively discussed and find that men who are not engaged in party politics, but wish to get done with the war in the shortest possible time, receive it quite favorably.

TO CHARLES SUMNER

PHILADELPHIA, May 16, 1862.

Startling news from Port Royal! What will the Administration do? I have written to the President this morning, telling him, among other things, that if he sustains Hunter I am sure the people will sustain him, and that, if he should feel obliged to modify Hunter's proclamation, it would be unwise to make such declarations of policy as would cripple him for future action. It is perfectly certain that measures similar to that proposed by Hunter will before long have to be adopted, and I have no doubt two months hence Hunter's proclamation would be received as the most natural thing in the world. But it seems to me that at the present time the issuing of such a proclamation, so startling in its propositions and so weak in argument, was premature and ill-advised, espe-

208 The Writings of [1862

cially as the thing was practically being done and there
was no necessity for ostentatiously proclaiming it to the
world and challenging public discussion. In my opinion
the best kind of a proclamation a commanding officer
can make would be something like this: "I know but
two classes of people in my department: loyal men and
rebels. All those that offer us aid and assistance will be
welcome; if they are slaves they shall be free; if slaves of
loyal masters, the latter may expect compensation from
the Government. No man who serves the Government
of the United States can be a slave." If the Administration should not deem it practicable to sustain Hunter's
act, a modification of his manifesto in this sense would,
perhaps, be the most satisfactory. At all events Hunter
must not be recalled. I see a statement in the *Herald*
which indicates that he is, but I trust this is not so. I
have no doubt you have already spoken to the President
about this matter. Would you be kind enough to let me
know how it stands?

One word about my personal affairs. I had a conversation with you last Wednesday. Immediately afterwards I saw the President again who repeated to me that
he did not want to see me in the Army unless he could
secure me a respectable command and influential position,
and that, if he could find none for me, he desired that I
should go back to Spain. Finally he promised me to
settle this matter as speedily as possible, and I then took
leave and returned to this city. I am now waiting for
orders and I am afraid I shall have to wait pretty long.
I should really prefer to remain here if I can have a sphere
of action sufficiently large. But I have placed this
matter entirely in the President's hands and shall be
governed by his decision. Would you perhaps have the
kindness to request him occasionally to end my suspense
as soon as possible?

FROM CHARLES SUMNER

SENATE CHAMBER, July 5, 1862.

Confidential.

My dear General: . . .[1] I wish you were here to tell
the President *the true way.* In vain will he appeal for troops
at the North, so it seems to many of us. I have insisted that
the appeal shall be made to the slaves, and the rear-guard of
the rebellion be changed into the advance guard of the Union.
He said that he would at once, if he did not fear that half the
Army would lay down their arms and three other States
would join the rebellion. I wish you were here to help. By
voice and presence you could do much—very—very much.
God bless you! Ever yours.

TO PRESIDENT LINCOLN

HEADQUARTERS 3D DIV., 11TH CORPS,
NEW–BALTIMORE, VA., Nov. 8, 1862.

Will you, after the great political defeat we have
suffered, listen a moment to the words of a true friend who
means to serve you faithfully, and in whose judgment you
once, perhaps, reposed some confidence?

The defeat of the Administration is owing neither to
your proclamations, nor to the financial policy of the
Government, nor to a desire of the people to have peace
at any price. I can speak openly, for you must know that
I am your friend. The defeat of the Administration is
the Administration's own fault.

It admitted its professed opponents to its counsels. It
placed the Army, now a great power in this Republic,
into the hands of its enemies. In all personal questions
to be hostile to the party of the Government seemed to be

---

[1] Two sentences about a military correspondence between Schurz and
Lincoln, of which part has not been found. See 18 *War Records*, 378–81,
398, 399.

14

a title to consideration. It forgot the great rule, that, if you are true to your friends, your friends will be true to you, and that you make your enemies stronger by placing them upon an equality with your friends. Is it surprising that the opponents of the Administration should have got into their hands the government of the principal States after they have had for so long a time the principal management of the war, the great business of the National Government?

Great sacrifices and enormous efforts had been made and they had been rewarded only by small results. The people felt the necessity of a change. Many of your friends had no longer any heart for the Administration as soon as they felt justified in believing that the Administration had no heart for them. I do not speak of personal favors but of the general conduct of the war. A change was sought in the wrong direction. This was the true cause of the defeat of your Government.

You have now made a change. This evening the news reaches us that the command of the Army of the Potomac has passed into new hands. But the change of persons means little if it does not imply a change of system. Let us be commanded by generals whose heart is [sic] in the war, and only by such. Let every general who does not show himself strong enough to command success, be deposed *at once*. Let every trust of power be accompanied by a corresponding responsibility, and all may be well yet.

There is but one way in which you can sustain your Administration, and that is by success; and there is but one thing which will command success, and that is *energy*. In whatever hands the State governments may be,—as soon as you are victorious, they will be obliged to support you; and if they were all in the hands of your friends,— if you do not give them victories, they will after a while be obliged to oppose you. Therefore let us have *energy* without regard to anything that may stand in your way. Let not the Government be endangered by tender considerations. If West Point cannot do the business, let West Point go down. Who cares? It is better that a thousand generals should fall than that the Republic should be jeopardized a single moment.

To-day we are still strong enough to meet the difficulties that stand against us. We do not know what we shall be to-morrow.

FROM PRESIDENT LINCOLN

EXECUTIVE MANSION,[1]
WASHINGTON, Nov. 10, 1862.

"Private & Confidential"

Gen. Schurz.

My dear Sir   Yours of the 8th was, to-day, read to me by Mrs. S[churz]. We have lost the elections; and

[1] In preparing this letter for publication the Editor was confronted with a somewhat perplexing problem. The rule in this work has been not to change the text of any document except in case of mistakes probably due to haste or to the oversight of some copyist or printer, long ago. It has, of course, been necessary to adopt rules for uniformity in regard to capitalization, punctuation etc.; thus making the meaning clearer, rather than changing it. It was found that if this Lincoln letter were made to conform to this practice, many changes would be necessary—so many that there was risk that at some future time, should the printed copy be compared with the original manuscript, one might infer that the liberties taken in this letter had been taken in other cases, which would be both erroneous and injurious. On the other hand, if the letter were reproduced as it was written, it might seem as if there were an attempt to make an invidious comparison, for hardly anyone's letter may well be printed *precisely* as written. However, in the present case it seems best to follow the manuscript in every detail. This makes the reproduction more realistic and may incidentally serve some historical or biographical purpose.

But, lest it should be inferred that Lincoln's other letters were penned with equal lack of care, the long letter of November 24, 1862, is also printed exactly as written. The few oversights in this latter letter indicate that those in the former were exceptional.

it is natural that each of us will believe, and say, it has been because his peculiar views was not made sufficiently prominent. I think I know what it was, but I may be mistaken. Three main causes told the whole story. 1. The democrats were left in a majority by our friends going to the war. 2. The democrats observed this & determined to re-instate themselves in power, and 3. Our newspapers, by vilifying and disparaging the administration, furnished them all the weapons to do it with. Certainly, the ill-success of the war had much to do with this.

You give a different set of reasons. If you had not made the following statements, I should not have suspected them to be true. "The defeat of the administration is the administrations own fault." (Opinion) "It admitted its professed opponents to its counsels." (Asserted as a fact) "It placed the Army, now a great power in this Republic, into the hands of it's enemys." (Asserted as a fact) "In all personal questions to be hostile to the party of the Government, seemed, to be a title to consideration." (Asserted as a fact) "If to forget the great rule, that if you arc true to your friends, your friends will be true to you, and that you make your enemies stronger by placing them upon an equality with your friends." "Is it surprising that the opponents of the administration should have got into their hands the government of the principal states, after they have had for a long time the principal management of the war, the great business of the national government."

I can not dispute about the matter of opinion. On the the three matters (stated as facts) I shall be glad to have your evidence upon them when I shall meet you. The plain facts, as they appear to me, are these. The administration came into power, very largely in a minority of the popular vote. Notwithstanding this, it distributed to it's party friends as nearly all the civil patronage as any administration ever did. The war came. The administration could not even start in this, without assistance outside of its party. It was mere nonsense to suppose a minority could put down a majority in rebellion. Mr. Schurz (now Gen. Schurz) was about

here then & I do not recollect that he then considered all
who were not republicans, were enemies of the government,
and that none of them must be appointed to military positions.
He will correct me if I am mistaken.   It so happened that very
few of our friends had a military education or were of the
profession of arms.   It would have been a question whether
the war should be conducted on military knowledge, or on
political affinity, only that our own friends (I think Mr.
Schurz included) seemed to think that such a question was
inadmissable.   Accordingly I have scarcely appointed a democrat to a command, who was not urged by many republicans and opposed by none.   It was so as to McClellan.   He
was first brought forward by the Republican Governor of
Ohio, & claimed, and contended for at the same time by
the Republican Governor of Pennsylvania.   I received rec-
ommendations from the republican delegations in Congress,
and I believe every one of them recommended a majority of
democrats.   But, after all many Republicans were appointed;
and I mean no disparagement to them when I say I do not
see that their superiority of success has been so marked as
to throw great suspicion on the good faith of those who are
not Republicans.   Yours truly,

A. LINCOLN

TO PRESIDENT LINCOLN

HEADQUARTERS 3D DIV., IITH CORPS,
CENTREVILLE, Nov. 20, 1862.

TO THE PRESIDENT OF THE UNITED STATES.

Dear Sir: Your favor of the 10th inst. did not reach me
until the 17th.   If there was anything in my letter of the
8th that had the appearance of presumption I ask your kind
indulgence.   You must forgive something to the sincerity
of my zeal, for there is no living being on this continent,
whose wishes for the success of your Administration are
more ardent than mine.   The consciousness of perfect

good faith gave me the boldness to utter my honest convictions without reserve. I do not know how many friends you have sincere enough to tell you things which it may not be pleasant to hear; I assure you, they are not the worst. In risking the amenities of undisturbed private relations they fulfil a duty, which many, who call themselves friends, have not the courage to understand and appreciate. In this spirit I wrote to you, with full confidence in the loftiness of your own way of thinking. If the opinions I expressed were unjust, it will be a happy hour for me when I shall be able conscientiously to acknowledge my error. But whatever I may have said it was but a mild and timid repetition of what a great many men say, whose utterances might perhaps have more weight with you than mine.

I fear you entertain too favorable a view of the causes of our defeat in the elections. It is of the highest importance, that, amidst the perplexities of your situation and the enormous responsibilities of your office, you should sift the true nature of the disaster to the very bottom. I throw myself upon your patient kindness in replying to some of your statements.

That a large proportion of Republicans have entered the Army, and that thereby the *party* vote was largely diminished, cannot be doubted. But you must recollect, that at the commencement of the war you were sincerely and even enthusiastically sustained by the *masses* of the people, and that the "Administration party" was not confined to the old Republican ranks. You had *the people* of the loyal States with you. This immense Administration party did not insist upon your regulating your policy strictly by the tenets of any of the old party platforms; they would have cheerfully sustained you in anything and everything that might have served to put down the rebellion. I am confident, you might have

issued your emancipation manifesto, you might have
dismissed your generals one after the other, long before
you did it—and a large majority of the people would have
firmly stood by you. All they wanted was merciless
energy and speedy success. You know it yourself, there
are now many prominent Democrats supporting you,
who go far beyond the program of the Chicago platform.

Whatever proportion of Republicans may have entered
the Army,—if the Administration had succeeded in preserving its hold upon the masses, your majorities would
at any moment have put the majorities of 1860 into the
shade and no insidious party contrivances could have
prevailed against you. But the general confidence and
enthusiasm yielded to a general disappointment, and there
were but too many Republicans, who, disturbed and confused by the almost universal feeling of the necessity of a
change, either voted against you or withheld their votes.
I *know* this to be a fact.

That some of our newspapers "disparaged and vilified
the Administration" may be true, although in our leading journals I have seen little else than a moderate and
well-measured criticism. I know of none that had ever
impeached your good faith or questioned your motives.
If there were no real and great abuses, the attacks on
your Administration were certainly unjustifiable. But
if there were, then, I think, the misfortune was not that
the abuses were criticised, but that the responsible individuals were not promptly and severely held to account.
It is my opinion, and I expect I shall hold it as long as I
live, that a party, in order to remain pure and efficient,
must be severe against its own members; it can disarm
the criticism of its opponents by justly criticising and
promptly correcting itself. But however that may be,
I ask you in all candor, what power would there have been
in newspaper-talk, what power in the talk of demagogues

based upon newspaper-talk, had the Administration been able to set up against it the evidence of great successes?

I feel that in regard to one important point I have not been quite clear in my letter of the 8th. When speaking of "your friends," I did not mean only those who in 1860 helped to elect you; I did not think of old, and, I may say, obsolete political obligations and affinities. But I meant all those, who fully understanding and appreciating the tendency of the revolution in which we are engaged, intend to aid and sustain you honestly in the execution of the tremendous task which has fallen to your lot. Nor did I, when speaking of the duty and policy of being true to one's friends, think of the distribution of favors in the shape of profitable offices. But I did mean that in the management of the great business of this revolution only such men should be permitted to participate, who answer to this definition of "friends" and on whose sympathies you can rely as securely as upon their ability.

I am far from presuming to blame you for having placed old Democrats into high military positions. I was also aware that McClellan and several other generals had been appointed on the recommendation of Republican governors and Members of Congress. It was quite natural that you appointed them when the necessities of the situation were new and pressing and everybody was untried. But it was unfortunate that you sustained them in their power and positions with such inexhaustible longanimity after they had been found failing—failing not only in a political but also in a military sense.

Was I really wrong in saying, that the principal management of the war has been in the hands of your opponents? Or will anybody assert, that such men as McClellan and Buell and Halleck and others of that school have the least sympathy with your views and principles, or that their

efficiency as military leaders has offered a compensation
for their deficiency of sympathy, since the first has in
eighteen months succeeded in effecting literally nothing
but the consumption of our resources with the largest and
best appointed army this country ever saw;—since the
second by his criminal tardiness and laxity endangered
even the safety of the metropolis of the Middle States,
and since the appearance of the third on the battlefield
of Shiloh served suddenly to arrest the operations of our
victorious troops and to make shortly afterwards the
great Army of the West disappear from the scene as by
enchantment, so as to leave the country open to the
enemy? Has it not been publicly stated in the newspapers
and apparently proved as a fact, that the enemy from
the commencement of the war has been continually
supplied with information by some of the confidential
subordinates of so important an officer as Adjutant-
General Thomas? Is it surprising that the people at
last should have believed in the presence of enemies at
our own headquarters, and in the unwillingness of the
Government to drive them out? As for me, I am far
from being inclined to impeach the loyalty and good faith
of any man; but the coincidence of circumstances is such,
that if the case were placed before a popular jury, I would
find it much easier to act on the prosecution than on the
defense.

You say that our Republican generals did no better;
I might reply, that between two generals of equal military
inefficiency I would in this crisis give a Republican the
preference. But that is not the question. I ask you
most seriously—what Republican general has ever had
a fair chance in this war? Did not McClellan, Buell,
Halleck and their creatures and favorites claim, obtain
and absorb everything? Were not other generals obliged
to go begging merely for a chance to do something for

their country, and were they not turned off as troublesome
intruders while your Fitzjohn Porters flourished?

No, sir, let us indulge in no delusions as to the true
causes of our defeat in the elections. The people, so
enthusiastic at the beginning of the war, had made
enormous sacrifices. Hundreds of millions were spent,
thousands of lives were lost apparently for nothing. The
people had sown confidence and reaped disaster and
disappointment. They wanted a change, and as an
unfortunate situation like ours is apt to confuse the minds
of men, they sought it in the wrong direction. I entreat
you, do not attribute to small incidents, the enlisting
of Republican voters in the Army, the attacks of the press
etc., what is a great historical event. It is best that you,
you more than anybody else in this Republic, should see
the fact in its true light and acknowledge its significance:
the result of the elections was a most serious and severe
reproof administered to the Administration. Do not
refuse to listen to the voice of the people. Let it not
become true, what I have heard said: that of all places
in this country it is Washington where public opinion is
least heard, and of all places in Washington, the White
House.

The result of the elections has complicated the crisis.
Energy and success, by which you would and ought to
have commanded public opinion, now form the prestige
of your enemies. It is a great and powerful weapon, and,
unless things take a favorable turn, troubles may soon
involve not only the moral power but the physical existence of the Government. Only relentless determination,
heroic efforts on your part can turn the tide. You must
reconquer the confidence of the people at any price.

One word in vindication of myself, the writer of this
letter. I pray you most earnestly not to attribute the
expressions of grief and anxiety coming from devoted men

like myself to a pettish feeling of disappointment in not
"seeing their peculiar views made sufficiently prominent."
When a man's whole heart is in a cause like ours, then, I
think, he may be believed not to be governed by small
personal pride. Besides, the spectacle of war is apt to
awaken solemn and serious feelings in the heart of one
who has some sympathy with his fellow-beings. I command a few thousands of brave and good fellows, entitled
to life and happiness just as well as the rest of us; and
when I see their familiar faces around the camp-fires and
think of it, that to-morrow they may be called upon to
die,—to die for a cause which for this or that reason is
perhaps doomed to fail, and thus to die in vain, and when
I hear the wailings of so many widows and orphans, and
remember the scenes of heartrending misery and desolation I have already witnessed—and then think of a possibility that all this may be for nothing—then I must
confess my heart begins sometimes to sink within me and
to quail under what little responsibility I have in this
business. I do not know, whether you have ever seen a
battlefield. I assure you, Mr. President, it is a terrible
sight. I am, dear sir,

Truly your faithful friend.

FROM PRESIDENT LINCOLN

Executive Mansion,
Washington, Nov. 24, 1862.

Gen. Carl Schurz

My dear Sir I have just received, and read, your
letter of the 20th. The purport of it is that we lost the
late elections, and the administration is failing, because the
war is unsuccessful; and that I must not flatter myself
that I am not justly to blame for it. I certainly know
that if the war fails, the administration fails, and that
I *will* be blamed for it, whether I deserve it or not. And

I ought to be blamed, if I could do better. You think I could do better; therefore you blame me already. I think I could not do better; therefore I blame you for blaming me. I understand you *now* to be willing to accept the help of men, who are not republicans, provided they have "heart in it." Agreed. I want no others. But who is to be the judge of hearts, or of "heart in it"? If I must discard my own judgment, and take yours, I must also take that of others; and by the time I should reject all I should be advised to reject, I should have none left, republicans, or others—not even yourself. For, be assured, my dear Sir, there are men who have "heart in it" that think you are performing your part as poorly as you think I am performing mine. I certainly have been dissatisfied with the slowness of Buell and McClellan; but before I relieved them I had great fears I should not find successors to them, who would do better; and I am sorry to add, that I have seen little since to relieve those fears. I do not clearly see the prospect of any more rapid movements. I fear we shall at last find out that the difficulty is in our case, rather than in particular generals. I wish to disparage no one—certainly not those who sympathize with me; but I must say I need success more than I need sympathy, and that I have not seen the so much greater evidence of getting success from my sympathizers, than from those who are denounced as the contrary. It does seem to me that in the field the two classes have been very much alike, in what they have done, and what they have failed to do. In sealing their faith with their blood, Baker, an Lyon, and Bohlen, and Richardson, republicans, did all that men could do; but did they any more than Kearney, and Stevens, and Reno, and Mansfield, none of whom were republicans, and some, at least of whom, have been bitterly, and repeatedly, denounced to me as secession sympathizers? I will not perform the ungrateful task of comparing cases of failure.

In answer to your question "Has it not been publicly stated in the newspapers, and apparently proved as a fact, that from the commencement of the war, the enemy was continually supplied with information by some of the confidential sub-

ordinates of as important an officer as Adjutant General
Thomas?" I must say "no" so far as my knowledge extends.
And I add that if you can give any tangible evidence upon
that subject, I will thank you to come to the City and do so.
Very truly your friend
A. LINCOLN

TO PRESIDENT LINCOLN

ARMY OF THE POTOMAC,
STAFFORD C. H., VA., Jan. 24, 1863.

.   .   .   .[1]

Permit me a few words about the recent occurrences
on the Rappahannock. I have spent several days there
and feel compelled to say to you that I have seen and
heard a great many things, which deeply distressed me.
Let me say to you that from what I have seen and heard
I am convinced the spirit of the men is systematically
demoralized and the confidence in their chief systematically broken by several of the commanding-generals.
I have heard generals, subordinate officers and men say
that they expect to be whipped anyhow, "that all these
fatigues and hardships are for nothing, and that they
might as well go home." Add to this, that the immense
army is closely packed together in the mud, that sickness
is spreading at a frightful rate, that in consequence of all
these causes of discouragement desertion increases every
day—and you will not be surprised if you see the army
melt away with distressing rapidity. Let us spread out
our wings, especially the right; let the cavalry be made
efficient and give the enemy no rest, and let every favorable moment be improved for making expeditions with
corps or grand divisions around the enemy's flanks.

[1] Two paragraphs about giving Gen. Stahel a cavalry-reserve corps.
See the next letter.

Only in this way we can accomplish something—only in this way we can preserve the Army.

TO PRESIDENT LINCOLN

CAMP NEAR FALMOUTH, Jan. 25, 1863.

I have just seen the Philadelphia *Inquirer*, which publishes a list of your nominations for major-general-ships containing my name but not that of General Stahel. You remember the conversations we have had upon that subject and my emphatic declaration that I would not be in any manner in General Stahel's way; that he yielded to me the command of the 11th Corps and would be satisfied with the command of the cavalry-reserve; that I accepted this sacrifice if he could be made a major-general as well as myself. You informed me kindly that this would be done. If there are circumstances preventing General Stahel's nomination together with mine, I feel in honor bound to respectfully decline the distinction you were kind enough to confer upon me, at the same time thanking you most sincerely for this great mark of friendly consideration. You will pardon me for this, for it has always been my principle to be true to my friends and to stand up to a word I once have given. I will much rather command the 11th Corps as a brigadier-general or not command it at all, than wear the two stars, setting aside a man who is worthy of preferment, deserves my friendship and to whom I had the honor to carry your promise of promotion.[1]

[1] The following letters show how averse Schurz was to turning this incident to his own advantage in any way, then or subsequently:—

"NEW YORK, Feb. 27, 1897.

"MAJOR GEO. W. DAVIS,

  "War Department.

"Dear Sir: In compliance with your request I herewith return the letter you have submitted to my inspection. The letter is unquestionably genuine. That it was not found on the files of the War Department does

TO LESLIE COMBS (INDIRECTLY)

NEAR CHATTANOOGA, Nov. 6, 1863.

GEO. D. PRENTICE, Editor of the Louisville *Journal:*

In your paper of November 3d I see a letter signed by Mr. Leslie Combs, in which the following allusion is made to me: "Our children have fought in every battlefield, and never one fled as Carl Schurz and his gang of freedom-shriekers did at Chancellorsville." I am not in the habit of replying to calumny and abuse springing from the impure inspirations of party spirit; but General Leslie Combs being a man of note, I deem it proper to avail myself of this opportunity to stop a slander which political enemies seem bent upon sustaining by frequent repetition.

I wish therefore to say, that in asserting that "Carl

---

not surprise me. Occasionally letters of a 'private and personal' nature would pass between President Lincoln and myself which did not go on the official files. President Lincoln, judging this one to be of such a character, probably withheld it for that reason. I do not remember whether it was answered by him in writing, and I have no means of ascertaining it because all my correspondence of the war period perished in a railroad fire. [See *post*, p. 375.]

"I do not know how this letter got into the hands of a third person. It occurs to me that Mr. Lincoln may have given it as a memento to General Stahel when that officer, as he probably did, called upon the President to offer his thanks for the promotion. This, however, is only a random guess.

"But, if you will pardon the question, is this letter, which certainly does not throw any light upon anything connected with the operations of the army, a proper document to be published in the *Rebellion Record?* To me it would seem quite doubtful, and this doubt I respectfully submit.

"Very sincerely yours,
"C. SCHURZ."

"HOTEL ARLINGTON, 18–20 WEST 25TH STREET,
"NEW YORK, May 26, 1912.

"FREDERIC BANCROFT, Esq.,

"My dear Sir: . . . Mr. Schurz's surmise that the letter was given to me by the President is correct, but I wonder why Mr. Schurz, with whom I had several war-time talks at various times, never made any reference to this matter. . . . Sincerely yours,

"JULIUS STAHEL."

Schurz fled at Chancellorsville," Mr. Combs *lies*. I choose the word *"lies"*—although with extreme reluctance and regret—upon due consideration of its meaning; for, if Mr. Leslie Combs has inquired into the facts, he must know that he is saying what is false; and, if he has made no such inquiry, then he gives with unpardonable levity the sanction of his name to a statement which is most injurious to another man's reputation, and which he does not know to be true. I wish to add that in saying, "Mr. Leslie Combs lies," I hold myself responsible for what I say.

This may seem equivalent to a challenge, and so it is. I do not, however, mean to fight a duel with Mr. Leslie Combs. Being a good pistol-shot, I might perhaps easily kill him, which I should not like to do; or, if he is equally skillful, he might kill me—and I should be sorry to die on so trifling an occasion; or we might not hurt each other, and then it would be a farce. Besides, I am opposed to dueling on principle.

But I challenge Mr. Leslie Combs to a different kind of a contest, which will be preferable to a common duel as a test of personal courage. I invite him to the hospitality of my headquarters in the camp of the Army of the Cumberland. I will share with him my tent, my blankets, my meals; but I invite him also to accompany me personally in the next battle, and not to leave me a single moment. There Mr. Leslie Combs may determine whether he will have the heart to repeat that calumny, or whether it would not be better for him and more honorable to retract it.

I trust, sir, you will give this letter the same publicity which you accorded to that of Mr. Leslie Combs.

Yours respectfully,

CARL SCHURZ.

THE TREASON OF SLAVERY[1]

. . . .

I have led you through this . . . summary of our
social and political history for the purpose of showing
that our present struggle is the natural outgrowth of
an antagonism of which we find the germs in the first
organization of American society. I have shown, also,
that the aristocratic element, after having identified itself
with the system of slavery, acted upon the command
of its necessities. Its principal crime consisted at the
beginning, and consists to-day, in its identifying itself
with slavery instead of yielding to the democratic principles upon which a healthy National organization could
be founded. But remaining faithful to slavery, it was
impelled by the irresistible power of logic, from step to
step, until at last it landed in the domain of high treason.
Finding slavery endangered by public opinion, it was
natural that it should shut itself up against that dangerous
influence. But being yoked together in a common National organization with the threatening influence of
the expansive democratic element, it was natural that it
should endeavor to control or suppress it by all the expedients of corruption and intimidation. But failing in this
finally, and still insisting upon the perpetuation of slavery,
it was natural that it should try to shut itself up more
effectually—to isolate itself completely, by breaking up
the National organization which held it under an influence
so dangerous to its existence. Thus slavery, impelled by
its necessities from step to step, was the real, the natural
traitor against the American nationality, and the Southern
people are only the victims of its inevitable treason. But
if slavery, the enemy of American nationality, could not

[1] Speech delivered at the Academy of Music, Brooklyn, Oct. 7, 1864.

15

act otherwise without giving itself up, how are you to act, the defenders of American nationality?

The answer would seem to every unprejudiced mind as plain as the question. Still, strange as it may appear at first sight, there is a difference of opinion. Only three lines of policy suggest themselves. The most fertile ingenuity could not invent any beyond these three. Either we must permit the slave aristocracy to isolate itself territorially as well as politically—that is, we must consent to the breaking up of the American nationality; or secondly, we must preserve our Union and nationality by striking down its enemies in arms and by extinguishing the social and political agency which in its nature is disloyal and anti-National; or, thirdly, we must invite the slave aristocracy back into the National organization, offering to it that supreme and absolute control of our National concerns without which it cannot insure its permanency in the Union.

On the first proposition the people have already pronounced their judgment. To accept it was impossible. The question has been discussed thousands of times; and every enlightened mind, every true American heart, has always arrived at the same conclusion. Considerations of policy, National existence, safety, liberty, civilization, peace, all lead to the same result. The old cry, "The Union must and shall be preserved!" is not a mere watchword of party. It is the instinctive outcry of the deepest convictions, of the immovable religious faith of the American mind. This conviction, this faith, is proclaimed by the thunder of our artillery; it is confirmed by our victories; it is sealed with the blood of the people. This question is no longer open to discussion.

But the conflict between the two other propositions is the real point at issue in our present controversy. Our opponents may speak of tyranny, but the violence of

their own denunciations gives the lie to their own assertions. It is dust thrown into the eyes of a deluded
multitude. They may no longer have the courage to say
that they are for slavery; they are still base enough to
say that they are not against it. All their tirades and
declamations hang loosely around this sentiment. The
true issue, divested of all its incidental questions, is this:
A nation ruled by the slave-power, or a nation governing
itself. For the first, they are ready to imperil victory
and peace and union; for the second, we are ready to
destroy slavery forever.

The second line of policy before mentioned has been
consistently acted upon by the party holding the reins
of government during the struggle. On some occasion
President Lincoln uttered the following words: "I am not
controlling events, but events control me." These
words, applicable of course only to the leading measures
of policy, have been denounced and ridiculed as a confession of weakness; I see in them a sign of a just understanding of his situation. Revolutionary developments
are never governed by the preconceived plans of individuals. Individuals may understand them, and shape their
course accordingly; they may aid in their execution and
facilitate their progress; they may fix their results in the
form of permanent laws and institutions—but individuals
will never be able to determine their character by their
own conceptions. Every such attempt will prove abor-
tive, and lead to violent reactions. A policy which is
so controlled by the spirit of the times, and is based upon
a just appreciation of circumstances, may, perhaps, not
be very brilliant, but it will be safe, and above all, eminently democratic. And I venture to suggest that a great
many of those who indulge in the highest sounding figures
of speech as to what great things they would do, if they
had the power, would hardly be capable of conceiving so

wise an idea as that which the President expressed in language so simple and so modest.

And thus the Government has steadily followed the voice of events—slowly, indeed, but never retracing a step. Slowly, did I say? We are apt to forget the ordinary relations of time, at a moment when the struggle of a century is compressing itself into the narrow compass of days and hours. What was to be done, and what was done, is plain. I showed you how, after the establishment of the first colonies, the democratic spirit natural to new organizations failed to absorb the aristocratic element, on account of the introduction of slavery. I showed you how the philosophy of the eighteenth century, and the lofty spirit of the Revolutionary period, failed in gradually abolishing slavery in consequence of an economic innovation. Those two great opportunities were lost; the full bearing of the question was not understood. But now the slave-power itself has made us understand it. Now, at last, slavery has risen in arms against our nationality. It has defied us, for our own salvation, to destroy it. Slavery itself, with its defiance, has put the weapon into our hands, and in obedience to the command of events the Government of the Republic has at last struck the blow. Treason has defied us, obliged us to strike it, and we have struck it on the head. The Government has not controlled events, but, resolutely following their control, proclaimed the emancipation of the slave. Mr. Lincoln was not the originator of the decree, he was the recorder of it. The executors are the people in arms.

But the opponents of the Government say by this act the war was diverted from its original object; that it was commenced for the restoration of the Union only, but was made a war for the abolition of slavery. It will not be difficult to show the shallowness of this subterfuge of bad consciences. Those who read history understandingly

will know that revolutionary movements run in a certain
determined direction; that the point from which they
start may be ascertained, but that you cannot tell beforehand how far they will go. The extent of their
progress depends upon the strength of the opposition
they meet; if the opposition is weak and short, the revolution will stop short also; but if the opposition is
strong and stubborn, the movement will roll on until
every opposing element in its path is trodden down and
crushed.

I invite our opponents to look back upon the war of
the Revolution. Was the Revolution commenced for
the achievement of independence from Great Britain?
No; it was commenced in opposition to the arbitrary
acts of the British Government; it was commenced for
the redress of specified grievances, and in vindication of
colonial rights and liberties. Far-reaching minds may
have foreseen the ultimate development, but it is well
known that some of the most energetic Revolutionary
characters disclaimed most emphatically all intention to
make the colonies independent not long before independence was actually declared. And how did they come to
divert the Revolutionary War from its original object?
The process was simple. They permitted themselves to
be controlled by events. In the course of the struggle they
came to the conclusion that the rights and liberties of the
colonies would not be secure as long as the British Government had the power to enforce arbitrary measures in this
country; they saw that British dominion was incompatible
with American liberty. Then independence was declared.
It was decreed by the logic of events; it was recorded by
Jefferson; it was enforced by Washington.

This was the way in which a struggle for a mere redress
of grievances was "perverted" into a struggle for the
abolition of British dominion. Is there anybody, to-day,

bold enough to assert that this perversion was illegitimate? Let us return to the crisis in which we are engaged.

We went into the war for the purpose of maintaining the Union, and preserving our nationality. Although it was the slave-power which had attempted to break up the Union, we did, at first, not touch slavery in defending the Union. No, with a scrupulousness of very doubtful merit, slavery was protected by many of our leaders—especially one of them, who at that time held the highest military command, made it a particular object not to hurt slavery while fighting against the rebellious slave-holder, and he exhausted all the resources of his statesmanship for that purpose. It is true he exhausted, at the same time, the patience of the people.

That statesmanship threatened to exhaust all our military and financial resources; but if, indeed, it did threaten to exhaust the resources of the rebellion, the threat was very gentle. You remember the results of that period of kid-glove policy, which the South found so very gentlemanly: reverse after reverse; popular discontent rising to despondency; ruin staring us in the face. The war threatened, indeed, to become a failure; and if the resolution of the Chicago Convention, which declared the war a failure, had special reference to the period when the distinguished candidate of the Democratic party was general-in-chief, then, it must be confessed, the Chicago Convention showed a certain degree of judgment.

Gradually it became clear to every candid mind that slavery, untouched, constituted the strength of the rebellion; but that slavery, touched, would constitute its weakness. The negro tilled its fields, and fed its armies; the negro carried its baggage and dug its trenches; and the same negro was longing for the day when he would be permitted to fight for the Union, instead of being forced to work for the rebellion. To oblige him to work for the rebellion, instead of permitting him to fight for the Union, would have been more than folly—it would have been a crime against the Nation.   To give him his freedom, then, was an act of justice not only to him, but to the American Republic.

If the rebellious slave-power had submitted, after the first six months of the war, it is possible that slavery might have had another lease of life.   But its resistance being vigorous and stubborn, and not only that, its resistance being crowned with success, it became a question of life or death—the death of the Nation, or the death of slavery.   Then the Government chose.   It chose the life of the Nation by the death of slavery; and the revolution rolled over the treasonable institution, and crushed it wherever it found it.

Could an act which undermined the strength of the enemy, and in the same measure added to our own— could that be called diverting the war from its original purpose?   Was not the object of the war to restore the Union?   How then could we refrain from using for our purposes an element which was certain to contribute most powerfully to that end?   Was it not the object of the war to make the Union permanent by restoring loyalty to the Union?   But by what means in the world can loyalty be restored, if it is not by crushing out the element which breeds disloyalty and treason as its natural offspring?

But if it is the opinion of our opponents that it was the original object of the war to lay the North helpless at the feet of the South, then it must be admitted the war is now much perverted from its original object.

The matter stands clear in the light of experience. Every man who professes to be for the Union, and shows any tenderness for an agency which is bound to destroy the Union, has in his heart a dark corner into which the spirit of true loyalty has not yet penetrated.   And on the other hand, every man, whatever his previous opinions may have been, as soon as he throws his whole heart into the struggle for the Union, throws at the same time his whole heart into the struggle against slavery.

Look at some of the brightest names which the history of this period will hand down to posterity; your own Daniel S. Dickinson, Benjamin F. Butler of Massachusetts, the venerable Breckenridge of Kentucky, the brave Andrew Johnson of Tennessee and many thousands of brave spirits of less note. You cannot say that they were abolitionists; but they are honestly for the death of slavery, because they are honestly for the life of the Nation.

Emancipation would have been declared in this war, even if there had not been a single abolitionist in America before the war. The measure followed as naturally, as necessarily, upon the first threatening successes of the rebellion, as a clap of thunder follows upon a flash of lightning. Nay, if there had been a lifelong pro-slavery man in the Presidential chair, but a Union man of a true heart and a clear head—such a man as will lay his hand to the plow without looking back—he would, after the first year of the rebellion, have stretched out his hand to William Lloyd Garrison, and would have said to him, "Thou art my man." Listening to the voice of reason, duty, conscience, he would have torn the inveterate prejudice from his heart, and with an eager hand he would have signed the death-warrant of the treacherous idol.

And you speak of diverting the war from its legitimate object! As in the war of the Revolution no true patriot shrank back from the conclusion that colonial rights and liberties could not be permanently secured, but by the abolition of British dominion, so in our times no true Union man can shrink back from the equally imperative conclusion that the permanency of the Union cannot be secured, but by the abolition of its arch-enemy—which is slavery. The Declaration of Independence was no more the natural, logical and legitimate consequence of the struggle for colonial rights and liberties than the emancipation proclamation is the natural, logical and legitimate consequence of our struggle for the Union. The emancipation proclamation is the true sister of the Declaration of Independence; it is the supplementary act; it is the Declaration of Independence translated from universal principle into universal fact. And the two great state papers will stand in the history of this country as the proudest monuments not only of American statesmanship, American spirit and American virtue, but also of the earnestness and good faith of the American heart. The fourth of July, 1776, will shine with tenfold luster, for its glory is at last completed by the first of January, 1863.

Thus the same logic of things which had driven the naturally disloyal slave aristocracy to attempt the destruction of the Union, impelled the earnest defenders of the Union to destroy slavery.

Still, we are told that the emancipation proclamation had an injurious effect upon the conduct of the war. This may sound supremely ridiculous at this moment, but it seems there is nothing too ridiculous for the leaders of the opposition to assert, and nothing too ridiculous for their followers to believe. Still let us hear them. They say that the anti-slavery policy of the Government divided the North and united the South. And who were these patriots who so clamorously complained of the divisions in the North? They were the same men who divided.

I will tell them what the anti-slavery policy of the Government did do.

It furnished a welcome pretext for those in the North whose loyalty was shaky, and it permanently attached to our colors four millions of hearts in the South whose loyalty was sound. It brought every man down to his true level. It made the negro a fighting patriot, and it made the pro-slavery peace Democrat a skulking tory. It added two hundred thousand black soldiers to our armies, and it increases their number daily.

I wish to call your special attention to this point. I will not discuss the soldierly qualities of the negro. Although on many bloody fields he has proved them, and although I consider a black man fighting for his own and our liberty far superior, as a soldier, to a white man who dodges a fight against slavery, yet, for argument's sake, I am willing to suppose that the negro soldier is best to be used as a garrison and guard soldier on our immense lines of railroads, in fortified places and posts. This, not even our opponents will deny. But do they not see that, in using him thus, we can release so many white veterans from such duty and send them forward to the battle-field? Do they not see that only in this way it becomes possible to effect those formidable concentrations of military power, and thus to achieve those glorious results, which have made the rebellion reel and the hearts of the Northern traitors quake? Do they not see that, while it may not be the negro who beats the enemy on the bat-tlefield, it is more than doubtful whether, without the negro reinforcements, we could hurl such strength against the enemy as makes victory sure? No wonder that there are opposed to the negro soldiers those whose cheeks grew pale when they heard of the taking of Atlanta, and of Sheridan whirling the rebels out of the Valley of Virginia.

The emancipation proclamation, I say, added two hundred thousand black soldiers to our armies, and it may indeed have kept some white ones away, who merely wanted an excuse for not going anyhow. They say a white soldier cannot fight by the side of the negro. I know of white soldiers who were very glad to see the negro fight by their side. Ask our brave men at Petersburg, along the Mississippi and on the Southern coast. Their cheers, when they saw the black columns dash upon the works of the enemy, did not sound like indignant protest against the companionship. But those dainty folks who raise the objection as a point of honor will, I candidly believe, indeed not fight by the side of the negro, for they are just the men who will not fight at all.

The emancipation proclamation and the enlistment of negroes had an injurious effect upon the war! and because the emancipation decree had an injurious effect upon the war, the war is a "failure"! Indeed, it looks much like it! The peace Democrats may call a man who undoubtedly is high authority with them, they may call Jefferson Davis himself upon the stand as a witness, to say what he thinks of this failure; they may call for the professional opinions of Lee, Johnston, Hood and Early, and I am willing to abide by it. Attorneys Grant, Sherman, Sheridan and Farragut have already entered their pleas in the case, and, methinks, the judicial bench of history is about to pronounce the final verdict. And when that verdict is out, the genius of justice will rejoice that the power of the slave aristocracy could be beaten down in spite of the united efforts and of the exhaustion of all its resources, and that the cause of liberty and Union could triumph without the support of those whose hearts were divided between God and mammon. Yes, freedom will at one blow have conquered the whole force of its adversaries—those that were in arms against it as open enemies, and those that imperilled its success as uncertain friends.

But the emancipation proclamation did us still another service. It is well known that at the beginning of the war not only the sympathies of the most powerful European Governments were against us, but that the sympathies of European nations were doubtful. Our armies were

beaten, our prospects looked hopeless and to the current
running against us we had to offer no counterpoise.   The
nations of Europe looked across the ocean with anxious
eyes, and asked: "Will not now, at last, the great blow be
struck against the most hideous abomination of this age?
Are they so in love with it that they will not even destroy
it to save themselves?"   For you must know every enlightened European is a natural anti-slavery man.   His
heart, although burdened with so many loads, has not been
corrupted by the foul touch of that institution, which seems
to demoralize everything that breathes its atmosphere.
And when they saw, to their utter astonishment and disgust, that at first slavery was not touched, their hearts
sunk within them, and they began to explain the reverses
we suffered by the moral weakness of our cause.

At last the emancipation proclamation came. A
shout of triumph went up from every liberty-loving heart.
Once more the friends of freedom in each hemisphere
joined in a common sympathy.   Once more the cause of
the American people became the cause of liberty the
world over.   Once more our struggle was identified with
the noblest aspirations of the human race.   Once more our
reverses found a response of sorrow in the great heart of
mankind, and our victories aroused a jubilant acclaim
which rolled around the globe.   Do you remember the
touching address of the working men of Manchester?
While the instincts of despotism everywhere conspired
against us, while the aristocracy of Great Britain covered
us with their sneering contempt, while the laboring men
in England began to suffer by the stopping of the cotton
supply, and the nobility and the princes of industry told
them that their misery was our fault, the great heart of
the poor man rose in its magnificence, and the English
laborer stretched his hard hand across the Atlantic to
grasp that of our President and he said: All hail, Libera-

tor! Although want and misery may knock at my doors,
mind it not. I may suffer, but be you firm! Let the
slave be free, let the dignity of human nature be vindicated, let universal liberty triumph! All hail, American
people! we are your brothers!

And this sympathy did not remain a mere idle exchange
of friendly feelings. That sympathy controlled public
opinion in Europe, and that public opinion held in check
the secret desires of unfriendly Governments. Mason
and Slidell slink from antechamber to antechamber
like two ticket-of-leave men, and they find written above
every door the inscription: "No slavery here!" No
Government would dare to recognize the slaveholding
Confederacy without loading itself down with the contempt and curses of the people. The irresistible moral
power of a great and good cause has achieved for us victories abroad no less signal than the victories our arms
have achieved for us at home. Our arms will lay the enemies of the Nation helpless at our feet, but Emancipation
has pressed the heart of the world to our hearts.

But our opponents are not moved by all this. They
come with their last pitiable quibble, and I beg your
pardon for answering that also. They say: "Your
emancipation proclamation was nothing but wind after
all. The proclamation did not effect the emancipation of
the slaves." It is true, slavery is not abolished by the
proclamation alone, just as little as by the mere Declaration of Independence the British armies were driven away
and the independence of the colonies established. But
that declaration was made good forever by the taking of
Yorktown, and I feel safe in predicting that our proclamation will be made as good forever by the taking of
Richmond. But there is one point at which all parallel
with the Revolution fails. If in those times a person had
proposed to make an anti-independence man comman-

der-in-chief, he would have been put into the madhouse,
while in our days those are running around loose who
seriously try to persuade the people to make an anti-
emancipation man President of the United States.

Yes, incredible as it may seem to all who are not initiated
into the mysteries of American politics, the idea is seriously
entertained to carry out that third line of policy of which
I spoke before—to invite the slave-power back into the
National organization, offering to it that supreme and
absolute control of our National concerns without which
it cannot insure its permanency in the Union, and, adroitly
enough, this program has been condensed into a single
euphonious sentence which is well apt to serve as the campaign cry of a party. It is this: The Union must be
restored "as it was."

We are frequently cautioned against visionaries in
politics, because with their extravagant schemes they are
apt to lead people into dangerous and costly experiments.
But the visionaries in innovations are harmless compared
with the visionaries who set their hearts upon restoring
what is definitively gone, and has become morally impossible; for while the former may find it difficult to make
people believe in the practicability of their novel ideas,
the latter not rarely succeed in persuading the multitude
that what had been may be again. Such a visionary was
Napoleon, who planned the restoration of the empire of
Charlemagne; he flooded Europe with blood, and failed.
But the restoration of the empire of Charlemagne was mere
child's play in comparison with the restoration of the
Union "as it was," and a task far more difficult than that
to which the genius of old Napoleon succumbed is by a
discriminating fate wisely set apart for our "young
Napoleon" to perform. We are, indeed, assured by his
friends that he will again exhaust all the resources of his
statesmanship for that purpose. This statesmanship

is indeed very obliging. It can hardly have recovered
from its first exhaustion, and now it tells us kindly that
it is ready to exhaust itself once more. It would be
uncivil to accept the sacrifice. We will take the good-will
for the deed and dispense with it. Still, I consider it an
evidence of appreciative judgment on the part of his
friends to have selected just that candidate for a task which
can be performed only in his characteristic manner; setting out with a grand flourish of promises and coming
back with a grander flourish of apologies.

Restore the Union "as it was"! Did you ever hear of
a great war that left a country in the same condition in
which it had found it? Did you ever hear of a great revolution which left the political and social relations of the
contending parties as they had been before the struggle?
And there are visionaries who believe that relations which
rested upon mutual confidence can be restored when that
confidence has been drowned in a sea of blood. Do you
really think you can ever restore the confidence "as it
was" between two companions, one of whom has been
detected in an attempt to rob and murder the other in his
sleep? By no process of reasoning can you prove—nay,
not even in the wildest flights of your imagination can
you conceive the possibility that the relations between a
dominant and an enslaved race can be placed upon the
ancient footing, when two hundred thousand men of the
enslaved race have been in arms against their masters,
and in arms, too, at the call of the supreme authority of
the Republic. You cannot leave them such as they are;
you cannot permit them even to remember that they have
fought for us as well as for themselves, without following
up the events which made them what they are, to the full
consummation of the freedom of the race. And, on the
other hand, you cannot keep the race in bondage without
reducing those who are now fighting for their own and our

freedom to their former state of subjection; and you cannot do this without inaugurating the most sweeping, the most violent and bloody reaction against justice and liberty the world ever witnessed. And you cannot provoke that reaction without provoking another revolution on its heels. And now you speak of restoring the Union "as it was"!

Such things have been tried before, and we find the consequences on the records of history. England had her restoration of the Stuart dynasty, and it led to the revolution of 1688. France had her restoration of the Bourbon dynasty, and it led to the revolution of 1830. And why these revolutions? Because the Stuarts tried a reaction against the principles sealed with English blood at Naseby; because the Bourbons tried a reaction against the principles sealed with French blood at the Bastile, and on a hundred battlefields. Might not America profit by the example? You think you can restore the cotton dynasty without provoking reaction and another revolution?

But for our opponents, it seems, history has no intelligible voice. We have only to shake hands with the rebels, and the past is blotted out. We have only to act as if nothing had happened, and all will be as it was before something did happen. This is their promise. I appeal to the people. If your leaders promised you to revive all those fallen in battle, and to gather up the blood spilt on so many fields, and to infuse it into the veins of the resurrected, the presumption upon your credulity could not be more extravagant. Are you so devoid of pride, are you so completely without self-respect, as to permit so gross an imposition to be presented to you, as if you were capable of being trapped by it? Will you suffer them to insult your understanding, and to stamp you as incorrigible fools, with impunity? This, indeed, is one of the

cases in which we do not know what to admire most—
the towering impudence of the imposters, or the unfathomable stupidity of the victims.   Let those who go into the
open trap of the jugglers glory in the reputation of the
folly.   But a man of sense cannot permit himself to be
gulled by so transparent an absurdity without despising
himself.   I call upon you to vindicate the fair fame of
the Americans, as an intelligent people!

But it would be unfair to presume that those who raised
the artful cry have merely done so for the purpose of setting
a trap for political idiots.   There is really something which
they do want to restore, and there they are in earnest.
They really do mean to revive one feature of the old
Union; not that fidelity to the eternal principles of justice
and liberty, which in the early times of this Republic was
the admiration of mankind, but another thing, which has
become an object of disgust to every patriotic heart, and
has succeeded in creating doubts in the practicability of
democratic institutions.   I have spoken of the demoralizing principle: "To the victors belong the spoils"; and
how, during the most disgraceful period of our history,
victory with the spoils could only be obtained by abject
subserviency to the slave aristocracy.   And now what
they mean to restore is slavery to its former power.
Again the South is to be a unit for the interests of slavery;
again the united Southern vote, with a few Northern
States, is to command our elections; again the knife
of secession is to be flourished over the head of the Nation;
again our legislators and the people are to be terrorized
with the cry: "Do what our Southern brethren want you
to do, or they will dissolve the Union once more!" and
the terrors of the past are to be used as a powerful means
of intimidation for the future.   Again this great Nation
is to be swayed not by reason but by fear; and again the
interests and the virtue of the people are to be traded away

16

for public plunder. And so they stand before the rebels as humble suppliants with this ignominious appeal: "We are tired of being our own masters; come back and rule us! We are tired of our manhood; come back and degrade us! We do |not| feel well in a Union firmly established; come back and threaten us! We are eager once more to sell out the liberties and honor of the people for the sweets of public plunder; come, oh! come back and corrupt us!"

And in this disgraceful supplication they call upon a great and noble people to join them; to join after deeds and sacrifices so heroic, after a struggle for the Nation's free and great future, so glorious; to join at a moment when at last victory crowns our helmets, and when the day of peace, bright and warm, dawns upon our dark and bloody field. Ah, if it could be, if the Nation could so basely forget her great past, and her greater future; if the Nation could so wantonly denude herself of all self-respect and shame and decency, and plunge into the mire of this most foul prostitution; if this could be, then, indeed, betrayed mankind could not hate us with a resentment too deep; all future generations could not despise us with a contempt too scorching; there would be no outrage on the dignity of human nature in the annals of the world for which this base surrender would not furnish a full apology. If it could be so, then every one of your great battles would be nothing but a mass-murder of the first degree; the war with its ruin and desolation would have been nothing but an act of wanton barbarism. Then be silent of your glorious exploits, you soldiers in the field; conceal your scars and mangled limbs, you wounded heroes: you mothers and wives and sisters, who wear your mourning with pride, hide your heads in shame—for the triumphant rebel sits upon the graves of our dead victories, whip in hand, and with a mocking grin laughs at the dastardly self-degradation of his conquerors.

It is difficult to speak about this with calmness; yet we must make the effort.

This, then, is our situation: We have to choose between two lines of policy, represented by two parties—the one fully appreciating the tendency of the movement, and resolutely following the call of the times; fully and honestly determined to achieve the great object of preserving the Nation, and with consistent energy using every means necessary for that purpose; striking the rebellion by crippling the strength of the traitors, and restoring loyalty by stopping the source of treason; a party, not infallible indeed, but inspired by the noblest impulses of the human heart, and impelled by the dearest interests of humanity; in full harmony with the moral laws of the universe, in warm sympathy with the humane and progressive spirit of our age. Let its policy be judged by its fruits; the heart of mankind beating for our cause; the once down-trodden and degraded doing inestimable service for our liberty as well as their own; the armies of the Union sweeping like a whirlwind over rebeldom, and the rebellion crumbling to pieces wherever we touch it. Would it be wise to abandon a course of policy, which, aside of [from] our moral satisfaction, has given us such material guarantees of our success? And what inducement is offered to us for leaving it? Is it a policy still clearer and more satisfactory to our moral nature? Is its success still more certain, a result still more glorious? Let us see what they present us?

A party which does not dare to advance a single clear and positive principle upon which it proposes to act; a party which gives us nothing but a vague assurance of its fidelity to the Union coupled with the proposition of stopping the war, which alone can lead to the restoration of the Union; giving us a platform which its candidate does not dare to stand upon, and a candidate who quietly submits to the assertions of his supporters that he will be obliged to stand on the platform; a party which was waiting two months for a policy, and then found its policy upset by events two days after it had been declared; a party floundering like a drunken man between a treacherous peace and a faithful war, between disunion that shall not be and a kind of union that cannot be; a party which is like a ship without compass and rudder, with a captain who declares that he will not do what he is hired to do, with a set of officers who swear that he shall do it, with a crew who were enticed on board by false pretences, and who are kept by the vague impression that there is something good in the kitchen, and that vessel bound for a port which does not exist on the map. Is not this picture true in every touch?

And why all this wild confusion of ideas and cross purposes? Why all these ridiculous absurdities in its propositions? Simply because that party refuses to stand upon the clear and irrevocable developments of history, and denies the stern reality of accomplished facts; because it repudiates the great and inexorable laws by which human events are governed; because it shuts its eyes against the manifest signs of the times; because, while pretending to save the Union, it protects the Union's sworn enemy; because it deems it consistent with loyalty to keep alive the mother of treason; in one word, because it insists upon saving slavery in spite of its suicidal crime. And to this most detestable monomania it is ready to subordinate every other principle, every other interest, every other consideration of policy. To save slavery it throws all imaginable impediments in the way of every measure of the Government directed against the main strength of the rebellion; to save slavery it would rather have seen our armies doomed to defeat by weakness than strengthened for victory by the colored element; to save slavery it would rather have seen foreign Governments interfere in favor of the rebellion than the heart of mankind attached to our cause by the glorious decree of liberty; to save slavery it insists upon interrupting the magnificent course of our victories by a cessation of hostilities, which would save the rebellion from speedy and certain ruin; to save slavery it is ready to sacrifice the manhood of the people, and to lay them at the feet of the rebel aristocracy as humble suppliants for an ignominious rule. And this rank madness you would think of placing at the helm of affairs in a crisis which will decide our future forever?

I invite those of our opponents whose heads and hearts are not irretrievably wrapt in self-deception, to mount with me for a moment a higher watch-tower than that of party. Look once more up and down the broad avenues of your history. Show me your men in the first great days of the Republic whose names shine with untarnished luster, the men whom you parade in the foremost ranks when you boast before the world abroad of your Nation's greatness; there is no one of them who did not rack his brain to find a way in which the Republic could be delivered of the incubus of slavery. But their endeavors were in vain. The masses of the people did not see the greatness of the danger; their eyes were blinded by the seductive shine of momentary advantages. Then at once began one of those great laws by which human affairs right themselves, to operate. It is the law that a great abuse, urged on by its necessities, must render itself insupportable and defy destruction. Slavery grew up under your fostering care; with its dimensions grew its necessities. It asked for security at home, and what it asked was given. It asked for its share in what we held in common; and what it asked was given. It asked for the lion's share, and accompanied its demand with a threat, and what it asked was given. Then it asked all that we held in common. It asked for a dictatorship, and the accompanying threat became a defiance. The people of the North rose up and said: "So far and no farther!" Then slavery, with fatal madness, raised its arm against the palladium which cannot be touched with impunity; it urged into our hands the sword of self-defence; with blind insolence it threw into the face of the Nation the final challenge: "Kill me or I will kill thee!" The challenge could not be declined; the Nation refused to be killed, and slavery had the full benefit of its defiance. Do you not see that this decree of self-destruction was written by a hand mightier than that of mortal man?

And you will stand up against it? What are you about to do? Stop and consider! Slavery is dying fast. Its life is ebbing out of a thousand mortal wounds. Even its nearest friends in rebeldom are standing around its deathbed in utter despair; even they give it up. Hardly anything remains to be done but to close its eyelids, and to write the coroner's verdict: "Slavery having challenged the American Nation to mortal combat, killed itself by running madly into the sword of its antagonist." There it lies. And you—you would revive it? What? That you should have served it when it was in the fulness of its power, that, with a violent stretch of charity, we may understand, although it revolted our hearts. But to revive it when it is dying! To think of galvanizing into new life the hideous carcass whose vitality is being extinguished by the hand of fate! To attempt to fasten anew and artificially upon the Nation a curse of which for a century she longed in vain to be rid, and which at last is being wiped out by the great process of providential retribution! To resuscitate and nurse to new power of mischief the traitress that fell in an attempt to assassinate the Republic! Revive slavery in the midst of the nineteenth century!

Have you considered the enormity of the undertaking! Look around you! You see a great Republic purified of her blackest stain, which sent a blush of shame to her cheeks when the world abroad pointed to it; you see the heart of a noble people relieved of the galling burden of wrong and guilt; you see the nations of the world stretching out to us their brotherly hands and cheering us on with their inspiriting acclamations; from the downtrodden and degraded on earth to the very angels in heaven you hear all good and generous hearts join in swelling chorus of gratitude and joy, for at last the great iniquity is tumbling down—and now strike heaven and earth in the face and revive it?   Now poison the future of the Republic again, now imperil the life of the Nation again and revive it? Are you in earnest?   Here we stand before an atrocity so appalling that we seek in vain for a parallel on the darkest pages of history; we search in vain the darkest corners of the human heart to find a motive or reason that might excuse a crime so ridiculous for its folly, a folly so disgraceful for its wickedness.

But, thank God, it is impossible!   You think you can stem the irresistible current of events with your contrivances of political legerdemain, with your peace-cry, which is treason, and your war-cry, which is fraud; with your hypocritical protests against a tyranny which does not exist, and your artful imposition of a "Union as it was," and cannot again be!   With these pigmy weapons you think you can avert the sweep of gigantic forces!   Poor schemers, you might as well try to bring a railroad train, running at full speed, back to its starting-point, by butting your little heads against the locomotive.   You might as well try to catch in your arms the falling waters of the Niagara in the midst of the cataract, to carry them back to their source.   In vain you sacrifice your honor for what is infamous.   In vain you jeopardize the life of the Nation for what is dead!   The doom of your cause is written in the stars.   If you love yourselves, and want to secure the respect of your children, then, I beseech you, leave the scandalous and hopeless task to the ignorant and brainless, who may show as an excuse for the mad attempt, the weakness of their minds; and to those hardened villains who have become as insensible to the secret lash of conscience as to the open contempt of mankind. But if you will not, then happy those of you whose names will sink into utter oblivion, for only they will escape the ignominious distinction of becoming a mark for the detestation of posterity.

Revive slavery in the midst of the nineteenth century! And you dare to hope that the American people will aid in this crazy attempt? In this crime against justice, liberty and civilization? In this treason against future generations? You dare to expect the American Nation to commit suicide that slavery may live? Poor man, desist! You are undone. You do not seem to know that he must fail who appeals to the cowardice of the American people. Step out of the way of the Nation who marches with firm step and a proud heart after the martial drumbeat of her destiny. She feels that the struggle of ages compresses itself into the portentous crisis of this hour. It is for coming centuries she fights; and already she sees before her what was once only a patriotic dream rise into magnificent, sunlit reality! Liberty! Liberty and Union! one and inseparable! now and forever!

TO THEODOR PETRASCH[1]

BETHLEHEM, PA., Oct. 12, 1864.[2]

My dearest Friend: . . . Now I must give you a little lecture. I do not share your opinion as to what we should

[1] Petrasch had been like a sympathetic older brother to Schurz in their school-boy days. Schurz's lasting gratitude and affection were beautifully expressed in his letters. Petrasch had lately come to the United States to live.   [2] Translated from the German.

not do in the present crisis. You would surely not have
judged so if you had shared in the great struggles which
are now over. You may have been surprised when I
defend the present Administration in public. But I
believe that a few words regarding my way of looking at
matters will make things clear to you. Every crisis in
human affairs has one principal question to which all
minor questions must be subordinated. We are engaged
in a war in which the existence of the Nation, indeed, in
which everything is involved. A party has risen in this
country that threatens to overthrow all the results of the
war, and that at a moment at which the final outcome is
hardly doubtful, if the policy introduced is firmly adhered
to. There can be no doubt that the Government has made
great mistakes; persons who are directing the fate of the
country are certainly far from ideal statesmen, though
not nearly as insignificant as their critics would represent
them to be. But that is of minor importance. The most
vital thing is that the policy of the party moves in the
right direction, that is to say, that the slaveholder be
vanquished and slavery abolished. Whether this policy
moves in that direction skilfully or awkwardly, slowly or
rapidly, is a matter of little consequence in comparison
with the question whether a policy should be adopted
that would move in another, a wrong and disastrous,
direction. Accordingly, it was easy for me to choose. I
did not hesitate one moment. If Frémont and McClellan
had been my bosom friends and the members of the
present Administration had been my deadly enemies, I
should nevertheless have supported the latter.

Counter-considerations of a personal nature, which you
mention, such as vindictive criticism, could have no
weight. If one wants to accomplish something worth
while, one must not allow trifles to interfere. I have long
since risen above that sort of thing. People may say

what they like of me. I do not expect thanks nor even appreciation. The only true reward is within ourselves. The satisfaction I crave, I have at all times, to-day as well as formerly; it consists in having my ideas, which I have expressed in my own manner, repeated and disseminated by many persons in their own manner. Whether my patent rights are respected by them, is a matter of indifference to me. Indeed, the real purpose of the propagation of ideas is best attained if their origin is forgotten. In this respect, I have seen and experienced much that afforded me great satisfaction. The signs of the times are now very favorable. The reëlection of the President is almost certain unless some great military misfortune overwhelms us and that is not to be expected. The results of the election will determine the results of the war, and the worst will then be over. I am sending you one of my speeches, which has been published by the Congressional Committee, and in which, if you will take the trouble to read it, you will find my opinion on the nature and real object of the present party strife elucidated more clearly than I could possibly do it in a letter.

I wish to enlighten you on two other points. You are underrating the President. I grant that he lacks higher education and his manners are not in accord with European conceptions of the dignity of a chief magistrate. He is a well-developed child of nature and is not skilled in polite phrases and poses. But he is a man of profound feeling, correct and firm principles and incorruptible honesty. His motives are unquestionable, and he possesses to a remarkable degree the characteristic, God-given trait of this people, sound common-sense. Should you read his official documents and his political letters, you would find this verified to a surprising extent. I know him from personal observation as well as anyone, and better than the majority. I am familiar with his motives. I have seen him heroically wage many a terrible struggle and work his way through many a desperate situation with strength born of loyalty to conviction. I have criticised him often and severely, and later I found that he was right. I also know his failings; they are those of a good man. That he has committed great errors in the endless embarrassments of his position, cannot be denied, but it can be explained. Possibly other persons, if in his position, would not have committed the same errors, but they would have committed others. Moreover, Lincoln's personality has a special importance in this crisis. Free from the aspirations of genius, he will never be dangerous to a liberal government. He personifies the people, and that is the secret of his popularity. His Administration is the most representative that the history of the world has ever seen. I will make a prophecy that may now sound peculiar. In fifty years, perhaps much sooner, Lincoln's name will be inscribed close to Washington's on this American Republic's roll of honor. And there it will remain for all time. The children of those who persecute him now, will bless him.

I wish to enlighten you on another point. You believe that this Government has treated me with great lack of consideration. These are the facts: I had rather a serious disagreement with my commander, General Hooker. He is a man with no firm moral force but he is a good soldier and in addition has the talent publicly to display his achievements in the most favorable light. Because of a wrong which he did me, I demanded an investigation, at which I fared very well and he very ill. But naturally I had to resign my command under him, so as to protect my own safety. Unfortunately, just at that time the reorganization of the Western Army was completed and the campaign about to begin, so that Sherman was unable to carry out his promise to give me a new command at

once.   Accordingly I voluntarily decided, while I waited
in Nashville, to assume direction of a recruiting-camp in
order not to be idle.   The Government had nothing to do
with this.   When I finally requested permission to report
at Washington, the Government immediately placed a
command at my disposal which was much larger than
my former one.   There are two reasons which prompted
me to decline this offer;   in the first place, my wife's
health made it desirable that I remain with my family for
a time;   and furthermore, the political situation was such
that I had a more important field of action here than anywhere else.   Therefore, I am where I am, voluntarily.
That these matters have been misrepresented in German
newspapers, is not surprising.   This gives me no concern.
I never think of publicly refuting such misrepresentations.
However, even if there had been ground for complaint,
my acts would have been the same.   In times like these,
more important matters than individual interests or
sensitiveness are at stake.   He who cannot rise above
them, should content himself with selling peanuts.   I
feel myself so uplifted by the splendid and hopeful trend
of affairs that I could make far greater sacrifices than
those which fate has demanded of me.   This is a great
people and this is their time of greatest trial.   We are in
the smelting-furnace, and the metal flows richly while the
dross turns to ashes.   We shall have a great future.   But
I must not begin this chapter.

TO MRS. SCHURZ[1]

RALEIGH, April 18, 1865.

I should have written yesterday if I had been able to
shake off the gloom that has settled upon me since the

[1] Translated from the German.

arrival of the news of the murder of Lincoln. A thunder-
clap from the blue sky could not have struck us more
unexpectedly and frightfully. Our good, good Lincoln!
Even now, whenever my thoughts drift to some other
object and then return to this terrible event, I am obliged
to ask myself whether it really can be true. The mur-
derer who did this deed has killed the best friend of
the South. It is really patricide. The people of the
South may thank God that the war is over. If this
army had been obliged to march once more upon the
enemy, not a single house would have been left standing
in their path. The soldiers sat about their camp-fires,
first in gloomy consternation; then you might everywhere
have heard the words, "We wish that the fight were not
over yet!" It is fortunate that it is over. If the war
were continued now, it would resemble the campaigns
of Attila. The evening after the arrival of the fearful
news, all the guards in the city were doubled, and after
dark the streets were all closed and every person who
ventured out was arrested, because it was feared that
the soldiers would vent their rage by setting fire to the
city. The precaution was by no means superfluous.
It will be long before I can live down these impressions.
Our triumph is no longer jubilant.

Sherman has been negotiating with Johnson for the
last two days. I fear that Sherman will attempt to excel
Grant as mediator, since Grant has excelled him as leader
in battle. Immediately after we had marched in here,
he committed a great mistake. He invited the rebel
governor of North Carolina, Vance, to return here, and
to summon his legislature to convene. Fortunately,
Vance has not yet come.[1]

[1] Before this was received by Mrs. Schurz, at Bethlehem, Pa., she wrote,
in German, Apr. 21, 1865: "Now you know all, and I see you sitting silent
and alone, and thinking, thinking, thinking! All that Lincoln has ever

TO CHARLES SUMNER

BETHLEHEM, PA., May 9, 1865.

The news the papers bring from the South leads me to believe that efforts are being made in Mississippi, Georgia and, it seems, in North Carolina also, to hurry those States back into the Union. In Mississippi a State convention is called to meet at Vicksburg on the 1st of June, and General Dana, who commands there, is openly countenancing the project. In Georgia, Governor Brown is trying to legislate the State back into the Union by a simple repeal of the act of secession.

It is more than probable that the persons engaged in these movements are new-fangled Unionists only made so by our military successes. In North Carolina, Vance has issued a proclamation as "Governor of North Carolina," dated on the 28th of April. I know from General Schofield's own lips that he is in favor of the restoration to power of Vance and his legislature; at least he was so before I left that State, and I apprehend that in the other States above named the military commanders will hardly be sufficiently on their guard against the machinations of the old leaders.

said to you, the little struggles you had with each other, and the joyous hours, all must now come back to you, and make you alternately glad and sorrowful. He has been laid to rest, and yesterday all the inhabitants of our little town went in a long procession to the cemetery, where we listened to a beautiful address by Dr. Fickard, and from there we went to the church, where there was wonderful music. It was my first long walk. I went with the children. We were all dressed in black, and I felt as though we were following an old, faithful father to his last resting-place. I could cry my heart out, and Dr. Fickard's address touched the hearts of all. Now, everything is calm again, and my overwhelming, irrepressible sorrow is subsiding. I keep thinking: he could not have died a happier death—without pain, in full view of his victories, so he fell like a hero. And as you have always said, after Washington, he is our greatest President, and the greatest of all emancipators. How happy I am that you have served him so faithfully!"

The attention of those in power cannot be too frequently and too urgently called to the necessity of binding the military commanders by the strictest and most imperative instructions, and I would entreat you to do so as often as you find an opportunity. I had a very full conversation with the President immediately before my departure from Washington. The objects he aims at are all [that] the most progressive friends of human liberty can desire. But it is his policy, and in many respects a correct one, to bring about these results practically without making them the subject of popular discussion in the shape of an openly announced program. This will work very well if he has the right instruments to carry out his ideas in the rebel States, or if, by giving minute instructions, he can make such instruments as he has work in the traces. But in this respect nothing should be neglected, and above all, *no time should be lost.* If we only make a vigorous start in the right direction the problem will be easily solved. But if too much latitude is given to the mischievous elements in the South for the next few weeks, it will be exceedingly difficult to set matters right again, and in this respect I fear everything from the military commanders. I have pressed this matter upon the attention of the President as strongly as I could, but, I apprehend, another effort in the same direction on your part would not be superfluous. There is no problem within our whole political horizon that demands more immediate attention at the present moment. A false step now will bring new and endless troubles upon us.

I received the two papers containing the Louisiana debate and am obliged to you.

TO PRESIDENT JOHNSON

BETHLEHEM, PA., May 13, 1865.

Permit me to avail myself of the privilege you gave me, to write to you whenever I had anything worthy of consideration to suggest.

A few days ago I found it stated in the papers that the trial of the conspirators[1] was to be conducted in secret. I did not believe it until I now see [sic] it confirmed. I do not hesitate to say that this measure strikes me as very unfortunate, and I am not surprised to find it quite generally disapproved. Yesterday I returned from Philadelphia where I had spent two days, and I can assure you that among the firmest supporters of the Administration I did not hear a single voice in favor of it. I admit, I do not know what objects are intended to be gained by secrecy. I take it for granted that they are of no futile character. But if it is important that the accused should be convicted and sentenced and that, perhaps with a view to further developments, the testimony as it appears should be kept from some conspirators still at large, it is of vastly greater importance that the trial should be absolutely fair, not only in spirit but also in appearance.

When the Government charged, before the whole world, the Chiefs of the rebellion with having instigated the assassination of Mr. Lincoln, it took upon itself the grave obligation to show that this charge was based upon evidence sufficient to bear it out. I am confident you would not have ventured upon this step had you not such evidence in your possession. But the Government is bound to lay it before the world in a manner which will command the respect even of the incredulous. You will admit that a military commission is an anomaly in the judicial system of this Republic; still I will not question here

[1] Against Lincoln and his Cabinet.

its propriety in times of extraordinary dangers. At all events, to submit this case to a military commission, a case involving in so pointed a manner the credit of the Government, was perhaps the utmost stretch of power upon which the Government could venture without laying itself open to the imputation of unfair play. But an order to have such a case tried by a military court behind closed doors, thus establishing a secret tribunal, can hardly fail to damage the cause of the Government most seriously in the opinion of mankind. The presumption will be that evidence was to be elicited by a court made up for the purpose, by means not fit to be divulged; and evidence brought forth under such circumstances will certainly lose in weight what it may gain in completeness.

I repeat, I am far from supposing that the Government is unable to make good its charge; but even if it should fail to do so and admit its failure in the broad daylight of an open court, it would stand in a better attitude before the world than if it succeeded in establishing its charge only by the unseen transactions of a secret tribunal appointed for the occasion. This is the most important state-trial this country ever had. The whole civilized world will scrutinize its proceedings with the utmost interest, and it will go far to determine the opinion of mankind as to the character of our government and institutions.

I am well aware that some of the public papers which are indulging in strong language about this matter have for some time been confessedly hostile to Mr. Stanton and avail themselves of this opportunity to give color to their attacks. I may assure you that I do not belong to that class. I greatly esteem him for the eminent services he has rendered and even for his disregard of popularity, and I should deeply regret to see the honors he has won, curtailed by so vulnerable an act. But still more have I at

heart the character of this Government and the success
of your Administration; you may count me among its
most zealous supporters and among your sincerest friends.
But because I am sincere I cannot refrain from laying
before you my apprehensions as to the consequences of
this measure, and from testifying to the unequivocal dis-
approbation it has already met with among those whose
opinions we are in the habit of respecting. It is still time
to throw open the doors of the court-room, and I would
entreat you not to hesitate.

Pardon me for this frank and unreserved expression of
my views. I considered it the duty of a loyal man and
the office of a friend.

TO CHARLES SUMNER

BETHLEHEM, PA., June 5, 1865.

The President's proclamation concerning the provisional
government of North Carolina must have convinced you
that the policy of the Administration with regard to the
negro-suffrage question is far from being satisfactorily
settled. I had a long conversation with Mr. Johnson
about it immediately before I left Washington. He
showed me the "Executive order" in the original draft,
and I urged him with all possible energy not to do [take]
any step that could not be retraced until the situation would have fully disclosed itself. I saw very soon
that he had committed himself in favor of making Mr.
Holden provisional governor; I then made an effort to
persuade him to strike out that one passage limiting the
right of suffrage to those qualified by the provisions of the
old North Carolina constitution. He listened so atten-
tively that I was almost sure he would heed my advice.
I proposed to him to appoint some sensible and reliable
person to supervise the political action of our military

commanders in the South, to work out instructions, to superintend their execution, to keep the Government advised of what is going on, etc. The proposition pleased him exceedingly, and he even went so far as to ask me, whether I would return to Washington at his bidding to aid him in this matter. I replied that, although my plans run in another direction, I would sacrifice two or three months for this object. I left and did [have] not hear[d] from him since, but the Executive order shows the drift of things. Southern delegations are crowding into Washington, and I fear the President permits his judgment to be controlled by their representations. I doubt whether any member of the Cabinet asserts his influence in a contrary direction. The Union men of the South are almost all governed by their old prejudices, and no good can be expected from them. If they are permitted to be the principal advisers of the President, the South will soon be again in the hands of the pro-slavery element.

I would entreat you to go to Washington as soon as you conveniently can. The President's opinions are quite unsettled on the most vital points. I fear he has not that clearness of purpose and firmness of character he was supposed to have. If he were still in Tennessee, his struggles with his old enemies would arouse his combativeness, and that would sustain him. But that element is wanting in his present situation.

I see Wendell Phillips has made a speech in favor of downright repudiation, and the opposition press is already accusing you of entertaining the same sentiments. An expression you used in your eulogy on Lincoln is quoted in support of the charge. I think it is important that you should avail yourself of the first opportunity to repel this imputation. That is one of the things which no man who wants to exercise an influence must be suspected of favoring.

Unless the President calls me, which I think he will not, I shall soon go to St. Louis and try to start a large journalistic enterprise. St. Louis, by its geographical situation, is destined to exercise an immense influence from Galena to New Orleans and from Louisville to the Rocky Mountains. There is the place for a great paper. What do you think of the plan? And if you approve of it, who are, in your opinion, the public men in Missouri likely to go into it?

Now pardon me for taxing your friendship a little. The war has exhausted me a little in a financial point of view, and I must try to make some money next winter by lecturing. Do you know a suitable person who would be able and willing to arrange for me a number of engagements in New England and northern New York, that would cover some six or seven weeks? Years ago, Mr. Charles Slack did that business for me, but I do not know whether he is still in Boston.

I shall remain here two or three weeks longer. May I expect an answer from you here?

TO PRESIDENT JOHNSON

BETHLEHEM, PA., June 6, 1865.

The passage in your Executive order concerning the provisional government of North Carolina, to which I had the honor to call your attention at our last interview, has, as I then anticipated, been generally interpreted as a declaration of policy on your part adverse to the introduction of negro suffrage. So far, it is treated with calmness by most of the papers, but it is sure to become a subject of general and fierce discussion—not only among extremists but among men of moderate views—as soon as the old pro-slavery and disloyal element, I mean the oath-taking rebels, will have reasserted their influence

in the Southern States. This will be the case as soon
as, under the present system, any independent political
action is allowed in the South, as it is now in Virginia.
The question of negro suffrage will then become the burning issue and is likely to have great influence upon the
attitude of political parties and upon the relations between
Congress and the Executive. It will depend upon events
whether any difference of opinion will assume the character
of direct opposition to the Administration, and events,
if we may judge from present symptoms, bid fair to give
sharpness to the controversy.

This would be an unfortunate thing. It is important
that your views on this point should not be misunderstood
by the country. There will soon be an opportunity for
an open declaration. The line of policy you have followed
with regard to North Carolina cannot be applied to her
neighbor South Carolina. The reason is simple. The
elective franchise and eligibility are limited by the old
South Carolina constitution by a property qualification
consisting in the ownership of a certain quantity of land
and a certain number of slaves. Suppose then, when the
turn of South Carolina comes, you order that, whereas
the property qualification prescribed by the old constitution of South Carolina can no longer remain in force in
consequence of the emancipation of the slaves, and there
being no other rule in the laws of that State to guide the
Executive, the task of restoring the State of South Carolina be placed in the hands of her *whole* people, and that
at the election of delegates to a convention *all* loyal
inhabitants of South Carolina without distinction be
permitted to vote. The reasons for this course will be
clear and acceptable to every fair-minded man, and, as
the order applies to *South Carolina*, not even the Democrats will find fault with it.

This will be consistent with the theory that secession

never carried the State out of the Union, and also with the fundamental principle that all constitutive action must proceed from the people. In theory as well as fact, this procedure will be far more *democratic* than the policy you have adopted with regard to North Carolina. It may be argued without doing violence to the rules of logic that, although secession never carried any of the States out of the Union, it did break up the existing State governments and completely suspended the Constitutional relations of the seceded States with the Government of the United States. This was a revolutionary proceeding, which placed the Government of the United States in a condition, and imposed upon it a task, not foreseen in the Constitution. Nor does the Constitution point out any remedies except those lying within the sphere of the military power. Strictly speaking, the appointment of a civil governor for a State by the Executive of the United States is an extra-Constitutional act; nor has, according to the accepted Constitutional theory, the President the power to order a governor of a State to call a convention of the people. You rely upon the implied powers and obey the necessity arising from the extraordinary and unforeseen circumstances. Now I ask, is not in this extra-Constitutional condition of things the most natural, and also *the most democratic* remedy to be found in a direct appeal to the original source of sovereignty, the whole body of the people of a State? And in what way can that be done more effectually than by calling State conventions to be elected by *all* the inhabitants of the respective States without distinction of rank, property or color, excluding only those who have disqualified themselves by acts of rebellion?

I think of elaborating these ideas and laying them before the public in a series of letters. By the time Congress meets, the necessity of taking a broad ground will probably have so far disclosed itself, that views like the above will be shared by a large majority of that body, and it would be very desirable to have a cordial understanding and coöperation established between that body and the Executive. When publishing those letters I should like to address them to you, unless it be disagreeable to you. It would not commit you in any way, but prepare the public mind for what inevitably must come. Have you any objection to it?[1]

Meanwhile pardon me for saying that, under existing circumstances, every measure which does not place the business of reconstruction upon the *broadest* ground will, in my humble opinion, tend to increase the difficulties which necessarily must arise, and hamper your future action.

It seems you have dropped the idea of appointing some one to supervise and aid the political action of our military commanders in the South. I still think it would be an excellent arrangement for keeping the Government well informed of what is going on, for keeping the military commanders well advised of what is expected of them, for facilitating business generally and for preventing a great many mistakes which otherwise are very likely to be made.

FROM CHARLES SUMNER

BOSTON, June 15, 1865.

Where is your speech? It is evident that we must create a public sentiment which shall insist upon just safeguards for the future.

You will be listened to—and read. I hope you will give us the opportunity.

[1] This question seems never to have been answered, except very indirectly by calling Schurz to Washington and requesting him to make the Southern trip that soon followed.

There seems to be a strange hallucination at Washington—
and a strange logic.

How can the President expect to organize governments on
the plan he is pursuing! Then how can he undertake to
put a governor over a State, and at the same time say that he
has not the power to recognize loyal people as voters!

I deplore the course he has taken. It divides the North,
and, if not arrested, will postpone the day of tranquillity
and reconciliation.

TO MRS. SCHURZ[1]

WASHINGTON, June 16, 1865.

Well, now I know what the President wants: I am to
visit the Southern States, in order to inform myself thoroughly on the conditions prevailing there, give my opinion
of them to the Government and make certain suggestions.
He complained of being unable to procure reliable information and, consequently, being always obliged to act
in the dark. I went at once to Stanton to talk the matter
over with him. Stanton's answer to my inquiry was that
he considered it absolutely necessary that I accept the
mission; that my report, even if it did not decide the
President's course of action, would be of the most vital
interest in the discussions of the next Congress; that the
President could not simply put my report into his pocket;
that my opinions and experiences would go to the public
officially, and could not fail to have some influence. But
if I declined, the President would be able later to say to
the radicals: "I have acted upon the information which
was at my command. I wished to send down one of your
own men to enlighten me about the state of affairs and
give me his advice, but he did not wish to go!"

Stanton is right. I told the President this morning that

[1] Translated from the German.

I wished first to know if the plan could be made feasible by the withdrawal of my resignation [from the Army], or otherwise, and that I would then give him my decision. There is to be a session of the Cabinet this afternoon, at which it is intended to discuss the matter.

FROM CHARLES SUMNER

BOSTON, June 22, 1865.

I have received both your letters.[1] The last is very interesting.

Of course the policy of the President *must break down.* It cannot succeed. I am pained that he commenced it.

I am glad that he has invited you to journey in the rebel States. You *must go.* Let me know the *extra* premium on your policy. The friends of the cause here will gladly pay it. I write this in earnest and as business. Send me the bill; and do you go at once on the journey.

But before you go, make one more effort to arrest the policy of the President. Every step that he takes is a new encouragement to (1) the rebels at the South, (2) the Democrats at the North and (3) the discontented spirits everywhere. It is a defiance to God and Truth.

Of course, we shall fight this battle, and, I know, we shall prevail. It cannot be that this great and glorious Republic is to sink to such an imbecile and shameful policy.

TO CHARLES SUMNER

BETHLEHEM, June 27, 1865.

Your note of the 25th inst. reached me to-day. I shall certainly accept the President's proposal.

As to the gentleman who accompanied the Freedmen's

---

[1] This seems to refer to letters in answer to Sumner's letter of June 15th and a note of the 19th. Neither the originals nor copies have been found.

commission, I should be glad to have him, but I am sorry not to have heard of him before. The Government will pay about $30 a month for "a clerk" to accompany me, and I have already engaged a young man of my acquaintance and cannot well back out, but I intended to use him more as a copyist and "major-domo" than anything else. The gentleman you speak of would in many respects be of vastly more use to me, and if, as you say, friends of the cause will be glad to send him with me, I shall of course be happy to take him, but all I can offer him would be to share the travelling accommodations which the Government furnishes me. For the rest of the expenses he would have to look to our friends who send him. If this is the understanding I will see what arrangements I can make at Washington and then telegraph you from there.

I shall probably leave this place for Washington on the 29th and then go to Charleston by the first steamer.

I shall endeavor to do my duty to the best of my ability, although the trip is indeed no pleasure excursion. But, I repeat, you and every friend of the cause that can afford it ought to go to Washington as soon as possible and remain there. The governors are appointed, but there ought to be no convention held before the meeting of Congress.

I wrote you a few lines day before yesterday; I hope you have received them. Please let me hear from you— *and go to Washington.*

TO CHARLES SUMNER

BETHLEHEM, PA., July 3, 1865.

. . . The President was sick when I was at Washington and I did not see him. I shall write him once more before I leave, to convince him that it would be good policy, under

existing circumstances, not to have any elections held in
the Southern States previous to the meeting of Congress.
This is a point of great importance, and it would be well
for our friends to make a united effort in that direction.
The President must be talked to as much as possible; he
must not be left in the hands of his old associations that
are more and more gathering around him. . . .[1]

<hr/>

FROM CHARLES SUMNER

BOSTON, July 11, 1865.

Send your second [newspaper] letter to Geo. L. Stearns, Esq.,
Boston.   He will give it a final direction, and will inform you.

I send a copy of the *Advertiser*, from which you will see the
type of correspondence.

Be of good cheer.   We shall win this battle easier than any
of the others.   No State will be allowed a Representative in
Congress unless under government founded on the consent
of the governed and Equality before the law.   On this we are
resolved.   And the disorganized States may make up their
minds to the consequence.

Let them begin at once with complete justice to the negro.
Preach this doctrine—talk it wherever you go.   You will be
sustained.

Morally and intellectually the country is already with us.
So are most of the politicians.   The rest must follow; and the
Administration will not be allowed to lag behind.

But you know all this, and, I am sure, will proclaim it.

<hr/>

TO CHARLES SUMNER

Confidential.   SAVANNAH, Aug. 2, 1865.

The convictions with which I came here are becoming
strengthened every day.   The military rule cannot be

<hr/>

[1] Several sentences before and several after this paragraph are omitted
because they refer to unimportant details of the Southern trip, about to
begin.

withdrawn for some time. The great rock we have to steer clear of, is a general collision between the whites and blacks, which, in my opinion, would be brought on at once by the withdrawal of our forces. We must have sensible, clear-headed people here to superintend the affairs of the colored people. A great many indiscretions are being committed that do much mischief. I have not discussed the question of negro suffrage in my [newspaper] correspondence because I want to reserve that for my official reports. I do not wish it known that I am writing for the *Advertiser*. You will easily divine the reason. It is important that the Government as well as the people should understand that things are very far from being ripe yet for the restoration of civil government.

· · · · · · ·

TO MRS. SCHURZ[1]

JACKSON, MISS., Aug. 27, 1865.

About my experiences in the South, I can tell you only a few generalities. I have found all of my preconceived opinions verified most fully, no, more than that. The real state of affairs leaves my expectations far behind. This is the most shiftless, most demoralized people I have ever seen. The influence of slavery has confused their moral conceptions, their childish, morbid self-complacency has not allowed them to approach, even in the slightest degree, a correct realization of their situation. At the present moment, society is in a state of complete dissolution and can only be held in check by iron force. All respect for the rights of personal property seems to have disappeared entirely. Everybody takes what he wants and seems completely to forget that this is what is called

[1] Translated from the German.

stealing. Since the negro is no longer a slave and no
longer costs a thousand dollars, his life is not deemed worth
a wisp of straw. I have a list of the murders committed
by Southern "gentlemen" upon negroes, which would
enrage the people of the North, if I were to submit it to a
mass-meeting there. If we were to remove our troops to-
day, the Southern States would swim in blood to-morrow.
I am expressing convictions based on experience, when I
say, that the only high light in his dark picture is the
conduct of the negro. Not only has the colored population passed from slavery to freedom without making a
single attempt to take vengeance for past sufferings, but
they are at this very moment engaged with laudable zeal
in the effort to found for themselves a substantial future.
Wherever a negro school is opened, it is full of children.
It is delightful to see the little woolly-headed pickaninnies
studying their spelling-books in the streets. The negroes
are unjustly accused of not wishing to work. They are
the only people here who do work. I have not seen one
white man in the fields. Strangely enough, only the
negroes have money; they are the only persons that do
not shrink from any sort of remunerative labor.

If I can only make my main report, I shall open the
eyes of the people of the North.

NEW ORLEANS, Sept. 2, 1865.

In Vicksburg I spent two days with General Slocum,
who had got into conflict with the governor of the State.
He welcomed me as a rescuer in the hour of need. Slocum
is entirely right in his opposition to the governor's plan
to organize a State militia, especially of the proposed
dimensions. If the Government disavows him and
supports the governor, it will be the most unwarranted
trick yet perpetrated at Washington. I did all that was
possible in the way of reports and telegraphic despatches.

If that does no good, it will not be my fault. If the President insists on taking a wrong course, in spite of all, he should not be surprised if, later, I take the field against him with the entire artillery that I am now collecting. He will find the guns rather heavy; but I still hope that it will not be necessary.

TO PRESIDENT JOHNSON

NEW ORLEANS, Sept. 5, 1865.

Private.

The enclosed paragraph[1] is clipped from one of to-day's New Orleans papers. I cannot deny that it was a painful surprise to me. You remember that I did not seek the mission on which I am at present employed. I accepted it thinking that I could render the country some service. The paragraph has the appearance of coming from one of the Government offices. The charge that I reported the information I gathered, to newspapers and not to you, is certainly unjust. You must have received my elaborate reports from every State I visited, and I am conscious of having done everything I could, to inform myself well, and to bring to your notice whatever I thought could be of interest and service to the Government.

That I have written some letters to newspapers is true; but in those letters I gave nothing that ought to have been kept secret. I think there could be no harm in my publishing incidents, anecdotes and observations that were

[1] "GEN. CARL SCHURZ TO BE RECALLED

"WASHINGTON, Aug. 22.

" It is understood that the course of General Schurz, now travelling in the South by orders from the Government, does not meet the approval of the President; and it is expected that he will be recalled soon. It is alleged that he writes for Northern newspapers his impressions of what he has seen, and publishes opinions as to what policy ought to be pursued towards the Southern States instead of making his reports directly to the War Department for the information of the President."

apt to entertain a newspaper reader, but in most cases not calculated to form part of an official report. Nor did I authorize any newspaper to mention my name in connection with those letters; on the contrary, I forbade it, and I regret to see that it has been done against my express directions.

The principal reason why I wrote those letters is well known to the Secretary of War, for I previously informed him of it. The compensation I receive from the Government is insufficient to cover the expenses incidental to my travels, aside from transportation and subsistence, and to provide for the wants of my family at the same time. I have no independent income; when I left the service I had but little laid up, and I am now obliged to depend upon the yield of my labors. In order to go South according to your desire, I had to give up all other engagements. If my suggestion to cancel my resignation [from the Army], had been accepted for the time being, I should have been above the necessity of doing something for the support of my family while travelling. But that suggestion not being accepted, I saw myself obliged, either to decline going, which, after your having selected me for this business, would have been inconsistent with my notions of duty, or to do something to make my going financially possible—especially as a trip so far South involved the payment of a considerable extra premium upon my life insurance. I informed the Secretary of War of all these circumstances.

And now to find myself abused in the newspapers for endeavoring to keep honestly above water while trying to serve the country; to see myself publicly threatened with a recall because I am obliged to make up with my own labor for the insufficiency of the compensation I receive from the Government, this, I must confess, is rather hard. It is a thing to which I ought not to be subjected, and I feel, unless you do indeed think that I have neglected my duty in some way which I at present fail to comprehend, I am justly entitled to some reparation before the public. It is exceedingly annoying to me to be preceded wherever I go, by a public announcement that the President does not approve of my conduct; and when I go home, to find the opinion spread abroad that I was *recalled* for violating my trust. If it was indeed deemed improper for me to write letters to newspapers, the Secretary of War might have told me so at the start, for I informed him of my being obliged to resort to it. He probably has my letter still in his possession.

I repeat, the paragraph has the appearance of coming from an authoritative source, and I leave it to you to decide whether I am not entitled to some manifestation on the part of the Government that will clear me of these damaging imputations and set me right before the public. There is no selfish motive in the world that would have induced me to accept this mission; there was neither pleasure, nor gain nor advancement in it. If I do not claim any praise for having accepted it under such circumstances, I certainly ought not to be left under the cloud of unjust censure. This mission will terminate my official connection with the Government; I should be sorry if the parting were darkened by any unpleasant incidents. I feel confident, however, if I leave it to your sense of justice to give me that reparation which I consider to be honestly due me, you will not permit me to suffer in standing and reputation.

TO EDWIN M. STANTON

BETHLEHEM, PA., Oct. 17, 1865.

At the close of our interview last Saturday you told me not to leave town without having seen the President, and that he was expecting me on that day. I did so; in fact, I considered it my duty to do so. I waited long and patiently to be admitted—a circumstance somewhat extraordinary considering that I had just returned from a three months' journey made at his own request. At last the doors were thrown open and I entered with the crowd. The President received me with civility, indeed, but with demonstrative coldness. I was painfully surprised, and availed myself of the first lull in our conversation to withdraw from an interview which under such circumstances could lead to no satisfactory results. I left town the same evening to see my family. My duty to see the President before leaving was fulfilled.

To-day I find in the Washington correspondence of the New York *Herald* the following paragraph:

The latest explanation of the disfavor into which General Carl Schurz seems to have fallen with the President is that during his recent trip through the Southern States, ostensibly on freedmen's affairs, his time was largely spent in efforts to organize the Republican party in that section. He is accused of attempting to convince the people of the States he travelled through that their readmission would be determined thereby.

This story is simply absurd. But since the thing has got into the newspapers and people are speculating about the cause of my "disfavor" with the President, it seems to me that I should be the first man to know something about the matter. I raise no claim of consideration upon the services I have rendered the party to which the President owes his elevation. But the position I occupy entitles me, I believe, to a frank explanation of whatever differences or misunderstandings there may be between us. I examine my conduct in vain to discover anything that could have been personally offensive to the President.

18

In my despatches, I gave him my views and impressions frankly and without reserve. It is quite possible that on some points the President's opinions and mine do not agree. I cannot suppose the President would make that the cause of a personal rupture. It may be that somebody has made some slanderous report about me. If so, I think they ought not to have been credited without my having been heard about it. Or if there be anything amiss of which I have at present no conception, the ordinary rules of propriety would serve to require that I should be asked what I have to say. I write to you about this matter because my appointment to the Southern mission passed through your hands; you encouraged me to take it, and our relations are—I have no reason to doubt—personally friendly. Will you be kind enough, as a mediator, to procure me the explanation to which I have, in my humble opinion at least, a just claim? After the reception I met with, I cannot apply to the President in person. I never received such treatment in my life. It is absolutely incomprehensible to me, and I should not like to expose myself to any more of it. I shall in all probability soon go West to take charge of a journalistic enterprise, and I am naturally anxious, before leaving the East, to have all these matters cleared up. By acceding to my request you will place me under great obligations. May I expect the favor of an early reply? It will find me here.

TO CHARLES SUMNER

BETHLEHEM, PA., Oct. 17, 1865.

I returned from my Southern trip on Thursday night, last, and had an interview with the President, Saturday. The information I bring with me is of considerable interest and importance; it might become of value in your Congressional deliberations. I am engaged in writing out a general report which the President seems by no means anxious to possess.

You have, perhaps, seen statements in the newspapers that I am in "disfavor." I wish to tell you confidentially that I myself believe it is so. He received me not, indeed, without civility, but with great coldness, asked me no questions about the results of my investigations and seemed to desire not to have any conversation about them at all. I accommodated him in that respect, withdrew from the interview as soon as I saw that it became very irksome, and left town the same night to see my family.

What the President's reasons are for treating me in so strange a manner I am at a loss to understand. The explanation given in the Washington despatches of yesterday's *Herald* is absurd. I cannot imagine what it can be unless he took offense at my reply to his despatch to me in the Sharkey–Slocum case.[1] But, then, he would have recalled me six weeks ago. That the views expressed in my letters to the President were radically at variance with his policy, is quite probable, but I do not see how, as a sensible and fair-minded man, he could make that the occasion for a personal rupture. In one word, I am completely in the dark. To-day I have written to Stanton requesting him to give or procure me some explanation.

Meanwhile, I am composing my report; when it is ready I shall present it, and then we shall see. I should be very glad to see you and Governor Andrew, the latter as the president of the Emigration Society, as soon as convenient. Can we meet at New York? I should prefer that to any other place. Please let me know at your earliest convenience when the meeting can be effected.

[1] See 3 *Reminiscences*, 189 ff., for ample details, which Schurz wrote with copies of the records before him.

In St. Louis they are making preparations to start a new paper for me. Gratz Brown is the principal mover in the matter. I consider it an enterprise of importance. It is necessary that the West and New England stand firmly together, and I have no doubt we can bring such a result about if proper measures be taken. If this journalistic enterprise succeeds, I shall be able to exercise a considerable influence in Missouri, Illinois and up and down the Mississippi as well as in the back country. I do not know whether they can get the necessary capital together on the spot. Can something be done in New England for this enterprise if there be a deficiency at St. Louis?

I stopped writing for the *Advertiser* as soon as I heard that my name was out and people were making a fuss about the matter. Now, let us meet as soon as possible. I have a great many things to tell you.

FROM CHARLES SUMNER

BOSTON, Oct. 20, 1865.

Private.

It is as I expected. It was so with the Chief Justice, who visited the South, by arrangement with the President, and who wrote to him from different places, until, at Mobile, he encountered proclamations, when he stopped. When he saw the President on his return nothing was said of his observation. It seems it was so with you.

I did not think the President in earnest when he invited you to make your tour. Since then he has been pushing forward his "experiment," and I doubt not, will push it further, if Congress does not assume jurisdiction of the whole subject.

Of course, you will make your report. But you ought as soon as possible to make a speech.

Governor Andrew says he can meet you in New York a week from to-morrow (Saturday). I fear that I cannot.

I wish you could give me briefly an outline of your impressions. My own convictions are now stronger than ever with regard to our duty. *The rebel States must not be allowed at once to participate in our Government.* This privilege must be postponed. Meanwhile all parties will be prepared for the great changes in their political relations. *There must be delay.* The President does not see this and every step that he takes is toward perdition.

Never was the way so clear or the opportunity so great. The President might have given peace to the country and made it a mighty example of justice to mankind. Instead of this consummation, he revives the old Slave Oligarchy, envenomed by war, and gives it a new lease of terrible power. This Republic cannot be lost; but the President has done very much to lose it. We must work hard to save it.

St. Louis is a central place. But I long to see you in Congress, where you can act directly by public speech on the country. But less than anybody, do you need Congress. You have already the public ear. I hope you will speak soon.

TO CHARLES SUMNER

BETHLEHEM, Nov. 13, 1865.

Your note of the 9th inst., together with the enclosed papers, reached me to-day. My report is ready and is being copied. It is quite voluminous, very full in the discussion of all the important points and has cost me considerable labor. I shall go to Washington to present it to the President probably before the end of the week. I intend to ask his permission to publish it at once so that it may be before the country when Congress meets. I consider it somewhat doubtful whether he will give that permission. If he does not, it will have to be asked for by Congress.[1] But if he does, it will be important to have

[1] As President Johnson ignored the request, Sumner introduced a resolution in the Senate calling for the report.

it out **without delay**. The question arises [as to] how to
publish it. For the newspapers it is too long. With the
accompanying documents, of which there are a considerable number, it will fill a volume of nearly 300 pages, and
the accompanying documents are as interesting and
instructive as the report itself. In fact, they form the
strength of the report as far as the establishment of facts
is concerned. I shall try to induce Lippincott in Philadelphia to publish it in the ordinary way. But if he should
refuse, can it be published in some other way? What do
you think? It is a strong document and will, I hope,
exercise an influence upon the attitude of Congress and
of the country.

· · · · · · ·

FROM CHARLES SUMNER

BOSTON, Nov. 15, 1865.

As soon as such a motion will be proper—immediately
after the President's message—I will call for your Report.
But I fear embarrassments.

It ought all to be printed with its annexes, as *mémoires
pour servir*.

Chambrun ought to have been with you before now. When
he left me, he intended to go, with a slight delay in New York,
direct to you.

The President's course is most disheartening. All that I
learn shows that he will persevere. Then comes a collision
with Congress, and inseparable confusion, and calamity.
The way of peace was very plain.

I have an article in the forthcoming *Atlantic*, entitled
"A Curiosity of Literature" but with "a moral" at the end
bearing on present affairs.

REPORT ON THE CONDITION OF THE SOUTH [1]

SIR:—When you did me the honor of selecting me for a mission to the States lately in rebellion, for the purpose of inquiring into the existing condition of things, of laying before you whatever information of importance I might gather, and of suggesting to you such measures as my observations would lead me to believe advisable, I accepted the trust with a profound sense of the responsibility connected with the performance of the task. The views I entertained at the time, I had communicated to you in frequent letters and conversations. I would not have accepted the mission, had I not felt that whatever preconceived opinions I might carry with me to the South, I should be ready to abandon or modify, as my perception of facts and circumstances might command their abandonment or modification. You informed me that your "policy of reconstruction" was merely experimental, and that you would change it if the experiment did not lead to satisfactory results. To aid you in forming your conclusions upon this point I understood to be the object of my mission, and this understanding was in perfect accordance with the written instructions I received through the Secretary of War.

These instructions confined my mission to the States of South Carolina, Georgia, Alabama, Mississippi, and the Department of the Gulf. I informed you, before

---

[1] This report accompanied President Johnson's message of Dec. 18, 1865, and is a part of Executive Document No. 11, House of Representatives, 39th Congress, 1st Session. The extensive and important documents that were printed with this report, and the direct references to those documents, have been omitted because the documents were so voluminous. In a few places the omission of these references has made it necessary for the Editor slightly to change the text, so that it will read smoothly; but, of course, the sense has been in no way altered. Whoever wishes to make a thorough study of this phase of reconstruction should consult the entire document.

leaving the North, that I could not well devote more than three months to the duties imposed upon me, and that space of time proved sufficient for me to visit all the States above enumerated, except Texas. I landed at Hilton Head, South Carolina, on July 15, visited Beaufort, Charleston, Orangeburg, and Columbia, returned to Charleston and Hilton Head; thence I went to Savannah, traversed the State of Georgia, visiting Augusta, Atlanta, Macon, Milledgeville and Columbus; went through Alabama, by way of Opelika, Montgomery, Selma and Demopolis and through Mississippi, by way of Meridian, Jackson and Vicksburg; then descended the Mississippi to New Orleans, touching at Natchez; from New Orleans I visited Mobile, Alabama, and the Teche country, in Louisiana, and then spent again some days at Natchez and Vicksburg, on my way to the North. These are the outlines of my journey.

Before laying the results of my observations before you, it is proper that I should state the *modus operandi* by which I obtained information and formed my conclusions. Wherever I went I sought interviews with persons who might be presumed to represent the opinions, or to have influence upon the conduct, of their neighbors; I had thus frequent meetings with individuals belonging to the different classes of society from the highest to the lowest; in the cities as well as on the roads and steamboats I had many opportunities to converse not only with inhabitants of the adjacent country, but with persons coming from districts which I was not able to visit; and finally I compared the impressions thus received with the experience of the military and civil officers of the government stationed in that country, as well as of other reliable Union men to whom a longer residence on the spot and a more varied intercourse with the people had given better facilities of local observation than my circumstances permitted me to enjoy. When practicable I procured statements of their views and experience in writing as well as of copies of official or private reports they had received from their subordinates or other persons. It was not expected of me that I should take formal testimony, and, indeed, such an operation would have required more time than I was able to devote to it.

My facilities for obtaining information were not equally extensive in the different States I visited. As they naturally depended somewhat upon the time the military had had to occupy and explore the country, as well as upon the progressive development of things generally, they improved from day to day as I went on, and were best in the States I visited last. It is owing to this circumstance that I cannot give as detailed an account of the condition of things in South Carolina and Georgia as I am able to give with regard to Louisiana and Mississippi.

Instead of describing the experiences of my journey in chronological order, which would lead to endless repetitions and a confused mingling of the different subjects under consideration, I propose to arrange my observations under different heads according to the subject-matter. It is true, not all that can be said of the people of one State will apply with equal force to the people of another; but it will be easy to make the necessary distinctions when in the course of this report they become of any importance. I beg to be understood when using, for the sake of brevity, the term "the Southern people," as meaning only the people of the States I have visited.

CONDITION OF THINGS IMMEDIATELY AFTER THE CLOSE OF THE WAR

In the development of the popular spirit in the South since the close of the war two well-marked periods can be distinguished. The first commences with the sudden collapse of the Confederacy and the dispersion of its armies, and the second with the first proclamation indicating the "reconstruction policy" of the Government. Of the first period I can state the characteristic features only from the accounts I received partly from Unionists who were then living in the South, partly from persons that had participated in the rebellion. When the news of Lee's and Johnston's surrenders burst upon the Southern country the general consternation was extreme. People held their breath, indulging in the wildest apprehensions as to what was now to come. Men who had occupied positions under the Confederate Government, or were otherwise compromised in the rebellion, ran before the Federal columns as they advanced and spread out to occupy the country, from village to village, from plantation to plantation, hardly knowing whether they wanted to escape or not. Others remained at their homes, yielding themselves up to their fate. Prominent Unionists told me that persons who for four years had scorned to recognize them on the street approached them with smiling faces and both hands extended. Men of standing in the political world expressed serious doubts as to whether the rebel States would ever again occupy their position as States in the Union, or be governed as conquered provinces. The public mind was so despondent that if readmission at some future time under whatever conditions had been promised, it would then have been looked upon as a favor. The most uncompromising rebels prepared for leaving the country. The masses remained in a state of fearful expectancy.

This applies especially to those parts of the country which were within immediate reach of our armies or had previously been touched by the war. Where Union soldiers had never been seen and none were near, people were at first hardly aware of the magnitude of the catastrophe, and strove to continue in their old ways of living.

Such was, according to the accounts I received, the character of that first period. The worst apprehensions were gradually relieved as day after day went by without bringing the disasters and inflictions which had been vaguely anticipated, until at last the appearance of the North Carolina proclamation substituted new hopes for them. The development of this second period I was called upon to observe on the spot, and it forms the main subject of this report.

RETURNING LOYALTY

It is a well-known fact that in the States south of Tennessee and North Carolina the number of white Unionists who during the war actively aided the Government, or at least openly professed their attachment to the cause of the Union, was very small. In none of those States were they strong enough to exercise any decisive influence upon the action of the people, not even in Louisiana, unless vigorously supported by the power of the General Government. But the white people at large being, under certain conditions, charged with taking the preliminaries of "reconstruction" into their hands, the success of the experiment depends upon the spirit and attitude of those who either attached themselves to the secession cause from the beginning, or, entertaining originally opposite views, at least followed its fortunes from the time that their States had declared their separation from the Union.

The first Southern men of this class with whom I came into contact immediately after my arrival in South Carolina expressed their sentiments almost literally in the following language: "We acknowledge ourselves beaten, and we are ready to submit to the results of the war. The war has practically decided that no State shall secede and that the slaves are emancipated. We cannot be expected at once to give up our principles and convictions of right, but we accept facts as they are, and desire to be reinstated as soon as possible in the enjoyment and exercise of our political rights." This declaration was repeated to me hundreds of times in every State I visited, with some variations of language, according to the different ways of thinking or the frankness or reserve of the different speakers. Some said nothing of adhering to their old principles and convictions of right; others still argued against the Constitutionality of coercion and of the emancipation proclamation; others expressed their determination to become good citizens, in strong language, and urged with equal emphasis the necessity of their home institutions being at once left to their own control; others would go so far as to say they were glad that the war was ended, and they had never had any confidence in the Confederacy; others protested that they had been opposed to secession until their States went out, and then yielded to the current of events; some would give me to understand that they had always been good Union men at heart, and rejoiced that the war had terminated in favor of the National cause, but in most cases such a sentiment was expressed only in a whisper; others again would grumblingly insist upon the restoration of their "rights," as if they had done no wrong; and indicated plainly that they would submit only to what they could not resist and as long as they could not resist it. Such were the definitions of "returning loyalty" I received from the mouths of a large number of individuals intelligent enough to appreciate the meaning of the expressions they used. I found a great many whose manner of speaking showed that they did not understand the circumstances under which they lived, and had no settled opinions at all except on matters immediately touching their nearest interests.

Upon the ground of these declarations, and other evidence gathered in the course of my observations, I may group the Southern people into four classes, each of which exercises an influence upon the development of things in that section:

1. Those who, although having yielded submission to the National Government only when obliged to do so, have a clear perception of the irreversible changes produced by the war, and honestly endeavor to accommodate themselves to the new order of things. Many of them are not free from traditional prejudice but open to conviction, and may be expected to act in good faith whatever they do. This class is composed, in its majority, of persons of mature age—planters, merchants, and professional men; some of them are active in the reconstruction movement, but boldness and energy are, with a few individual exceptions, not among their distinguishing qualities.

2. Those whose principal object is to have the States without delay restored to their position and influence in the Union and the people of the States to the absolute control of their home concerns. They are ready, in order to attain that object, to make any ostensible concession that will not prevent them from arranging things to suit their taste as soon as that object is attained. This class comprises a considerable number, probably a large majority, of the professional politicians who are extremely active in the reconstruction movement. They are loud in their praise of the President's reconstruction policy, and clamorous for the withdrawal of the Federal troops and the abolition of the Freedmen's Bureau.

3. The incorrigibles, who still indulge in the swagger which was so customary before and during the war, and still hope for a time when the Southern Confederacy will achieve its independence. This class consists mostly of young men, and comprises the loiterers of the towns and the idlers of the country. They persecute Union men and negroes whenever they can do so with impunity, insist clamorously upon their "rights," and are extremely impatient of the presence of the Federal soldiers. A good many of them have taken the oaths of allegiance and amnesty, and associated themselves with the second class in their political operations. This element is by no means unimportant; it is strong in numbers, deals in brave talk, addresses itself directly and incessantly to the passions and prejudices of the masses, and commands the admiration of the women.

4. The multitude of people who have no definite ideas about the circumstances under which they live and about the course they have to follow; whose intellects are weak, but whose prejudices and impulses are strong, and who are apt to be carried along by those who know how to appeal to the latter.

Much depends upon the relative strength and influence of these classes. In the course of this report you will find statements of facts which may furnish a basis for an estimate. But whatever their differences may be, on one point they are agreed: further resistance to the power of the National Government is useless, and submission to its authority a matter of necessity. It is true, the right of secession in theory is still believed in by most of those who formerly believed in it; some are still entertaining a vague hope of seeing it realized at some future time, but all give it up as a practical impossibility for the present. All movements in favor of separation from the Union have, therefore, been practically abandoned, and resistance to our military forces, on that score, has ceased. The demonstrations of hostility to the troops and other agents of the Government, which are still occurring in some localities, and of which I shall speak hereafter, spring from another class of motives. This kind of loyalty, however, which is produced by the irresistible pressure of force, and consists merely in the non-commission of acts of rebellion, is of a negative character, and might, as such, hardly be considered independent of circumstances and contingencies.

OATH-TAKING

A demonstration of "returning loyalty" of a more positive character is the taking of the oaths of allegiance and amnesty prescribed by the General Government. At first the number of persons who availed themselves of the opportunities offered for abjuring their adhesion to the cause of the rebellion was not very large, but it increased considerably when the obtaining of a pardon and the right of voting were made dependent upon the previous performance of that act. Persons falling under any of the exceptions of the amnesty proclamation made haste to avert the impending danger; and politicians used every means of persuasion to induce people to swell the number of voters by clearing themselves of all disabilities. The great argument that this was necessary to the end of reconstructing their State governments, and of regaining the control of their home affairs and their influence in the Union, was copiously enlarged upon in the letters and speeches of prominent individuals, which are before the country and need no further comment. In some cases the taking of the oath was publicly recommended in newspapers and addresses with sneering remarks, and I have listened to many private conversations in which it

was treated with contempt and ridicule. While it was
not generally looked upon in the States I visited as a very
serious matter, except as to the benefits and privileges
it confers, I have no doubt that a great many persons took
it fully conscious of the obligations it imposes, and honestly
intending to fulfil them.

The aggregate number of those who thus had qualified
themselves for voting previous to the election for the
State conventions was not as large as might have been
expected. The vote obtained at these elections was
generally reported as very light—in some localities
surprisingly so. It would, perhaps, be worth while for
the Government to order up reports about the number of
oaths administered by the officers authorized to do so,
previous to the elections for the State conventions; such
reports would serve to indicate how large a proportion
of the people participated in the reconstruction movement
at that time, and to what extent the masses were represented in the conventions.

Of those who have not yet taken the oath of allegiance,
most belong to the class of indifferent people who "do not
care one way or the other." There are still some individuals who find the oath to be a confession of defeat
and a declaration of submission too humiliating and too
repugnant to their feelings. It is to be expected that the
former will gradually overcome their apathy, and the
latter their sensitiveness, and that, at a not remote day,
all will have qualified themselves, in point of form, to
resume the right of citizenship. On the whole, it may be
said that the value of the oaths taken in the Southern
States is neither above nor below the value of the political
oaths taken in other countries. A historical examination
of the subject of political oaths will lead to the conclusion
that they can be very serviceable in certain emergencies
and for certain objects, but that they have never insured

the stability of a government, and never improved the
morals of a people.

FEELING TOWARDS THE SOLDIERS AND THE PEOPLE OF THE NORTH

A more substantial evidence of "returning loyalty"
would be a favorable change of feeling with regard to the
Government's friends and agents, and the people of the
loyal States generally. I mentioned above that all
organized attacks upon our military forces stationed in
the South have ceased; but there are still localities where
it is unsafe for a man wearing the Federal uniform or
known as an officer of the Government to be abroad outside of the immediate reach of our garrisons. The
shooting of single soldiers and Government couriers was
not unfrequently reported while I was in the South, and
even as late as the middle of September, Major Miller,
assistant adjutant general of the commissioner of the
Freedmen's Bureau in Alabama, while on an inspecting
tour in the southern counties of that State, found it
difficult to prevent a collision between the menacing
populace and his escort. His wagon-master was brutally
murdered while remaining but a short distance behind
the command. The murders of agents of the Freedmen's
Bureau have been noticed in the public papers. These
and similar occurrences, however, may be looked upon
as isolated cases, and ought to be charged, perhaps, only
to the account of the lawless persons who committed
them.

But no instance has come to my notice in which the
people of a city or a rural district cordially fraternized
with the army. Here and there the soldiers were welcomed as protectors against apprehended dangers; but
general exhibitions of cordiality on the part of the popula-

tion I have not heard of. There are, indeed, honorable individual exceptions to this rule. Many persons, mostly belonging to the first of the four classes above enumerated, are honestly striving to soften down the bitter feelings and traditional antipathies of their neighbors; others, who are acting more upon motives of policy than inclination, maintain pleasant relations with the officers of the Government. But, upon the whole, the soldier of the Union is still looked upon as a stranger, an intruder—as the "Yankee," "the enemy." It would be superfluous to enumerate instances of insult offered to our soldiers, and even to officers high in command; the existence and intensity of this aversion is too well known to those who have served or are now serving in the South to require proof. In this matter the exceptions were, when I was there, not numerous enough to affect the rule. In the documents accompanying this report you will find allusions confirming this statement. I would invite special attention to the letter of General Kirby [T. Kilby] Smith.

This feeling of aversion and resentment with regard to our soldiers may, perhaps, be called natural. The animosities inflamed by a four years' war, and its distressing incidents, cannot be easily overcome. But they extend beyond the limits of the army, to the people of the North. I have read in Southern papers bitter complaints about the unfriendly spirit exhibited by the Northern people—complaints not unfrequently flavored with an admixture of vigorous vituperation. But, as far as my experience goes, the "unfriendly spirit" exhibited in the North is all mildness and affection compared with the popular temper which in the South vents itself in a variety of ways and on all possible occasions. No observing Northern man can come into contact with the different classes composing Southern society without noticing it. He may be received in social circles with

great politeness, even with apparent cordiality; but soon
he will become aware that, although he may be esteemed
as a man, he is detested as a "Yankee," and, as the
conversation becomes a little more confidential and throws
off ordinary restraint, he is not unfrequently told so; the
word "Yankee" still signifies to them those traits of
character which the Southern press has been so long in
the habit of attributing to the Northern people; and
whenever they look around them upon the traces of the
war, they see in them, not the consequences of their own
folly, but the evidences of "Yankee wickedness." In
making these general statements, I beg to be understood
as always excluding the individual exceptions above
mentioned.

It is by no means surprising that prejudices and resentments, which for years were so assiduously cultivated
and so violently inflamed, should not have been turned
into affection by a defeat; nor are they likely to disappear
as long as the Southern people continue to brood over
their losses and misfortunes. They will gradually subside
when those who entertain them cut resolutely loose from
the past and embark in a career of new activity on a
common field with those whom they have so long considered their enemies. Of this I shall say more in another
part of this report. But while we are certainly inclined
to put upon such things the most charitable construction,
it remains nevertheless true, that as long as these feelings
exist in their present strength, they will hinder the growth
of that reliable kind of loyalty which springs from the
heart and clings to the country in good and evil fortune.

SITUATION OF UNIONISTS

It would have been a promising indication of returning
loyalty if the old, consistent, uncompromising Unionists

of the South, and those Northern men who during the war settled down there to contribute to the prosperity of the country with their capital and enterprise, had received that measure of consideration to which their identification with the new order of things entitled them. It would seem natural that the victory of the National cause should have given those who during the struggle had remained the firm friends of the Union, a higher standing in society and an enlarged political influence. This appears to have been the case during that "first period" of anxious uncertainty when known Unionists were looked up to as men whose protection and favor might be of high value. At least it appears to have been so in some individual instances. But the close of that "first period" changed the aspect of things.

It struck me soon after my arrival in the South that the known Unionists—I mean those who during the war had been to a certain extent identified with the National cause —were not in communion with the leading social and political circles; and the further my observations extended the clearer it became to me that their existence in the South was of a rather precarious nature. Already in Charleston my attention was called to the current talk among the people, that, when they had the control of things once more in their own hands and were no longer restrained by the presence of "Yankee" soldiers, men of Dr. Mackey's stamp would not be permitted to live there. At first I did not attach much importance to such reports; but as I proceeded through the country, I heard the same thing so frequently repeated, at so many different places and by so many different persons, that I could no longer look upon the apprehensions expressed to me by Unionists as entirely groundless. I found the same opinion entertained by most of our military commanders. Even Governor Sharkey, in the course of a conversation I had

with him in the presence of Major-General Osterhaus,
admitted that, if our troops were then withdrawn, the
lives of Northern men in Mississippi would not be safe.
To show that such anticipations were not extravagant,
I would refer to the letter addressed to me by General
Osterhaus. He states that he was compelled to withdraw
the garrison from Attala county, Mississippi, the regiment
to which that garrison belonged being mustered out, and
that when the troops had been taken away, four murders
occurred, two of white Union men, and two of negroes.
(He informed me subsequently that the perpetrators
were in custody.) He goes on to say: " There is no
doubt whatever that the state of affairs would be intolerable for all Union men, all recent immigrants from the
North, and all negroes, the moment the protection of the
United States troops were withdrawn." General Osterhaus informed me of another murder of a Union man by
a gang of lawless persons, in Jackson, about the end of
June. General Slocum, in his order prohibiting the
organization of the State militia in Mississippi, speaks of
the "outrages committed against Northern men, Government couriers and negroes." He communicated to me
an official report from Lieutenant-Colonel Yorke, commanding at Port Gibson, to General Davidson, pointing
in the same direction. General Canby stated to me that
he was obliged to disband and prohibit certain patrol
organizations in Louisiana because they indulged in the
gratification of private vengeance. Lieutenant Hickney,
assistant commissioner of the Freedmen's Bureau, at
Shreveport, Louisiana, in a report addressed to Assistant
Commissioner Conway, says: " The life of a Northern
man who is true to his country and the spirit and genius
of its institutions, and frankly enunciates his principles,
is not secure where there is not a military force to protect
him." Mr. William King, a citizen of Georgia well-

known in that State, stated to me in conversation: " There
are a great many bad characters in the country, who would
make it for some time unsafe for known Union people
and Northerners who may settle down here to live in this
country without the protection of the military." The
affair of Scottsborough, in the military district of northern
Alabama, where a sheriff arrested and attempted to
bring to trial for murder Union soldiers who had served
against the guerillas in that part of the country, an
attempt which was frustrated only by the prompt interference of the district commander, has become generally
known through the newspapers. It is not improbable
that many cases similar to those above mentioned have
occurred in other parts of the South without coming to
the notice of the authorities.

It is true these are mere isolated cases, for which it
would be wrong to hold anybody responsible who was not
connected with them; but it is also true that the apprehensions so widely spread among the Unionists and Northern men were based upon the spirit exhibited by the
people among whom they lived. I found a good many
thinking of removing themselves and their families to
the Northern States, and if our troops should be soon
withdrawn, the exodus will probably become quite extensive unless things meanwhile change for the better.

ASPECT OF THE POLITICAL FIELD

The status of this class of Unionists in the political
field corresponds with what I have said above. In this
respect I have observed practical results more closely in
Mississippi than in any other State. I had already left
South Carolina and Georgia when the elections for the
State conventions took place. Of Alabama, I saw only
Mobile after the election. In Louisiana, a convention,
a legislature and a State government had already been

elected, during and under the influence of the war, and I left before the nominating party conventions were held; but I was in Mississippi immediately after the adjournment of the State convention, and while the canvass preparatory to the election of the legislature and of the State and county officers was going on. Events have since sufficiently developed themselves in the other States to permit us to judge how far Mississippi can be regarded as a representative of the rest. Besides, I found the general spirit animating the people to be essentially the same in all the States above mentioned.

The election for the State convention in Mississippi was, according to the accounts I have received, not preceded by a very vigorous and searching canvass of the views and principles of the candidates. As I stated before, the vote was very far from being full, and in most cases the members were elected not upon strictly defined party issues, but upon their individual merits as to character, intelligence and standing in society. Only in a few places the contest between rival candidates was somewhat animated. It was probably the same in Alabama, Georgia and South Carolina.

The Mississippi convention was, in its majority, composed of men belonging to the first two of the four classes above mentioned. There were several Union men in it of the inoffensive, compromising kind—men who had been opposed to secession in the beginning, and had abstained from taking a prominent part in the rebellion unless obliged to do so, but who had, at least, readily acquiesced in what was going on. But there was, as far as I have been able to ascertain, only one man there who, like the Unionists of East Tennessee, had offered active resistance to the rebel authorities. This was Mr. Crawford, of Jones county; he was elected by the poor people of that region, his old followers, as their acknowledged leader, and his may justly be looked upon as an exceptional case. How he looked upon his situation appears from a speech he delivered in that convention, and especially from the amended version of it placed into my hands by a trustworthy gentleman of my acquaintance who had listened to its delivery. But several instances have come to my knowledge, in which Union men of a sterner cast than those described as acquiescing compromisers were defeated in the election, and, aside from Mr. Crawford's case, none in which they succeeded.

The impulses by which voters were actuated in making their choice appeared more clearly in the canvass for State officers, Congressmen, and members of the legislature, when the antecedents and political views of candidates were more closely scrutinized and a warmer contest took place. The population of those places in the South which have been longest in the possession of our armies is generally the most accommodating as to the new order of things; at least the better elements are there in greater relative strength. A Union meeting at Vicksburg may, therefore, be produced as a not unfavorable exponent of Mississippi Unionism. Among the documents attached to this report you will find three speeches delivered before such a meeting—one by Mr. Richard Cooper, candidate for the attorney-generalship of the State; one by Hon. Sylvanus Evans, candidate for Congress; and one by Colonel Partridge, candidate for a seat in the legislature. The speakers represented themselves as Union men, and I have learned nothing about them that would cast suspicion upon the sincerity of their declarations as far as they go; but all three qualified their Unionism by the same important statement.

MR. COOPER: In 1850 I opposed an attempt to break up the United States Government, and in 1860 I did the same.

I travelled in Alabama and Mississippi to oppose the measure. (Applause.) But after the State did secede, I did all in my power to sustain it. (Heavy applause.)

MR. EVANS: In 1861 I was a delegate from Lauderdale county to the State convention, then and in 1860 being opposed to the act of secession, and fought against it with all my powers. But when the State had seceded, I went with it as a matter of duty, and I sustained it until the day of the surrender with all my body and heart and mind. (Great applause.)

COLONEL PARTRIDGE: He was a Union man before the war and a soldier in the war. He had performed his duty as a private and an officer on the battlefield and on the staff.

These speeches, fair specimens of a majority of those delivered by the better class of politicians before the better class of audiences, furnish an indication of the kind of Unionism which, by candidates, is considered palatable to the people of that region. And candidates are generally good judges as to what style of argument is best calculated to captivate the popular mind. In some isolated localities there may be some chance of success for a candidate who, proclaiming himself a Union man, is not able to add, "but after the State had seceded I did all in my power to sustain it," although such localities are certainly scarce and difficult to find.

It is not so difficult to find places in which a different style of argument is considered most serviceable. Your attention is respectfully invited to a card addressed to the voters of the sixth judicial district of Mississippi by Mr. John T. Hogan, candidate for the office of district attorney. When, at the commencement of the war, Kentucky resolved to remain in the Union, Mr. Hogan, so he informs the constituency, was a citizen of Kentucky; because Kentucky refused to leave the Union Mr. Hogan left Kentucky. He went to Mississippi, joined the rebel army, and was wounded in battle; and because he left his native State to fight against the Union, "therefore," Mr. Hogan tells his Mississippian constituency, "he cannot feel that he is an alien in their midst, and, with something of confidence in the result, appeals to them for their suffrages." Such is Mr. Hogan's estimate of the loyalty of the sixth judicial district of Mississippi.

A candidate relying for success upon nothing but his identification with the rebellion might be considered as an extreme case. But, in fact, Mr. Hogan only speaks out bluntly what other candidates wrap up in lengthy qualifications. It is needless to accumulate specimens. I am sure no Mississippian will deny that if a candidate there based his claims upon the ground of his having left Mississippi when the State seceded, in order to fight for the Union, his pretensions would be treated as a piece of impudence. I feel warranted in saying that Unionism absolutely untinctured by any connection with, or at least acquiescence in the rebellion, would have but little chance of political preferment anywhere, unless favored by very extraordinary circumstances; while men who, during the war, followed the example of the Union leaders of East Tennessee, would in most places have to depend upon the protection of our military forces for safety, while nowhere within the range of my observation would they, under present circumstances, be considered eligible to any position of trust, honor, or influence, unless it be in the county of Jones, as long as the bayonets of the United States are still there.

The tendency of which in the preceding remarks I have endeavored to indicate the character and direction, appeared to prevail in all the States that came under my observation with equal force, some isolated localities excepted. None of the provisional governments adopted the policy followed by the late "military government"

of Tennessee: to select in every locality the most reliable
and most capable Union men for the purpose of placing
into their hands the positions of official influence.   Those
who had held the local offices before and during the rebellion were generally reappointed, and hardly any discrimination made.   If such wholesale reappointments
were the only thing that could be done in a hurry, it may
be asked whether the hurry was necessary.   Even in
Louisiana where a State government was organized during
the war and under the influence of the sentiments which
radiated from the camps and headquarters of the Union
army, and where there is a Union element far stronger
than in any other of the States I visited, even there, men
who have aided the rebellion by word and act are crowding
into places of trust and power.   Governor Wells, when
he was elected lieutenant-governor of Louisiana, was
looked upon and voted for as a thorough Unionist; but
hardly had he the patronage of the State government in
his hands, when he was carried along by the seemingly
irresistible current.   Even members of the "Conservative
Union party," and friends of Governor Wells, expressed
their dissatisfaction with the remarkable "liberality"
with which he placed men into official positions who had
hardly returned from the rebel army, or some other place
where they had taken refuge to avoid living under the
flag of the United States.   The apprehension was natural
that such elements would soon obtain a power and influence which the governor would not be able to control
even if he wished.   Taking these things into consideration,
the re-nomination of Governor Wells for the governorship can certainly not be called a victory of that Union
sentiment to which he owed his first election.

While I was in New Orleans an occurrence took place
which may be quoted as an illustration of the sweep of
what I might call the *reactionary movement.* When

General Shepley was military governor of Louisiana, under General Butler's *régime*, a school board was appointed for the purpose of reorganizing the public schools of New Orleans. A corps of loyal teachers was appointed, and the education of the children was conducted with a view to make them loyal citizens. The National airs were frequently sung in the schools, and other exercises introduced, calculated to impregnate the youthful minds of the pupils with affection for their country. It appears that this feature of the public schools was distasteful to that class of people with whose feelings they did not accord.

Mr. H. Kennedy, acting mayor of New Orleans, early in September last, disbanded the school board which so far had conducted the educational affairs of the city, and appointed a new one. The composition of this new school board was such as to induce General Canby to suspend its functions until he could inquire into the loyalty of its members. The report of the officer intrusted with the investigation shows that a large majority of the members had sympathized with the rebellion, and aided the Confederate Government in a variety of ways. But as no evidence was elicited proving the members legally incapable of holding office, General Canby considered himself obliged to remove the prohibition, and the new school board entered upon its functions.

The real substance, stripped of all circumlocutions, of an editorial taken from the New Orleans *Times*, of September 12, evidently written in defense of the measure, can be expressed in a few words: "The schools of New Orleans have been institutions so intensely and demonstratively loyal as to become unpopular with those of our fellow-citizens to whom such demonstrations are distasteful, and they must be brought back under 'popular control' so as to make them cease to be obnoxious in that par-

ticular." It was generally understood, when the new
school board was appointed, that a Mr. Rodgers was to
be made superintendent of public schools. In Major
Lowell's report to General Canby this Mr. Rodgers
figures as follows:

Mr. Rodgers, the candidate for the position of superintendent
of public schools, held the same office at the commencement
of the war. His conduct at that time was imbued with extreme
bitterness and hate towards the United States, and, in his
capacity as superintendent, he introduced the "Bonnie Blue
Flag" and other rebel songs into the exercises of the schools
under his charge. In histories and other books where the
initials "U. S." occurred he had the same erased, and "C. S."
substituted. He used all means in his power to imbue the
minds of the youth intrusted to his care with hate and malignity towards the Union. He has just returned from the late
Confederacy, where he has resided during the war. At the
time he left the city to join the army he left his property in
the care of one Finley, who claims to be a British subject
but held the position of sergeant in a Confederate regiment of
militia.

No sooner was the above mentioned prohibition by General
Canby removed than Mr. Rodgers was actually appointed, and he now presides over the educational interests of New Orleans. There is something like system in
such proceedings.

Similar occurrences, such as the filling with rebel officers
of professorships in the Military Institute of Louisiana,
where formerly General Sherman held a position, have
already become known to the country, and it is unnecessary to go into further details. Many cases of this
description are not of much importance, in themselves,
but serve as significant indications of the tendency of
things in the South.

It is easily understood that, under such circumstances,

Unionists of the consistent, uncompromising kind do not play an enviable part. It is a sad fact that the victory of the National arms has, to a great extent, resulted in something like a political ostracism of the most loyal men in that part of the country. More than once have I heard some of them complain of having been taunted by late rebels with their ill fortune; and it is, indeed, melancholy for them to reflect that, if they had yielded to the current of public sentiment in the rebel States instead of resisting it, their present situation and prospects would be much more pleasing. Nor is such a reflection calculated to encourage them, or others, to follow a similar course if similar emergencies should again arise.

WHAT HAS BEEN ACCOMPLISHED

While the generosity and toleration shown by the Government to the people lately in rebellion have not met with a corresponding generosity shown by those people to the Government's friends, it has brought forth some results which, if properly developed, will become of value. It has facilitated the re-establishment of the forms of civil government, and led many of those who had been active in the rebellion to take part in the act of bringing back the States to their Constitutional relations; and if nothing else were necessary than the mere putting in operation of the mere machinery of government in point of form, and not also the acceptance of the results of the war and their development in point of spirit, these results, although as yet incomplete, might be called a satisfactory advance in the right direction. There is, at present, no danger of another insurrection against the authority of the United States on a large scale, and the people are willing to reconstruct their State governments, and to send their Senators and Representatives to Congress.

But as to the moral value of these results, we must not indulge in any delusions. There are two principal points to which I beg to call your attention. In the first place, the rapid return to power and influence of so many of those who but recently were engaged in a bitter war against the Union, has had one effect which was certainly not originally contemplated by the Government. Treason does, under existing circumstances, not appear odious in the South. The people are not impressed with any sense of its criminality. And, secondly, there is, as yet among the Southern people an *utter absence of national feeling*. I made it a business, while in the South, to watch the symptoms of "returning loyalty" as they appeared not only in private conversation, but in the public press and in the speeches delivered and the resolutions passed at Union meetings. Hardly ever was there an expression of hearty attachment to the great republic, or an appeal to the impulses of patriotism; but whenever submission to the National authority was declared and advocated, it was almost uniformly placed upon two principal grounds: That, under present circumstances, the Southern people could "do no better"; and then that submission was the only means by which they could rid themselves of the Federal soldiers and obtain once more control of their own affairs. Some of the speakers may have been inspired by higher motives, but upon these two arguments they had principally to rely whenever they wanted to make an impression upon the popular mind. If any exception is to be made to this rule it is Louisiana, in whose metropolis a different spirit was cultivated for some time; but even there, the return in mass of those who followed the fortunes of the Confederate flag during the war does not appear to have a favorable influence upon the growth of that sentiment. While admitting that, at present, we have perhaps no right to expect anything better than this submission—loyalty which springs from necessity and calculation—I do not consider it safe for the Government to base expectations upon it, which the manner in which it manifests itself does not justify.

The reorganization of civil government is relieving the military, to a great extent, of its police duties and judicial functions; but at the time I left the South it was still very far from showing a satisfactory efficiency in the maintenance of order and security. In many districts robbing and plundering were going on with perfect impunity; the roads were infested by bands of highwaymen; numerous assaults occurred, and several stage lines were considered unsafe. The statements of Major-General Woods, Brigadier-General Kilby Smith and Colonel Gilchrist give a terrible picture of the state of things in the localities they refer to. It is stated that civil officers are either unwilling or unable to enforce the laws; that one man does not dare to testify against another for fear of being murdered, and that the better elements of society are kept down by lawless characters under a system of terrorism. From my own observation I know that these things are not confined to the districts mentioned in the documents above referred to. Both the governors of Alabama and Mississippi complained of it in official proclamations. Cotton, horse and cattle stealing was going on in all the States I visited on an extensive scale. Such a state of demoralization would call for extraordinary measures in any country, and it is difficult to conceive how, in the face of the inefficiency of the civil authorities, the removal of the troops can be thought of.

In speaking above of the improbability of an insurrectionary movement on a large scale, I did not mean to say that I considered resistance in detail to the execution of the laws of Congress and the measures of the Government impossible. Of all subjects connected with the negro question I shall speak in another part of this report. But there is another matter claiming the attention and foresight of the Government. It is well known that the levying of taxes for the payment of the interest on our National debt is, and will continue to be, very unpopular in the South. It is true, no striking demonstrations have as yet been made of any decided unwillingness on the part of the people to contribute to the discharge of our National obligations. But most of the conversations I had with Southerners upon this subject led me to apprehend that they, politicians and people, are rather inclined to ask money of the Government as compensation for their emancipated slaves, for the rebuilding of the levees on the Mississippi, and various kinds of damage done by our armies for military purposes, than, as the current expression is, to "help paying the expenses of the whipping they have received." In fact, there are abundant indications in newspaper articles, public speeches, and electioneering documents of candidates, which render it eminently probable that on the claim of compensation for their emancipated slaves the Southern States, as soon as readmitted to representation in Congress, will be almost a unit. In the Mississippi convention the idea was broached by Mr. Potter, in an elaborate speech, to have the late slave States relieved from taxation "for years to come," in consideration of "debt due them" for the emancipated slaves; and this plea I have frequently heard advocated in private conversations. I need not go into details as to the efforts made in some of the Southern States in favor of the assumption by those States of their debts contracted during the rebellion. It may be assumed with certainty that those who want to have the Southern people, poor as they are, taxed for the payment of rebel debts, do not mean to have them taxed for the purpose of meeting our National obligations.

20

But whatever devices may be resorted to, present indications justify the apprehension that the enforcement of our revenue laws will meet with a refractory spirit, and may require sterner measures than the mere sending of revenue officers into that part of the country.

THE NEGRO QUESTION—FIRST ASPECTS

The principal cause of that want of national spirit which has existed in the South so long, and at last gave birth to the rebellion, was, that the Southern people cherished, cultivated, idolized their peculiar interests and institutions in preference to those which they had in common with the rest of the American people. Hence the importance of the negro question as an integral part of the question of union in general, and the question of reconstruction in particular.

When the war came to a close, the labor system of the South was already much disturbed. During the progress of military operations large numbers of slaves had left their masters and followed the columns of our armies; others had taken refuge in our camps; many thousands had enlisted in the service of the National Government. Extensive settlements of negroes had been formed along the seaboard and the banks of the Mississippi, under the supervision of army officers and treasury agents, and the Government was feeding the colored refugees, who could not be advantageously employed, in the so-called contraband camps. Many slaves had also been removed by their masters, as our armies penetrated the country, either to Texas or to the interior of Georgia and Alabama. Thus a considerable portion of the laboring force had been withdrawn from its former employments. But a majority of the slaves remained on the plantations to which they belonged, especially in those parts of the country which were not touched by the war, and where, consequently, the emancipation proclamation was not enforced by the military power. Although not ignorant of the stake they had in the result of the contest, the patient bondmen waited quietly for the development of things. But as soon as the struggle was finally decided, and our forces were scattered about in detachments to occupy the country, the so far unmoved masses began to stir. The report went among them that their liberation was no longer a mere contingency, but a fixed fact. Large numbers of colored people left the plantations; many flocked to our military posts and camps to obtain the certainty of their freedom, and others walked away merely for the purpose of leaving the places on which they had been held in slavery, and because they could now go with impunity. Still others, and their number was by no means inconsiderable, remained with their former masters and continued their work on the field, but under new and as yet unsettled conditions, and under the agitating influence of a feeling of restlessness. In some localities, however, where our troops had not yet penetrated and where no military post was within reach, planters endeavored and partially succeeded in maintaining between themselves and the negroes the relation of master and slave, partly by concealing from them the great changes that had taken place, and partly by terrorizing them into submission to their behests. But aside from these exceptions, the country found itself thrown into that confusion which is naturally inseparable from a change so great and so sudden. The white people were afraid of the negroes, and the negroes did not trust the white people; the military power of the National Government stood there, and was looked up to, as the protector of both.

Upon this power devolved the task to bring order into that chaos. But the order to be introduced was a new order, of which neither the late masters nor the late slaves had an adequate conception. All the elements of society being afloat, the difficulties were immense. The military officers and agents of the Freedmen's Bureau, to whom the negroes applied for advice and guidance, either procured them such employment as could be found, or persuaded them to return to their plantations and to continue in the cultivation of the crops, promising them that their liberty, rights, and interests should be protected. Upon the planters they urged the necessity of making fair and equitable contracts with the freedmen, admonishing them to treat their laborers as free men ought to be treated. These efforts met with such success as the difficulties surrounding the problem permitted to expect. Large numbers of negroes went back to the fields, according to the advice they had received, but considerable accumulations still remained in and around the towns and along the seaboard, where there was no adequate amount of profitable employment for them. The making and approving of contracts progressed as rapidly as the small number of officers engaged in that line of duty made it possible, but not rapidly in proportion to the vast amount of work to be accomplished. The business experience of many of the officers was but limited; here and there experiments were tried which had to be given up. In numerous cases contracts were made and then broken, either by the employers or the laborers, and the officers in charge were overwhelmed with complaints from both sides. While many planters wanted to have the laborers who had left them back on their plantations, others drove those that had remained away, and thus increased the number of the unemployed. Moreover, the great change had burst upon the country in the midst of the agricultural labor season when the crops that were in the ground required steady work to make them produce a satisfactory yield, and the interruption of labor, which could not but be very extensive, caused considerable damage. In one word, the efforts made could not prevent or remedy, in so short a time, the serious disorders which are always connected with a period of precipitous transition, and which, although natural, are exceedingly embarrassing to those who have to deal with them.

The solution of the social problem in the South, if left to the free action of the Southern people, will depend upon two things: (1) upon the ideas entertained by the whites, the "ruling class." of the problem, and the manner in which they act upon their ideas; and (2) upon the capacity and conduct of the colored people.

OPINIONS OF THE WHITES

That the result of the free labor experiment made under circumstances so extremely unfavorable should at once be a perfect success, no reasonable person would expect. Nevertheless, a large majority of the Southern men with whom I came into contact announced their opinions with so positive an assurance as to produce the impression that their minds were fully made up. In at least nineteen cases of twenty the reply I received to my inquiry about their views on the new system was uniformly this: " You cannot make the negro work without physical compulsion." I heard this hundreds of times, heard it wherever I went, heard it in nearly the same words from so many different persons, that at last I came to the conclusion that this is the prevailing sentiment among the Southern people. There are exceptions to this rule but, as far as my information extends, far from enough to affect the rule.

Unfortunately the disorders necessarily growing out of the transition state continually furnished food for argument. I found but few people who were willing to make due allowance for the adverse influence of exceptional circumstances. By a large majority of those I came in contact with, and they mostly belonged to the more intelligent class, every irregularity that occurred was directly charged against the system of free labor. If negroes walked away from the plantations, it was conclusive proof of the incorrigible instability of the negro, and the impracticability of free negro labor. If some individual negroes violated the terms of their contract, it proved unanswerably that no negro had, or ever would have, a just conception of the binding force of a contract, and that this system of free negro labor was bound to be a failure. If some negroes shirked, or did not perform their task with sufficient alacrity, it was produced as irrefutable evidence to show that physical compulsion was actually indispensable to make the negro work. If negroes, idlers or refugees crawling about the towns, applied to the authorities for subsistence, it was quoted as incontestably establishing the point that the negro was too improvident to take care of himself, and must necessarily be consigned to the care of a master. I heard a Georgia planter argue most seriously that one of his negroes had shown himself certainly unfit for freedom because he impudently refused to submit to a whipping. I frequently went into an argument with those putting forth such general assertions, quoting instances in which negro laborers were working faithfully, and to the entire satisfaction of their employers, as the employers themselves had informed me. In a majority of cases the reply was that we Northern people did not understand the negro, but that they (the Southerners) did; that as to the particular instances I quoted I was probably mistaken; that I had not closely investigated the cases, or had been deceived by my informants; that they *knew* the negro would not work without compulsion, and that nobody

could make them believe he would. Arguments like
these naturally finished such discussions. It frequently
struck me that persons who conversed about every other
subject calmly and sensibly would lose their temper as
soon as the negro question was touched.

EFFECTS OF SUCH OPINIONS, AND GENERAL TREATMENT OF THE NEGRO

A belief, conviction, or prejudice, or whatever you may
call it, so widely spread and apparently so deeply rooted
as this, that the negro will not work without physical
compulsion, is certainly calculated to have a very serious
influence upon the conduct of the people entertaining it.
It naturally produced a desire to preserve slavery in its
original form as much and as long as possible—and you
may, perhaps, remember the admission made by one of
the provisional governors, over two months after the
close of the war, that the people of his State still indulged
in a lingering hope slavery might yet be preserved—or to
introduce into the new system that element of physical
compulsion which would make the negro work. Efforts
were, indeed, made to hold the negro in his old state of
subjection, especially in such localities where our military
forces had not yet penetrated, or where the country was
not garrisoned in detail. Here and there planters succeeded for a limited period to keep their former slaves in
ignorance, or at least doubt, about their new rights; but
the main agency employed for that purpose was force and
intimidation. In many instances negroes who walked away
from the plantations, or were found upon the roads, were
shot or otherwise severely punished, which was calculated
to produce the impression among those remaining with
their masters that an attempt to escape from slavery
would result in certain destruction. A large proportion

of the many acts of violence committed is undoubtedly
attributable to this motive.   For the sake of illustration
I will give some instances:

Brigadier-General Fessenden reported to Major-General
Gillmore from Winnsboro', South Carolina, July 19th, as
follows:

The spirit of the people, especially in those districts not
subject to the salutary influence of General Sherman's army,
is that of concealed and, in some instances, of open hostility,
though there are some who strive with honorable good faith
to promote a thorough reconciliation between the Government
and their people. A spirit of bitterness and persecution
manifests itself towards the negroes. They are shot and
abused outside the immediate protection of our forces by
*men who announce their determination to take the law into their
own hands, in defiance of our authority*. To protect the negro
and punish these still rebellious individuals it will be necessary
to have this country pretty thickly settled with soldiers.

I received similar verbal reports from other parts of
South Carolina. To show the hopes still indulged in by
some, I may mention that one of the sub-district commanders, as he himself informed me, knew planters within
the limits of his command who had made contracts with
their former slaves *avowedly* for the object of keeping
them together on their plantations, so that they might
have them near at hand, and thus more easily reduce
them to their former condition, when, after the restoration
of the civil power, the "unconstitutional emancipation
proclamation" would be set aside.

Cases in which negroes were kept on the plantations,
either by ruse or violence, were frequent enough in South
Carolina and Georgia to call forth from General Saxton
a circular threatening planters who persisted in this
practice with loss of their property, and from Major-

General Steedman, commander of the Department of Georgia, an order bearing upon the same subject. At Atlanta, Georgia, I had an opportunity to examine some cases of the nature above described. While I was there, 9th and 10th of August, several negroes came into town with bullet and buckshot wounds in their bodies. From their statements, which, however, were only corroborating information previously received, it appeared that the reckless and restless characters of that region had combined to keep the negroes "where they belonged."[1] Several freedmen were shot in the attempt to escape, others succeeded in eluding the vigilance of their persecutors; large numbers, terrified by what they saw and heard, quietly remained under the restraint imposed upon them, waiting for better opportunities. The commander of the sub-district and post informed me that bands of guerillas were prowling about within a few miles of the city, making it dangerous for soldiers and freedmen to show themselves outside of the immediate reach of the garrison, and that but a few days previous to my arrival a small squad of men he had sent out to serve an order upon a planter, concerning the treatment of freedmen, had been driven back by an armed band of over twenty men, headed by an individual in the uniform of a rebel officer.

As our troops in Georgia were at that time mostly concentrated at a number of central points, and not scattered over the State in small detachments, but little information was obtained of what was going on in the interior of the country. A similar system was followed in Alabama, but enough has become known to indicate the condition of things in localities not immediately under the eye of the military. In that State the efforts

[1] These quotation-marks were made in Mr. Schurz's copy, doubtless by himself.

made to hold the negro in a state of subjection appear to
have been of a particularly atrocious nature. Rumors
to that effect which reached me at Montgomery induced
me to make inquiries at the post hospital. The records
of that institution showed a number of rather startling
cases which had occurred immediately after the close of
the war, and some of a more recent date; all of which
proved that negroes leaving the plantations and found on
the roads, were exposed to the savagest treatment. A
statement signed by the provost marshal at Selma,
Alabama, Major J. P. Houston, says:

There have come to my notice officially twelve cases, in
which I am morally certain the trials have not been had yet,
that negroes were killed by whites. In a majority of cases
the provocation consisted in the negroes' trying to come to
town or to return to the plantation after having been sent
away. The cases above enumerated, I am convinced, are
but a small part of those that have actually been perpetrated.

In a report to General Swayne, assistant-commissioner
of the Freedmen's Bureau in Alabama, communicated
to me by the general, Captain Poillon, agent of the bureau
at Mobile, says of the condition of things in the south-
western part of the State, July 29th:

There are regular patrols posted on the rivers, who board
some of the boats; after the boats leave they hang, shoot or
drown the victims they may find on them, and all those
found on the roads or coming down the rivers are almost
invariably murdered. . . . The bewildered and terrified
freedmen know not what to do—to leave is death; to remain
is to suffer the increased burden imposed upon them by the
cruel taskmaster, whose only interest is their labor, wrung
from them by every device an inhuman ingenuity can devise;
hence the lash and murder are resorted to to intimidate those

whom fear of an awful death alone causes to remain, while patrols, negro dogs, and spies disguised as Yankees, keep constant guard over these unfortunate people.

In a letter addressed to myself, September 9th, Captain Poillon says:

Organized patrols, with negro hounds, keep guard over the thoroughfares; bands of lawless robbers traverse the country, and the unfortunate who attempts to escape, or he who returns for his wife or child, is waylaid or pursued with hounds, and shot or hung.

In Mississippi I received information of a similar character. Lieutenant-Colonel, P. J. Yorke, post commander at Port Gibson, Mississippi, reported to General Davidson, on August 26th, that a "county patrol" had been organized by citizens of his sub-district, which, for reasons given, he had been obliged to disband; one of these reasons in his own language, was:

The company was formed out of what they called picked men, *i. e.*, those only who had been actually engaged in the war, and were known as strong disunionists. The negroes in the sections of country these men controlled were kept in the most abject slavery and treated in every way contrary to the requirements of General Orders No. 129, from the War Department.

As late as September 29th, Captain J. H. Weber, agent of the Freedmen's Bureau, reported to Colonel Thomas, assistant-commissioner of the Bureau in the State of Mississippi, as follows:

In many cases negroes who left their homes during the war, and have been within our military lines, and having provided homes here for their families, going back to get their wives

and children, have been driven off and told that they could
not have them.   In several cases guards have been sent to
aid people in getting their families; in many others it has been
impracticable, as the distance was too great.   In portions of
the northern part of this district the colored people are
kept in slavery still.   The white people tell them that they
were free during the war, but the war is now over, and they
must go to work again as before.   The reports from sub-
commissioners nearest that locality show that the blacks are
in a much worse state than ever before, the able-bodied being
kept at work under the lash, and the young and infirm driven
off to care for themselves.   As to protection from the civil
authorities, there is no such thing outside of this city.

The conviction, however, that slavery in the old form
cannot be maintained has forced itself upon the minds of
many of those who ardently desired its preservation.
But while the necessity of a new system was recognized
as far as the right of property in the individual negro is
concerned, many attempts were made to introduce into
that new system the element of physical compulsion,
which, as above stated, is so generally considered indispensable.   This was done by simply adhering, as to the
treatment of the laborers, as much as possible to the
traditions of the old system, even where the relations
between employers and laborers had been fixed by contract.   The practice of corporal punishment was still
continued to a great extent, although, perhaps, not in so
regular a manner as it was practised in times gone by.
It is hardly necessary to quote any documentary evidence
on this point; the papers [originally] appended to this
report are full of testimony corroborating the statement.
The habit is so inveterate with a great many persons as
to render, on the least provocation, the impulse to whip
a negro almost irresistible.   It will continue to be so until
the Southern people will have learned, so as never to

forget it, that a black man has rights which a white man
is bound to respect.

Here I will insert some remarks on the general treatment of the blacks as a class, from the whites as a class.
It is not on the plantations and at the hands of the planters
themselves that the negroes have to suffer the greatest
hardships. Not only the former slaveholders, but the
non-slaveholding whites, who, even previous to the war,
seemed to be more ardent in their pro-slavery feelings
than the planters themselves, are possessed by a singularly
bitter and vindictive feeling against the colored race
since the negro has ceased to be property. The pecuniary
value which the individual negro formerly represented
having disappeared, the maiming and killing of colored
men seems to be looked upon by many as one of those
venial offences which must be forgiven to the outraged
feelings of a wronged and robbed people. Besides, the
services rendered by the negro to the National cause
during the war, which make him an object of special
interest to the loyal people, make him an object of particular vindictiveness to those whose hearts were set
upon the success of the rebellion. The number of murders
and assaults perpetrated upon negroes is very great; we
can form only an approximative estimate of what is going
on in those parts of the South which are not closely
garrisoned, and from which no regular reports are received,
by what occurs under the very eyes of our military authorities. As to my personal experience, I will only mention
that during my two days' sojourn at Atlanta one negro
was stabbed with fatal effect on the street, and three were
poisoned, one of whom died. While I was at Montgomery
one negro was cut across the throat evidently with intent
to kill, and another was shot, but both escaped with their
lives. Several papers [originally] attached to this report
give an account of the number of capital cases that

occurred at certain places during a certain period of
time. It is a sad fact that the perpetration of those
acts is not confined to that class of people which might
be called the rabble. Several "gentlemen of standing"
have been tried before military commissions for such
offences.

These statements are naturally not intended to apply
to all the individuals composing the Southern people.
There are certainly many planters who, before the rebellion, treated their slaves with kindness, and who now
continue to treat them as free laborers in the same manner.
There are now undoubtedly many plantations in the
South on which the relations between employers and
employés are based upon mutual good will. There are
certainly many people there who entertain the best
wishes for the welfare of the negro race, and who not
only never participated in any acts of violence, but who
heartily disapprove them. I have no doubt, a large
majority can, *as to actual participation*—not, however,
as to the bitter spirit—offer a good plea of not guilty. But
however large or small a number of people may be guilty
of complicity in such acts of persecution, those who are
opposed to them have certainly not shown themselves
strong enough to restrain those who perpetrate or favor
them. So far, the *spirit of persecution* has shown itself
so strong as to make the protection of the freedman by
the military arm of the Government in many localities
necessary—in almost all, desirable. It must not be
forgotten that in a community a majority of whose
members is peaceably disposed, but not willing or not
able to enforce peace and order, a comparatively small
number of bold and lawless men can determine the
character of the whole. The rebellion itself, in some of
the Southern States, furnished a striking illustration of
this truth.

GENERAL IDEAS AND SCHEMES OF WHITES CONCERNING THE
FREEDMEN

Some of the planters with whom I had occasion to
converse expressed their determination to adopt the
course which best accords with the spirit of free labor, to
make the negro work by offering him fair inducements,
to stimulate his ambition and to extend to him those
means of intellectual and moral improvement which are
best calculated to make him an intelligent, reliable and
efficient free laborer and a good and useful citizen.   Those
who expressed such ideas were almost invariably professed
Union men, and far above the average in point of mental
ability and culture.   I found a very few instances of
original secessionists also manifesting a willingness to
give the free-labor experiment a fair trial.   I can represent
the sentiments of this small class in no better way than
by quoting the language used by an Alabama judge in a
conversation with me.

I am one of the most thoroughly whipped men in the South
[said he]; I am a genuine old secessionist, and I believe now,
as I always did, we had the Constitutional right to secede.
But the war has settled that matter, and it is all over now.
As to this thing of free negro labor, I do not believe in it, but
I will give it a fair trial.   I have a plantation and am going
to make contracts with my hands, and then I want a real
Yankee to run the machine for me; not one of your New
Yorkers or Pennsylvanians, but the genuine article from
Massachusetts or Vermont—one who can not only farm, but
sing psalms and pray and teach school—a real abolitionist,
who believes in the thing just as I don't believe in it.   If he
does not succeed, I shall consider it proof conclusive that you
are wrong and I am right.

I regret to say that views and intentions so reasonable
I found confined to a small minority.   Aside from the

assumption that the negro will not work without physical compulsion, there appears to be another popular notion prevalent in the South, which stands as no less serious an obstacle in the way of a successful solution of the problem. It is that the negro exists for the special object of raising cotton, rice and sugar *for the whites*, and that it is illegitimate for him to indulge, like other people, in the pursuit of his own happiness in his own way. Although it is admitted that he has ceased to be the property of a master, it is not admitted that he has a right to become his own master. As Colonel Thomas, assistant-commissioner of the Freedmen's Bureau in Mississippi, in a letter addressed to me, very pungently expresses it:

The whites esteem the blacks their property by natural right, and, however much they may admit that the relations of masters and slaves have been destroyed by the war and by the President's emancipation proclamation, they still have an ingrained feeling that the blacks at large belong to the whites at large, and whenever opportunity serves they treat the colored people just as their profit, caprice or passion may dictate.

An ingrained feeling like this is apt to bring forth that sort of class legislation which produces laws to govern one class with no other view than to benefit another. This tendency can be distinctly traced in the various schemes for regulating labor which here and there see the light.

Immediately after the emancipation of the slaves, when the general confusion was most perplexing, the prevalent desire among the whites seemed to be, if they could not retain their negroes as slaves, to get rid of them entirely. Wild speculations were indulged in, how to remove the colored population at once and to import white laborers to fill its place; how to obtain a sufficient supply of coolies, etc., etc. Even at the present moment the removal of the freedmen is strongly advocated by those who have the traditional horror of a free negro, and in some sections, especially where the soil is more adapted to the cultivation of cereals than the raising of the staples, planters appear to be inclined to drive the negroes away, at least from their plantations. I was informed by a prominent South Carolinian in July, that the planters in certain localities in the northwestern part of his State had been on the point of doing so, but better counsel had been made to prevail upon them; and Colonel Robinson, 97th United States Colored Infantry, who had been sent out to several counties in southern Alabama to administer the amnesty oath, reported a general disposition among the planters of that region to "set the colored people, who had cultivated their crops during the summer, adrift as soon as the crops would be secured, and not to permit the negro to remain upon any footing of equality with the white man in that country." The disposition to drive away all the negroes from the plantations was undoubtedly confined to a few districts; and as far as the scheme of wholesale deportation is concerned, practical men became aware that, if they wanted to have any labor done, it would have been bad policy to move away the laborers they now have before others were there to fill their places. All these devices promising at best only distant relief, and free negro labor being the only thing in immediate prospect, many ingenious heads set about to solve the problem, how to make free labor compulsory by permanent regulations.

Shortly after the close of the war some South Carolina planters tried to solve this problem by introducing into the contracts provisions leaving only a small share of the crops to the freedmen, subject to all sorts of constructive

21

charges, and then binding them to work off the indebtedness they might incur. It being to a great extent in the power of the employer to keep the laborer in debt to him, the employer might thus obtain a permanent hold upon the person of the laborer. It was something like the system of peonage existing in Mexico. When these contracts were submitted to the military authorities for ratification, General Hatch, commanding at Charleston, at once issued an order prohibiting such arrangements. I had an opportunity to examine one of these contracts, and found it drawn up with much care, and evidently with a knowledge of the full bearings of the provisions so inserted.

I had a conversation with Mr. W. King, of Georgia, a gentleman of good political sentiments and undoubtedly benevolent intentions. He recommends a kind of guardianship to be exercised by the employer over the freedman. He is a fair representative, not of the completely unprejudiced, but of the more liberal-minded class of planters, and his sayings show in what direction even those who are not actuated by any spirit of bitterness against the negro seek a way out of their perplexities.

MUNICIPAL REGULATIONS

The motives and spirit bringing forth such ideas found a still clearer expression in some attempted municipal regulations. In no State within the range of my observation had, at the time of my visit, so much progress been made in the reorganization of local government as in Louisiana. In most of the parishes, the parish authorities had exercised their functions for some time; in others the organization was less complete. Governor Wells informed me that he had filled the parish offices with men recommended to him by the people of the parishes, and it is fair to assume that in most cases the appointees represented the views and sentiments of the ruling class. Some of the local authorities so appointed furnished us an indication of the principles upon which they thought it best to regulate free labor within their jurisdiction.

Mr. W. B. Stickney, agent of the Freedmen's Bureau at Shreveport, Louisiana, reported to the assistant-commissioner of the bureau in Louisiana as follows:

August 1.—The following is a literal copy of a document brought to this office by a colored man, which is conclusive evidence that there are those who still claim the negro as their property:

"This boy Calvin has permit to hire to whom he pleases, but I shall hold him as my property until set free by Congress. July 7, 1865. (Signed.) E. V. TULLY."

The spirit of the above also made its appearance in another form, in the action of the police board of the parish of Bossier, which was an attempt to revive at once the old slave laws, and to prevent the freedmen from obtaining employment (away) from their former masters. The gist of the enactment alluded to is contained in the paragraph directing the officers on patrol duty "to arrest and take up all idle and vagrant persons running at large without employment and carry them before the proper authorities, to be dealt with as the law directs." A regulation like this certainly would make it difficult for freedmen to leave their former masters for the purpose of seeking employment elsewhere. The matter was submitted to Brevet Major-General Hawkins, commanding western district of Louisiana, who issued an order prohibiting the parish police forces from arresting freedmen unless for positive offence against the law.

Clearer and more significant was the ordinance passed by the police board of the town of Opelousas, Louisiana.

It deserves careful perusal. Among a number of regulations applying exclusively to the negro, and depriving him of all liberty of locomotion, the following striking provisions are found:

Section 3. No negro or freedman shall be permitted to rent or keep a house within the limits of the town *under any circumstances*, and any one thus offending shall be ejected and *compelled to find an employer* or leave the town within twenty-four hours. The lessor or furnisher of the house leased or kept as above shall pay a fine of ten dollars for each offence.

Sec. 4. No negro or freedman shall reside within the limits of the town of Opelousas *who is not in the regular service of some white person or former owner.*

Section 8. No freedman shall sell, barter or exchange any articles of merchandise or traffic within the limits of Opelousas without permission in writing from his employer or the mayor or president of the board.

This ordinance was at first approved by a lieutenant-colonel of the United States forces having local command there, and it is worthy of note that thereupon the infection spread at once, and similar ordinances were entertained by the police boards of the town of Franklin and of the parish of St. Landry. The parish ordinance of St. Landry differs from the town ordinances of Opelousas and Franklin in several points, and wherever there is any difference, it is in the direction of greater severity. It imposes heavier fines and penalties throughout, and provides, in addition, for a system of corporal punishment. It is also ordained

that the aforesaid penalties shall be *summarily enforced*, and that it shall be the duty of the *captain or chief of patrol* to see that the aforesaid ordinances are promptly executed. While the town ordinances provide that a negro who does not find an employer shall be compelled to leave the town, the parish or county ordinance knows nothing of letting the negro go, but simply *compels* him to find an employer. Finally, it is ordained "that it shall be the duty of every *citizen* to act as a police officer for the detection of offenses and the apprehension of offenders, who shall be immediately handed over to the proper captain or chief of patrol."

It is true, an "organization of free labor" upon this plan would not be exactly the reëstablishment of slavery in its old form, but as for the practical working of the system with regard to the welfare of the freedman, the difference would only be for the worse. The negro is not only not permitted to be idle, but he is positively prohibited from working or carrying on a business for himself; he is *compelled* to be in the "regular service" of a white man, and if he has no employer he is *compelled* to find one. It requires only a simple understanding among the employers, and the negro is just as much bound to his employer "for better and for worse" as he was when slavery existed in the old form. If he should attempt to leave his employer on account of non-payment of wages or bad treatment he is *compelled* to find another one; and if no other will take him he will be *compelled* to return to him from whom he wanted to escape. The employers, under such circumstances, are naturally at liberty to arrange the matter of compensation according to their tastes, for the negro will be compelled to be in the regular service of an employer, whether he receives wages or not. The negro may be permitted by his employer "to hire his own time," for in the spirit and intent of the ordinance his time never properly belongs to him. But even the old system of slavery was more liberal in this respect, for such "permission to hire his own time" "shall never extend over seven days at any one time." (Section 4.) The sections providing for the "*summary*" enforcement of the penalties and placing

their infliction into the hands of the "chief of patrol"
—which, by the way, throws some light upon the objects
for which the militia is to be reorganized—place the
freedmen under a sort of permanent martial law, while
the provision investing every white man with the power
and authority of a police officer as against every black
man subjects them to the control even of those individuals
who in other communities are thought hardly fit to control
themselves. On the whole, this piece of legislation is a
striking embodiment of the idea that although the former
owner has lost his individual right of property in the
former slave, "the blacks at large belong to the whites
at large."

Such was the "organization of free labor" ordained
by officials appointed by Governor Wells, and these
ordinances were passed while both the emancipation
proclamation and a provision in the new constitution of
Louisiana abolishing slavery in that State forever were
recognized as being in full force. It is needless to say
that as soon as these proceedings came to the knowledge
of the Freedmen's Bureau and the department commander they were promptly overruled. But Governor
Wells did not remove the police boards that had thus
attempted to revive slavery in a new form.

The opposition to the negro's controlling his own labor,
carrying on business independently on his own account
—in one word, working for his own benefit—showed
itself in a variety of ways. Here and there municipal
regulations were gotten up heavily taxing or otherwise
impeding those trades and employments in which colored
people are most likely to engage. An ordinance passed
by the common council of Vicksburg is an illustration.
A letter from Colonel Thomas says:

You will see by the city ordinance that a drayman, or hack-
man, must file a bond of five hundred dollars, in addition to

paying for his license.   The mayor requires that the bondsmen must be freeholders.   The laws of this State do not, and never did, allow a negro to own land or hold property; the white citizens refuse to sign any bonds for the freedmen.   The white citizens and authorities say that it is for their interest to drive out all independent negro labor; that the freedmen must hire to white men if they want to do this kind of work.

I found several instances of a similar character in the course of my observations, of which I neglected to procure the documentary evidence.

It may be said that these are mere isolated cases; and so they are.   But they are the local outcroppings of a spirit which I found to prevail everywhere.   If there is any difference, it is in the degree of its intensity and the impatience or boldness with which it manifests itself. Of the agencies which so far restrained it from venturing more general demonstrations I shall speak in another part of this report.

EDUCATION OF THE FREEDMEN

It would seem that all those who sincerely desire to make the freedman a freeman in the true sense of the word, must also be in favor of so educating him as to make him clearly understand and appreciate the position he is to occupy in life, with all its rights and corresponding duties, and to impart to him all the knowledge necessary for enabling him to become an intelligent coöperator in the general movements of society.   As popular education is the true ground upon which the efficiency and the successes of free-labor society grow, no man who rejects the former can be accounted a consistent friend of the latter.   It is also evident that the education of the negro, to become general and effective after the full restoration of local government in the South, must be

protected and promoted as an integral part of the
educational systems of the States.

I made it a special point in most of the conversations
I had with Southern men to inquire into their views with
regard to this subject. I found, indeed, some gentlemen
of thought and liberal ideas who readily acknowledged
the necessity of providing for the education of the colored
people, and who declared themselves willing to coöperate
to that end to the extent of their influence. Some
planters thought of establishing schools on their estates,
and others would have been glad to see measures taken to
that effect by the people of the neighborhoods in which
they lived. But whenever I asked the question whether
it might be hoped that the legislatures of their States or
their county authorities would make provisions for negro
education, I never received an affirmative, and only in
two or three instances feebly encouraging, answers. At
last I was forced to the conclusion that, aside from a small
number of honorable exceptions, the popular prejudice
is almost as bitterly set against the negro's having the
advantage of education as it was when the negro was a
slave. There may be an improvement in that respect,
but it would prove only how universal the prejudice was
in former days. Hundreds of times I heard the old
assertion repeated, that "learning will spoil the nigger
for work," and that "negro education will be the ruin of
the South." Another most singular notion still holds a
potent sway over the minds of the masses—it is, that the
elevation of the blacks will be the degradation of the whites.
They do not understand yet that the continual contact
with an ignorant and degraded population must necessarily lower the mental and moral tone of the other classes
of society. This they might have learned from actual
experience, as we in the North have been taught, also
by actual experience, that the education of the lower

orders is the only reliable basis of the civilization as well
as of the prosperity of a people.

The consequence of the prejudice prevailing in the
Southern States is that colored schools can be established
and carried on with safety only under the protection of
our military forces, and that where the latter are withdrawn the former have to go with them.   There may be
a few localities forming exceptions, but their number is
certainly very small.   Chaplain Joseph Warren, superintendent of education under the Freedmen's Bureau in
Mississippi, after describing the general spirit of opposition
to the education of the negroes exhibited in Mississippi
and enumerating the reasons assigned for it, says:

In view of these things I have no doubt but that, if our
protection be withdrawn, negro education will be hindered in
every possible way, including obstructions by fraud and violence.   I have not the smallest expectation that, with the
State authorities in full power, a Northern citizen would be
protected in the exercise of his Constitutional right to teach
and preach to the colored people, and shall look for a renewal
of the fearful scenes in which Northerners were whipped,
tarred and feathered, warned off and murdered, before the war.

In the letter of General Kilby Smith occurs the following statement referring to the condition of things in
Mobile, Alabama:

Threats were made to destroy all school-houses in which
colored children were taught, and in two instances they were
fired.   The same threats were made against all churches in
which colored people assembled to worship, and one of them
burned.   Continued threats of assassination were made against
the colored preachers, and one of them is now under special
guard by order of Major-General Woods.

While I was in Louisiana General Canby received a
petition, signed by a number of prominent citizens of

New Orleans, praying him "to annul Order No. 38, which authorizes a board of officers to levy a tax on the taxpayers of the parish of Orleans to defray the expense of educating the freedmen." The reasons given for making this request are as follows:

Most of those who have lost their slaves by the rebellion, and whose lands are in the course of confiscation, being thus deprived of the means of raising corn for their hungry children, have not anything left wherewith to pay such a tax. The order in question, they consider, violates that sacred principle which requires taxation to be equal throughout the United States. *If the freedmen are to be educated at public expense, let it be done from the treasury of the United States.*

Many of the signers of this petition, who wanted to be relieved of the school tax on the ground of poverty, were counted among the wealthy men of New Orleans, and they forgot to state that the free colored element of Louisiana, which represents a capital of at least thirteen millions and pays a not inconsiderable proportion of the taxes, contributes at the same time for the support of the schools for whites, from which their children are excluded.

While travelling in the South I found in the newspapers an account of an interview between General Howard and some gentlemen from Mississippi, in which a Dr. Murdoch, from Columbus, Mississippi, figured somewhat conspicuously. He was reported to have described public sentiment in Mississippi as quite loyal, and especially in favor of giving the colored race a good education. I inquired at the Freedmen's Bureau whether anything was known there of a feeling so favorable to negro education among Dr. Murdoch's neighbors. It appears that the feeling of Dr. Murdoch's neighbors at Columbus was not only not in favor of negro education, but that, according to the report of the agent of the Freedmen's Bureau

at that place, "the citizens of the town are so prejudiced
against the negroes that they are opposed to all efforts
being made for their education or elevation"; that "the
people will not give rooms or allow the children of their
hired freedmen to attend the schools," and that the citizens of the place have written a letter to the officers, saying, "that they would respectfully ask that no freedmen's
schools be established under the auspices of the bureau,
as it would tend to disturb the present labor system, and
take from the fields labor that is so necessary to restore
the wealth of the State." It seems Dr. Murdoch's
neighbors do not form an exception to the general rule.
In this connection I may add that several instances have
come to my notice of statements about the condition of
things in the late rebel States, being set afloat by Southerners visiting the North, which would not bear close
investigation. The reason, probably, is that gentlemen
are attributing their own good intentions to the rest of
their people with too great a liberality.

Having thus given my experience and impressions with
regard to the spirit actuating the Southern people concerning the freedman and the free-labor problem, and before
inquiring into their prospective action, I beg leave to
submit a few remarks on the conduct of the negro.

THE FREEDMAN

The first Southern men with whom I came into contact
after my arrival at Charleston designated the general
conduct of the emancipated slaves as surprisingly good.
Some went even so far as to call it admirable. The
connection in which they used these laudatory terms
was this: A great many colored people while in slavery
had undoubtedly suffered much hardship and submitted
to great wrongs, partly inseparably connected with the

condition of servitude, and partly aggravated by the individual wilfulness and cruelty of their masters and overseers. They were suddenly set free; and not only that: their masters, but a short time ago almost omnipotent on their domains, found themselves, after their defeat in the war, all at once face to face with their former, slaves as a conquered and powerless class. Never was the temptation to indulge in acts of vengeance for wrongs suffered more strongly presented than to the colored people of the South; but no instance of such individual revenge was then on record, nor have I since heard of any case of violence that could be traced to such motives. The transition of the Southern negro from slavery to freedom was untarnished by any deeds of blood, and the apprehension so extensively entertained and so pathetically declaimed upon by many, that the sudden and general emancipation of the slaves would at once result in "all the horrors of St. Domingo," proved utterly groundless. This was the first impression I received after my arrival in the South, and I received it from the mouths of late slaveholders. Nor do I think the praise was unjustly bestowed. In this respect the emancipated slaves of the South can challenge comparison with any race long held in servitude and suddenly set free. As to the dangers of the future, I shall speak of them in another connection.

But at that point the unqualified praise stopped and the complaints began: the negroes would not work; they left their plantations and went wandering from place to place, stealing by the way; they preferred a life of idleness and vagrancy to that of honest and industrious labor; they either did not show any willingness to enter into contracts, or, if they did, showed a stronger disposition to break them than to keep them; they were becoming insubordinate and insolent to their former owners; they indulged

in extravagant ideas about their rights and relied upon
the Government to support them without work; in one
word, they had no conception of the rights freedom gave,
and of the obligations freedom imposed upon them.
These complaints I heard repeated with endless variations
wherever I went. Nor were they made without some
show of reason. I will review them one after another.

Unwillingness to work.—That there are among the
negroes a good many constitutionally lazy individuals
is certainly true. The propensity to idleness seems to
be rather strongly developed in the South generally,
without being confined to any particular race. It is also
true that the alacrity negroes put into their work depends
in a majority of cases upon certain combinations of
circumstances. It is asserted that the negroes have a
prejudice against working in the cultivation of cotton, rice
and sugar. Although this prejudice, probably arising
from the fact that the cotton, rice and sugar fields remind
the former slave of the worst experiences of his past life,
exists to some extent, it has not made the freedmen now
on the plantations unwilling to cultivate such crops as
the planters may have seen fit to raise. A few cases of
refusal may have occurred. But there is another fact
of which I have become satisfied in the course of my
observations, and which is of great significance: while
most of the old slaveholders complain of the laziness
and instability of their negro laborers, the Northern men
engaged in planting, with whom I have come into contact,
almost uniformly speak of their negro laborers with
satisfaction, and these Northern men almost exclusively
devote themselves to the cultivation of cotton. A good
many Southern planters, in view of the fact, expressed
to me their intention to engage Northern men for the
management of their plantations. This circumstance
would seem to prove that under certain conditions the

negro may be expected to work well. There are two
reasons by which it may be explained: first, that a Northern man knows from actual experience what free labor is,
and understands its management, which the late slaveholder, still clinging to the traditions of the old system,
does not; and then, that the negro has more confidence
in a Northern man than in his former master. When a
Northern man discovers among his laboring force an
individual that does not do his duty, his first impulse is
to discharge him, and he acts accordingly. When a late
slaveholder discovers such an individual among his
laborers, his first impulse is to whip him, and he is very
apt to suit the act to the impulse. Ill treatment is a
doubtful encouragement for free laborers, and it proves
more apt to drive those that are still at work away than
to make the plantation attractive to others. But if the
reasons above stated are sufficient to explain why the
negroes work better for Northern than for Southern men,
it will follow that a general improvement will take place
as soon as the latter fulfil the same conditions—that is,
as soon as Southern men learn what free labor is and how
to manage it in accordance with its principles, and as soon
as they succeed in gaining the confidence of the colored
people.

In the reports of officers of the Freedmen's Bureau
you will find frequent repetitions of the statement that
the negro generally works well where he is decently
treated and well compensated. Nor do the officers of
the Freedmen's Bureau alone think and say so. Southern
men, who were experimenting in the right direction,
expressed to me their opinion to the same effect. Some
of them told me that the negroes on their plantations
worked "as well as ever," or even "far better than they
had expected." It is true the number of planters who
made that admission was small, but it nearly corresponded

with the number of those who, according to their own statements, gave free negro labor a perfectly fair trial, while all those who prefaced everything they said with the assertion that "the negro will not work without physical compulsion," could find no end to their complaints. There are undoubtedly negroes who will not do well under the best circumstances, just as there are others who will do well under the worst.

In another part of this report I have already set forth the exceptional difficulties weighing upon the free-labor experiment in the South during this period of transition. The sudden leap from slavery to freedom is an exciting event in a man's life, and somewhat calculated to disturb his equanimity for a moment. People are on such occasions disposed to indulge themselves a little. It would have shown much more wisdom in the negroes if all of them had quietly gone to work again the next day. But it is not reasonable to expect the negroes to possess more wisdom than other races would exhibit under the same circumstances. Besides, the willingness to work depends, with whites as well as blacks, somewhat upon the nature of the inducements held out, and the unsatisfactory regulation of the matter of wages has certainly something to do with the instability of negro labor which is complained of. Northern men engaged in planting almost uniformly pay wages in money, while Southern planters, almost uniformly, have contracted with their laborers for a share in the crop. In many instances the shares are allotted between employers and laborers with great fairness; but in others the share promised to the laborers is so small as to leave them in the end very little or nothing. Moreover, the crops in the South looked generally very unpromising from the beginning, which naturally reduced the value falling to the lot of the laborer. I have heard a good many freedmen complain that, taking all things into consideration, they really did not know what they were working for except food, which in many instances was bad and scanty; and such complaints were frequently well founded. In a large number of cases the planters were not to blame for this; they had no available pecuniary means, and in many localities found it difficult to procure provisions. But these unfavorable circumstances, combined with the want of confidence in Southern men, were well calculated to have an influence upon the conduct of the negro as a laborer.

I have heard it said that money is no inducement which will make a negro work. It is certain that many of them, immediately after emancipation, had but a crude conception of the value of money and the uses it can be put to. It may, however, be stated as the general rule, that whenever they are at liberty to choose between wages in money and a share in the crop, they will choose the former and work better. Many cases of negroes engaged in little industrial pursuits came to my notice, in which they showed considerable aptness not only for gaining money, but also for saving and judiciously employing it. Some were even surprisingly successful. I visited some of the plantations divided up among freedmen and cultivated by them independently without the supervision of white men. In some instances I found very good crops and indications of general thrift and good management; in others the corn and cotton crops were in a neglected and unpromising state. The excuse made was in most cases that they had obtained possession of the ground too late in the season, and that, until the regular crops could be harvested, they were obliged to devote much of their time to the raising and sale of vegetables, watermelons etc., for the purpose of making a living in the meantime.

On the whole I feel warranted in making the following

statement: Many freedmen—not single individuals, but whole "plantation gangs"—are working well; others do not. The difference in their efficiency coincides in a great measure with a certain difference in the conditions under which they live. The conclusion lies near, that if the conditions under which they work well become general, their efficiency as free laborers will become general also, aside from individual exceptions. Certain it is, that by far the larger portion of the work done in the South is done by freedmen.

Vagrancy.—Large numbers of colored people left the plantations as soon as they became aware that they could do so with impunity. That they could so leave their former masters was for them the first test of the reality of their freedom. A great many flocked to the military posts and towns to obtain from the "Yankees" reliable information as to their new rights. Others were afraid lest by staying on the plantations where they had been held as slaves they might again endanger their freedom. Still others went to the cities, thinking that there the sweets of liberty could best be enjoyed. In some places they crowded together in large numbers, causing serious inconvenience. But a great many, probably a very large majority, remained on the plantations and made contracts with their former masters. The military authorities, and especially the agents of the Freedmen's Bureau, succeeded by continued exertions in returning most of those who were adrift to the plantations, or in finding other employment for them. After the first rush was over the number of vagrants grew visibly less. It may be said that where the Freedmen's Bureau is best organized there is least vagrancy among the negroes. Here and there they show considerable restlessness, partly owing to local, partly to general causes. Among the former, bad treatment is probably the most prominent;

22

among the latter, a feeling of distrust, uneasiness, anxiety about their future, which arises from their present unsettled condition. It is true, some are going from place to place because they are fond of it. The statistics of the Freedmen's Bureau show that the whole number of colored people supported by the Government since the close of the war was remarkably small and continually decreasing. This seems to show that the Southern negro, when thrown out of his accustomed employment, possesses considerable ability to support himself. It is possible, however, that in consequence of short crops, the destitution of the country and other disturbing influences, there may be more restlessness among the negroes next winter than there is at present. Where the results of this year's labor were very unsatisfactory, there will be a floating about of the population when the contracts of this year expire. It is to be expected, however, that the Freedmen's Bureau will be able to remedy evils of that kind. Other emancipatory movements, for instance the abolition of serfdom in Russia, have resulted in little or no vagrancy; but it must not be forgotten that the emancipated serfs were speedily endowed with the ownership of land, which gave them a permanent moral and material interest in the soil upon which they lived. A similar measure would do more to stop negro vagrancy in the South than the severest penal laws. In every country the number of vagrants stands in proportion to the number of people who have no permanent local interests, unless augmented by exceptional causes, such as war or famine.

Contracts.—Freedmen frequently show great disinclination to make contracts with their former masters. They are afraid lest in signing a paper they sign away their freedom, and in this respect they are distrustful of most Southern men. It generally requires personal assurances from a United States officer to make them feel safe. But

the advice of such an officer is almost uniformly followed.
In this manner an immense number of contracts has been
made, and it is daily increasing. A Northern man has no
difficulty in making contracts, and but little in enforcing
them. The complaints of Southern men that the contracts are not well observed by the freedmen are in
many instances well founded. The same can be said of
the complaints of freedmen with regard to the planters.
The negro, fresh from slavery, has naturally but a crude
idea of the binding force of a written agreement, and it
is galling to many of the planters to stand in such relations as a contract establishes to those who formerly were
their slaves. I was, however, informed by officers of the
Freedmen's Bureau, and by planters also, that things
were improving in that respect. Contracts will be more
readily entered into and more strictly kept as soon as the
intimate relations between labor and compensation are
better understood and appreciated on both sides.

Insolence and insubordination.—The new spirit which
emancipation has awakened in the colored people has
undoubtedly developed itself in some individuals, especially young men, to an offensive degree. Hence cases
of insolence on the part of freedmen occur. But such
occurrences are comparatively rare. On the whole, the
conduct of the colored people is far more submissive than
anybody had a right to expect. The acts of violence
perpetrated by freedmen against white persons do not
stand in any proportion to those committed by whites
against negroes. Every such occurrence is sure to be
noticed in the Southern papers, and we have heard of but
very few.

When Southern people speak of the insolence of the
negro, they generally mean something which persons
who never lived under the system of slavery are not apt
to appreciate. It is but very rarely what would be

called insolence among equals. But, as an old planter said to me, "our people cannot realize yet that the negro is free." A negro is called insolent whenever his conduct varies in any manner from what a Southern man was accustomed to when slavery existed.

The complaints made about the insubordination of the negro laborers on plantations have to be taken with the same allowance. There have been, no doubt, many cases in which freedmen showed a refractory spirit, where orders were disobeyed, and instructions disregarded. There have been some instances of positive resistance. But when inquiring into particulars, I found not unfrequently that the employer had adhered too strictly to his old way of doing things. I hardly heard any such complaints from Northern men. I have heard planters complain very earnestly of the insubordinate spirit of their colored laborers because they remonstrated against the practice of corporal punishment. This was looked upon as a symptom of an impending insurrection. A great many things are regarded in the old slave States as acts of insubordination on the part of the laborer which, in the free States, would be taken as perfectly natural and harmless. The fact is, a good many planters are at present more nervously jealous of their authority than before, while the freedmen are not always inclined to forget that they are free men.

Extravagant notions.—In many localities I found an impression prevailing among the negroes that some great change was going to take place about Christmas. Feeling uneasy in their present condition, they indulged in the expectation that Government intended to make some further provision for their future welfare, especially by ordering distributions of land among them. To counteract this expectation, which had a tendency to interfere seriously with the making of contracts for the next season,

it was considered necessary to send military officers, and
especially agents of the Freedmen's Bureau, among them,
who, by administering sound advice and spreading correct
information, would induce them to suit their conduct to
their actual circumstances. While in the South I heard
of many instances in which this measure had the desired
effect, and it is to be expected that the effect was uniformly
good wherever judicious officers were so employed.

Impressions like the above are very apt to spread among
the negroes, for the reason that they ardently desire to
become freeholders. In the independent possession of
landed property they see the consummation of their
deliverance. However mistaken their notions may be
in other respects, it must be admitted that this instinct
is correct.

Relations between the two races.—There are whites in
the South who profess great kindness for the negro.
Many of them are, no doubt, sincere in what they say.
But as to the feelings of the masses, it is hardly necessary
to add anything to what I have already stated. I have
heard it asserted that the negroes also cherish feelings
of hostility to the whites. Taking this as a general
assertion, I am satisfied that it is incorrect. The negroes
do not trust their late masters because they do not feel
their freedom sufficiently assured. Many of them may
harbor feelings of resentment towards those who now ill-
treat and persecute them, but as they practiced no revenge
after their emancipation for wrongs suffered while in
slavery, so their present resentments are likely to cease
as soon as the persecution ceases. If the persecution
and the denial of their rights as freemen continue, the
resentments growing out of them will continue and spread.
The negro is constitutionally docile and eminently good-
natured. Instances of the most touching attachment of
freedmen to their old masters and mistresses have come

to my notice. To a white man whom they believe to
be sincerely their friend they cling with greater affection
than even to one of their own race. By some Northern
speculators their confidence has been sadly abused.
Nevertheless, the trust they place in persons coming
from the North, or in any way connected with the Government, is most childlike and unbounded. There may be
individual exceptions, but I am sure they are not numerous.
Those who enjoy their confidence enjoy also their affection.
Centuries of slavery have not been sufficient to make
them the enemies of the white race. If in the future a
feeling of mutual hostility should develop itself between
the races, it will probably not be the fault of those who
have shown such an inexhaustible patience under the
most adverse and trying circumstances.

In some places that I visited I found apprehensions
entertained by whites of impending negro insurrections.
Whenever our military commanders found it expedient to
subject the statements made to that effect by whites to close
investigation, they uniformly found them unwarranted
by fact. In many instances there were just reasons for
supposing that such apprehensions were industriously
spread for the purpose of serving as an excuse for further
persecution. In the papers [originally] annexed to this
report you will find testimony supporting this statement.
The negro is easily led; he is always inclined to follow
the advice of those he trusts. I do, therefore, not consider a negro insurrection probable as long as the freedmen
are under the direct protection of the Government and
may hope to see their grievances redressed without resorting to the extreme means of self-protection. There
would, perhaps, be danger of insurrections if the Government should withdraw its protection from them, and if,
against an attempt on the part of the whites to reduce
them to something like their former condition, they

should find themselves thrown back upon their own resources. Of this contingency I shall speak below.

Education.—That the negroes should have come out of slavery as an ignorant class is not surprising when we consider that it was a penal offence to teach them while they were in slavery; but their eager desire to learn and the alacrity and success with which they avail themselves of every facility offered to them in that respect, has become a matter of notoriety. The statistics of the Freedmen's Bureau show to what extent such facilities have been offered and what results have been attained. As far as my information goes, these results are most encouraging for the future.

PROSPECTIVE—THE REACTIONARY TENDENCY

I stated above that, in my opinion, the solution of the social problem in the South did not depend upon the capacity and conduct of the negro alone, but in the same measure upon the ideas and feelings entertained and acted upon by the whites. What their ideas and feelings were while under my observation, and how they affected the contact of the two races, I have already set forth. The question arises, what policy will be adopted by the "ruling class" when all restraint imposed upon them by the military power of the National Government is withdrawn, and they are left free to regulate matters according to their own tastes? It would be presumptuous to speak of the future with absolute certainty; but it may safely be assumed that the same causes will always tend to produce the same effects. As long as a majority of the Southern people believe that "the negro will not work without physical compulsion," and that "the blacks at large belong to the whites at large," that belief will tend to produce a system of coercion, the enforcement of which will be aided by the hostile feeling against the negro now prevailing among the whites, and by the general spirit of violence which in the South was fostered by the influence slavery exercised upon the popular character. It is, indeed, not probable that a general attempt will be made to restore slavery in its old form, on account of the barriers which such an attempt would find in its way; but there are systems intermediate between slavery as it formerly existed in the South, and free labor as it exists in the North, but more nearly related to the former than to the latter, *the introduction of which will be attempted.* I have already noticed some movements in that direction, which were made under the very eyes of our military authorities, and of which the Opelousas and St. Landry ordinances were the most significant. Other things of more recent date, such as the new negro code submitted by a committee to the legislature of South Carolina, are before the country. They have all the same tendency, because they all spring from the same cause.

It may be objected that evidence has been given of a contrary spirit by the State conventions which passed ordinances abolishing slavery in their States, and making it obligatory upon the legislatures to enact laws for the protection of the freedmen. While acknowledging the fact, I deem it dangerous to be led by it into any delusions. As to the motives upon which they acted when abolishing slavery, and their understanding of the bearings of such an act, we may safely accept the standard they have set up for themselves. When speaking of popular demonstrations in the South in favor of submission to the Government, I stated that the principal and almost the only argument used was, that they found themselves in a situation in which "they could do no better." It was the same thing with regard to the abolition of slavery; wherever abolition was publicly advocated, whether in popular meetings or

in State conventions, it was on the ground of necessity—
not unfrequently with the significant addition that, as
soon as they had once more control of their own State
affairs, they could settle the labor question to suit themselves, whatever they might have to submit to for the
present.   Not only did I find this to be the common talk
among the people, but the same sentiment was openly
avowed by public men in speech and print.   Some declarations of that kind, made by men of great prominence,
have passed into the newspapers and are undoubtedly
known to you.   The current sentiment is expressed in
the language of a candidate for a seat in the State convention of Mississippi.   It is a card addressed to the
voters of Wilkinson county, Mississippi, by Gen. W.
L. Brandon.   The General complains of having been
called "an unconditional, immediate emancipationist
—an abolitionist."   He indignantly repels the charge
and avows himself a good pro-slavery man.

But, fellow-citizens [says he], what I may in common with
you have to submit to, is a very different thing.   Slavery
has been taken from us; the power that has already practically
abolished it threatens totally and forever to abolish it.   *But
does it follow that I am in favor of this thing?   By no means.*
My honest conviction is, we must accept the situation as it is,
*until we can get control once more of our own State affairs.   We
cannot do otherwise and get our place again in the Union, and
occupy a position and exert an influence that will protect us against
greater evils which threaten us.*   I must, as any other man who
votes or holds an office, submit *for the time* to evils I cannot
remedy.

General Brandon was elected on that platform, and
in the convention voted for the ordinance abolishing
slavery, and imposing upon the legislature the duty to
pass laws for the protection of the freedmen.   And General

Brandon is certainly looked upon in Mississippi as an honorable man, and an honest politician. What he will vote for when his people have got once more control of their own State affairs, and his State has regained its position and influence in the Union, it is needless to ask. I repeat, his case is not an isolated one. He has only put in print what, as my observations lead me to believe, a majority of the people say even in more emphatic language; and the deliberations of several legislatures in that part of the country show what it means. I deem it unnecessary to go into further particulars.

It is worthy of note that the convention of Mississippi —and the conventions of other States have followed its example—imposed upon subsequent legislatures the obligation not only to pass laws for the protection of the freedmen in person and property, but also *to guard against the dangers arising from sudden emancipation.* This language is not without significance; not the blessings of a full development of free labor, but only the dangers of emancipation are spoken of. It will be observed that this clause is so vaguely worded as to authorize the legislatures to place any restriction they may see fit upon the emancipated negro, in perfect consistency with the amended State constitutions; for it rests with them to define what the dangers of sudden emancipation consist in, and what measures may be required to guard against them. It is true, the clause does not authorize the legislatures to reëstablish slavery in the old form; but they may pass whatever laws they see fit, stopping short only one step of what may strictly be defined as "slavery." Peonage of the Mexican pattern, or serfdom of some European pattern, may under that clause be considered admissible; and looking at the legislative attempts already made, especially the labor code now under consideration in the legislature of South Carolina, it appears not only

possible, but eminently probable, that the laws which
will be passed to guard against the dangers arising from
emancipation will be directed against the spirit of
emancipation itself.

A more tangible evidence of good intentions would
seem to have been furnished by the admission of negro
testimony in the courts of justice, which has been conceded
in some of the Southern States, at least in point of form.
This being a matter of vital interest to the colored man,
I inquired into the feelings of people concerning it with
particular care. At first I found hardly any Southern
man that favored it. Even persons of some liberality
of mind saw seemingly insurmountable objections. The
appearance of a general order issued by General Swayne
in Alabama, which made it optional for the civil authorities either to admit negro testimony in the State courts
or to have all cases in which colored people were concerned
tried by officers of the bureau or military commissions,
seemed to be the signal for a change of position on the
part of the politicians. A great many of them, seeing
a chance for getting rid of the jurisdiction of the Freedmen's Bureau, dropped their opposition somewhat suddenly and endeavored to make the admission of negro
testimony in the State courts palatable to the masses by
assuring them that at all events it would rest with the
judges and juries to determine in each case before them
whether the testimony of negro witnesses was worth
anything or not. One of the speeches delivered at
Vicksburg, already referred to in another connection,
furnishes a specimen of that line of argument.

In my despatch from Montgomery, Alabama, I sug-
gested to you that instructions be issued making it part
of the duty of agents of the Freedmen's Bureau to appear
in the State courts as the freedmen's next friend, and to
forward reports of the proceedings had in the principal

cases to the headquarters of the bureau. In this manner it would have been possible to ascertain to what extent the admission of negro testimony secured to the colored man justice in the State courts. As the plan does not seem to have been adopted, we must form our conclusions from evidence less complete. Among the [originally] annexed documents there are several statements concerning its results, made by gentlemen whose business it was to observe. The opinions expressed in these papers are uniformly unfavorable. It is to be hoped that at other places better results have been attained. But I may state that even by prominent Southern men, who were anxious to have the jurisdiction of the State courts extended over the freedmen, the admission was made to me that the testimony of a negro would have but little weight with a Southern jury. I frequently asked the question, "Do you think a jury of your people would be apt to find a planter who has whipped one of his negro laborers guilty of assault and battery?" The answer almost invariably was, " You must make some allowance for the prejudices of our people."

It is probable that the laws excluding negro testimony from the courts will be repealed in all the States lately in rebellion if it is believed that a satisfactory arrangement of this matter may in any way facilitate the "readmission" of the States, but I apprehend such arrangements will hardly be sufficient to secure to the colored man impartial justice as long as the feelings of the whites are against him and they think that his rights are less entitled to respect than their own. More potent certainly than the laws of a country are the opinions of right and wrong entertained by its people. When the spirit of a law is in conflict with such opinions, there is but little prospect of its being faithfully put in execution, especially where those who hold such opinions are the same who have to administer the laws.

The facility with which Southern politicians acquiesce in the admission of negro testimony is not surprising when we consider that the practical management of the matter will rest with their own people. I found them less accommodating with regard to "Constitutional amendment." Nine-tenths of the intelligent men with whom I had any conversation upon that subject expressed their willingness to ratify the first section, abolishing slavery throughout the United States, but not the second section, empowering Congress "to enforce the foregoing by appropriate legislation." I feel warranted in saying that, while I was in the South, this was the prevailing sentiment. Nevertheless, I deem it probable that the "Constitutional amendment" will be ratified by every State legislature, provided the Government insists upon such ratification as a *conditio sine qua non* of readmission. It is instructive to observe how powerful and immediate an effect the announcement of such a condition by the Government produces in Southern conventions and legislatures. It would be idle to assume, however, that a telegraphic despatch, while it may beat down all parliamentary opposition to this or that measure, will at the same time obliterate the prejudices of the people; nor will it prevent those prejudices from making themselves seriously felt in the future. It will require measures of a more practical character to prevent the dangers which, as everybody that reads the signs of the times must see, are now impending.

THE MILITIA

I do not mean to say that the Southern people intend to retrace the steps they have made as soon as they have resumed control of their State affairs. Although they regret the abolition of slavery, they certainly do not

intend to reëstablish it in its old form. Although they
are at heart opposed to the admission of negro testimony
in the courts of justice, they probably will not reënact
the laws excluding it. But while accepting the "abolition
of slavery," they think that some species of serfdom,
peonage or some other form of compulsory labor is not
slavery, and may be introduced without a violation of
their pledge. Although formally admitting negro testimony, they think that negro testimony will be taken
practically for what they themselves consider it "worth."
What particular shape the reactionary movement will
assume it is at present unnecessary to inquire. There
are a hundred ways of framing apprenticeship, vagrancy
or contract laws, which will serve the purpose. Even
the mere reorganization of the militia upon the old footing
will go far towards accomplishing the object. To this
point I beg leave to invite your special attention.

The people of the Southern States show great anxiety
to have their militia reorganized, and in some instances
permission has been given. In the case of Mississippi
I gave you my reasons for opposing the measure under
existing circumstances. They were, first, that county
patrols had already been in existence, and had to be disbanded on account of their open hostility to Union people
and freedmen. Second, that the governor proposed to
arm the people upon the ground that the inhabitants
refused to assist the military authorities in the suppression
of crime, and that the call was addressed, not to the loyal
citizens of the United States, but expressly to the "young
men who had so distinguished themselves for gallantry"
in the rebel service. And third, because the State was still
under martial law, and the existence of organized and
armed bodies not under the control of the military
commander was inconsistent with that state of things.

But there are other more general points of view from

which this question must be looked at in order to be appreciated in its most important bearings. I may state, without fear of contradiction, that, in every case where permission was asked for reorganizing the militia, the privilege or duty of serving in that armed organization was intended to be confined to the whites. In the conversations I had with Southern men about this matter, the idea of admitting colored people to the privilege of bearing arms as a part of the militia was uniformly treated by them as a thing not to be thought of. The militia, whenever organized, will thus be composed of men belonging to one class, to the total exclusion of another. This concentration of organized physical power in the hands of one class will necessarily tend, and is undoubtedly designed, to give that class absolute physical control of the other. The specific purpose for which the militia is to be reorganized appears clearly from the uses it was put to whenever a local organization was effected. It is the restoration of the old patrol system which was one of the characteristic features of the régime of slavery. The services which such patrols are expected to perform consist in maintaining what Southern people understand to be the order of society. Indications are given in several of the [originally] accompanying documents. Among others, the St. Landry and Bossier ordinances define with some precision what the authority and duties of the "chief patrols" are to be. The militia, organized for the distinct purpose of enforcing the authority of the whites over the blacks, is in itself practically sufficient to establish and enforce a system of compulsory labor without there being any explicit laws for it; and, being sustained and encouraged by public opinion, the chief and members of "county patrols" are not likely to be over-nice in the construction of their orders. This is not a mere supposition, but an opinion based upon experience already gathered. As I stated above, the reorganization of the county patrol system upon the basis here described will result in the establishment of a sort of permanent martial law over the negro.

It is, therefore, not even necessary that the reaction against that result of the war, which consists in emancipation, should manifest itself by very obnoxious legislative enactments, just as in some of the slave States slavery did not exist by virtue of the State constitution. It may be practically accomplished, and is, in fact, practically accomplished whenever the freedman is not protected by the Federal authorities, without displaying its character and aims upon the statute book.

NEGRO INSURRECTIONS AND ANARCHY

That in times like ours, and in a country like this, a reaction in favor of compulsory labor cannot be ultimately successful, is as certain as it was that slavery could not last forever. But a movement in that direction can prevent much good that might be accomplished, and produce much evil that might be avoided. Not only will such a movement seriously interfere with all efforts to organize an efficient system of free labor, and thus very materially retard the return of prosperity in the South, but it may bring on a crisis as dangerous and destructive as the war of the rebellion itself.

I stated above that I did not deem a negro insurrection probable as long as the freedmen were assured of the direct protection of the National Government. Whenever they are in trouble, they raise their eyes up to that power, and although they may suffer, yet, as long as that power is visibly present, they continue to hope. But when State authority in the South is fully restored, the Federal forces withdrawn and the Freedmen's Bureau abolished, the colored man will find himself turned over to the mercies of those whom he does not trust. If then an attempt is made to strip him again of those rights which he justly thought he possessed, he will be apt to feel that he can hope for no redress unless he procure it himself. If ever the negro is capable of rising, he will rise then. Men who never struck a blow for the purpose of gaining their liberty, when they were slaves, are apt to strike when, their liberty once gained, they see it again in danger. However great the patience and submissiveness of the colored race may be, it cannot be presumed that its active participation in a war against the very men with whom it again stands face to face, has remained entirely without influence upon its spirit.

What a general insurrection of the negroes would result in, whether it would be easy or difficult to suppress it, whether the struggle would be long or short, what race would suffer most, are questions which will not be asked by those who understand the problem to be, not how to suppress a negro insurrection, but how to prevent it. Certain it is, it would inflict terrible calamities upon both whites and blacks, and present to the world the spectacle of atrocities which ought to be foreign to civilized nations. The negro, in his ordinary state, is docile and good-natured; but when once engaged in a bloody business, it is difficult to say how far his hot impulses would carry him; and as to the Southern whites, the barbarous scenes the country has witnessed since the close of the rebellion indicate the temper with which they would fight the negro as an insurgent. It would be a war of extermination, revolting in its incidents, and with ruin and desolation in its train. There may be different means by which it can be prevented, but there is only one certain of effect: it is, that the provocations be avoided which may call it forth.

But even if it be prevented by other means, it is not

23

'the only danger which a reactionary movement will bring upon the South. Nothing renders society more restless than a social revolution but half accomplished. It naturally tends to develop its logical consequences, but is hindered by adverse agencies which work in another direction; nor can it return to the point from which it started. There are, then, continual vibrations and fluctuations between two opposites which keep society in the nervous uneasiness and excitement growing from the lingering strife between the antagonistic tendencies. All classes of society are intensely dissatisfied with things as they are. General explosions may be prevented, but they are always imminent. This state of uncertainty impedes all successful working of the social forces; people, instead of devoting themselves with confidence and steadiness to solid pursuits, are apt to live from hand to mouth, or to indulge in fitful experiments; capital ventures out but with great timidity; the lawless elements of the community take advantage of the general confusion and dissatisfaction, and society drifts into anarchy. There is probably at the present moment no country in the civilized world which contains such an accumulation of anarchical elements as the South. The strife of the antagonistic tendencies here described is aggravated by the passions inflamed and the general impoverishment brought about by a long and exhaustive war, and the South will have to suffer the evils of anarchical disorder until means are found to effect a final settlement of the labor question in accordance with the logic of the great revolution.

THE TRUE PROBLEM—DIFFICULTIES AND REMEDIES

In seeking remedies for such disorders, we ought to keep in view, above all, the nature of the problem which is to be solved. As to what is commonly termed "reconstruction," it is not only the political machinery of the States and their constitutional relations to the General Government, but the whole organism of Southern society that must be reconstructed, or rather constructed anew, so as to bring it in harmony with the rest of American society. The difficulties of this task are not to be considered overcome when the people of the South take the oath of allegiance and elect governors and legislatures and members of Congress and militia captains. That this would be done had become certain as soon as the surrenders of the Southern armies had made further resistance impossible, and nothing in the world was left, even to the most uncompromising rebel, but to submit or to emigrate. It was also natural that they should avail themselves of every chance offered them to resume control of their home affairs and to regain their influence in the Union. But this can hardly be called the first step towards the solution of the true problem, and it is a fair question to ask, whether the hasty gratification of their desire to resume such control would not create new embarrassments.

The true nature of the difficulties of the situation is this: The General Government of the republic has, by proclaiming the emancipation of the slaves, commenced a great social revolution in the South, but has, as yet, not completed it. Only the negative part of it is accomplished. The slaves are emancipated in point of form, but free labor has not yet been put in the place of slavery in point of fact. And now, in the midst of this critical period of transition, the power which originated the revolution is expected to turn over its whole future development to another power which from the beginning was hostile to it and has never yet entered into its spirit, leaving the class in whose favor it was made completely without

power to protect itself and to take an influential part
in that development. The history of the world will be
searched in vain for a proceeding similar to this which
did not lead either to a rapid and violent reaction, or to
the most serious trouble and civil disorder. It cannot be
said that the conduct of the Southern people since the
close of the war has exhibited such extraordinary wisdom
and self-abnegation as to make them an exception to the
rule.

In my despatches from the South I repeatedly expressed
the opinion that the people were not yet in a frame of
mind to legislate calmly and understandingly upon the
subject of free negro labor. And this I reported to be
the opinion of some of our most prominent military
commanders and other observing men. It is, indeed,
difficult to imagine circumstances more unfavorable for
the development of a calm and unprejudiced public
opinion than those under which the Southern people are
at present laboring. The war has not only defeated their
political aspirations, but it has broken up their whole
social organization. When the rebellion was put down,
they found themselves not only conquered in a political and military sense, but economically ruined. The
planters, who represented the wealth of the Southern
country, are partly laboring under the severest embarrassments, partly reduced to absolute poverty. Many who
are stripped of all available means, and have nothing but
their land, cross their arms in gloomy despondency,
incapable of rising in a manly resolution. Others, who
still possess means, are at a loss how to use them, as their
old way of doing things is, by the abolition of slavery,
rendered impracticable, at least where the military arm
of the government has enforced emancipation. Others
are still trying to go on in the old way, and that old way
is in fact the only one they understand, and in which they

have any confidence. Only a minority is trying to adopt the new order of things. A large number of the plantations, probably a considerable majority of the more valuable estates, is under heavy mortgages, and the owners know that, unless they retrieve their fortunes in a comparatively short space of time, their property will pass out of their hands. Almost all are, to some extent embarrassed. The nervous anxiety which such a state of things produces extends also to those classes of society which, although not composed of planters, were always in close business connection with the planting interest, and there was hardly a branch of commerce or industry in the South which was not directly or indirectly so connected. Besides, the Southern soldiers, when returning from the war, did not, like the Northern soldiers, find a prosperous community which merely waited for their arrival to give them remunerative employment. They found, many of them, their homesteads destroyed, their farms devastated, their families in distress; and those that were less unfortunate found, at all events, an impoverished and exhausted community which had but little to offer them. Thus a great many have been thrown upon the world to shift as best they can. They must do something honest or dishonest, and must do it soon, to make a living, and their prospects are, at present, not very bright. Thus that nervous anxiety to hastily repair broken fortunes, and to prevent still greater ruin and distress, embraces nearly all classes, and imprints upon all the movements of the social body a morbid character.

In which direction will these people be most apt to turn their eyes? Leaving the prejudice of race out of the question, from early youth they have been acquainted with but one system of labor, and with that one system they have been in the habit of identifying all their interests. They know of no way to help themselves but the one they

are accustomed to. Another system of labor is presented
to them, which, however, owing to circumstances which
they do not appreciate, appears at first in an improvising
light. To try it they consider an experiment which
they cannot afford to make while their wants are urgent.
They have not reasoned calmly enough to convince themselves that the trial must be made. It is, indeed, not
wonderful that, under such circumstances, they should
study, not how to introduce and develop free labor, but
how to avoid its introduction, and how to return as much
and as quickly as possible to something like the old order
of things. Nor is it wonderful that such studies should
find an expression in their attempts at legislation. But
the circumstance that this tendency is natural does not
render it less dangerous and objectionable. The practical
question presents itself: Is the immediate restoration of
the late rebel States to absolute self-control so necessary
that it must be done even at the risk of endangering one
of the great results of the war, and of bringing on in those
States insurrection or anarchy, or would it not be better
to postpone that restoration until such dangers are passed?
If, as long as the change from slavery to free labor is
known to the Southern people only by its destructive
results, these people must be expected to throw obstacles
in its way, would it not seem necessary that the movement
of social "reconstruction" be kept in the right channel
by the hand of the power which originated the change,
until that change can have disclosed some of its beneficial
effects?

It is certain that every success of free negro labor will
augment the number of its friends, and disarm some of
the prejudices and assumptions of its opponents. I am
convinced one good harvest made by unadulterated free
labor in the South would have a far better effect than all
the oaths that have been taken, and all the ordinances

that have as yet been passed by Southern conventions.
But how can such a result be attained? The facts enumerated in this report, as well as the news we receive from
the South from day to day, must make it evident to
every unbiased observer that unadulterated free labor
cannot be had at present, unless the National Government
holds its protective and controlling hand over it. It
appears, also, that the more efficient this protection of
free labor against all disturbing and reactionary influences,
the sooner may such a satisfactory result be looked for.
One reason why the Southern people are so slow in accommodating themselves to the new order of things is, that
they confidently expect soon to be permitted to regulate
matters according to their own notions. Every concession made to them by the Government has been taken
as an encouragement to persevere in this hope, and,
unfortunately for them, this hope is nourished by influences from other parts of the country. Hence their
anxiety to have their State governments restored *at once*,
to have the troops withdrawn, and the Freedmen's Bureau
abolished, although a good many discerning men know
well that, in view of the lawless spirit still prevailing, it
would be far better for them to have the general order
of society firmly maintained by the Federal power until
things have arrived at a final settlement. Had, from the
beginning, the conviction been forced upon them that
the adulteration of the new order of things by the admixture of elements belonging to the system of slavery would
under no circumstances be permitted, a much larger
number would have launched their energies into the new
channel, and, seeing that they could do no "better,"
faithfully coöperated with the Government. It is hope
which fixes them in their perverse notions. That hope
nourished or fully gratified, they will persevere in the
same direction. That hope destroyed, a great many will,

by the force of necessity, at once accommodate themselves
to the logic of the change.   If, therefore, the National
Government firmly and unequivocally announces its
policy not to give up the control of the free-labor reform
until it is finally accomplished, the progress of that reform
will undoubtedly be far more rapid and far less difficult
than it will be if the attitude of the Government is such
as to permit contrary hopes to be indulged in.

The machinery by which the Government has so far
exercised its protection of the negro and of free labor in
the South—the Freedmen's Bureau—is very unpopular
in that part of the country, as every institution placed
there as a barrier to reactionary aspirations would be.
That abuses were committed with the management of
freedmen's affairs; that some of the officers of the bureau
were men of more enthusiasm than discretion, and in
many cases went beyond their authority: all this is certainly true.   But, while the Southern people are always
ready to expatiate upon the shortcomings of the Freedmen's Bureau, they are not so ready to recognize the
services it has rendered.   I feel warranted in saying that
not half of the labor that has been done in the South this
year, or will be done there next year, would have been or
would be done but for the exertions of the Freedmen's
Bureau.   The confusion and disorder of the transition
period would have been infinitely greater had not an
agency interfered which possessed the confidence of the
emancipated slaves; which could disabuse them of any
extravagant notions and expectations and be trusted;
which could administer to them good advice and be
voluntarily obeyed.   No other agency, except one placed
there by the National Government, could have wielded
that moral power whose interposition was so necessary
to prevent Southern society from falling at once into the
chaos of a general collision between its different elements.

That the success achieved by the Freedmen's Bureau is
as yet very incomplete cannot be disputed. A more
perfect organization and a more carefully selected person-
nel may be desirable; but it is doubtful whether a more
suitable machinery can be devised to secure to free labor
in the South that protection against disturbing influences
which the nature of the situation still imperatively
demands.

IMMIGRATION

A temporary continuation of National control in the
Southern States would also have a most beneficial effect
as regards the immigration of Northern people and
Europeans into that country; and such immigration
would, in its turn, contribute much to the solution of the
labor problem. Nothing is more desirable for the South
than the importation of new men and new ideas. One
of the greatest drawbacks under which the Southern
people are laboring is, that for fifty years they have been
in no sympathetic communion with the progressive ideas
of the times. While professing to be in favor of free trade,
they adopted and enforced a system of prohibition, as
far as those ideas were concerned, which was in conflict
with their cherished institution of slavery; and, as almost
all the progressive ideas of our days were in conflict with
slavery, the prohibition was sweeping. It had one peculiar effect, which we also notice with some Asiatic nations which follow a similar course. The Southern people
honestly maintained and believed, not only that as a
people they were highly civilized, but that their civilization was the highest that could be attained, and ought
to serve as a model to other nations the world over. The
more enlightened individuals among them felt sometimes
a vague impression of the barrenness of their mental life,

and the barbarous peculiarities of their social organization; but very few ever dared to investigate and to expose the true cause of these evils. Thus the people were so wrapt up in self-admiration as to be inaccessible to the voice even of the best-intentioned criticism. Hence the delusion they indulged in as to the absolute superiority of their race—a delusion which, in spite of the severe test it has lately undergone, is not yet given up; and will, as every traveller in the South can testify from experience, sometimes express itself in singular manifestations. This spirit, which for so long a time has kept the Southern people back while the world besides was moving, is even at this moment still standing as a serious obstacle in the way of progress.

Nothing can, therefore, be more desirable than that the contact between the Southern people and the outside world should be as strong and intimate as possible; and in no better way can this end be subserved than by immigration in mass. Of the economic benefits which such immigration would confer upon the owners of the soil, it is hardly necessary to speak.

Immigration wants encouragement. As far as this encouragement consists in the promise of material advantage, it is already given. There are large districts in the South in which an industrious and enterprising man, with some capital, and acting upon correct principles, cannot fail to accumulate large gains in a comparatively short time, as long as the prices of the staples do not fall below what they may reasonably be expected to be for some time to come. A Northern man has, besides, the advantage of being served by the laboring population of that region with greater willingness.

But among the principal requisites for the success of the immigrant are personal security and a settled condition of things. Personal security is honestly promised by the thinking men of the South; but another question

is, whether the promise and good intentions of the thinking
men will be sufficient to restrain and control the populace,
whose animosity against "Yankee interlopers" is only
second to their hostile feeling against the negro. If the
military forces of the Government should be soon and
completely withdrawn, I see reasons to fear that in many
localities immigrants would enjoy the necessary security
only when settling down together in numbers strong
enough to provide for their own protection. On the
whole, no better encouragement can be given to immigration, as far as individual security is concerned, than the
assurance that the National Government will be near to
protect them until such protection is no longer needed.

The South needs capital. But capital is notoriously
timid and averse to risk itself, not only where there
actually is trouble, but where there is serious and continual danger of trouble. Capitalists will be apt to consider
—and they are by no means wrong in doing so—that no
safe investments can be made in the South as long as
Southern society is liable to be convulsed by anarchical
disorders. No greater encouragement can, therefore,
be given to capital to transfer itself to the South than the
assurance that the Government will continue to control
the development of the new social system in the late rebel
States until such dangers are averted by a final settlement
of things upon a thorough free-labor basis.

How long the National Government should continue
that control depends upon contingencies. It ought to
cease as soon as its objects are attained; and its objects
will be attained sooner and with less difficulty if nobody
is permitted to indulge in the delusion that it will cease
before they are attained. This is one of the cases in which
a determined policy can accomplish much, while a half-
way policy is liable to spoil things already accomplished.
The continuance of the National control in the South,

although it may be for a short period only, will cause some inconvenience and expense; but if thereby destructive collisions and anarchical disorders can be prevented, justice secured to all men, and the return of peace and prosperity to all parts of this country hastened, it will be a paying investment. For the future of the Republic, it is far less important that this business of reconstruction be done quickly than that it be well done. The matter well taken in hand, there is reason for hope that it will be well done, and quickly too. In days like these great changes are apt to operate themselves rapidly. At present the Southern people assume that free negro labor will not work, and therefore they are not inclined to give it a fair trial. As soon as they find out that they must give it a fair trial, and that their whole future power and prosperity depend upon its success, they will also find out that it will work, at least far better than they have anticipated. Then their hostility to it will gradually disappear. This great result accomplished, posterity will not find fault with this Administration for having delayed complete "reconstruction" one, two, or more years.

Although I am not called upon to discuss in this report the Constitutional aspects of this question, I may be pardoned for one remark. The interference of the National Government in the local concerns of the States lately in rebellion is argued against by many as inconsistent with the spirit of our Federal institutions. Nothing is more foreign to my ways of thinking in political matters than a fondness for centralization of military government. Nobody can value the blessings of local self-government more highly than I do. But we are living under exceptional circumstances which require us, above all, to look at things from a practical point of view; and I believe it will prove far more dangerous for the integrity of local self-government if the National control in the South be discontinued—while by discontinuing it too soon, it may be rendered necessary again in the future—than if it be continued, when by continuing it but a limited time all such future necessity may be obviated. At present these acts of interference are but a part of that exceptional policy brought forth by the necessities into which the rebellion has plunged us. Although there will be some modifications in the relations between the States and the National Government, yet these acts of direct interference in the details of State concerns will pass away with the exceptional circumstances which called them forth. But if the social revolution in the South be now abandoned in an unfinished state, and at some future period produce events provoking new and repeated acts of direct practical interference,—and the contingency would by no means be unlikely to arise,—such new and repeated acts would not pass over without most seriously affecting the political organism of the Republic.

NEGRO SUFFRAGE

It would seem that the interference of the National authority in the home concerns of the Southern States would be rendered less necessary, and the whole problem of political and social reconstruction be much simplified, if, while the masses lately arrayed against the Government are permitted to vote, the large majority of those who were always loyal, and are naturally anxious to see the free-labor problem successfully solved, were not excluded from all influence upon legislation. In all questions concerning the Union, the National debt, and the future social organization of the South, the feelings of the colored man are naturally in sympathy with the views and aims of the National Government. While the Southern white fought against the Union, the negro did all he could to aid it; while the Southern white sees in the National Government his conqueror, the negro sees in it his protector; while the white owes to the National debt his defeat, the negro owes to it his deliverance; while the white considers himself robbed and ruined by the emancipation of the slaves, the negro finds in it the assurance of future prosperity and happiness. In all the important issues the negro would be led by natural impulse to forward the ends of the Government, and by making his influence, as part of the voting body, tell upon the legislation of the States, render the interference of the National authority less necessary.

As the most difficult of the pending questions are intimately connected with the status of the negro in Southern society, it is obvious that a correct solution can be more easily obtained if he has a voice in the matter. In the right to vote he would find the best permanent protection against oppressive class-legislation, as well as against individual persecution. The relations between the white and black races, even if improved by the gradual wearing off of the present animosities, are likely to remain long under the troubling influence of prejudice. It is a notorious fact that the rights of a man of some political power are far less exposed to violation than those of one who is, in matters of public interest, completely subject to the will of others. A voter is a man of influence; small as that influence may be in the single individual, it becomes larger when that individual belongs to a numerous class of voters who are ready to make common cause with him for the protection of his rights. Such an individual is an object of interest to the political parties that desire to have the benefit of his ballot. It is true, the bringing face to face at the ballot-box of the white and black races may here and there lead to an outbreak of feeling, and the first trials ought certainly to be made

while the National power is still there to prevent or repress
disturbances; but the practice once successfully inaugurated under the protection of that power, it would probably
be more apt than anything else to obliterate old antagon-
isms, especially if the colored people—which is probable,
as soon as their own rights are sufficiently secured—
divide their votes between the different political parties.

The effect of the extension of the franchise to the colored
people upon the development of free labor and upon the
security of human rights in the South being the principal
object in view, the objections raised on the ground of the
ignorance of the freedmen become unimportant. Practical
liberty is a good school, and, besides, if any qualification
can be found, applicable to both races, which does not
interfere with the attainment of the main object, such
qualification would in that respect be unobjectionable.
But it is idle to say that it will be time to speak of negro
suffrage when the whole colored race will be educated,
for the ballot may be necessary to him to secure his
education. It is also idle to say that ignorance is the
principal ground upon which Southern men object to
negro suffrage, for if it were, that numerous class of
colored people in Louisiana who are as highly educated, as
intelligent and as wealthy as any corresponding class
of whites, would have been enfranchised long ago.

It has been asserted that the negro would be but a
voting machine in the hand of his employer. On this
point opinions seem to differ. I have heard it said in the
South that the freedmen are more likely to be influenced
by their schoolmasters and preachers. But even if we
suppose the employer to control to a certain extent the
negro laborer's vote, two things are to be taken into
consideration: (1) The class of employers, of landed
proprietors, will in a few years be very different from
what it was heretofore; in consequence of the general

breaking up, a great many of the old slaveholders will be obliged to give up their lands and new men will step into their places; and (2) the employer will hardly control the vote of the negro laborer so far as to make him vote against his own liberty. The beneficial effect of an extension of suffrage does not always depend upon the intelligence with which the newly admitted voters exercise their right, but sometimes upon the circumstances in which they are placed; and the circumstances in which the freedmen of the South are placed are such that, when they vote only for their own liberty and rights, they vote for the rights of free labor, for the success of an immediate important reform, for the prosperity of the country, and for the general interests of mankind. If, therefore, in order to control the colored vote, the employer, or whoever he may be, is first obliged to concede to the freedman the great point of his own rights as a man and a free laborer, the great social reform is completed, the most difficult problem is solved, and all other questions it will be comparatively easy to settle.

In discussing the matter of negro suffrage I deemed it my duty to confine myself strictly to the practical aspects of the subject. I have, therefore, not touched its moral merits nor discussed the question whether the National Government is competent to enlarge the elective franchise in the States lately in rebellion by its own act; I deem it proper, however, to offer a few remarks on the assertion frequently put forth, that the franchise is likely to be extended to the colored man by the voluntary action of the Southern whites themselves. My observation leads me to a contrary opinion. Aside from a very few enlightened men, I found but one class of people in favor of the enfranchisement of the blacks; it was the class of Unionists who found themselves politically ostracised and looked upon the enfranchisement of the loyal negroes as the

salvation of the whole loyal element.   But their numbers
and influence are sadly insufficient to secure such a result.
The masses are strongly opposed to colored suffrage;
anybody that dares to advocate it is stigmatized as a
dangerous fanatic; nor do I deem it probable that in the
ordinary course of things prejudices will wear off to such
an extent as to make it a popular measure.   Outside of
Louisiana only one gentleman who occupied a prominent
political position in the South expressed to me an opinion
favorable to it.   He declared himself ready to vote for
an amendment to the constitution of his State bestowing
the right of suffrage upon all male citizens without distinction of color who could furnish evidence of their
ability to read and write, without, however, disfranchising
those who are now voters and are not able to fulfil that
condition.   This gentleman is now a member of one of
the State conventions, but I presume he will not risk his
political standing in the South by moving such an amendment in that body.

The only manner in which, in my opinion, the Southern
people can be induced to grant to the freedman some
measure of self-protecting power in the form of suffrage,
is to make it a condition precedent to "readmission."

DEPORTATION OF THE FREEDMEN

I have to notice one pretended remedy for the disorders
now agitating the South, which seems to have become
the favorite plan of some prominent public men.   It is
that the whole colored population of the South should
be transported to some place where they could live completely separated from the whites.   It is hardly necessary
to discuss not only the question of right and justice,
but the difficulties and expense necessarily attending the
deportation of nearly four millions of people.   But it

24

may be asked, what would become of the industry of the
South for many years, if the bulk of its laboring population were taken away?   The South stands in need of an
increase and not of a diminution of its laboring force to
repair the losses and disasters of the last four years.
Much is said of importing European laborers and Northern
men; this is the favorite idea of many planters who want
such immigrants to work on their plantations.   But they
forget that European and Northern men will not come to
the South to serve as hired hands on the plantations, but
to acquire property for themselves, and that even if the
whole European immigration at the rate of 200,000 a
year were turned into the South, leaving not a single man
for the North and West, it would require between fifteen
and twenty years to fill the vacuum caused by the deportation of the freedmen.   Aside from this, the influx
of Northern men or Europeans will not diminish the
demand for hired negro labor; it will, on the contrary,
increase it.   As Europeans and Northern people come in,
not only vast quantities of land will pass from the hands
of their former owners into those of the immigrants, but
a large area of new land will be brought under cultivation,
and as the area of cultivation expands, hired labor, such
as furnished by the colored people, will be demanded in
large quantities.   The deportation of the labor so demanded would, therefore, be a very serious injury to the
economical interests of the South, and if an attempt were
made, this effect would soon be felt.

It is, however, a question worthy of consideration
whether it would not be wise to offer attractive inducements and facilities for the voluntary migration of freedmen to some suitable district on the line of the Pacific
railroad.   It would answer a double object: (1) It would
aid in the construction of that road, and (2) if this
migration be effected on a large scale it would cause a

drain upon the laboring force of the South; it would make the people affected by that drain feel the value of the freedmen's labor, and show them the necessity of keeping that labor at home by treating the laborer well, and by offering him inducements as fair as can be offered elsewhere.

But whatever the efficiency of such expedients may be, the true problem remains, not how to remove the colored man from his present field of labor, but how to make him, where he is, a true freeman and an intelligent and useful citizen.   The means are simple: protection by the government until his political and social status enables him to protect himself, offering to his legitimate ambition the stimulant of a perfectly fair chance in life, and granting to him the rights which in every just organization of society are coupled with corresponding duties.

CONCLUSION

I may sum up all I have said in a few words.   If nothing were necessary but to restore the machinery of government in the States lately in rebellion in point of form, the movements made to that end by the people of the South might be considered satisfactory.   But if it is required that the Southern people should also accommodate themselves to the results of the war in point of spirit, those movements fall far short of what must be insisted upon.

The loyalty of the masses and of most of the leaders of the Southern people, consists in submission to necessity. There is, except in individual instances, an entire absence of that national spirit which forms the basis of true loyalty and patriotism.

The emancipation of the slaves is submitted to only in so far as chattel slavery in the old form could not be kept up. But although the freedman is no longer considered the property of the individual master, he is considered the slave of society, and all independent State legislation will share the tendency to make him such. The ordinances abolishing slavery, passed by the conventions under the pressure of circumstances, will not be looked upon as barring the establishment of a new form of servitude.

Practical attempts on the part of the Southern people to deprive the negro of his rights as a freeman may result in bloody collisions, and will certainly plunge Southern society into restless fluctuations and anarchical confusion. Such evils can be prevented only by continuing the control of the National Government in the States lately in rebellion until free labor is fully developed and firmly established, and the advantages and blessings of the new order of things have disclosed themselves. This desirable result will be hastened by a firm declaration on the part of the Government, that National control in the South will not cease until such results are secured. Only in this way can that security be established in the South which will render numerous immigration possible, and such immigration would materially aid a favorable development of things.

The solution of the problem would be very much facilitated by enabling all the loyal and free-labor elements in the South to exercise a healthy influence upon legislation. It will hardly be possible to secure the freedman against oppressive class legislation and private persecution, unless he be endowed with a certain measure of political power.

As to the future peace and harmony of the Union, it is of the highest importance that the people lately in rebellion be not permitted to build up another "peculiar institution" whose spirit is in conflict with the fundamental principles of our political system; for as long as they cherish interests peculiar to them in preference to those they have in common with the rest of the American people, their loyalty to the Union will always be uncertain.

I desire not to be understood as saying that there are no well-meaning men among those who were compromised in the rebellion. There are many, but neither their number nor their influence is strong enough to control the manifest tendency of the popular spirit. There are great reasons for hope that a determined policy on the part of the National Government will produce innumerable and valuable conversions. This consideration counsels lenity as to persons, such as is demanded by the humane and enlightened spirit of our times, and vigor and firmness in the carrying out of principles, such as is demanded by the national sense of justice and the exigencies of our situation.

In submitting this report I desire to say that I have conscientiously endeavored to see things as they were, and to represent them as I saw them. I have been careful not to use stronger language than was warranted by the thoughts I intended to express. A comparison of the tenor of the [originally] annexed documents with that of my report, will convince you that I have studiously avoided over statements. Certain legislative attempts at present made in the South, and especially in South Carolina, seem to be more than justifying the apprehensions I have expressed.

Conscious though I am of having used my best endeavors to draw, from what I saw and learned, correct general conclusions, yet I am far from placing too great a trust in my own judgment, when interests of such magnitude are at stake. I know that this report is incomplete, although as complete as an observation of a few months could enable me to make it. Additional facts might be elicited, calculated to throw new light upon the subject. Although I see no reason for believing that things have changed for the better since I left the South, yet such may be the case. Admitting all these possibilities, I would entreat you to take no irretraceable step towards relieving the States lately in rebellion from all National control, until such favorable changes are clearly and unmistakably ascertained.

To that end, and by virtue of the permission you honored me with when sending me out to communicate to you freely and unreservedly my views as to measures of policy proper to be adopted, I would now respectfully suggest that you advise Congress to send one or more "investigating committees" into the Southern States, to inquire for themselves into the actual condition of things, before final action is taken upon the readmission of such States to their representation in the legislative branch of the government, and the withdrawal of the National control from that section of the country.

I am, sir, very respectfully, your obedient servant,

CARL SCHURZ.

His Excellency ANDREW JOHNSON,
President of the United States.

FROM CHARLES SUMNER

WASHINGTON, Xmas Day, [1865.]

I am in the midst of your Report, which I find all that I expected; very able, elaborate, complete, full of facts and ideas.[1] Let me suggest that in your speech you present a

[1] On Jan. 6, 1866, Schurz wrote to Mrs. Schurz: "My Report scored a great success with the Members of Congress. Sumner proposed to the Senate to have 100,000 copies printed. The House also asked for it. The President expressed himself to a Senator in this way: 'The only great mistake I have yet made was to send Schurz to the South.'— I believe it!"

vivid, vigorous portraiture of the condition of things in the
rebel States.   Of course, this will not preclude a presentment
also of the ideas involved.

Meeting Sir Fred. Bruce at dinner Sat. evening, I found he
had been prodigiously impressed by the power of [Thaddeus]
Stevens's speech.   He evidently put it before [Henry J.]
Raymond's.

Until the Committee gives us the facts Congress will occupy
itself with the ideas.   This discussion will go on for months.
I do not see how it can be stopped; nor do I think it desirable
to stop it.   At last the evidence, as reported, will show the
necessity of interference by Congress.   Now, to my mind the
single point to be reached is *the assertion of jurisdiction by
Congress*.

One person will reach this point by one road and another
by another road.   Provided it is reached, it is not of much
importance how this is accomplished.   Therefore, I hope that
all will speak and ventilate their theories; for, though differing,
I feel sure that a large majority will concur in asserting Congressional jurisdiction; and this is the main thing.

Meanwhile, the President and Seward press their policy.
Alas! alas! unhappy country.   Good-bye.

TO HEINRICH MEYER

DETROIT, June 10, 1866.[1]

We had our household goods sent from the East by
rail.[2]   Two large boxes had just arrived at the station
when a fire broke out and destroyed not only the buildings
but all the goods there.   Among these were our boxes.
They contained our most valued possessions and their
loss is irreparable.   You may know how M. [Mrs. Schurz]

[1] Translated from the German.

[2] After passing the winter of 1865–66 in Washington as correspondent
of the New York *Tribune*, Schurz became editor-in-chief of the Detroit
Post.

valued the letters which she had received from me.   A
box containing all these was destroyed.   They contained
not only a record of all the closest mutual relations of our
lives, but, in part, a very detailed sketchy diary-account
of all the important and interesting events I have been
connected with during the past fourteen years.   M. had collected and arranged them with the greatest care, even to
the scraps of paper on which I had written to her during
the war, on the battlefield or on the march.   The letters
were of quite indescribable value to us.   They would
have been the most splendid legacy to our children.
When they were lost, we felt as though part of our lives
had been taken from us, and as though we could see our
past only dimly, through a veil.   You can imagine how
severe the blow was to us, and even now, when we speak
of it, we can hardly repress our tears.   I do not believe
that we shall ever become reconciled to this loss.

And there were other heavy losses.   First among these
are all my manuscripts, collected materials and notes,
extracts etc. etc.; then a lot of letters from prominent
persons, for example, from Lincoln,[1] then all our pictures,
large photographs, of which we had a very pretty collection—fortunately the albums with the portraits were
in the trunks; then all our music, and the most valuable
of my war relics, my old, shot-riddled Division flag, my
sword; then my entire military library and the greater part
of my books on political economy and history . . . and
my entire, very valuable, collection of military and geo-
graphic maps, among them complete sets of atlases with
detailed maps of all the campaigns of Frederick the Great,
Napoleon, the Arch-Duke Charles, the Russian-Turkish
wars and large maps of all parts of Europe; finally, the
entire little collection of books, etc.,—all gone.

[1] Fortunately about a dozen Lincoln letters were not among the lost
treasures, and a few of them are first published in this work.

THE LOGICAL RESULTS OF THE WAR[1]

MR. PRESIDENT AND FELLOW-CITIZENS:—No discerning man can survey the present situation of affairs in this Republic without perceiving that, although the war is over, the country is not yet at peace. There is a fierce contest going on between the Executive and Legislative branches of the National Government, in which the masses of the people are called upon to take sides. In the South we see symptoms of dangerous fermentation sporadically breaking out in bloody deeds. In the North the war of opinions is carried on with passionate violence. A gathering of men, euphoneously styling itself " The National Union Convention," has already called upon the people of the South not to submit if the policy adopted by the Congress of the United States should prevail. Everywhere the air is heavy with threats and apprehensions.

This state of things, surprising and alarming as it may appear, is by no means without precedent. Look over the history of the world, and you will find that every great reformatory movement in society, every revolution in favor of popular rights, every sudden onward stride in the progress of civilization, has had to pass through two distinct periods: first, the struggle for its achievement, and then the struggle for the preservation of its results; the first, the period of action; the second, the period of reaction.

When the struggles of the first period are over and the victory seems decided, the discomfited forces of society gradually wake up from the torpor of their defeat; the energies and vigilance of the victors are relaxed by a sanguine delusion of security and the generous emotions engendered by success. The defeated party presently

[1] Speech delivered at Philadelphia, Sept. 8, 1866.

rallies for an attempt to recover what it has lost, the victors are off their guard, and the results of the victory are again put in question. These results will be safe only if the victors have been wise enough to have them firmly imbedded in political forms of institutions so well fixed and fortified that the tide of the reaction, however furious, cannot shake or move them. But these results may again be lost or grievously impaired, if the victors in foolish confidence have neglected to surround them with impregnable safeguards. New, protracted and dangerous struggles will inevitably be the consequence. History teaches us this lesson on thousands of its most instructive pages, and no true statesman will close his eyes against it.

That period of reaction after our glorious victory for National Union and human liberty has now come upon us and it is the more formidable and dangerous as one of the great powers of the state has made himself its agent and champion. I shall attempt to analyze its nature and the situation in which it has placed us, with fairness, but without reserve; and I invite you to follow my reasoning with that intellectual honesty which shrinks from no conclusions of logic.

When the civil war had come to a close, the problem presented itself of what is commonly called reconstruction. The principal difficulty of that problem consisted then, and consists now, in this: The political system of this Republic rests upon the right of the people to control their local concerns in their several States by the operations of self-government, subject to certain restrictions imposed by the National Constitution, and in the right to co-operate with one another in the government of the whole. This system was not to be changed in the work of reconstruction; but it was evident also that if reconstruction was to accomplish only the mere setting in motion again of the machinery of government as it had been previous to the war, and nothing else, it would have forthwith invested the very people who had been in rebellion against the Government with the power in a great measure to control the very results which had been won, and against which they had struggled; and this would have been a surrender of the consequences of our victory to the discretion of the defeated.

Here was a difficulty which struck the mind of every candid man at first sight. The immediate and unconditional restoration of the rebel States to the absolute control of their home affairs and to power in the General Government, was so obviously incompatible with the best interests and sacred obligations of the Republic, so manifestly against all common-sense, that when one of the greatest heroes of the war, led astray by a too generous error of judgment, admitted it as one of the stipulations of an armistice, the people, startled out of their equanimity by the mistake, raised a general outcry against him all over the loyal States; the President himself repudiated the proposition with the utmost promptness and decision, and some of the journals which now advocate a similar policy were among the loudest in their expressions of indignant denunciation, calling it either madness or treason. The hero I speak of undoubtedly soon saw his error, and the country remembers nothing but the gratitude it owes him.

In fact, all those who had been faithful to the National cause during the war substantially agreed, at its close, on two points with almost unbroken unanimity: First, that as speedily as possible all the attributes of our democratic system of government should be restored; but, second, that the rebel States could not be reinstated in the full control of their local affairs, in their full participation in the government of the Republic, until, by the imposition of irreversible stipulations, it should have been rendered

impossible for them to subvert or impair any of the results
of the war, or to violate any of the obligations the Republic
had taken upon herself. This appeared so reasonable,
and, in fact, so absolutely a dictate of common-sense, that
no man with any pretensions to patriotism or statesmanship objected to it.

Least of all did Andrew Johnson object to it. No man
insisted more strenuously that the participants in the
rebellion must be punished and stripped of all political
power and social influence, and that the government of
the States, as well as of the Nation, must be confided exclusively to the tried and ever-faithful friends of the Republic.
Nay, he was so fierce and radical in those days that many
of us began to be seriously alarmed lest, by shedding the
blood of too many victims, by too severe exactions, by too
merciless and sweeping a proscription, he offend the
humane spirit of this age, and cast a shadow upon the fair
escutcheon of this Republic. We have learned to know
him better by this time. Nobody fears that he will hang
too many traitors now. He tells us that he is going the
round of the circle, and is just now at the other end;
and we have every reason to believe it. But let that
pass.

Cast a look back upon the days immediately following
the close of the war—those days of promise! How easy
was it then to accomplish all that would have saved the
Nation from the throes of the struggle we are to-day
engaged in! Then the people of the rebel States had not
yet rallied from the torpor of the defeat. Far from
thinking of another fight, they thought of nothing but
of the necessity of submission. In tremulous anxiety
they awaited the verdict of the conqueror. They expected nothing better than that we should dictate the
terms of peace. If anybody had told them that we would
not, they would not have believed him. They dreamed

of nothing but punishment, of wholesale hanging and confiscation; and the imposition of any sort of government that would permit them to live and to retain what they had saved from the disasters of the war, would have been welcomed by them as an act of grace and favor. Nothing appeared to them more natural than that the participants in the rebellion should be excluded from office, influence and power—nay, from the franchise even; and that the functions of government should be confined to the tried and faithful friends of the National cause. Even negro suffrage, universal, unrestricted, would then have been accepted as one of the bitter but irresistible consequences of the war.

Let it not be said that, in thus describing the condition of the Southern people at that time, I am gloating over the prostration of a defeated enemy, or that it would have been ungenerous to take advantage of their helplessness. Whatever the President's friends may think, I am one of those who still consider the rebellion one of the great crimes in history; and victorious Liberty, firmly planting her heel upon the neck of defeated crime, would have been no unwelcome sight to me.

Yes, how easy would it have been then at that moment to accomplish all that was needful. While the South was thus passive, in the North also all that insidious opposition which had dogged the Government during the war, vanished before the glory of our victory. When the Southern lion of treason was struck down, the Northern curs of treason took to their kennels. The Government stood unhampered. There was not a sensible man in the North who did not expect, nay, who did not desire, that the Government should and would assert the rights of victory and leave nothing undone to give the Republic the fullest measure of security for the future; and to all the hopeful germs of liberty, justice, equality and progressive civilization which sleep in our political system, the freest scope of development.

Hardly anybody doubted that this would be done. It was looked upon as a foregone conclusion. And if the Government had resolutely adopted even the boldest policy of reform, all the generous and patriotic elements of American society would have coöperated with cheerful alacrity.

I repeat, how easy it would have been then to fortify the great results of the war, with all their promise of glorious development, in Constitutional safeguards so strong and impregnable that the reactionary movement, however violent, would have dashed itself to atoms against them! Nay, seeing its utter hopelessness, it would perhaps not even have been seriously attempted. How easy would it have been to lay broad and deep the foundations on which the political life of this Republic might have developed itself to the full realization of those sublime ideals of universal liberty, equal rights and impartial justice, which stand as the supreme guiding stars in the heart of every true friend of the human kind.

In the life of nations, as in the life of individuals, we see here and there standing out in bold relief, moments of great opportunity—moments when by simply following the manifest logic of events mighty consummations may be reached, which, if the auspicious hour be suffered to pass, will sometimes require ages of bitter and dangerous struggles to accomplish. Such a moment of great opportunity had arrived for the American Republic immediately after the close of the civil war. Truly, it did not require a bold and daring genius or profound statesman at the head of affairs to seize it. It required simply a man who would faithfully follow the common impulse of the hour. It required only a man of sincere sympathy with the best ideas of this great age; not a great man, but merely an

honest man. Alas, that our good President was dead!
That at such a moment Abraham Lincoln's great heart,
his true and tender sympathies with the lowly children
of humanity, his pure and unerring instincts of right and
liberty, his unselfish purpose to be equally just to all,
should have been lost to us! If he had lived, whatever
hesitations we might have had to pass through, no man
who knew him will doubt that the peace of the country
would have been safe and the triumph of liberty and
justice certain. Alas, that the good President is dead!
We have learned to measure the greatness of our loss by
what he left behind him.

The first great opportunity was thrown away, and the
man who cheated the Nation out of it has committed a
crime against the glory and happiness of the American
Republic which the flatteries of millions of sycophants
will not be sufficient to gloss over, and which centuries
of repentance cannot wash out. And how was the great
opportunity thrown away?

President Johnson took the work of reconstruction into
his own hands and began to develop a scheme of policy.
He issued proclamations appointing provisional governors
for the rebel States, and ordered them to call State conventions. Was not the work of reconstruction to be
placed exclusively into the hands of loyal men? Of course
is was; Andrew Johnson had said so! He had solemnly
declared that if there were but five thousand men of tried
loyalty in a State, theirs must be the government.

But political power in the States naturally belongs to
those who have the right to vote and to be voted for.
Andrew Johnson began by prescribing the qualifications
of voters. The loyal blacks were at once excluded from
the suffrage; the right of voting was to be confined to the
loyal whites. But who were the loyal whites?   The
President issued a proclamation of amnesty and declared

that all participants in the rebellion should be regarded as loyal men if they would take the oath of allegiance, fourteen specially enumerated classes excepted. Thus, while the ballot-box was withheld from the loyal blacks, it was placed in the hands of a vast majority of those who had stood up against the Government of the Republic. Then the President opened his special pardon bank, and one after another the leaders of the rebellion were declared loyal, and enabled to place themselves once more at the head of their political followers.

A child might have foreseen the consequences. The true Union element was everywhere helplessly overwhelmed by rebel majorities. The conventions and legislatures fell into the hands of those who had stood against us in the civil war. The elective executive offices of the States were presently exercised by the leaders in the rebellion, and the whole machinery of the State governments was restored to their control.

Thus the reaction was fairly started. It commenced when the President first opened to the late rebels the road to power, and gained in strength as that power was obtained. It is true Andrew Johnson himself deemed it necessary to impose upon them conditions precedent to their full restoration. He demanded that their State conventions should declare the secession ordinances null and void, which, however, not all of them did. But that was a mere matter of form—good as far as it went. Such declarations in words, however, would never prevent another rebellion. He demanded that they should repudiate the rebel debt, a demand which was but partially complied with. But not insisting upon a provision to be embodied in the Federal Constitution, the President left it open to have a repeal at any time of the State laws by which the rebel debt was set aside. He demanded of them that their legislatures should ratify the

Constitutional amendment prohibiting slavery; but he left it to them to fix by State law the social and political *status* of the emancipated slaves, thus to reduce them to slavery again in all but the name, and to prevent the development of free labor.

There the President stopped. These demands partially complied with, he pronounced the rebel States fit to be restored to their full Constitutional rights and privileges, and declared himself satisfied; and not only that, he insisted that he being satisfied everybody else should be satisfied also, and presently he declared everybody a traitor whose satisfaction was not complete. But the late rebels were indeed satisfied. In their most sanguine dreams they had never expected such magnanimity—a magnanimity which put the Nation's friends at the mercy of the Nation's enemies! They were indeed satisfied; and no sooner had their satisfaction inspired them with the desire to give cheers for Andrew Johnson than their gratitude went so far as to couple them with cheers for Jefferson Davis.

The reactionary movement chose for its first objective point persons obnoxious to the rebel element; first, the freed negroes; and then, as the President's policy gradually developed itself and became more encouraging, the white Union men of the South and Northern settlers. The South had fought for slavery; the emancipation of the slaves was for the rebels the most grievous result of their failure, and every freed negro reminded them of their defeat. Against the freedmen, therefore, the first fury of the reactionary movement directed itself. At that period I was myself in the South, and I know of what I affirm. I myself visited the hospitals and the prisons; I myself saw the lifeless bodies, the mangled limbs, the mutilated heads, of not a few of the victims. I myself listened to their sorrowful tales and those of their friends.

25

I will not go into details. I will not attempt to draw the
veil from that dark drama of blood and horror which
makes the heart sick; for if ever the history of the countless
murders and acts of fiendish persecution then perpetrated
in the South should be traced and told, case after case, a
picture of atrocities would reveal itself to the eyes of the
world—a picture so revolting that the nineteenth century would blush for itself, and it would seriously be
doubted whether it were best for humanity to take that
country from the savage Indian and surrender it to the
more barbarous rule of white men who call themselves
civilized.

I say I was myself in the South shortly after the close
of the war and when the President's policy was bearing
its first fruits. President Johnson had honored me with
a confidential mission to investigate the condition of
things in the late rebel States, and I endeavored to show
myself worthy of that confidence by honestly reporting
what I had seen and heard and what I conscientiously
understood to be true. Subsequently it appeared to me
as if I had misunderstood the nature of my mission.
But I dare to assert that every truthful man who knows
what has occurred in the South will testify that if the
official statements I have made convey erroneous impressions at all, they do so only by their studied mildness.
My report has not had the good fortune of winning the
applause or of exercising an influence upon the mind of
him who sent me; but I console myself with the confident
belief that in this country no individual, however powerful,
can seal the eyes of the people by merely closing his own.

I have heard it said that the acts of barbarous persecution to which the freedmen were, and, for aught I know,
are still exposed, were merely isolated occurrences, and do
not authorize general conclusions. Can it be that in a
community where public opinion stigmatizes the murder

of a negro as a crime, assassination is permitted to stalk abroad with impunity in open daylight? Still I will waive this point, and say that the character of the majority shall be judged only by the majority's acts.

It was not by the crimes committed upon individual freedmen alone that the reaction against emancipation manifested itself. While murder affected only the individual, legislation affected the class; and it was by legislation enacted by the majority as represented in conventions and legislatures that the war against free labor was systematized. And what do we behold? Here is Mississippi declaring the penal and criminal laws formerly enacted against slaves in full force against freedmen, and by special acts depriving the freedmen of the right to acquire real property, and thus to own homes for themselves and their children. Here is Alabama, her legislation placing upon the freedmen similar disabilities. Here is South Carolina—the same South Carolina which the other day walked arm in arm with Massachusetts—with a black code, reëstablishing even the names of "master" and "servant," only transferring the whipping business from the master to the town magistrate. Here is North Carolina, with her old black laws still unrepealed. Here is Louisiana, with a labor code which delivers the plantation laborer almost helpless into the hands of the planter. Here is Virginia, with a vagrant law calculated to make the freedman a vagrant, and the vagrant a slave again.

In my official report, I predicted that if the reactionary movement in the South be left unchecked, it would result in the introduction, by legislation, or, in the absence of laws, by practical appliances, of some system of labor intermediate between free labor and slavery, but having more of the attributes of the latter than of the former. Has not my prediction been verified by fact? To be sure, the President affects not to believe it, for it is a truth

hardly recommendatory of his policy.   But I do not ask
the President to believe *me*.   He himself testifies to the
truth of what I have said, by his own acts.   All over the
South his military officers, his agents acting under his
orders and by his authority, have been busy for some time
setting aside and overruling State laws and judicial proceedings, because they were too glaringly incompatible
with the decree of emancipation.   It appears the President
must, after all, have had an inkling of what was going on.
I bring to the President the President's own testimony.
Will he condescend to believe himself? or does he, perhaps, know himself so well as to have no faith in his own
character for truth and veracity?

   And what does all this prove?   It proves that the people
lately in rebellion, as soon as they saw their State governments once more in their hands, saw also a chance to turn
their power to account in a reactionary movement against
emancipation.   It shows that they were determined not
to permit the emancipated slave to become a true freeman,
nor a system of true free labor to supplant that of slavery.
It shows that they used their power in that direction as
far as the General Government suffered them to go; and
Heaven knows, President Johnson, although anxious to
keep up appearances, suffered them to go far enough.

   But the reactionary movement did not confine itself
to the blacks; the whites, too, came in for their share.
No sooner did the people lately in rebellion see the road
to political power reopened to them by the President's
reconstruction policy than they malignantly turned upon
those Southern men who had refused to espouse the cause
of the rebellion, and those Northerners who, during and
after the war, imported into the South their capital, intelligence, enterprise and civilization.   You see the people
lately in rebellion not only not permitting the loyalists
of the South to control the powers of Government, but

refusing even to share it with them. Fidelity to the South
—that is, participation in the rebellion—has become an
absolute requisite for political trust, influence and power;
identification with the National cause, a badge of disgrace;
and the tried loyalists of the South, the same men into
whose hands the President promised to place the work of
reconstruction, to the exclusion of rebels, find themselves
rudely ostracised from political life.

Nor does the reaction stop there. Hardly had the
President's policy had time to be understood when a
malignant spirit of hostility began to follow the Northern
emigrant in all the relations of life. Every man was
spotted who refused to sell his loyal principles along with
his calico; and the Southern Union men, in the same
measure as they had been faithful to the Government,
were sneered at, howled at, spit upon as traitors to the
Southern cause, and soon found themselves the outcasts
of Southern society. And presently the torch and the
pistol came again into play. Houses were burned to
smoke out men of loyal sentiments. Democratic committees gave, and are now giving, men who fought under
the flag of the country, notice to quit under penalty of
death; and to the many cowardly murders committed in
secret are now added wholesale butcheries in broad daylight and under the inspiration of the constituted authorities. Did you listen to tales of horror and woe coming
from the lips of the faithful men now here appealing to
your sympathy? And why are they here? Because, as
even one of the President's court organs sneeringly asserted—and certainly Andrew Johnson himself would
not impeach the veracity of his own mouthpiece—because
this very convention of Southern Unionists would not
have been permitted to meet in any one of the rebel
States! Here they are—the men who most faithfully
clung to the Republic in the hour of her greatest need—

here they are, ostracized from political life, cast out from Southern society, persecuted by murderous malignity even to their very firesides; many of them driven away by bloodthirsty rebel mobs, exiles again from their homes, because they stood by their country.

Can it be that in the great struggle for the Union the tried and self-sacrificing Unionists of the South are the worst-defeated party? Shameful, incredible as it may seem, yet so it is. Under the heels of the rebellion when the rebellion broke out, they are still more under the heels of the rebels since the rebellion is vanquished; for then they looked up with hope, and now they look down almost with despair. Here they are, taking refuge under the shield of the loyal North, to enjoy the poor privilege of giving expression to their grief.

And there is the South: those who but recently fought against us, again wielding the powers of government in their States; flaunting before our eyes the declaration that in rising to destroy the Union they did no wrong; boasting of the rebellion as the pride and glory of their history; insolently defying and sneering at those who conquered them; making complicity in treason a test for political distinction; spitting upon tried loyalty to the National cause as a mark of disgrace; seeking to legislate and whip into servitude and misery those whom we have emancipated; persecuting as intruders those of us who have gone to live with them; tolerating no opinion which is not their own; driving away and murdering like outlaws the most faithful friends of the Union and of liberty; repeating the horrors of Fort Pillow on the streets of Memphis and New Orleans, and all this in the name of Southern rights and Andrew Johnson! Not only "the South for Southerners" is the cry, for the Southern Union men are Southerners also, but "the South for rebels." Such are the fruits of the reaction sprung from the President's policy. Do you recognize them! It is slavery; slavery dead only in name, but its spirit revived by the treacherous policy of one who had sworn that it should never rise again. There it is, ambitious of power, impatient of restraint, overbearing in its ascendancy, brutal in its resentments, merciless with its murderous resentment, writing again its signature on the pages of American history in characters of blood.

I know the President's friends will say that I exaggerate. I wish I had exaggerated. But let them read the testimony of our military commanders whom a protracted residence in the South has enabled to form a judgment; let them scan the list of Southern State officers and inquire into their past career and their present doings; let them look over the records of Southern legislatures and study the character of their enactments; let them search the Southern press as an exponent of Southern sentiment; let them run their eyes over the lists of killed and wounded Union men, white as well as black, whom the reaction has already laid low; let them read General Sheridan's dispatches, which the President was so exceedingly slow in bringing to the knowledge of the people; let them listen to the words of those true men of the South who have laid the woful story of their sorrows before us; nay, let them for one moment be honest with themselves, and grant an audience to the misgivings of their own hearts, and within themselves they will hear a voice giving a lie to the whitewashing talk with which they strive to deceive the people.

Thus the reaction in the Southern States is almost complete. "Almost," I say; not quite. Whatever encouragement the President may have given them, and however far they may have been urged on by it, still they labored under one restraint. There was something which operated as a check and prevented still wilder abuses of power. When they had gained supreme control in their States, there was still another thing to be gained, and that was their old controlling power in the government of the Nation. They had their governors, they had their legislatures, their judges, their municipal officers— but their seats in Congress were still to be won. They had conquered all the ground except one position, but that position was the key to the battlefield. While all other points were surrendered to them by treacherous complicity, that one position was garrisoned by a host of faithful men; for, thank Heaven, the spirit of the loyal people which gave victory to the National arms gave also to the country a Congress true to the cause of freedom.

Against that rock the waves of the reaction have so far dashed in vain. Even the late rebels, strong as were their impulses, and great their confidence in the subserviency of their new friend, Andrew Johnson, knew well that the great American Republic was not yet absolutely ruled by the dictatorial assumptions of the President, and that to gain admission to Congress, the will of Congress, representing the people, would have to be consulted. In order to accomplish this, they had to win our good opinion, and in order to win our good opinion they had to restrain themselves in their mad reactionary career. But even then, when common-sense might have told them that they must stoop to conquer, their fury proved stronger than the necessity of deception; and the South entered the Philadelphia wigwam with the blood of Memphis and New Orleans upon her garments.

And now, after all this, the loyal people are summoned to surrender what Congress has so firmly maintained. Suppose for a moment this were done; can the consequences be doubtful? If the people lately in rebellion have done what they did do while they knew that they could gain something by merely restraining themselves, what will they do when they have won all they want without restraining themselves?

Mark my words: You admit the late rebel States to representation and power in the National Government such as they are, unconditionally; you remove the brakes from the reactionary movement without having first secured and fortified the results of the war by amendments to the Federal Constitution; and I predict the reaction will go so far as to call in question all legislation that was had during the absence from Congress of the eleven rebel States. Whether so atrocious a movement will ultimately succeed, will rest with the people; but it is certain that if the President's policy prevail it will be attempted, and the attempt will not be checked before having plunged the Republic into disasters of the wildest confusion.

I speak deliberately, and I am sure no thoughtful student of history will deny that reactions, like revolutions, have an almost irresistible tendency to go to extremes, and will never stop until they reach them, unless they find insuperable obstacles in their way; and if there ever was a people on the face of the globe inclined to rush on to extremes with mad precipitation, it is the people of the rebel States.

Look the matter square in the face. Here is a Congress of which Southern men and Northern Johnson men form a majority; for such is the design of our opponents. The Southern delegations are there, unshackled by any of the Constitutional amendments now before the people. As a matter of course the test oath will at once be repealed. The South loudly demands the repeal; the President is in favor of it; and such being the case, where would the Johnson men find spirit enough to refuse it? The test oath repealed, the representative men of the South—that is, those who represented and led the South during the rebellion—will at once find their way to Congressional seats;

and as by the emancipation of the slaves the representation of the Southern States will be largely increased, there will be more representative men of the South in Congress, and their power will be greater than ever before. Will the increase of their power be calculated to render them more modest in their pretensions?

Next in order comes the breaking down of all Congressional legislation for the protection of the emancipated slaves. All the obstacles which stand in the way of their reducing the freedmen to some sort of servile subjection will again be overturned without delay. The repeal of the Freedmen's Bureau and the civil-rights acts will be considered a matter of course; and it will give President Johnson, the modest man who would not be a dictator at any price, particular satisfaction to get rid of that power which enables him to protect the rights of the lowly children of the Republic, and which, for that reason, perhaps, he considers so dangerous a temptation. Woe to the negro, then, who, upon the solemn promise given by the Nation, attempted to be a freeman! Thrice woe, then, to the colored man who, when the country in the hour of danger called him under arms, took up his musket and with gallant devotion staked his life for the life of the Republic! All the pent-up resentments which the disastrous struggles and the bitter disappointments of years have accumulated in the Southern heart will come down upon his doomed head without restraint or moderation, and the Government for which he had sacrificed his blood will have withdrawn its protecting arm from him, and he will stand there a bloody monument of American treachery.

Next in order will come the demand of compensation for the emancipated slaves and the damage done by our armies while operating against the rebels in the Southern States. Does anybody doubt that such extravagant

claims will be preferred? Why, of the men elected to
Congress in the Southern States last year, a vast majority
were elected upon the distinct pledge that this demand
for compensation would be preferred and insisted upon.
Every Southern man will tell you that the Southern
members, with the exception of a few members from
Tennessee, and perhaps Arkansas, will be a solid unit
upon that very question; and, in fact, if the rebel States
be readmitted unconditionally, such as they are, will it
not be natural? How many thousand millions they will
demand, who knows? At any rate, they will demand
enough to have a good many millions to spare, with which
to buy up the necessary number of Northern doughfaces.
And you will keep in mind that I am reasoning upon the
supposition that the majority in Congress be composed
of Southerners and Northern Johnson men, whose incor-
ruptibility may be considered not quite above temptation
since the consciences of so many of them have proved
unable to resist mere visions of something to eat.

Next in order come the pensions paid to disabled
soldiers and sailors and to the widows and orphans of
those who lost their lives in the struggle against the
rebellion. Will the late rebels consent to help pay pensions to those, or to the widows and orphans of those
who subjugated them, while nothing is given to the rebel
soldiers who defended them? Look into the Southern
press; listen to the speeches of their candidates for office,
and you will find the answer. No sooner will the rebel
States be admitted, unconditionally such as they are,
than the alternative will be put to us either to stop paying
pensions to Northern invalids, widows and orphans, or to
pay them likewise to those whose claims are based upon
services rendered to the rebel cause. Can such a thing
be thought of? The tender-hearted Johnsonites, who
wept together with their Southern friends at the Phila-

delphia Convention, will hardly be capable of refusing
to Southern heroes the pittance of fifty or sixty millions
a year, whatever Northern taxpayers may think of it.

Finally, we arrive at the National debt. That the
Southern people should be loath to pay the cost of the
whipping they have received is natural enough. They
cannot reasonably be expected to do so willingly. Such
is human nature, and such is certainly Southern human
nature. Let that Southern human nature be restored to
power and influence in the National Government, and
what reasonable man will doubt that every possible
impediment will be thrown in the way of all legislation
necessary to provide for the satisfaction of the just claims
of our National creditors, unless we consent to assume the
rebel debt also? I do not pretend to say that the masses
of the South would be in favor of paying the rebel debt.
What they would be most in favor of would be to pay no
debt at all. But the creditors of the late Confederate
Government would indeed be very much in favor of giving some value to their Confederate bonds, and being the
most influential men of the South, they will not find it
difficult to persuade the Southern masses that if any debt ·
is to be paid at all the Confederate debt is entitled to
payment as well as any other, if not even more. Who
doubts that the people lately in rebellion will be very well
convinced of this. Then operations will commence for
the assumption of the rebel debt. The Southern members
of Congress will be an almost solid unit for it. It will be
necessary to buy up Northerners enough to make a
majority. Do you think this impossible? The Confederate debt is estimated at about four billion dollars.
Suppose the Confederate creditors combine and set one
hundred million, or two hundred million, or five hundred
million dollars, of their Confederate bonds apart as a
general corruption fund; suppose an agent of the Con-

federate bondholder approaches a Northern doughface
in this wise: "Sir, I offer you a million dollars in Confederate bonds at one cent on the dollar, the payment to
be made by you ten days after the assumption of the
Confederate debt by the United States. Now, sir, I
offer you this as a fair business transaction, and not as a
bribe." Suppose this offer be made, is it not probable that
a good many of those who are willing to sell their souls
for a post-office will take it and vote for the assumption
of the Confederate debt? To refuse anything to a Southern man is already a task of tremendous difficulty to a
Northern doughface; but to refuse that something with a
million dollars attached to it, would not that appear to
most of our Johnson men an unjustifiable act of vindictiveness, calculated to alienate the hardly reconciled feelings
of our erring, but now so sweetly repentant brethren?

It is true a Northern representative, after having voted
for such a measure, would never again be able to confront
his constituents; but what of that? With a million or so
in his pocket, a Northern doughface who never could
stand up against the frown of his Southern masters, will
feel quite independent in the face of the contempt of his
countrymen. He is accustomed to it anyhow, and the
money will sweeten the sensation. Here is a premonitory
symptom of what is to come; no sooner had the news of
the Philadelphia Johnson Convention reached the Stock
Exchange of London than there was an immediate rise
in Confederate bonds. Who is stupid enough not to understand this? And what would be the consequence of
assumption? Every augmentation of our National debt
will proportionately diminish the value of our securities.
The assumption of the rebel debt will be equivalent to the
repudiation of at least half of our National obligations;
our National creditors will be robbed of their just dues;
our National faith will be broken; and the Republic

will stand ruined in her credit and covered with eternal disgrace.

Do not dismiss this as a mere wild alarm. Read the history of representative governments, and you will find that more than one financial scheme has been carried through, just as foul as this, and apparently far more hopeless. And what may we not look for at a moment like this, when the President openly uses the whole patronage of the Government as a machinery of corruption, and familiarizes his followers with the idea that conscience is a marketable commodity?

Truly, these are no wild alarms, and the country may indeed congratulate itself, if, after the supposed success of the Johnson policy, the reaction stops even there. It is not only possible, but probable, that with one gigantic sweep they will attempt to brush away all the legislation passed by Congress during the absence of the eleven rebel States, and all that was done by the Southern conventions and legislatures called and organized upon the basis of the provisional governments instituted by the President. We see already the premonitory symptoms. The President himself, by questioning in his veto messages the legality of Congressional legislation in the absence of the eleven States, has directed the reaction into that channel and indicated the current it must take. One of the President's principal spokesmen, Mr. Ewing, of Ohio, has published an elaborate argument intended to prove that bills passed by the present Congress over the President's veto have not the validity of laws; and a supreme [court] Judge in North Carolina openly pronounces the convention called in that State by order of the President, an illegal and revolutionary body, and the constitution adopted by it null and void. Is it possible not to perceive where such arguments must lead us? And is there a single result of the war, except the slaughtering of half a million of men and rivers of blood and tears, which they do not involve?

But I hear it said that the people of the rebel States do not at all contemplate such things. Have they not shown the insincerity of their repentance and the meekness of their disposition at the Philadelphia Convention? "Oh," exclaims Senator Doolittle, in a fine burst of tearful sentimentality, "Oh, if the whole American people could have seen, as we saw, South Carolina and Massachusetts walking arm-in-arm!" Let me tell that ecstatic Senator that the whole American people have seen the performance and have seen right through it too. A meeting called for consultation; a consultation in which the managers did not dare to permit anybody to express an honest opinion for fear of bursting up the whole concern; a frank exchange of views, where everybody acted as a special policeman to keep everybody else still. And by a jugglery so contemptible, by a dumb puppet-show so clumsy, these gentlemen think they can deceive a people so wide-awake as the Yankees. Nay, the humbug was even too transparent for Southern eyes. Look over the Southern press and you will see that they either scornfully repudiate the whole performance as an act of barefaced hypocrisy, or, on the supposition that there are people in the North who absolutely insist on being bamboozled, accept and approve it as a trap in which fools can be caught by Copperheads.

But I am told that, in a Congress organized upon the Johnson plan, the representatives of the rebel States will at all events constitute only a minority, and that, if they carry the reactionary movement too far, the Northern Johnson men will resist them. Ah, their virtue has already shown most wonderful powers of resistance! Look at their representative men. Here is Mr. Doolittle. When the civil-rights bill was passed in the Senate, Mr.

Doolittle happened to be absent. The next day he took the floor declaring that he would have voted Aye had he been present, and asked the privilege of recording his vote in favor of that excellent measure. At that time it was understood that the President approved of it. A few days afterward the President vetoed the bill. Mr. Doolittle made haste to record his vote in favor of sustaining the veto and has ever since been denouncing that excellent measure as one of the abominations of the age. There is his independence of conviction! Here is Mr. Raymond. He voted for the Constitutional amendment now before the people. He expressed his hope that the President would accept it and recommend it to the Southern States for adoption. The President not long afterward declared himself against the Constitutional amendment; and we see Mr. Raymond, in his address laid before the Philadelphia Convention, inform the Southern people that they would be cowards and unworthy of freedom if they submitted to so cruel an outrage. Ah, there is virtue in the Johnson men! They resist the South? How many of the renegade Republicans are there who have not time and again given the lie to their professions of the day before, and who do not now every hour eat up their own words along with their "bread and butter"? And they are to be relied upon as the men to stem a reactionary current which they themselves have helped to set and keep in motion. If you want to know how far they are capable of sinking, look and see how far they have sunk already. When the news of the New Orleans riots and the connection of the President with that revolting butchery flashed over the country, the heart of every honest man was palpitating with indignation. Was it not then time for these fast friends of Andrew Johnson to tell him, "We have followed you so far, but we cannot go with you into deeds of blood?"

But what did they do? Not one of them had spirit enough to condemn openly what must have sickened their inmost hearts. With indecent haste they rushed forward to approve the President's acts and to whitewash the assassins of Louisiana. Nay, for men who are capable of so monstrous a self-debasement, there is no depth of infamy into which they will not be ready to descend.

And thus the reactionary movement rushes on. The atrocities it has already achieved, after having won the machinery of the State governments, I have described to you. I have endeavored to unfold before you its prospective program, to be carried when the late rebel States are unconditionally restored to power in the National Government. And now we behold the President of the United States prostituting the whole power of his office, by using it as a machinery of intimidation and bribery, putting up at auction the patronage of the Government, the price to be paid in consciences, and leaving, as he himself says, his Presidential dignity behind him—indeed, he leaves it so far behind that the two will never again come together—promenading his bad grammar and clownish egotism across the country to bully a brave and noble people into acquiescence; behind him the encouraging shouts of the rebel States; around him all the disloyal elements of the North, which, during the war, conspired for the overthrow of the Republic, together with a bevy of political hirelings, who carry their principles in their pockets, and are ready to sell out, along with their better convictions, the whole great future of their country; and the whole of this disgusting company, President, rebels, Copperheads and renegades, vying with each other in threats of another civil war if their nefarious designs are successfully resisted.

Such is the situation of affairs at this moment; such the difficulties which surround us; such the dangers which threaten us. Can these difficulties be overcome? Can these dangers be averted? We have no time to stop and discuss whether and how, they can be, for every patriotic heart in the country will respond, "*They must be.*"

It is true the first golden opportunity after the victory of our arms, when we might have accomplished with ease what now may cost us the fiercest struggles,—that first great opportunity has been treacherously frittered away, never to return; but it is not too late yet. A faithful Congress is still guarding the key position of the battle-field, and nobody need despair as long as behind a faithful Congress there stands a faithful people.

I stated at the beginning of my remarks that in order to render the reaction harmless, the great results achieved by the war must be so firmly imbedded into our political institutions as to be impregnable by any sudden movement. This can only be done by throwing the safeguard of the Constitution around them. A mere law can be repealed by a simple accidental majority in the legislatures without any Congress; a mere party platform may be pushed aside by the very men who made it, even without the formality of a vote; but a Constitutional provision cannot be overcome unless two-thirds of Congress and three-fourths of the States concur in striking it out.

The Thirty-ninth Congress proceeded upon this idea. It embodied some of the safeguards to be built up around the results of our great National struggle, in a Constitutional amendment which is now submitted to the people for approval.

The provisions of that Constitutional amendment are known to you. It declares citizens all persons born or naturalized in the United States, and provides that such citizens shall be protected in the enjoyment of equal civil rights in whatever State they may reside. It fixes the basis of representation so that if, in any State the franchise be denied to any class of citizens, except for participation in rebellion or other crime, the number of Representatives shall be reduced in proportion. It provides that the leaders of rebellion shall not be eligible to political office, unless Congress, by a two-thirds vote, remove the disability. Finally, it provides that the validity of the National debt of the United States, including debts incurred by the payment of pensions or bounties, shall not be questioned, and that no rebel debt shall be assumed and no claim for the loss of emancipated slaves be held legal and paid.

I will confess that as a general plan of reconstruction, as a foundation for the future political development of this great Republic, this Constitutional amendment never appeared to me broad enough. I believe not only in the ability, but also in the right, of man to govern himself. I believe that the only safe basis for democratic institutions to rest upon, consists in the integrity of self-government, and the integrity of self-government consists in no man's being excluded from participation in it by disabilities which he cannot overcome. I believe that to place the government of the late rebel States upon a reliable loyal foundation, you must enfranchise all the loyal men, black as well as white, thus effecting a safe reconstruction of the whole Republic by enlarging the democratic basis of our political system. I believe that the Republic owes it to the emancipated slaves whom she promised to make truly and forever free, either to protect them by the arm of the Federal Government, or to enable them to protect themselves, and that the development of free labor and the cause of democratic government requires the enfranchisement of the negro just as much as the negro needs it for his own protection. I believe that this Republic will have achieved true glory and secured lasting peace only when she metes out impartial justice to all her children.　This would have been, in my opinion, not only the safest basis of reconstruction, but the most glorious achievement of this age, and the best warrant for the future development of our National strength, prosperity and greatness.　If for this I am villified as an advocate of negro suffrage, I am willing to take the abuse and to stand by my convictions.

That the Constitutional amendment falls short of this, I heartily deplore.　Still, I fondly hope that we shall yet reach the great consummation, and the very obstreperousness of the rebel States may hasten it on.　But such as the Constitutional amendment is, as far as it goes, is it not in itself good?　Is it not necessary?　What objection can there be to it?　Is it wrong that the civil rights of American citizens should be placed directly under the shield of the National Constitution?　Is it not perfectly proper and just that if the people of a State exclude the negroes from the right of suffrage, they should not have the advantage of counting them in the basis of representation—an advantage which would give one rebel soldier in South Carolina three times as much political power as is wielded by a Union soldier in Massachusetts.

Is it not proper that if Massachusetts and South Carolina are to walk arm-in-arm, they should at least be equals at the ballot-box?　Who but those who want to see the National debt repudiated will object to its being secured by a Constitutional provision?　Is not this absolutely necessary in the face of the dangers which threaten us?　Or is it, perhaps, wrong and unwise that by excluding the instigators of the rebellion from political office, we should make it impossible for those who but yesterday strove to destroy the Republic, to govern it again to-morrow?　To be sure, Mr. Johnson's friends say that to keep such gentlemen out of office is a great outrage.　Is it not significant that Mr. Johnson's friends never call it an outrage when the rebels keep Union men out of office because they are Union men?

Show me in the history of the world a single example of a great rebellion, the suppression of which was attended with such mildness and magnanimity. If there were any proof wanted to demonstrate the greatness of that magnanimity, it would be found in the fact that the same men whose lives were forfeited by the law, and who but yesterday escaped the halter, are to-day vociferously complaining of our cruelty because we do not just yet want them to rule us to-morrow. Nay, the provisions of the Constitutional amendment are so evidently just and proper that it has neither been attacked on its own merits by the President, who certainly is not disinclined to attack everything that comes from that body which "hangs upon the verge of the government," nor even by the distinguished gentlemen who did all the speaking for the Philadelphia Convention.

But here we encounter the great staple argument of the Johnson party. It is that, however proper, just and necessary the provisions of the Constitutional amendment may be, the Government has no right to make its ratification a condition precedent to the readmission of the rebel States; they always have been States; they have never ceased to be States; they are States now; and as such they are entitled to all the rights and privileges of other States. I will not follow our opponents into a metaphysical disquisition on the nature of a State, for it is not necessary for the purpose of proving the utter absurdity of their position.

Who does not know that a great civil war is subject to the same rules of public law as a foreign war? Is it not a principle of common-sense as well as a principle approved by every publicist of note since the world has had a literature, that the victor in a civil war, as well as in an

international conflict, has a right to protect himself
against immediate and prospective danger? Is it not the
very height of insanity to say that the Government of the
United States has no right to provide for the future security of the Republic because the defeated rebels regain
all their rights at the moment of their failure, and by the
very fact of their defeat? Here is Vattel, book 3, section
201, 44, 45:

When the conqueror has subdued a hostile nation, he may,
if prudence so require, render her incapable of doing mischief
with the same ease in the future. . . . If the safety of the
State lies at stake, our precaution and foresight cannot be
extended too far. Must we delay to avert our ruin until
it becomes inevitable? . . . An injury gives a right to provide for our future safety by depriving the unjust aggressor
of the means of injuring us."

Would it not be an act of folly unprecedented in the
history of nations to neglect so absolutely necessary a
precaution in our case? Is it possible that men with
any pretensions to sanity should attempt to deny the
justice of a principle so self-evident; a principle equally
approved by common-sense and public law? That President Johnson should ever have taken so absurd a position
I can explain only upon one theory. He frequently tells
us in his unfortunately not unfrequent speeches that he
commenced his political career as a village alderman, at
Greenville, Tennessee, and that he then rose, step by step,
until he reached the Presidency of the United States.
It seems, when the President finds himself in a tangle, he
is still in the habit of applying to the Dogberry of Greenville for a Constitutional argument.

But the President's own acts give the lie to his theories.
Has he not himself imposed upon the rebel States conditions precedent to readmission? Did he not order them

to ratify the Constitutional amendment prohibiting slavery
and to repudiate the rebel debt, expressly telling them
that they would not be readmitted until they should have
done so? And if he can do that why not Congress? Has
the alderman of Greenville grown so big as to absorb in
himself all the powers of the Government, leaving nothing
to the representatives of the people?

But he did not stop even there. He appointed governors and ordered them to call State conventions. He
kept the governors of his appointment still in office after
the people of the rebel States had elected their own. Nay,
when their elected governors were already in office, and
the legislatures working, he set aside laws passed by
those legislatures and approved by those governors, on
his own authority, by mere executive order; and after
all this, he still dares to speak of those States as being entitled to just the same rights as New York or Massachusetts. Would he have dared to attempt similar things
in Pennsylvania? I apprehend the sturdy yeomanry of
the Keystone State would have shown him the difference between their State and conquered Mississippi in
the twinkling of an eye. Nay, if his theory were correct,
if the conquered communities of the South were really
entitled to the same rights and privileges as the loyal
States of the Union, he would, by his very acts of flagrant
interference with the legitimate rights of the States, have
committed a high crime against the Constitution of the
United States, and Jack Rogers of New Jersey ought to
have moved his impeachment long ago to give Senator
Cowan of Pennsylvania an opportunity to pronounce him
guilty.

Here I will leave Mr. Johnson and his friends to their
self-imposed task of proving that the great men who made
the Constitution were such consummate fools as to render
the Government of the United States Constitutionally

unable, after having conquered a great rebellion, to provide for the future security of the Republic by imposing conditions upon the defeated enemy.   They are profound Constitutional lawyers, I presume, and I wish them joy.

In the meantime, I trust no honest and patriotic man will find it difficult to understand this aspect of the question.   In the course of the war the Government wanted money, and called upon the people for loans under the distinct and solemn promise that the lender should have his interest and principal as provided by law.   This constituted our obligation to the National creditor.   The Government wanted aid and coöperation inside of the rebellious States, and called upon the Union men of the South to come forward, under the distinct understanding that they should not be abandoned to the tender mercies of the rebels.   This constituted our National obligations to the Union men of the South.   The Government wanted to weaken the enemy and increase its forces in the field, and it called upon the negro to take part in the conflict, under the distinct and solemn promise that his race should be forever and truly free.   This constituted our National obligation to the negro.

Great as is my respect for our fundamental law, I do not hesitate to affirm that these obligations, as to their binding force, stand upon a level with the Constitution itself.   If there were nothing in the Constitution of the United States providing means, or expressly indicating a mode in which those obligations shall be fulfilled, would it not still be the great duty of the Republic to fulfil them? If it was Constitutional to make those promises, must it not be equally Constitutional to clear away all obstacles which might prevent us from keeping them?   If it is our duty to pay the National debt and to secure their rights to the loyalists and freedmen of the South, is it not also our duty, not only to do all that is necessary to that end,

but also to prevent such obstacles being thrown in our way
as might render our ability to fulfil our obligations uncertain?   It is clear, therefore, that if the unconditional
readmission of the rebel States might become in the least
degree prejudicial to our National obligations, it is not only
the right, but it is the sacred duty, of the Government to
keep the rebel States from representation and power in our
National concerns, until they shall have bound themselves,
by the strongest and most irreversible guarantees, to respect the great obligations the Republic has to perform.
If we have a President whose moral perceptions are so
obtuse that he does not understand that duty, every true
American should sink upon his knees and thank Heaven
that we have a Congress which does.

Let no man deceive himself.   It is in vain to resort to
Constitutional quibbles.   It is in vain to speak upon the
mutual aversion of the races.   It is in vain to say: "Let
us trust the rebels; they have been so clever at the Philadelphia Convention they will at last do justice to the
National creditor, to the Southern Union man and to the
negro; let us try the experiment, and put power into their
hands."   It is in vain to speak of favorable possibilities.
We have no right to make experiments with the lives,
liberties and property of our friends.   We have no right
to content ourselves with a vague prospect that the investment of the rebels with political power may possibly not
result in a breach of our National obligations.   We have
no right to be satisfied with anything short of the positive
assurance that our National obligations are Constitutionally beyond the reach of the reconstructed rebels, so that if
they have the desire, they have not the power, to do mischief.   We ourselves have to vouch for the discharge of
these solemn obligations, and it would be downright
treachery to delegate even the smallest part of them to
other people whose intentions are uncertain.   We have

given our promise for value received in money and in blood. It was under the banner of the Stars and Stripes that this bargain was fairly struck, and that banner will bear a blot of eternal disgrace unless the compact be honestly carried out.

I declare here before the American people, and I call to witness every honest man on the face of the globe, if, after having taken the money of the National creditor, upon the distinct promise that his interest should be fairly secured; if, after having called upon the Southern loyalist for coöperation, upon the distinct promise that his rights should be protected; if, after having summoned the negro to the battlefield, upon the distinct and solemn promise that his race should be forever and truly free; if, after having done all this, the Government of this Republic restores the rebel States to the full enjoyment of their rights and the full exercise of their power in the Union, without previously exacting such irreversible stipulations and guarantees as will fully, and beyond peradventure, secure the National creditor, the Southern Union man and the emancipated negro against those encroachments upon their rights which the reaction now going on is bringing with it, it will be the most unnatural, the most treacherous, the most dastardly act ever committed by any nation in the history of the world. It will be such an act as will render every man who participates in it unfit forever to sit in the company of gentlemen.

You remember the scorn and contempt with which the rebels spoke about the "mean-spirited Yankee." Do this, betray those who stood by you in the hour of need, and at that moment you will deserve it all. Do this, and your bitterest enemy in the South will have a right to ask the negro, "Did we not tell you the Yankees would cheat you?" And the negro will have to reply, "You did; and you were right." Not because they hated you, but be-

cause they despised you, the people of the South ventured
upon the rebellion. Do this, betray your friends into
the hands of their enemies, and they will despise you more
than ever before, and you will have to say to yourselves
that you deserve it.

And yet a policy like this I have heard designated as
the "Lincoln and Johnson policy." In the name of
common decency, in the name of the respect we owe to
the memory of our martyred President, I solemnly protest
against this insidious coupling of names. The Lincoln
policy! I knew Abraham Lincoln well; and at times
when many earnest and true men were dissatisfied with
his ways, and when I myself could not resist an impulse
of impatience, yet I never lost my faith in him, because I
knew him well. The workings of his mind were slow;
but the pure and noble sympathies of his heart, true as
the magnet needle, always guided them to the polar star
of universal justice. He was not one of those bold
reformers who will go far ahead of the particular requirements of the hour; he laboriously endeavored to comprehend what the situation demanded, and when he once
clearly understood it, at once he planted his foot, and no
living man ever saw Abraham Lincoln make a step back-
ward. His march was ahead, and each dawning day
found him a warmer advocate of the progressive ideas
of our great age.

I have heard it said, and it is one of the staple arguments of Mr. Johnson's friends, that Abraham Lincoln
would never have imposed upon the rebel States a condition precedent to restoration because it was not in the
Baltimore platform. If Mr. Lincoln had been assassi-
nated in the year 1862, they might, with equal justice,
have said, because emancipation was not in the Chicago
platform of 1860, he would never have been in favor of
emancipation. I undertake to say he would have been

as firm an advocate of impartial suffrage to-day as he was of emancipation, had he lived to see how necessary the one is to secure and complete the other. True, he never ranted about the hanging and impoverishing of traitors, but in his soul slept the sublime ideal of merciful justice and just mercy. He would not have thought of taking bloody revenge on the Union's enemies, but he would never have ceased to think of being just to the Union's friends. Abraham Lincoln and this "policy"! He would rather have suffered himself to be burnt at the stake than to break or endanger the pledge he had given to the Southern Union man when he called upon him for assistance, and to the negro soldier, when he summoned him to the field of battle; and if he could rise from the dead and walk among us to-day, we would see him imploring mercy upon the accursed souls of his assassins. But even his large heart, with its inexhaustible mine of human kindness, would have no prayer for those who strive to undo, or culpably suffer to be undone, the great work which was the crowning glory of his life.

Let Andrew Johnson's friends look for arguments wherever they choose, but let the grave of the great martyr of liberty be safe against their defiling touch. In the name of the National heart I protest against the infamous trick of associating Abraham Lincoln with a policy which drove into exile the truest men of the South, and culminated in the butchery of New Orleans. If Andrew Johnson has chosen his pillory, let him stand there alone, enveloped in the incense of bought flattery, adored by every villain in the land, and loaded down with the maledictions of the down-trodden and degraded.

Americans, the lines are drawn, and the issues of the contests are clearly made up.

You want the Union fully restored. We offer it to you—a Union based upon universal liberty, impartial justice and equal rights, upon sacred pledges faithfully fulfilled, upon the faith of the Nation nobly vindicated; a Union without a slave and without a tyrant; a Union of truly democratic States; a Union capable of ripening to full maturity all that is great and hopeful in the mind and heart of the American people; a Union on every square foot of which free thought may shine out in free utterance; a Union between the most promising elements of progress, between the most loyal impulses in every section of this vast Republic; in one word, a Union between the true men of the North and the true men of the South.

The reactionists, with their champion, Andrew Johnson, also offer you a Union—a Union based upon deception unscrupulously practiced, upon great promises treacherously violated, upon the National faith scandalously broken; a Union whose entrails are once more to be lacerated by the irrepressible struggle between slavery and liberty; a Union in a part of which the rules of speech will be prescribed by the terrorism of the mob, and free thought silenced by the policeman's club and the knife of the assassin; a Union tainted with the blood of its truest friends and covered with the curses of its betrayed children; a Union between the fighting traitors of the South and the scheming traitors of the North; a Union between the New York rioters of 1863 and the Memphis and New Orleans rioters of 1866.

You want magnanimity to a beaten foe. We offer it to you. We demand no blood, no persecution, no revenge. We only insist that when the Republic distributes the charitable gift of pardon and grace, the safety and rights of her faithful children are entitled to the first consideration. We are ready to grasp the hand of the South. We only want first to ascertain whether the blood of our slaughtered friends is already dried on it. Peace and good-will to all men is the fondest wish of our heart and we are anxious to give and secure it even to the bitterest of our enemies as soon as they show an honest willingness to grant it to all of our friends.

The reactionists, with their champion, Andrew Johnson, speak, too, of magnanimity. Magnanimity! What magnanimity is this which consists in forgiveness to the Union's enemies and forgetfulness to the Union's friends? which puts the dagger into the hands of the former with which to strike at the lives of the latter? Magnanimity, indeed! It is mercy in the prostituting embrace of treason; it is persecution and murder in the garb of grace.

Are the American people sunk so deeply—can they be so completely lost to all sense of decency and honor—that such an insult to their common-sense, and to the generous impulses of their hearts, should be offered to them with impunity? Or is it possible that those who but yesterday would have defied the world in arms, should to-day, with craven pusillanimity, recoil before the difficulties which the revived hopes of defeated traitors oppose to their onward march? I appeal to your understandings. Let the clear, practical eye of the American be turned upon the task immediately before us, and see how simple it is. You have but to speak and the dangers which surround you will vanish. Let the National will rise up from the ballot-boxes of November with a strength which laughs at resistance, and with a clearness of utterance which admits of no doubt, and the reaction which now surges against you like a sea of angry waves will play around your feet like the harmless rivulet set running by an April shower. Even Andrew Johnson's damaged intellect will quickly perceive that, although he may succeed in buying up a few forlorn wretches, it is a hopeless enterprise to debauch the great heart of the American people. He will learn in season that it would indeed be highly imprudent for him to think of dictatorship, and that if he ventured too far in his treacherous course, the American people are not incapable of remembering what he has so strenuously impressed upon their minds, that "treason must be made odious," and that "traitors must be punished." The late rebels will soon understand that those who defeated them in the field still live; and that it will be a wise thing for the South to lose no time in accommodating themselves to a necessity from which there is no escape. Nay, even to our friend, Henry Ward Beecher, it may finally become clear that by boldly and unflinchingly insisting upon what is right, the Union can just as quickly, and far more firmly, be restored than by accepting with fidgety impatience that which is wrong. But above all, our loyal friends in the South, white and black, whose cry for help is to-day thrilling the heart of every just man in the land, will raise their heads with proud confidence, feeling that they do not stand alone among their enemies, but that as they, in the gloomiest hours of danger, were true to the Republic, the Republic, so help her, God, will be true to them.

Yes, let the National will once more make itself understood to friend and foe, and the dangers which are now hanging over us like a black cloud will quickly clear away. Before its thunder tones the armed legions of the rebellion could not stand; before it the iniquitous designs of the reaction will soon vanish in utter hopelessness. Andrew Johnson's wretched brigade will be dispersed as by a whirlwind; the arm of the daring demagogue, which is now so defiantly lifted against the popular conscience, will fall palsied by his side, and the truly loyal men of America will quickly, justly and firmly restore the shaken fabric of the Union.

We have passed through gloomy days of late; days of

grievous disappointment, of deep humiliation, of sorrowful anxiety. But when the other night I stood upon the balcony of the Union League House and saw the countless multitude surging below, a multitude greater in number than the hosts which marched with Sherman to the sea, or the Army of the Potomac when it swept over the ramparts of Richmond, and that multitude, as once our batallions were summoned to the battlefield by the paternal voice of Abraham Lincoln, now following the solemn call of the same voice issuing from the grave; and when I saw from that ocean of human faces radiating forth the electric light of intelligence and love of liberty; and when I thought that the volcanic bursts of enthusiasm there were but one throb of the patriotic emotions which are to-day again swelling the great heart of the loyal North, then my soul felt itself lifted out of the gloom of dark apprehensions and I ceased to fear for the future of the Republic. Then it became certain again to my mind, that the great people of the New World, who fought a four years' battle of conscience, have not forgotten their exalted mission on earth, and that the very gates of hell cannot shake their mighty determination to wield, with a firm hand, the National power, until justice is done to all, and until, with safety to all, the Republic can be set afloat upon the broadest channel of self-government.

We have already heard the triumphant morning gun of Vermont, booming with increased volume. Far off San Francisco has merrily responded; old Maine in the North stands ready to send us a cheering echo, and all over the land our hosts are mustering with the inspiring confidence that to march on is to conquer.

Our time has come. Forward into line, Republicans! This is to be the final battle of the war. Let it be the greatest victory of right and justice.

TO HEINRICH MEYER

DETROIT, Nov. 8, 1866.[1]

No political victory has ever been more complete than that of the Republican majority in Congress and no defeat more humiliating than that of the President. But such a victory was, indeed, very necessary. In almost all of the Southern States the men who had started the rebellion were again holding the political power in their hands and a violent, often even a bloody, reaction had begun. The abolition of slavery and the introduction of free labor was again at stake. Everywhere the negro population was oppressed by laws which only stopped short of the re-introduction of slavery, and the President vetoed every bill designed to prevent this state of affairs. He insisted on leaving a free hand to the former rebels and on allowing them unconditionally to take part in the Government of the country.

Johnson is a very narrow man, obstinate and stubborn to an unscrupulous degree. He is vain like all persons who are not clever enough to see how little they know, and in spite of his past successes he is still hampered by the bad qualities of his low origin. He is a born demagogue and if he were a man of great talent he might in his present position become a menace to the Republic.

Well, we have succeeded in mastering Johnson at the right moment, and during the rest of his Administration Congress will rule the country without paying much attention to him. He may congratulate himself if he escapes an indictment and an impeachment. The mischief he has done so far consists in his having inflamed the South to bitter revolt against Congress and in having delayed the work of reconstruction so that it will require

[1] Translated from the German.

more time than necessary. Let us hope that matters may now proceed peaceably.

TO MRS. SCHURZ

St. Louis, Sept. 4, 1867.[1]

I enjoy my journalistic work[2] in every respect but one: I find that I scatter my best ideas in innumerable articles, without being able to work them out as a complete whole. If I should try to do so the articles would be too long for use in a newspaper. Consequently the thoughts I have and wish to express can produce no satisfactory effect— they are like a thousand scattered raindrops falling singly. The advantage formerly of my speeches and lectures was that I could work them out at my leisure, giving great care to the minutest detail and to the polishing of every phrase. The result was a harmonious tableau designed to make a deep and lasting impression. I can no longer devote myself to such work, I have neither the leisure, the quiet nor the concentration. In journalism one is obliged to pay attention to hundreds of things which are trifles in themselves, but these trifles take all the time in which one is capable of concentrated work and when the day's task is done one is exhausted and in need of rest. That is the reason I have not been able to write any of the things I was planning to do this summer, although my mind is full of ideas that are waiting to be expressed. It is a pity— is it not?—that I am not rich and able to work as I should like. I should accomplish much more. But it can't be helped, and, after all, the thought that a comfortable old age can be secured for us all is gratifying and worth some sacrifices, all the more if it can be gained by my own efforts.

[1] Translated from the German.
[2] On the St. Louis *Westlische Post*, of which he had recently become one of the editors and owners.

THE ROAD TO PEACE—A SOLID, DURABLE PEACE[1]

MR. PRESIDENT AND FELLOW-CITIZENS:—What the country stands most in need of is a final settlement of the difficulties connected with our civil war. The people of this country want peace—a solid, durable peace. This want is acknowledged by both political parties, and both speak of peace as the true end of their respective policies. But while they profess to agree as to the object to be accomplished, they widely disagree as to the means to be employed. First, the Republican party steps before you and points out to you what it has accomplished. It speaks thus: "See here what we have done. We have carried on a great war against those who wanted to disrupt the Republic for the purpose of making slavery the corner-stone of a new empire. We have reconstructed the disorganized rebel States upon the basis of universal liberty and equal rights. We have enabled the whole people thereof to set up governments of their own; and behold eight of these States have already resumed their old places in the Union; only three are still behind, and in a short space of time those three will also have gone through the required preliminary process, and then the great work for which we have struggled and labored so long will be consummated. We offer you peace, therefore, upon the basis of a restored Union, of results already accomplished and of a state of things already existing." Thus speaks the Republican party. The Democrats hold a different language. They say: "All you have done, since the close of the war, for the restoration of the Union counts for nothing. Your reconstruction measures are unconstitutional, revolutionary and void." In the words of the Democratic candidate for the Vice-Presidency, which are but a violent construction of the Democratic platform, "these laws

[1] Speech delivered at Library Hall, Chicago, Sept. 19, 1868.

must be trampled in the dust, the army must be sent into the South, and disperse the newly erected State governments with the bayonet, and the Senate of the United States must be compelled to submit to our dictation. We offer peace to the people, not on the basis of accomplished results, of an existing state of things, but the existing state of things must first be overturned, by force of arms if need be, and upon its ruins we shall commence again to build up something which, after new struggles and conflicts, shall give peace to the country." This, as its platform and the manifestoes of its candidates clearly show, is the purpose of the Democratic party. It is evident that the Republicans, placing themselves upon the ground of results already accomplished, have the advantage in argument; for the Democrats will not persuade the prudent and patriotic people of this Republic to overthrow that which exists and to launch into new struggles, troubles and uncertainties, unless they clearly show that that which has been accomplished is intrinsically bad, and that they have something better to put in its place. Permit me, then, first, to pass in review the reconstruction policy carried out by Congress, and the objections to it brought forward by the Democratic party.

If a true, durable peace was to issue from the struggles of our civil war, it was above all things necessary that the causes of strife should be removed. But what were these causes? They consisted in two facts. First, that in the South there existed a peculiar interest and institution —namely, slavery and the aristocratic class government inseparable from involuntary labor, which in its very nature was antagonistic to the fundamental principles upon which our democratic system of government rests; and, secondly, that the Southern people cherished that institution and interest peculiar to themselves far above those they had in common with the rest of the American

people. Those are the sources of the irrepressible conflict. The slave-power demanded supreme control in our
National Government, which it justly deemed necessary
for its existence. Free-labor society justly refused to yield
that supreme control, because such a surrender would
have been incompatible with its highest interests. The
irrepressible conflict ripened into a crisis, and the civil
war ensued. It was, therefore, the logical tendency of the
war, as carried on by free labor, to stop the sources from
which the conflict had sprung—that is, to destroy slavery
and to break the power of aristocratic class government
in the South. That logic was followed; slavery was abolished; but by the mere overthrow of the rebellion and the
abolition of slavery, only the destructive part of the
great problem was solved.

Now, something was to be put in the place of slavery;
a new organization of a positive character was to be given
to Southern society, so as to prevent the return of aristocratic class government with its evil consequences. Here
commenced the constructive, creative part of the problem
to be solved. What new organization of society was that
to be? If it was to prevent the growing up again of local
interests and institutions antagonistic to those of the rest
of the American people; if it was to obviate the recurrence
of irrepressible conflicts; if it was to lay the foundation of a
durable and solid National peace, it had to be such as to
secure entire harmony between the social and political
institutions of the different sections of the country and the
controlling principles of our democratic system of government. What are these controlling principles? We find
them laid down in the grand old charter of American
liberty—"All men are created equal, and have certain
inalienable rights," and "governments derive their just
powers from the consent of the governed." What does
this mean in its practical application? It means that

society shall impose no duties unless they be coupled with corresponding rights; that no class of people shall have the exclusive privilege of governing another class; that every human being is entitled to a measure of liberty and of political rights, which enables him to pursue his own happiness in every legitimate way, which secures to him all necessary power to protect himself against usurpation and which opens to him the way to obtain that development of his mental and moral faculties which he may be capable of. In one word, in the place of slavery the system of free labor was to be planted, surrounded with the political institutions necessary to guarantee its existence and development. This was the great problem to be solved by what is called the work of reconstruction. When attempting this business, we had, above all things, to consider one of the most important circumstances. According to our Constitutional system, the National Government could not, like the Emperor of Russia after the emancipation of the serfs, permanently hold the progress of the new order of things in its protecting hand. It could only start and give direction to the movement, then turn it over with certain restrictions to the local majorities in the several States, to the operation of local self-governments. The character and propensities of the different elements of the Southern people became then a matter of great concern. The population of the South could be divided into three classes: First, the large majority of whites, who were long pro-slavery men, and who had directly or indirectly taken part in the rebellion for the perpetuation of slavery. Second, the white Union people, who, during the war, had supported the Government and had gradually adopted its anti-slavery policy, but who were too weak in numbers to exercise any considerable political influence. And, third, the colored people, who had been emancipated by the war, and whose interests were, therefore, most closely identified with the new order of things. The question naturally arose, in what manner can the new order of things, free labor and the democratic organization of society, be safely committed to a population so composed?

The first proposition broached was that the master class of the South, the whites, should, within certain loose limitations, have the exclusive control of political power in the Southern States and, therefore, of the development of the new order of things. It was first brought forward in one of the military capitulations concluded between General Sherman and the rebel General Joe Johnston, one of the main stipulations of which was that the rebel general should surrender his army on the express condition of the restoration to office of the rebel governors, legislatures, State and municipal officers.

Do you remember the cry of indignation which arose all over this land when the news of this treaty went abroad? Mark well; I do not mean to say anything against General Sherman. He committed then an error which those are most liable to commit who are capable of the highest virtues. It was an error of over-generosity to a beaten enemy. He has since recognized that error, and that he has done so he proves most clearly by now going hand in hand with General Grant, and using what influence he has at his disposal to make General Grant President of the United States. When we now pronounce the name of Sherman we do not think of the error he committed, but we think only of the magnificent deeds he has performed for this Republic, and of the profound gratitude we all owe him. But although the people had rejected that treaty with so much emphasis, the same idea was taken up and has been adhered to with wonderful tenacity by a man who is so unfortunate as to consider every favor of accident a deserved tribute to his genius, and who construes his rise from the position of alderman at Greenville, Tennessee, to the Presidency, as a Divine commission, unmistakably commanding him to assume the special direction of the universe—a man whose belief in his own powers and wisdom is so intense that he candidly thinks if the universe does not commit itself to the opinions he proclaims as his, that universe will make itself most egregiously ridiculous, and ought to be held to account for its indecent exposure. I mean Andrew Johnson. And from his hands the proposition went boldly into the Democratic platform.

When that piece of boastful inconsistency, which he called his "policy," had been for some time in operation, Mr. Johnson said in one of his messages, that the people of the South (meaning the Southern whites) had, on the whole, done as well as could be expected. I candidly declared I was then, and am now, of the same opinion— yes, "the Southern States have done as well as could be expected." Let us now see what we had a right to expect of them. Look back with me to the close of the war. The present generation of Southern whites had, from early childhood, been taught that slavery was not only right, but necessary. They had, on their own ground, never seen any other system of labor in operation. It was the only one they understood. With it all their doings and hopes of success were inseparably connected. All their ways of thinking, their social habits, their political theories and aspirations, and even their religious doctrines, revolved around slavery as the great central axis. They believed in it—they idolized it—they clung to it with a sort of religious superstition—they shut out from their minds all progressive ideas hostile to it, and their imagination was utterly incapable of realizing a condition of things in the South without it. The Presidential election of 1860 at last dealt a fatal blow to that political ascendancy of the South, without which they felt that slavery could not prosper in the Union. They did not hesitate a moment; they staked at once their all on the cast of war. After a fierce struggle of four years, they succumbed. They had sacrificed their peace, the prosperity of their country, their all, for slavery. They lost the battle and lost slavery with it.

What, then, could we, after all this, expect of them? Had we a right to expect that they would all at once drop their life-long notions, their inveterate prejudices, their violent propensities, their lawless habits and their whole love of slavery, while they were still denouncing the act of emancipation as an act of robbery, as a crime against the very order of nature? Had we a right to expect that they would, in good faith, welcome the system of free labor which they did not understand, of whose blessings they knew nothing and which had come down upon them as would a thunderbolt, first making itself known by its destructive force? And if, indeed, they might have been made to submit to all this under the relentless pressure of power and necessity, had we a right to expect that they would, in good faith, secure and develop what was so strange and distasteful to them if we put the power over it into their own hands? There never was a privileged class which gave up its privileges of its own free will and choice; there never was one that made important concessions unless they were extorted from it; there never was one which, after being compelled to surrender its privileges, did not take advantage of every available chance to recover them? Is there anything in the character of the Southern whites to make them an exception to this rule? Whatever their good qualities may be, the only three things which might have induced them to abandon their privileges without irresistible necessity are just those which they are most deficient in—a just regard for the rights of others, a correct appreciation of the spirit and tendency of this age and common-sense generally.

In saying this I am not indulging in mere speculation. In 1865 and 1866 we had occasion to witness the doings of the Southern legislatures, elected by the Southern whites, under the auspices of Mr. Johnson's policy. The results are before us as matter of history. And what are they? No sooner did the master-class feel in possession of authority and power again than it sought at once a chance for a reaction in the direction of its old pro-slavery notions, and it availed itself of that chance with refreshing alacrity. Here vagrance laws were enacted calculated to tie the colored laborer to his late owner by the most arbitrary legal obligations. There the negro was forbidden to acquire real estate and thus to have a home for himself and his children. In another place contract laws were devised compelling the colored man virtually to sell himself for a certain specified time under severe penalties. In still another State the old slave code was boldly restored to force, and so on. Is that free labor? And after all this, Andrew Johnson, in one of his messages, congratulated the country upon the fact that the Southern people had done even better than he had expected. Heaven knows what his expectations may have been; they must have been even worse than mine. But what did all this prove? It proved that the Southern whites, instead of securing and developing free labor, endeavored only to find a new form of slavery, another peculiar institution. Instead of placing society upon a democratic basis, they sought only a new foundation for aristocratic class government. I repeat, these are not mere speculations. These are hard, incontestable facts; but facts which might easily have been foreseen. "Lead us not into temptation," is the text of the prayer. But the gift of exclusive power to the Southern whites was bound to

lead them into a temptation which might have become
dangerous to virtue itself, and which naturally proved
irresistible to those who desired nothing better than an
opportunity to sin.   Yes, they surely have done as well,
under the circumstances, as we had a right to expect; but
they did not do as well as it was our duty to demand.   And
just here is the "rub."   If nothing better could be expected of the Southern whites than that they would take
advantage of every chance to build up another peculiar
institution, an interest antagonistic to the fundamental
principles of democratic government, and thus plant the
seeds of another irrepressible conflict to disturb the future
of this Republic, then it was folly, it was absurdity, it was
a crime, to place in their hands exclusively all political
power in the Southern States.   The Southern gentleman
showing himself unfit to secure the establishment of free
labor and the harmony of our institutions, which is necessary for the peace of the country, the American people
could not afford to jeopardize the peace of the country
for the Southern gentleman's accommodation.   It was our
solemn duty to look out for other classes of the Southern
people, of whom we had a right to expect that they would
accomplish the end.

Congress at last took the work of reconstruction out
of Andrew Johnson's hands into its own.   It was indeed
high time.   That sublime ruler of the universe was making a wonderful muddle of it.   It cannot be said that
Congress proceeded with haste and harshness in the
matter of reconstruction.   It gave Andrew Johnson's
hopeless experiment a fair trial, and only when it had
become manifest that the restriction of the suffrage to the
whites would lead to a decided reaction in favor of involuntary labor and aristocratic class government, Congress slowly groped its way toward a logical, efficient and
clearly defined policy.

The question to be decided put itself to Congress in a
very simple form: If for the harmony and peace of the
Republic it is necessary to establish free labor in the
South, and to secure and develop it through the operation
of self-government, you must not put the political power,
the right of suffrage, into the hands of pro-slavery people
who do not want free labor, excluding from it a majority
of those who do want free labor. If you want to establish
democratic government in the South, and to prevent
the return of aristocratic class rule, you must not confine
the right of suffrage to one class, but you must extend it
over the masses of the people without arbitrary distinction.
And, finally, assuming a sincere devotion to the fundamental principles of our government to be the essential
condition of true loyalty to the Republic—if you want to
have loyal governments in the South, you must not appoint disloyalists, by habit and disposition, to lord it over
the loyal men, but enable the loyal men *en masse* to counteract the power of those who are inclined to be traitors.
Such were the considerations by which Congress in its
reconstruction policy was governed. Are they not as
logical and self-evident as the rule of three? Can conclusions be more imperative? The manner in which
Congress acted upon these conclusions was equally simple.
First, it kept the whole rebel country under the immediate
control of the National Government, through its military
arm, for the purpose of restoring the disturbed order of
society, of protecting persons and property, and of enforcing rights and redressing wrongs, where no other efficient
means for that end could be found. Then Congress
called upon the people of the South to form State constitutions in harmony with the new order of things, and to
rebuild upon that basis their State and municipal governments. Congress called upon the Southern people, I say;
not like Mr. Johnson, upon one class of the people, and

that class, too, the same which in its majority had made
the rebellion for the perpetuation of slavery; but Congress,
according to good democratic doctrine, appealed to the
whole people of the South—high and low, white and black
—to give themselves a political organization in which free
labor might be safe, and to take their governments into
their own hands. Then the Southern people went to
work to rebuild their State governments, and no sooner
was the political organization of the State perfected
according to the conditions prescribed, and the local authorities fairly constituted, than Congress withdrew the
protecting and controlling arm of the military power
and turned the affairs of the reconstructed State again into
the broad channel of self-government. This, then, is the
sum and substance of the reconstruction policy of Congress.
These are the principles upon which it rests, these the
means it has employed, these the ends it has designed to
reach. Thus eight of the late rebel States have been
restored to their old places in the Union. The three yet
behind will regain their places in a short period of time,
and the great end, so devoutly wished and so laboriously
struggled for, the restoration of the American Union, upon
the basis of universal liberty, impartial justice and equal
rights, will be a grandly consummated fact. Upon this
we offer peace to the country, and, conscious of the recti-
tude of our intentions, we confidently and proudly appeal
to the enlightened judgment of the American people and
the sympathies of civilized mankind.

If there is a Democrat within the reach of my voice who
will only throw off, for a single moment, the shackles of
party prejudice, and whose ear is still open to the voice
of conscience and reason, I appeal to him. Let him look
at what has been done with an unclouded eye. Are not
the principles upon which this work of reconstruction is
based reasonable, sound, just and eminently democratic?

Were not the conclusions drawn from these principles logical and absolutely imperative? Were not the means employed for their execution, proper and even necessary? Can that Democrat tell me how, after the close of the war, when on Southern soil bloodshed and persecution were the order of the day, when class seemed to be arrayed against class, and man against man, how, then, the disturbed order of society could be righted without the interference of the military power? Can he tell me how the relations between the late master and the late slave, which, by sudden emancipation, had been thrown into chaos, could be prevented from degenerating into bloody conflicts, without the benevolent interposition of the National Government? Can he tell me how the development of free labor in the South could be insured except by giving the laborer that share of political power, without which he could not protect and defend his rights against the attacks of the late master-class which acrimoniously disputed them? Did he ever think of this: that Congress had absolutely no choice but such governments as this, based on impartial suffrage, and the governments of Southern whites exclusively, which means governments of the pro-slavery rebel majority; yes, that there was this inevitable stubborn alternative which admitted of no shirking or subterfuge —either these governments or rebel governments? Does the honest, patriotic Democrat hear that? And when this alternative is put before him plainly, bluntly, stubbornly, and he has to choose between the two, where will his choice fall? Where will his reason and conscience as a man, where his duty as a patriotic citizen, where his devotion to human liberty, and where his love of peace, lead him?

But here the voice of his party summons him, declaring that the reconstruction measures of Congress are unconstitutional, usurpations, null and void, frightening him with

negro supremacy, with the most atrocious despotism the
world ever saw, that had been established over the South
—telling him, in the language of the Democratic candidate
for the Vice-Presidency, that these laws must be trampled
into the dust; that all that has been done for the restoration of the Union, since the close of the war, must be
destroyed again, and that the Democratic President, to be
elected, must send the army into the South to drive out
the reconstructed State governments at the point of the
bayonet.   Indeed, if a proposition so atrocious, jeopard-
izing the peace of the country and the very existence of
the Republic, does not find an excuse in the most conclusive, the most irresistible reasons, we shall be justified in
regarding it as the hallucination of a madman, or as a
criminal plot of malicious enemies to their country.

Let us see what these reasons are.   They shall have
our candid consideration.   First, then, the Congressional
policy of reconstruction is denounced by the Democratic
party as unconstitutional.   This is not the first time that
the Democratic party has flourished this favorite weapon,
which it seems to claim as all its own.   Do you remember
the winter and spring of 1861, when the rebellion first
raised its head, and when every true man, following the
warm impulse of patriotism and the voice of conscience,
jumped forthwith at the conclusion, "If the life of the
Republic is attempted by force, force must be used to
save it"?   Do you remember it?   Then you remember,
also, how the Democracy then gave vent to its patriotism
in this profound Constitutional conundrum—"The Southern States may not have the Constitutional power to
secede from the Union, but the Government of the Republic has no Constitutional right to keep them in the Union."
Had not the matter been so terribly serious, the world
would have been convulsed with laughter when a great
political party, with solemn air, blurted out so unfathom-

able and shameless an absurdity. But so it was. The great Constitutional argument against coercion enunciated by the Democratic President, Buchanan, and sustained by the party leaders and organs, with the criminal threat that, if the soldiers of the Union marched out to coerce the rebellious South, a fire would be kindled in their rear.

Such was the Democratic construction of the Constitution then. What would have been the consequence if the American people had accepted it! The American people would have acknowledged, before the whole world, that this Government had no right and no power to defend its own existence. It would have presented the doleful and ridiculous spectacle of a government tumbling to pieces at the first show of resistance, from inherent constitutional inconsistency. This boasted experiment, this beacon-light of liberty-loving humanity, would have become the laughing-stock of the whole world, and for centuries the advocates of despotism would have triumphantly pointed to this most ridiculous failure as often as a friend of liberty dared to pronounce the word Republic.

The South would have gone her own way after her first success; she would have proved an insolent and exacting neighbor. War would have been the inevitable consequence. No national bonds would then have held together the East and the West; conflicts of interests would have led to new separations; these, to new collisions. Despised abroad, the little republics would have exhausted and ruined one another by incessant warfare among themselves, and America, once the hope of the oppressed, the pride of the free and the terror of the devotees of despotism, would have become the sport of foreign powers. Such would have been the inevitable consequence had the American people accepted the Democratic construction of the Constitution in 1861.

And what is the Democratic construction of the Constitution now? It is exactly the same in spirit, only different in terms: That the rebel States immediately after, and by the very fact of the defeat of the rebellion, became at once just as rightful and competent States in the Union again, as though they had never rebelled; that the Government of the Republic had, after the rebellion, no other authority over the rebel States, than to recognize them as reinstated in all their rights and powers as States of this nation. In other words, that the Government of this Republic had no right to provide for its future security by dictating terms of peace to a defeated aggressor. I need not go into a legal argument on this point. I will not quote decisions of the Supreme Court, nor attempt a new definition of the powers the Constitution confers upon Congress when it authorizes it to receive new States, and enjoins upon the United States to guarantee to the several States a republican form of government. The country has already been overwhelmed with legal ingenuity upon this subject. I will address myself simply to your common-sense.

What does it mean that rebel States, after and by the very fact of the defeat of the rebellion, were at once restored to all their rights, privileges and powers in the Union just as if they had never rebelled? Nobody will pretend that, while the rebel States were actually making war upon the Government of this Republic, they were then entitled to any Constitutional privileges and any exercise of Constitutional powers in that Government. But the Democrats do pretend that the rebels, as soon as they were coerced by force of arms to cease their resistance, lapsed, by the very fact of their defeat, again into these Constitutional privileges and powers. Thus rights forfeited by successful resistance were regained by defeat. In other words, you, brave soldiers of the Union, thought

28

you had whipped the rebels into submission, but how mistaken you are! It turns out that you have whipped the rebels only into power again. Did you understand it so? The victorious party, just because it is victorious, has no other authority over the defeated aggressor than to recognize him as an equal in rights, privileges and powers, just because that aggressor is defeated. Is not this absurd on its very face? Is it possible that the Government of this Republic should, after a war, have no right to provide for its future safety by imposing terms of peace upon a defeated aggressor? True, this may not be, in so many words, stated in the Constitution, neither is the right of the Government to coerce seceding States granted there in express terms. But is there no such thing as a power inherent in a government, as such, as a vital condition of its existence? Are there no rights and powers arising from the law of nature that may be applied to governments, from the necessity of things? Is there a Democratic jurist in this assembly—I summon him as a witness. Can he point out to me in a single textbook, from the beginning of legal literature down to the present day, a single sentence in which the faintest doubt is expressed as to the right of a government after a war—no matter whether an international war or a war between a government and its rebellious subjects—to provide for its future safety by dictating terms of peace to a defeated enemy? If there is a Democratic historian in this assembly, will he point out to me a single instance in the annals of the world, where, after a war, the victorious government did not claim the right, and where its right was not recognized, to dictate terms of peace to the defeated enemy? Why, look at two men fighting on the street. One has been assailed by another; he wrestles with him and throws him down; and he will not let him up again until the defeated assailant is so disabled that

he can inflict no further injury, or until he promises that
he will not attempt it again. What is that man doing?
He exercises the natural right to provide for his future
security by dictating terms of peace to his defeated
aggressor.

The Democrats are in the habit of prating to us about
the wisdom of the great men who formed the Constitution
of the United States. Yes, the Fathers of the Constitution
were great men. They were among the wisest of their
generation. And now the Democrats will make us believe that these same Fathers of the Constitution were
such consummate blockheads as to deprive the Government of this Republic of a right which every government
has possessed and exercised since mankind had a history,
and which every government, from the very necessity of
things, will possess and exercise until the end of things.
Nay, a right which every loafer on the street will claim
and exercise as a natural right when assailed by another
loafer. In support of such a right we do not need the
authority of Vattel, Puffendorf and Grotius. We do not
need a broad display of legal ingenuity or of metaphysical
reasoning. We hear it asserted by the common-sense of
mankind. We find it confirmed in the nature of things.
We see it written in the book of manifest necessity. It is
a right which a government must have, if it has a right to
exist at all.

And this the Democrats undertake to deny. Where
would the acceptance of their doctrine lead us? Just to
the same consequences into which the country would have
drifted had, in 1861, the American people accepted the
doctrine that the Government of the Republic does not
possess the right to coerce rebellious States. I repeat,
the two doctrines, although different in terms, are essentially the same in spirit. They mean, simply, that the
Government of this Republic has no right to defend its

own existence against aggression organized upon a large scale. If you run this doctrine to its logical consequences, then a State can, as such, not be held to account for an act of rebellion, for a rebellion is the act of individuals, while individuals ought not to be held to account for an act of rebellion if, in committing it, they merely followed their allegiance to the State. Who, then, is to be held to account for the rebellion? Nobody; for the State is covered by the responsibility of the individual, while the responsibility of the individual is covered by the State. Accept this position, and rebellion will be a mere pastime, which can result only in the acquisition of new rights by success, and the preservation of old rights by failure. The National power will be a mere football, to be tossed about at pleasure by daring sectional minorities. Disputed questions of general concern will not be decided by the largest number of votes, but by the greatest fighting capacity of this or that political faction. And the Republic must insensibly drift into disgrace, ruin and the chaos of universal anarchy, Yes, the principle the Democrats now maintain is identical with the doctrine of the unconstitutionality of coercion, which, logically, means nothing but the right of secession. And well may the Southern leaders say—as they boastfully tell us every day—if the Democratic construction of the Constitution prevails, they have, even after their defeat, at last won what they fought for. What then, is the great Democratic Constitutional doctrine? It is an attempt to twist the Constitution into a rope with which to strangle the Republic. There I will leave it, to the contemplation of a patriotic people.

The next great objection raised by our opponents against the Republican policy consists in the assertion that Congress has subjected the South to the most odious and oppressive military despotism the world ever saw. Upon this subject that mournful statesman from Wis-

consin, Senator Doolittle, who affords himself and the
world so much amusement by his sepulchral wit, as well as
his exhilarating profundity, has grown particularly eloquent. In a speech made by him in the city of Washington some time ago, he delivered himself of the following
wonderful disclosures:

They (meaning the Republicans in Congress) have established from the Potomac to the Rio Grande a military despotism
more absolute than any other in any civilized country within
the last two hundred years. If you sit down by the grave of
Washington you sit in the shadow of a military government
more despotic and absolute than any in Poland or Hungary
or Ireland. They have heaped upon the people of the South
more of oppression and of indignity than can be found in all
the history of Europe since the barbarous proceedings of the
Duke of Alva against the Dutch Republic.

When such childish nonsense is uttered by a sensational
penny-a-liner, or a little demagogue at a ward meeting,
or Andrew Johnson, we let it pass; but when a grave
Senator of the United States, who pretends to respecta-
bility, rises before the people and compares the military
governments in the South with the atrocities committed
in Hungary and Poland, he deserves chastisement. He
must be either more ignorant than the merest schoolboy
ought to be, or have a fondness for wilful misrepresenta-
tion incompatible with the character of a gentleman. I
understand Senator Doolittle has been travelling in
Europe. It appears he might have spent the time very
profitably in requesting some little German boy to give
him a bit of elementary information upon European
affairs. He might then have learned that, after the
failure of the Hungarian revolution, a long row of gal-
lowses was erected, on which the most prominent of the
Hungarian generals were hung. He might have learned

that, after the downfall of the Polish insurrection, the
Russian sword raged among the helpless victims without
mercy; that every whisper against the victorious government was punished with death; that immeasurable chain-
gangs of men and women were driven across thousands
of miles of sterile country, to drag out their miserable
lives in the snows of Siberia. He might have learned
that even in civilized France, after the wholesale butchery
of the 2d of December, 1851, hundreds of men were
transported, to find a speedy death in the miasmas of
Cayenne. That is military despotism in Europe. Where
has the Senator his ears and his eyes that he knows
nothing of this? If the military governments in the South
had been like the military despotisms in Hungary, Poland
and France, men like the rebel Generals Preston and Forrest
would long ago have expired on the gallows instead of
presuming to give a Vice-President to the United States.
Wade Hampton would have been moldering under the
ground instead of dictating Democratic platforms and
trying to starve loyal negroes into voting the Democratic
ticket. Henry A. Wise's redoubtable tongue would now
be food for worms instead of proclaiming the approaching
victory of the lost cause, and thousands of Southern ladies
and gentlemen would now be shivering among the icebergs
of Alaska, instead of killing negroes and spitting in the
faces of Southern Unionists. Military despotism, indeed!
Show me a single gallows, in this great Republic, where a
single man expired for participation in the rebellion—
for the miserable Wirz was not hung because he was a
rebel, but because he had murdered thirteen thousand of
our brave boys by starvation. Show me a single prison
where a single man has been held captive for treason!
Yes, there was one, Fortress Monroe, where Jefferson
Davis was fed on fried oysters and spring chickens, and
where the hall before his prison-cell was covered with a

thick carpet, lest the step of the sentinel should disturb
the sweet slumbers of the rebel chief. But even he is now
released, to have his ears tickled with the cheers of the
blockade runners of Liverpool. There is Mr. Doolittle's
military despotism. Does that Senator really mean to
lie when he prates about the atrocities of Hungary and
Poland? No, I acquit him of that; he possesses in an
eminent degree the faculty of talking nonsense in perfect
good faith. He has succeeded in fortifying his native
stupidity with a bulwark of ignorance which I recognize
as fairly impregnable. I will leave him to his glory.
Military despotism! You will search the annals of the
world in vain for a rebellion, after the failure of which the
vanquished were treated with such merciful mildness,
with such boundless generosity by the conquerors, as they
were here. The very insolence with which those who, but
yesterday, strove to destroy the Republic, insist upon
ruling it to-day, is irrefutable proof of the fact.

But I am, indeed, willing to admit that our military
governments in the South may be called despotisms, if
we apply to them the Democratic standard of liberty.
Since the Democratic party identified itself with the slave-
power, it has always held this as one of its fundamental
doctrines: That true liberty consists in the right of one
man to strip another man of his rights. The Southern
Democrat did not consider himself a free man if he was
not permitted to "wallop a nigger" whenever it pleased
him, and the Northern Democrat insisted that this inalienable privilege be scrupulously respected. That one
man should have a right to hold another man as his slave
was, in the opinion of the Democrats, one of the essential
conditions, without which free institutions could not exist;
and that this right of one class of society over another
should be extended over the Territories of this Republic
was demanded by the Democracy in the name of self-

government. The abolition of slavery has not yet succeeded in curing the Democratic party of this atrocious
notion. Still they maintain that true liberty consists in
the right of one man, especially a Southern man, to deprive
another of his rights—and just this is the reason for their
opposition to our military governments in the South.
For what was the object of these military governments?
Not to assert an undue governmental authority over the
people of the Southern States, but to prevent one class
of Southern people from asserting an undue and tyrannical
authority over another class. What a terrible thing!
The inalienable right of the Southern Democrat to "wallop
the nigger" has been ruthlessly invaded, and more than
that; as from his right to whip a negro, the Southern man
derived his right to hang an Abolitionist, so he now derives
from his right to rebel against the Republic a new right
to persecute and shoot a Radical; but this right, too,
has been most provokingly interfered with by the military authorities. What a fearful innovation! Hence the
rage of the Democracy. Hence the cry about the most
atrocious despotism the world ever saw. Hence the
doleful lamentation that the Constitution is now surely
going to the dogs. It is the raving wrath of baffled
tyranny; it is the furious howl of the wolf against whose
cruel voracity the lamb is sheltered by the shepherd.
Do you want proof? You have heard of the nine hundred
and thirty-nine murders committed in Texas in an incredibly short space of time. You remember, also, that under
Sheridan's military administration, by the vigorous
watchfulness of that faithful patriot, the number of
murders was signally reduced. You remember, further,
that under Hancock's administration the number of
murders fearfully increased. This is a matter of history.
And for protecting the victims glorious Phil. Sheridan
was denounced as a tyrant, while Hancock was praised

as a second Washington for respecting the Democratic liberty of the assassin.

If you want to measure the effect which this nefarious doctrine—that true liberty consists in the right of one man to deprive of his rights another—has had upon the political development of the country, see what it has made of the Democratic party itself. No sooner had that party wedded itself to that atrocious heresy than it became at once incapable of any progressive idea. The world marched on, but that party remained lashed to its savage idol with a chain it could not break. Look at its platforms from year to year, from decade to decade. Not a single proposition for the intellectual and moral advancement of society. Not a thought for the elevation of human nature. Nothing but a dreary and hopeless repetition of the old song, that one class of men must have the freedom to tyrannize over another, and that when one man deprives another of his rights nobody has a right to interfere. This year some credulous men and women deluded themselves into the belief that the Democratic party could become an engine of progress. Preposterous expectation! The temptation was indeed great, the prospect enticing, but there is the New York platform, and the candidates' manifestoes, and what do you behold? Ranting denunciations of Congress, because it contrived to secure the rights of the emancipated slave against the rapacity of the master-class and the fierce demand that that master-class must be reinstated, even at the point of the bayonet, if need be, in the Constitutional right to strip of his right whomsoever it pleases. No, I will not be unjust to the Democratic platform; it does recognize the fact that secession has been defeated and slavery abolished. Aye, indeed, four years—which in days like these amount to half a century—four years it hobbles painfully after the greatest events of our times, and reluctantly comes at last

to the conclusion that something has happened which
can not be denied. If that is progress, the Democratic
party has shown something like a progressive spirit. If
it goes on at that rate, it will, at the end of the nineteenth
century, recognize the fact that a locomotive is a better
engine of transportation than a wheelbarrow, and a steam-
boat a swifter conveyance than Noah's ark. But even
the poor acknowledgment of great consummations contained in the New York platform is already fiercely repudiated by the Southern Democrats, and it is loudly
proclaimed there that the right of secession holds as good
as ever, and that if slavery has been abolished, it was a
great wrong, and ought to be remedied. So you see the true
spirit of the Democracy which lives in the South stands
aghast at the folly of this progressive feat, and confidently
proclaims that those are fools who think it could improve.
It is this Democratic doctrine of true liberty that has been
the great curse of the Republic. It has poisoned our
political life by leading the popular mind into channels of
vicious logic, and debauching the hearts of the multitude
with its artful defense of wrong. It has made man the
enemy of man, and thus produced an irrepressible conflict.
It has stirred up all the bitter contests of the last thirty
years, and plunged the country into the bloodiest civil
wars, and it will do so again unless we at last cut out and
eject this prolific abomination from our political system.
In the war the first cut was made, and our military governments only followed up the surgical operation.

I would be the last man on earth to sound the praise
of military rule, as such. I would denounce it even in
this case, had it not been the necessary means of transition from the reign of wrong to the reign of right. To
give security and order to Southern society in a period
of chaotic confusion; to render possible the appeal which
was taken to the whole Southern people, without distinc-

tion of class or color, and to disappear again as soon as
these people had given themselves a political organization
—such was the purpose for which it was instituted, and
such the end it has accomplished. Nowhere on the face
of the earth has military rule been devoted to such a
glorious cause as this—to wipe out that most pernicious
of atrocities, that, in the name of liberty, one man should
claim the right to deprive of his rights another; to clear
the track for the government of the people, for the people,
and by the people, on every inch of ground on which the
American flag throws its shadow. Only the friends of
tyranny will call this despotism; but it will stand blessed
in the memories of coming generations as the pioneer of
order, freedom and justice.

The third great Democratic objection to the Republican
policy of reconstruction is that we have oppressed the
Southern people, by bestowing the elective franchise
upon the colored men of the South, while the negro is
still so very stupid. Yes, it is true that Congress has
secured the right of voting to the colored people of the
South, and it is also true that in point of intelligence and
education the negro stands below the average of the
whites. Why did Congress secure to the negro the right
of voting? I have said it already: Because there was no
other alternative but between governments of the rebel
majority on one, and governments based upon impartial
suffrage on the other hand; because it was necessary to
protect free labor, which could be done only by giving the
laborer the political means with which to protect his own
rights. Now, as to the intelligence and education of the
negro, is it not a little singular that the Democratic party
has suddenly become so very fastidious with regard to
the intellectual qualifications of voters? I never heard
of it that the Democracy had refused admission to their
party to a man on the ground that he was too stupid for

them. On the contrary, it is a well-known fact that the Democrats insist upon the right of a certain class which notoriously does not shine by its intelligence, to vote at every election not only once, but four or five times, and the more stupid the man, the oftener he is to vote. Now, I will readily admit that an intelligent exercise of the suffrage is a most desirable thing, but I deny that it is the most important consideration, when we have to determine what class of people shall, and what class shall not, vote. The strength of the democratic system of government does not consist in the whole mass of voters clearly and minutely understanding every question submitted to them in all its bearing, most desirable as such understanding may be. The strength of the democratic system of government consists in the fact that the whole mass of citizens have the right to vote; that this right to them is a stimulus to inform themselves and to take a lively interest in public affairs, and thus becomes a powerful engine of popular education; that they have in their hands the means to preserve and enforce the equality of all before the law, and thus prevent the growth of privilege and monopoly and aristocratic class government which might settle themselves upon the neck of the people. The vote of the individual is guided in a great measure by instincts, his traditions, the nature of his nearest interests and the circumstances under which he lives. And it is not difficult to show that these agencies may sometimes impel the most ignorant to vote more wisely than the shrewdest and most accomplished. Take this example: If, in 1861, the people of the Southern States voted upon the question whether those States should secede from the Union for the purpose of perpetuating slavery; if then in the South the vote of the blacks had been taken with that of the whites, do you think the negroes would have voted for secession, that slavery might be preserved? Stupid

they may be, but they would not have been stupid enough
for that. No; following their irresistible instinct, they
would have voted that the Union remain together and
that slavery be abolished. And in voting thus they would
have voted ten thousand times more wisely and patriotically than the wisest heads of the rebel aristocracy whom
you might have seen assembled the other day in the
Democratic Convention at New York. See what would
have been the result of negro voting then. The Union
would not have been disrupted; the five hundred thousand
brave young men, whose blood has soaked the battlefields
of the Union, would still be among us, and the country
would not now groan under a National debt of twenty-
five hundred millions of dollars. I appeal to any Democrat who may hear me, if he could recall those days of
1861, if he could avert from this Republic the calamities
we have gone through, if he could thereby save the lives
of half a million of our noblest sons, if he could spare the
country the embarrassments springing from our burden
of debt—if he could do that by permitting the negro to
vote, would he not willingly cast aside all his haughty
prejudice of race, his specious scruples about the negro's
ignorance, and say to the black man: "Go, in the name
of God, and vote." He would be a monster in human
shape, and would deserve to be spurned from human
society, if he did not sink upon his knees and thank Heaven
for the chance. For this, unfortunately, it is too late.
But should not every good man eagerly grasp at a similar
possibility as it presents itself to-day? What are the
negroes of the South doing with their suffrage now? It
is one of those false impressions which have for years been
assiduously disseminated by the Democrats that we, the
Republicans, have nothing in our heads but the negro;
that all we have done we did for the exclusive benefit of
the black man. Is this true? I for one am free to confess

that if there had been no other object in view, I should have been no less zealous in striving to vindicate the outraged dignity of nature in the meanest child of the human family and to lift the yoke of cruel injustice from his neck. But is it true? Look at our past history. In 1856 and 1860 we Republicans fought for the exclusion of slavery from the territories. We conquered. See what has become of those territories. They have grown up into rich, civilized, powerful, progressive States, inhabited by an intelligent, prosperous, progressive, happy people. And who are these people who are now enjoying the benefit of our victory? Are they negroes? No; they are white people like you and myself. We saved the territories for the white laborer in saving them from slavery; and then we were taunted with having nothing in our heads but the interests of the black man. So it was when we emancipated the slaves. Is there a sane man now who will deny that the abolition of slavery is a great blessing, not to the negro alone, but to the whole people, and will be a greater blessing still to our children and our children's children? We liberated only four millions of blacks, but we delivered thirty millions of whites from the odious yoke of grasping aristocracy. We did care for the negro, not as a negro, but as a wronged member of the human family. We were wronged in him. In righting him, we only righted ourselves. Ask yourselves, was not the vote given to the colored man in the South that he might render us all a great service at the ballot-box of the South? What is he voting for? He votes that the whip which tortured him while in slavery may remain away from his back. He votes, therefore, that free labor be permanently established and successfully developed; that the equality of the rights of all before the law be maintained; that the restoration of aristocratic class government in the South, and of similar things at war with true

democratic government, be prevented. He votes, therefore, to help us in extinguishing the germs of other conflicts,
and in securing the necessary harmony between the social
and political institutions of the several States, and the
fundamental principles of our democratic system. In
doing that, does he not thereby give us his most valuable,
nay, indispensable, aid in laying down broad and deep
the only safe and durable basis for national peace, good
understanding and prosperous development? Are not
the colored voters of the South, therefore, in preventing
new irrepressible conflicts, in helping us to secure a solid
peace, rendering the country as inestimable a service as
they would have rendered us in 1861, had they then been
permitted by their votes, to avert civil war with all its
calamities? Would it not be folly, criminal folly, to
reject this service? Can we afford to reject it? Free
labor must be established; the restoration of aristocratic
class government, with its disloyal tendencies, must be
prevented. The interests of the American people, the
peace of the country, imperatively demand it. The pro-
slavery whites will not help us to accomplish this object;
we must have the help of the colored element. There is
no choice. What sane, patriotic man can hesitate? Let
me say to you, this great American Republic—and were
she ten times greater—cannot afford to despise a necessary
service, which can only be rendered by the poorest of her
children—and Heaven forbid that she should. Great as
she is, she will honor herself by readily accepting and
thankfully acknowledging it.

But is it not *just because* the colored people of the South
are to render the Republic this great service, that the
Democratic party so strenuously objects to their having
the right to vote? See how the case lies: The colored
people of the South, desirous to keep their newly acquired
rights unimpaired, have mostly come to the very natural

conclusion that the same men who gave them their liberty can be best relied upon to secure it to them. They are, therefore, strongly inclined to vote Republicans into power, and in doing this, every fair-minded man will admit, they show eminent good sense. But it is just this evidence of good sense which makes the Democrats so very savage in denouncing the colored people as unworthy the right of suffrage. In fact, the Democrats do not want to deprive the negro of his vote because he does not vote intelligently enough, but because he votes, in the main, altogether too intelligently for them. On the other hand, a negro who votes the Democratic ticket for the purpose of raising pro-slavery men, the natural enemies of free labor, to office and power, must evidently be a very stupid fellow—unless he is dishonest enough to trade his vote away for a consideration. But just such Democratic negroes are received by the Democrats with open arms. Even Wade Hampton, the very flower of the Southern chivalry, condescends to fraternize with them, and you all have heard of the negro Democrat Williams, from Tennessee, who had a seat in the National Democratic Convention, and who was no longer treated as the despised "nigger" Williams, but was called "Mr." Williams, while some went so far as to call him "The Honorable Mr. Williams." Since they thus receive negroes, who have so little sense or honesty as to support the enemies of their own rights, with open arms, it is no longer a qualification of intelligence for the negro voter which the Democrats insist upon, but it is evidently a qualification of stupidity. To the intelligent negro voter they object, but when a negro is only stupid enough to support his enemies by voting the Democratic ticket, the Democrats are ready, apparently, and for the present at least, to welcome him as a man and a brother.

I know very well there is a strong ingredient of deviltry

in these professions of friendship for the colored Democrat.
The Southern chivalry, with characteristic candor, ask
the confiding negro for his vote that they may disfranchise
him afterward. "Be my friend, colored brother, and give
me power that I may rob thee of thy rights." I do not
think that this game of deception is particularly chivalrous;
but whatever the ultimate designs of the Southern Democrats may be, it will, under the present circumstances,
have a good effect. This is not the first time that the
devil, without knowing it, has served the church. The
Southern Democrats indulge in the delusion that by means
of the negro vote they can carry some of the late rebel
States, and thereby defeat the Presidential candidate of
the Republican party. For this purpose they fervently
embrace the negro in order to squeeze Democratic votes
out of him. Perhaps they have reason to chuckle over
this or that colored man who has gone into the trap. But
the calculation of the Southern Democrats is wrong in
one important point. We have votes enough in the North
to elect Grant and Colfax. The Democrats will not have
the power to disfranchise the negroes again, and in the
meantime the Southern chivalry is gradually falling into
the habit of embracing the colored brother to obtain his
vote—all of which is very proper. As soon as by another
Republican victory the reconstruction policy of Congress
has once become an irreversible fact, so that the colored
population can not again be stripped of its rights, it will
not matter how large a proportion of the negro vote goes
to the Democracy; for the great cause of free labor and
equal rights will then have achieved a decisive triumph by
the mere fact of the negro having become a universally
recognized voter, and each party bidding for his vote by
supporting his rights and interests.

The rights of the emancipated class being out of danger,
the negro vote will then naturally divide itself between

29

the different parties, and there is the solution of that
fearful question of the war of races, with which the Democrats have endeavored to frighten our nervous brethren.
Political parties will no longer think of a war of races
when they think of gaining negro votes for their respective
tickets.   The Southern Democrats are now going through
a preparatory course, and for a beginning they do ad-
mirably well.   At present, to be sure, there is a great
deal of knavery in the background.   But another Republican victory, and they will swear, and believe it themselves, that they never thought of disfranchising the negro.
They will ask for negro votes in good faith—and welcome
all they can obtain.   Free labor will be safe, and the
races will live in peace.   The chivalry will have deceived
and cheated itself.

But, negro supremacy!   Our opponents tell us that
colored suffrage must, necessarily, result in negro supremacy in the South.   Horrible, most horrible to contemplate!   Let us look this spectral apparition calmly
in the face.   There are in the Southern States 9,000,000
whites, and there are 3,500,000 negroes.   The whites, as
the Democrats assure us, are the superior, and the negroes
the inferior race.   And now the same Democrats come to
tell us that 3,500,000 of the inferior race of negroes will
surely trample into the dust 9,000,000 of their superiors.
Well, if that really were so; if the whites of the South were
really such a miserable set that 9,000,000 of them could
be trodden under foot by 3,500,000 poor negroes, then
they would not deserve anything better, and we can hardly
pity them.   Is it not astonishing?   What a tremendous
fellow the negro has suddenly become!   Formerly we
heard it said that a Southern gentleman was equal to at
least five Northern men.   Now it turns out, on Democratic authority, that a Southern gentleman is not the
equal of one half of a negro.   Oh, how are the mighty

fallen! This is indeed a most melancholy state of things. I apprehend our philanthropic friends in Boston will have to move in the matter, and try to get up a "New England Southern gentlemen's relief and protection society"—president, Wendell Phillips. But if we may believe some Democratic authorities, the case is still more desperate than I have stated it. General Frank P. Blair gives us to understand, in the speech with which he accepted his nomination, that the supremacy of the whole white race in this Republic is in peril to be upset by the negroes, and something must speedily be done to avert so dreadful a calamity. This, certainly, is still more alarming. The whole population of the United States amounts to about forty millions—thirty-six millions of whites and four millions of blacks. Nobody will deny that, under such circumstances, the supremacy of the white race is in the most imminent danger. What shall we do? Where shall we turn for help? Fortunately, every great crisis brings forth its great man, and the great man of this crisis is found. He is there to put himself into the breach for the white race. General Frank P. Blair himself is going to do it. He has said so; and he is as good as his word. He will march boldly and fearlessly at the head of the thirty-six millions of whites, and then let the four millions of blacks come on! We defy them! There has been some anxious and profound speculation in this country as to what the Blair family is intended for in the order of the universe. It is discovered now. The Blair family is destined to rescue the thirty-six millions of proud Caucasian whites in this country from the atrocious tyranny of four millions of blacks. Yes, the Blair family will do it—or perish in the attempt.

Seriously speaking, when the Democratic leaders sound the alarm about the dangers of negro supremacy, what a glorious confidence they must have in the unfathomable stupidity of their followers! If it is true that in two or three of the Southern States the colored people outnumber the whites, while in all the others the whites are in an overwhelming majority, and that a number of whites are disfranchised for participation in the rebellion, is it not equally true that the whites possess nearly all the real property, all the capital, all the social influence, all the advantage of education, all the political experience, and that of this vast enginery of social and political power the colored people, just emerged from slavery, are almost wholly destitute? And yet, in spite of all this, the blacks are to tread the whites in the dust? If, indeed, the nine millions are not enough to stand their ground against the three and a half millions of blacks, we are ready to send them a reinforcement of carpet-baggers to help them maintain their white preponderance. I do not say this jokingly; I am in earnest. Is not every man who emigrates to the South from the Northern States or from Europe, a white man? The negroes do not find the Ku-Klux atmosphere of the South so pleasing as to be attracted by it. Yes, every emigrant Southward-bound is a white man, and he helps to fortify the ascendancy of the white race there. And if the Southern people were not so foolish as to drive away new-comers who do not agree with them in politics, with petty annoyances and persecutions, and even bloody threats and violence, there would probably have been an increase of the white population in the South of one or two millions since the close of the war.

Indeed, it is a singular sort of infatuation, of lunacy, I might almost say, which possesses the Southern people in this respect. What they want for the restoration and development of their prosperity is immigration, capital, industry, an influx of new and stirring elements. They recognize this in the abstract; but when immigrants do present themselves, the Southern whites demand that the

new-comers shall think and act just as they do; and if
these new-comers entertain and express principles and
ideas materially differing from those traditional in the
South, they are denounced as vile carpet-baggers and
rascally scalawags, and threatened with expulsion by
force if they do not go voluntarily. But if those new-
comers really did accommodate themselves to the traditional Southern ways of thinking and acting, what would
they be good for? Look at the Northern States, from
which the most useful of those immigrants come. The
people of the Northern States have attained their high
degree of prosperity and civilization just because they
do not think and act as the Southern people are wont to
do. They owe their culture, their wealth, their social
advancement to the very fact that, unlike the Southern
people, they admit and encourage the utmost freedom of
inquiry and discussion; that they recognize and protect
the dignity of labor in the meanest laborer; that no class
of society can claim rights and privileges for itself which
are not also granted and secured to the other classes. If,
now, as the Southern people will have it, immigrants
coming from the North give up all these principles and
rules of action, their main value to the South will be lost,
their energy and enterprise will be hampered, their capacity for progressive improvement will be emasculated.
What the Southern people want is not an increase, not a
reinforcement of their old stock of ideas and habits of life;
they have entered upon a new order of things, and they
want new thoughts, new impulses, new energies, new rules
of action. They want what differs from their traditional
notions, just because it differs from them.

Under such circumstances, it sounds so sadly ludicrous
when we hear them indignantly complain that their
"first men," their old tried statesmen, are thrown aside for
new-comers. Well, what is the damage? What have their

old and tried Southern statesmen—their Davises, their
Toombses, their Slidells, and their Masons—what have
they done for the South?   They have simply shown their
utter incapacity to comprehend the irresistible tendency
of this age against slavery and all kindred systems of
social organization.   Modern Don Quixotes, they insisted
upon perpetuating and raising to dominant power institutions which were manifestly doomed to destruction by
the progressive spirit of the nineteenth century.   To this
crazy infatuation they have sacrificed the peace, the
prosperity, even the lives, of hundreds of thousands of the
Southern people.   They have been the ruin of their
country.   And now the Southern whites insist upon dig-
ging them up again from their political graves to the ruin
of their country once more.   What a senseless idea!
The merest adventurer of the class they contemptuously
call "carpet-baggers," if his interests and sympathies
are in any way identified with the new order of things,
is of ten times more real value to the South than the most
renowned of the old and tried statesmen, who, with incorrigible stubbornness, are still worshipping their old broken
idols.   The Southern people ought to remember that, as
the Scripture says, "new wine should not be put into old
bottles, lest the old bottles burst and the new wine be
spilled."   And methinks most of those old Southern
bottles have already done such an amount of bursting
that they ought to be let alone.   Nay, instead of repelling
with barbarous fierceness what they really need, let the
Southern people welcome every man who comes to them
to identify his interest with theirs.   Let them welcome
him the more heartily if he brings new ideas and new
energies to supply their deplorable deficiencies.   Let them
not complain that among the first comers there are many
adventurers, for it is always the adventurer who has to
blaze the track where men are called upon to launch into

uncertainties.   In this, as in many other cases, the adventurer forms the vanguard of civilization.   Not until they
can settle down in safety, the solid and cautious men will
follow to risk their fortunes.   Do they want to know what
carpet-baggers can do?   Let them look at that towering
monument, that crowning glory of progressive and enterprising carpet-baggerdom—the city of Chicago.   In this
way the white race in the South will receive a wonderful strength of reinforcement—reinforcements of men who
will not permit the blacks to trample into the dust the
whites, and are much less afraid of it; nor will they permit
the whites to trample into the dust the blacks, but they
will see to it that both races work harmoniously together,
respecting one another's rights, and thus promoting the
civilization and prosperity of all.   The fear of being trodden under foot by 3,500,000 negroes may then cease, even
with the most tremulous of the nine and more millions of
whites, and the harrowing spectacle of the tragic and
bloody self-sacrifice of the Blair family may then safely
be spared us.   So much for that silliest of all party humbugs—the Democratic cry about negro supremacy.

Finally, the last great argument of the Democratic
party is, that the Republican policy can not give peace
to the country, because the majority of the Southern
whites will not submit to it.   Ah, indeed, they will not
submit!   I am by no means inclined to judge harshly of
the Southern whites.   I have treated them here without
passion or prejudice, as a fit subject of pathological
inquiry.   As we pity a sick man for his bodily ailments,
so we give our sympathy, and, if possible, our aid to those
who are afflicted with mental and moral infirmities for
which they are not entirely responsible.   The notions,
habits and influences under which the present generation
of the Southern whites have grown up, are not of their
own making.   They have come upon them as traditions

and their effects were but natural. We may regard them
less as crimes than as misfortunes, but we must deal with
them as facts. The South is our "sick man." For his
disease we must find a remedy, and the remedy we select
must correspond with a careful diagnosis of the ailment.
The disease in this case has been an inordinate craving
for unlawful power and dominion. This craving was
stimulated by the intoxicating influence of flattery and
subserviency on the part of the Northern Democrats,
and by the hope of success, to such an extent that it at
last resulted in the delirium tremens of the secession
movement. The victories of the Union army broke the
fit, and the patient, when the intoxicating cup of pride
and great expectations was taken away, showed some
symptoms of improvement. But, unfortunately, the
"sick man" has been operated upon by Democratic
doctors once more. The worst stimulant imaginable
in such a case is false hope; and false hope has been administered to him without stint—the false hope of a return
to controlling power, of a reaction in the direction of
aristocratic class government, founded upon a new system
of serfdom—the false hope of restoration and revenge.
Yes; the Democratic doctors seem to have acted upon the
theory that this patient, inclined to delirium, can best be
cured by pouring alcohol down his throat by the gallon.
No wonder that the disease approaches another crisis,
and it is high time that the rational system of cure should
be resumed. And what is this rational system? In dis-
eases of this nature, false hope is poison. Nothing is better
calculated to cure the most vicious appetite than the
evident impossibility of its gratification, and, fortunately,
the medicine is in our hands, and the physician stands
ready to administer it.

Indeed, the Democrats tell us that our policy will not
produce peace, because the Southern whites will not sub-

mit to it. Is this not rather disingenuous? Have not
the Democrats told their Southern friends day after day
for three years: Do not submit to this Radical tyranny!
You would be cowards, you would be unworthy to be
called freemen if you did submit! Have not the Democrats
besought, implored them: Resist, resist to the last! We
will help you! And after having addressed to them these
frantic invocations they coolly turn round to us and say:
" You see, your policy must fail, for they will not submit
to it at all, at all."

Ah, the late rebel will not submit, then, at all, at all,
to what the American people are likely to resolve upon.
It appears to me this argument is a little out of date.
Seven years ago there might have been some point in it,
but since then we have learned that the white people of
the South can be made to submit to things which do not
entirely suit their fancy. And we have a modest gentleman at the head of our Presidential ticket who has practically proved that, in an emergency, he knows exactly
how to do it. His name is Ulysses S. Grant. You
remember a certain day in April, 1865, when General Lee
fell back with his army upon Appomattox Courthouse,
and when General Grant demanded of him an unconditional surrender. What! General Lee, the proud
Southern, the very chieftain of the Southern chivalry,
looking down upon the rest of mankind with so much
high-born contempt; General Lee throw down his sword
and surrender his invincible Southern legions to that poor
little Northern mud-sill, a late tanner from Illinois!
Do you think it suited his fancy? Neither his nor that
of his followers. Why, then, did he surrender? Because
he felt that Grant had thrown his mighty arm around him,
ready to squeeze out of him the last breath of life, if he
showed the least hesitation. He submitted because he
knew that it was impossible to resist. Thus we have

learned from the history of our own days, that even Southern gentlemen will submit to evident necessity. Should we not profit by the lesson? Let us show the Southern reactionists that the loyal people who fought a four years' war for Union, liberty and equal rights, are still alive, and that they still are the same people; that they still cherish the same principles, and still march under the same flag; that no threats can frighten and no seductive allurements swerve them from the path of right. Let us show the Southern people this, by elevating upon our shields once more the very man who led us through war to victory, and who will lead us through victory to peace—and they will soon grow as tired of resisting, as after the fall of Richmond they grew tired of fighting; they will, after a little explosion of rant, submit as gracefully as General Lee surrendered at Appomattox Courthouse. The late rebels of the South may all be as brave as Lee—and yet they will submit as soon as they see that the loyal people in their righteous demands are as firm as Grant. Here, indeed, is the medicine for the sick man of the South, ready for use. It is not yet too late for a cure.

Let it not be said that this means a brutal reign of physical force. It is the application of an irresistible moral power by the imposing assertion of an unbending National will. And no fitter man than General Grant could be found to serve as its representative. Let me repeat what I said of him at the commencement of the campaign: "He knows the Southern people and they know him. They have been in rather close and lively contact, and understand one another. He has given them evidence of his unbending determination in a conflict, and of his generosity after victory. They know that when he demanded an unconditional surrender, he meant it to be unconditional; they know also that he treated the

vanquished with magnanimous forbearance. The people
of the South will therefore have no reason to fear that he
will act with the vindictive spirit of an exasperated partisan,
and no reason to hope that iniquity and factious resistance
will meet from him with weak indulgence." They know
that he is not a man of extreme notions, of extravagant
fancies; that he will impose nothing upon the people
which is unjust, improper, unreasonable or oppressive.
But they know, also, that when he has once conceived,
in accordance with the popular will, what is right, down
he will plant his foot, and neither the power of all rebeldom,
nor the very gates of hell, will stagger him. As Andrew
Johnson and the Democratic party stirred up the most
vicious elements of Southern society to new hope and
activity, so Grant's election will put a tremendous damper
upon all reactionary aspirations, and give new encouragement and moral power to those men who, in the spirit
of peace and justice, strive to confirm the new order of
things. Yes, a firm and faithful people, and at their
head a firm and faithful leader, that is the true medicine
for the sick man of the South. I repeat, in disease of
this nature, nothing is better calculated to cure the most
vicious appetite than the evident impossibility of its
gratification. There will be boisterous incorrigibles, no
doubt, but they will gradually mope, and rant, and swear,
and drink themselves to death. They will die by self-
combustion. And peace to their ashes! But those elements
of Southern society which have vitality in them will rise
up to new life. All men of sense will cut loose from false
hopes, will throw behind them the past, and turn their
eyes upon the future. The spirit of persecution will have
to yield to the spirit of improvement. In a country like
this, habits form quickly, and, before Grant's Administration is over, the new order of things will have deeply
entered into the habits of Southern society. Then even

the carpet-bagger will soon be welcomed in the South for
the new ideas and energies he brings, and all sores will
presently be forgotten in a new common prosperity.
Such is the peace which the firmness of the loyal people
promises and which it is bound to achieve.

Wade Hampton tells us that this will be for the South
"the peace of the graveyard." Aye, Wade Hampton, it
will be a graveyard in one sense, and we mean to dig
the graves broad and deep. In that graveyard will be
buried the pro-slavery aristocracy of the South, with its
foolish fancies and its grasping pretensions of superiority
and dominion. There will be buried the false civilization
of the South, which elevated the few upon the neck of the
oppressed many. There will be buried that most abominable of all heresies, that true liberty consists in the right
of one class of men to deprive of their rights another class;
and let us hope that the corpse of the Democratic party
will be laid by its side. There will be buried the irrepressible conflict, which, during so many years, has disturbed
the peace of the country and swallowed up a million of
lives and untold millions of treasure. There will be buried
out of sight and memory, this age of blood and tears, of
violence and injustice, to make room for a new and better
order of things. A graveyard, indeed; but from those
graves will spring up free labor with its abundant fields
and busy workshops. There will spring up the schoolhouse for all the children of the people to join all classes
of society together for mutual improvement in the onward
march of a common civilization. There will spring up
that progressive public spirit which will recognize that
one part of the people will best promote its own interest
by aiding in the advancement of all others. There will
spring up true loyalty to the Republic, for then the interests and institutions most cherished by the South will
be just those it has in common with the rest of the

American people. And finally, upon the grave of iniquity, will grow the flower of peace, that true and enduring peace of common liberty and rights mutually respected.

What do the Democrats offer us for this? Look at their platform. Indeed, it promises you peace, but before that peace is to come they mean to go through some preliminary operations. And what are they? A trifle. The reconstruction measures of Congress, the laws of the land, are only to be trampled in the dust. The Southern State governments are only to be dispersed by force of arms. The Senate of the United States is only to be coerced into submission, so General Blair tells us, and all this to put all political power in the Southern States again into the hands of the whites of the South, an overwhelming majority of whom were active participants in the rebellion, and life-long enemies of free-labor society, based upon equal rights. These are the Democratic preliminaries of peace. Indeed! Is this all? And do not say that I exaggerate; for General Blair's letter, by which he secured his nomination, is but the logical construction of the Democratic platform. What can it mean, that denunciation of the reconstruction measures of Congress as unconstitutional, revolutionary and void, if it does not mean that the results of these measures are to be set aside at any price, even at the price of a forcible revulsion! Trample into the dust the laws! Disperse the Southern State governments at the point of the bayonet! Restore the late rebels to power in their States by force! Compel the Senate to submit! Look at it calmly and dispassionately. This is not a quiet legislative process. For this there is but one name—it is a counter-revolution in the fullest sense of the term. Do you know what that signifies? Look into the history of the world. Counter-revolutions mean *revenge*. They are the explosion of resentments long laid up; of hate and vindictiveness panting for action. You may know where they begin, but you cannot tell where they will end. They are propelled by passion, and passion outruns control. If you want to understand the full bearing of the Democratic program of counter-revolution, look at the men who are to execute it. There is Horatio Seymour. He, a respectable gentleman! Pleasant, plausible, smooth. Not a man of a ferocious temper by any means; but scan his political career from its first commencement to the present day, and what do you find? A sickly shrinking from great responsibilities; a continual effort to reach his ends by small means, by petty contrivances; a lack of true manhood. He has not even courage enough to say what he wants, and obtains his nominations for office by declining. He has never another word to say for his own expressed convictions of right as soon as he finds them overruled by his friends. He made an emphatic declaration in favor of paying the bonds in gold but a few days before the Democratic Convention, and then accepted the greenback platform without a murmur, as a matter of course. He loudly proclaimed himself a dishonored man if he should take the Democratic nomination for the Presidency, and then he very politely took it. He has been accused of wilful, mendacious misrepresentations of facts—facts open to everybody, but I candidly declare I believe he has not moral force enough to distinguish truth from falsehood. In one word, he is made to be the tool of a stronger will. In private life a sweet-tempered, kind-hearted gentleman, he is, in a position of power, just the man to be swayed by the passions of other people. If President, he would perhaps recoil before the counter-revolutionary program of his friends, but at the decisive moment he would feel that his delicate constitution needed a washing in the surf at Newport, or the strengthening perfumes of the far-off pineries in

Wisconsin. The stern business of the hour he would leave to men of stronger will and fiercer disposition. He would be like potter's clay in their hands. And certainly men of stronger will and fiercer disposition would not be wanting around him.

There is General Blair. True, his lucubrations on negro supremacy are ludicrous enough, but it will not do to speak lightly of his ability. There is power in his organization. He has that stuff in him which, developed by a high moral sense, might have made him a Brutus, but which, turned into the channel of unprincipled ambition and bitter vindictiveness, is well apt to make him a Catiline. He is essentially a revolutionary character; a mind fertile of expedients, a reckless determination which stops at nothing, and all the dangerous incentives springing from a situation in which he has all to gain and nothing to lose. I can hardly conceive of a counter-revolutionary leader more daring, reckless and dangerous than he. Preston and Forrest knew well what they were doing when they proposed and seconded his nomination. What will Horatio Seymour be with such a man at his elbow? Such a man will bend or break him like a reed across his knees.

But there would be even stronger powers than Blair ready and eager to take the counter-rebellion in their own hands. Who made the Democratic platform and the nominations? Vallandigham, Wade Hampton, Preston, Forrest. Do you know them? Did you not hear the old rebel yell which greeted the counter-revolutionary program in the New York Convention? Do you not hear it now ringing over the Southern country? Do you not hear the leaders of the late rebellion openly proclaim that a Democratic victory will be a victory of the "lost cause"; that their will must again rule the land, and that as they have fought once they are ready to fight again?

Did you not read what the bloody Forrest said to a Northern journalist, that, if another conflict occurred, there would be no quarter for any Radical within his reach, and measures would be taken that not a victim would escape him. Do you not hear all over the South threats no less savage than these?

You may be told that these are fanciful exaggerations. Alas! no. Look at the more prudent of the Democratic leaders, how they grow pale at the indiscreet sincerity of their Southern friends. Upon their troubled faces you read the proof of what I say. Listen to them, how they, with nervous anxiety, whisper "Hush! hush!" lest the ardent Southerner betray too much of what is to come, and the people, forewarned, should block the game! It is in vain. The tendency of a counter-revolution is a thing too big for concealment. Lee and Beauregard may roar even more gently than sucking doves—the rebel element of the South has shown its hand again, and we have seen the dagger in the sleeve. Is it not natural after all? Can it be otherwise? May not Andrew Johnson say, again, that the late rebels are doing just as well as we have a right to expect of them? Look at that fearful spectacle in the Democratic National Convention. The Democratic party clamoring for the overthrow of the laws! For the restoration to uncontrolled sway of the rebel majority in the Southern States! Promising them, as Wade Hampton kindly informs us, that they shall have all, all they desire, much more than they openly dare to express! Nay, the Democratic candidate for the Vice-Presidency formally appealing to the arbitrament of arms, of another fight, and assuring them that the government of the Republic once in Democratic hands, he will take the lead! Is it a wonder that the morbid imagination of the Southerner eagerly seizes upon these appeals and promises, and that, intoxicated with new

hopes, they seriously speak of the "lost cause" regained?
Is it surprising that the insane invocation of force against
the reconstructed governments should have violently
stirred up the worst impulses, the fiercest passions of the
Southern populace, like the rallying cry of another
rebellion?

And these men, with the reckless habits of slave society,
with all their pent-up wrath, their violent resentments,
their wild vindictiveness, excited to fever heat by the
promise of victory, and the prospect of undivided power,
these are the men to take into their hands the counter-
revolution in their own States, and to unite with the most
unscrupulous class of Northern demagogues in the control
of the National Government. Where would they stop?
I will not attempt to predict what atrocities their hot
thirst of revenge will bring forth in the Southern States.
There we have already witnessed things which humanity
must blush for, and which, for the honor of the American
name, we would be happy to hide from the eyes of the
world. But which of those great conquests for the cause
of liberty and human rights, which we consider the most
glorious results of the war, would be safe? Would free
labor be safe? Which of the laws enacted for its protection would be respected? The laws passed by Southern
legislatures, or the civil rights act? They have already
been denounced as unconstitutional and void. The
fourteenth Constitutional amendment? Already a Northern lawyer has been found to perform for the South the
menial service of pronouncing it invalid, because its ratification was brought about by the agency of the military
governments. The Constitutional amendment, abolishing
slavery? The same reasoning brought against the fourteenth amendment will be urged against it, and already
the late slaveholders are eagerly calling over the rolls of
the late slaves, determined to reclaim them as property,

30

or have compensation for them in money. Will the National debt be safe? Already we hear it denounced as an accursed debt, contracted in the unholy cause of oppression, and you can not read the Democratic platform with an unprejudiced mind without seeing in its financial propositions the hideous design of repudiation grinning out between every two words. Will you say that this is mere speculation? I do not speak of things that will, but that have been already threatened and attempted. Will you say that the Senate will stand in the way? General Blair tells you plainly that the Senate will be compelled to submit, and the late rebels proclaim, with fierce exultation, that they stand ready to respond to another appeal to arms. What safeguard then of free labor; what obligation of the National honor will be safe? The counter-revolution is ready to roll over them all with the force of an avalanche, and nothing is required to set it in motion but that you should put power into the hands of those who are ready to commence the terrible work. If the Democratic platform means anything, it means this. This is its logic. It can mean nothing else.

Is this a promise of peace? The threatened overthrow of all the most glorious results of this grand period of our history, an attempt to disgrace the American name in the eyes of all mankind by the spoliation of the National creditor, the power of the Republic wielded by the most turbulent elements in the land—a reign of greed and revenge—can that be peace? You ask me whether I think that they can ultimately succeed in all they contemplate? No; thank Heaven—it cannot be; not as if the desire were wanting, but I am confident, as long as but one spark of love of liberty, of honesty, of self-respect, of National pride, is alive in the hearts of the American people, such enormities cannot ultimately succeed. Even if the American people should now so far forget themselves

as to fall into the ignominious trap, the burning shame
would give them no rest, and in four years they would
certainly sweep this party of conspirators from the face
of the earth. Succeed, no; but you put power into their
hands, and it will surely be attempted. Do you know
what that means? Neither did the rebellion succeed;
but do you remember what the mere attempt has cost us?
American patriots, have you already forgotten the terrors
of the battlefield, the agonies of the prisoners' camp, the
rivers of blood and the sea of tears? Have you forgotten
the untold millions of treasure you have poured into the
gulf of the great conflict? And now you would permit
and encourage the attempt again? Are we little children?
are we a people of lunatics, that we should wantonly reopen all those fearful questions again, which have stag-
gered the Republic on its foundations, covered the land
with calamity and distress, plunged the Nation in mourning, and sorely tried the spirit even of the bravest—
reopen them again, wantonly, recklessly, when at one
blow we can close them forever?

Merchants, manufacturers, farmers, laboring men,
shall I speak to you of the public debt, our National credit,
of the currency, of the taxes you pay, of our material
prosperity? I have not pronounced these words, perhaps,
and yet, have I not spoken of these things all the time?
Is there a man, understanding his own interests, so insane
as to believe that the burdens which weigh upon us can
be lightened, that credit and confidence can be restored,
that our prosperity can be promoted by putting power
into the hands of men who are so reckless of the peace
of the country? You want peace, order and undisturbed
development of our National resources; you want the
Southern markets to open, and the whole South again to
become an addition to the wealth of the land. How can
you, then, think of placing at the helm of affairs the very

men whose avowed purpose is to reopen the questions which have so long been disturbing our repose, to continue the wild agitations which so long have beem prostrating credit, confidence and prosperity, and to make the South again, for years to come, the theater of desolating civil commotions? Can you be crazy enough to embark your fortunes on a sea of uncertainty like this, the whole sky overhung with threatening storm-clouds? And if you belonged to those whose patriotism is tied up in their pockets, and whose hearts have never been warmed by generous emotions, remember—and the most selfish of you should write it in indelible letters upon your strong box—you cannot endanger the peace of the country without plotting your own ruin.

Democrats of the North, a last appeal to you. Not for ourselves will I speak, but to you I will say a word for the poor South, whose friends you profess to be. Did you ever consider what your friendship has made of that unfortunate country? For more than a generation you have excited and stimulated the worst pro-slavery passions in the Southern people. You, children of the free North, could not love slavery for its own sake; you could not believe that so flagrant an abomination could successfully resist the progressive spirit of the nineteenth century, and yet did you not encourage that insane resistance—resistance to the last—with your insidious acclamations and your promises of aid? Is it not true that, but for that artful encouragement the Southern people would have recognized the impossibility of perpetuating slavery, and that, abandoning their false hopes, they might have long ago commenced, by a gradual and peaceable reform, to accomplish that which has now been accomplished by the terrors of revolution and war? That the peaceable and salutary course of reform was not commenced in time, you, Northern Democrats, you are responsible for it. But

more.   Brave as the Southern people may be, they would
scarcely have dared to raise their hands in rebellion against
this Republic had they not been assured that the people
of the North would not fight, or, if they did, that there
would be Northern people enough to rise in aid of the
rebellion.   You, Northern Democrats, caused them to
indulge in this fatal delusion; you goaded them on to the
path of rebellion, blood and destruction.   But, still more.
In 1864, when the back of the rebellion was already broken,
and when speedy submission might have spared us many
grievous sacrifices, you, Northern Democrats, then declared the war a failure on our side; you then encouraged
the Southern people to persevere, to hope, to fight on.
And thus the slaughter and destruction continued.   But
still more.   At last the rebellion was vanquished, and the
Southern people lay prostrate at the feet of the conqueror
exhausted, impoverished, lacerated, bleeding.   So far
your friendship had brought them.   There was but one
way for them to rise to new life, peace and prosperity.
It was by giving up all those old wild dreams of sectional
power; by abandoning all thought of the possibility of a
reaction; by accepting readily all the new order of things
would bring; by devoting themselves, without looking
back, to the reparation of their losses; by averting their
eyes from the past and turning them full upon the future.
And who will deny that after the first stunning effect of
their defeat such was their disposition, and that this disposition would have been strengthened by a firm and
uncompromising attitude on the part of the North?   Thus
their wounds might have been quickly healed, and their
life restored to health and vigor.   But what did you do,
Northern Democrats?   No sooner was there a chance for
their regeneration than you hastened again to pour into
their minds the poison of false hope.   You stimulated their
pride with flattery.   You stirred up their feverish imagina-

tions by showing them the deceitful picture of a possible reaction. By wild harangues you excited them to stubborn resistance to the new order of things. You inflamed their worst passions by appealing to their worst prejudices; and, alas! they believed you once more. And now see what you have done. The South, in a new attack of that delirium which the defeat of the rebellion had happily abated, and the repulsive manifestations of which you yourselves now vainly endeavor to restrain; the old terrorism, the old violence, the old mania for the exercise of unrighteous power; and thus three years since the end of the war have been wantonly squandered—three years, which might have given them peace, but for you. And yet, if you are not blind to the signs of the times, you know that all the hopes you have excited are vain. You know what they are struggling for can never be restored, and what they are struggling against is bound to come. You must know that this will be a Republic of free labor and equal rights. And yet you are still pouring oil into the flame of their madness—nay, you are urging the sword into their hands, which you know they can raise only for self-destruction. Democrats of the North, are your consciences dead? Have you no hearts, no pity for your Southern victims! Have their destroyed cities, their devastated fields, have the hundreds of thousands of their sons whose blood they have sacrificed at your instigation, not yet given you your fill? Shall the agony of those whom you have goaded on from error to error, from crime to crime, from disaster to disaster, be continued forever? Will you never give them a chance to return to reason? What have the poor Southern people done to you, that you should never cease to persecute them with your cruel, relentless, murderous, fiendish friendship? Is it not as if the policy of your party were born of the love of mischief for mischief's sake? When contemplating this appalling spectacle, does it not appear questionable to yourselves which was the most terrible curse for the South, the institution of slavery or the friendship of the Democratic party? Is there no human feeling in your hearts which moves you—no voice of conscience which compels you to desist from this most cruel wickedness?

If there is not, then we, Republicans, have to find the remedy. As we delivered the South of slavery, so we have now to deliver the Southern people of the most malicious of their enemies—who call themselves their friends; of a friendship whose very touch is disaster and disgrace, whose continuance would be death. And this will be the crowning consummation of all our conquests. How shall we accomplish it? Republicans, no man can read the signs of the times to-day, without feeling that this struggle is already decided, and our victory certain. Already the glorious guns of New England are reverberating with increased volume. We hear the irresistible tramp of the old grand army of freedom again, and the whole American sky rings with the triumphant shout: "We are coming! We are coming!" Against this invincible power the very hosts of pandemonium will rear themselves up in vain. Ah, how contemptibly silly are those who dared to dream that the great American Nation would be cowardly enough to throw away, with wanton levity, the great fruits of their grandest struggle for liberty and justice. Yes, success is certain; but take care lest that very certainty diminish our efforts and deprive our triumph of its highest value.

Mark what I say. One of those meager victories which leave the beaten enemy the hope of a future revulsion of fortune, will not suffice now. We must strike down the wicked faction opposed to us with such crushing force that even the most sanguine of them can never expect again to revive it under the load of universal condemnation; that even the most credulous of Southern reactionists must recognize every Democratic promise of aid as a piece of impotent deception, and that the whole Southern people must open their eyes and behold their treacherous seducers in the North so deeply accursed by the enlightened opinion and the patriotism of the American Republic that, whatever their desire for mischief may be, their power is annihilated forever. Only then we shall take away from the Democracy their greatest faculty for evil, their ability to cheat their victims, with a show of strength. Only then we shall deliver the poor South of the most terrible of curses, their false friends. Only then we shall rid this country of the most dangerous element of trouble: a conspiracy against the vital principles of our Government, nourished by false hopes.

American patriots, now is your time! Your duty calls you with trumpet tones. Let no true man to whom speech is given now be silent. Let none whose heart ever was fired by the divine breath of liberty, now stand idle. There are those who are still wavering between right and wrong. Not a moment let there be lost. Speak to them the language of great principles; assault their understanding with irrefutable arguments; storm their hearts with solemn appeals. The greatest victory ever achieved is within our grasp. It rests with us to make it the final one. Up, then, and be doing! Now is the time to make the American people brothers once more, by writing upon the very frontispiece of this Republic in characters of burning light, that even the wickedest must read it and bow his head; that even the blind must feel the electric flash, the great law of our future: Liberty and Equal Rights for all and forever! Peace through Justice.

TO BENJAMIN F. LOAN[1]

JEFFERSON CITY, [Mo.], Jan. 7, 1869.

A paper has been presented to me, signed by a large number of senators and representatives, inviting you and me to address a caucus of the Radical members of the legislature in explanation of our views on pending questions. Friends of yours have been circulating statements concerning my political principles and opinions calculated to prejudice the minds of members of the Radical party against me. I have been informed that some of these statements are countenanced by you. Believing that you do not desire to do me any injustice, I shall be very glad to meet you in the caucus and hear you repeat those of the charges which thus have been made against me and which you consider well founded, so that I may have an opportunity to publicly admit or deny them. This, it seems to me, would be no more than fair. I need hardly assure you that in any discussion I shall meet you in a kindly and courteous spirit. It is my earnest desire to remove all bitterness of feeling from the Senatorial contest and to preserve the harmony and strength of the Radical party intact. No means can be more conducive to this end than a public and frank explanation of what differences there may be between us. You would oblige me by signifying to me your pleasure in regard to this matter.

JEFFERSON CITY, Jan. 7, 1869.

The misrepresentations I referred to in my letter of this morning consist mainly in this: Your friends assert that I, by immediately enfranchising those who are excluded from the suffrage for participation in the rebellion, intend to throw the State into the hands of the rebels. And I

[1] Schurz's rival as Republican candidate for U. S. Senator. See 3 *Reminiscences*, 294 ff.

am informed that this statement is countenanced by you.

Hoping to meet you this evening.

JEFFERSON CITY, Jan. 7, 1869.

In reply to your last note I desire to say that you have entirely misconstrued my language. I am *not* in favor of immediately enfranchising the rebels, and I cannot understand how you could construe my words in that way.

We have been invited to address the Radical caucus *to-night* and not to-morrow night. I shall be there according to invitation and shall speak even should you not meet me. The misrepresentations, the echo of which I find in your letter, have gone far enough and I desire to stop them.

ON BEING CHOSEN UNITED STATES SENATOR[1]

MR. PRESIDENT AND GENTLEMEN OF THE GENERAL ASSEMBLY:—For the high honor and trust you have conferred upon me I give you my heartfelt thanks, but not on my personal account alone. Without attaching too great a significance to what you have done, I may say that my election to the Senate of the United States under the existing circumstances is an evidence of the liberal and progressive spirit moving the people of Missouri. You have broken through all those prejudices and set aside all those traditional considerations which formerly were almost decisive in determining the action of legislative bodies on questions like this. Locality, foreign birth, time of residence, all this spoke against me, and as an offset I had nothing to show but some faithful efforts in behalf of the cause of the

[1] Remarks before the joint session of the Missouri general assembly, Jefferson City, Jan. 20, 1869, copied from the *Missouri Democrat*, St. Louis, Jan. 21, 1869.

Union, liberty and equal rights, and the generous confidence of many friends in my ability to render to the State and our common cause some service in the higher law-giving body of this Republic. By this act you have proclaimed to the world that the people of Missouri have risen above those prejudices and narrow-minded notions which are so apt to cloud the judgment of politicians, and that Missouri throws wide open her gates to all who have the heart and will and ability to coöperate in achieving the great destinies of the country, offering them a hearty welcome with full assurance of generous appreciation. It is therefore not so much for the high distinction with which you have honored me personally, as for this shining proof of a progressive spirit and large-minded liberality that I most sincerely thank you. And if I am proud of anything, it is that in an act of such significance I should have been found worthy to act as an humble instrument.

I shall not entertain you with pompous promises as to what I am going to do and to accomplish, but believe me when I say that I stand here with the profoundest consciousness of the duties and obligations I owe to you and to the country, and that I shall faithfully devote the best energies of my manhood to the great task of justifying your choice.

Gentlemen, we have vast and difficult problems to solve together. The civil war which lies behind us has delivered us of two great evils, but it has also loaded heavy burdens upon our shoulders. But, tremendous as these burdens may appear, I am convinced that with the wonderful natural resources of our country and the almost inexhaustible laboring force resting in the brains and arms of our people, they will be like a plaything in our hands as soon as we have once secured the development of things on a permanent basis, thus giving a solid peace to the Republic and enabling ourselves to combine all the energies of the Nation for the promotion of the general welfare.

In order to arrive at that permanent basis we must endeavor to close up the distracting agitations which have sprung from our civil conflict. The body-politic needs rest, but it can and it will have no undisturbed repose as long as there are classes of men who have to struggle for their rights. Our democratic system of government can stand with security only upon the foundation of impartial justice and right, equal to all. It is not in consideration of the loyalty of the negro alone that we strive to extend the right of suffrage to the colored people. It is our interest, no less than theirs; it is the general interest of society which demands that the laboring man, whatever his race or his color, should possess the political rights wherewith to defend his freedom, independence and manhood, and that all those stimulants of improvement should be furnished to him, which are calculated to raise him to the highest measure of usefulness. Thus we shall only be just to ourselves in being just to them.

To protect and secure the free development of the new order of things it has been found necessary to take away the power for mischief from the hands of those who during the great National crisis stood up against us as enemies to the good cause. This was necessary and therefore justifiable. A few days ago I declared here in your presence as my opinion—which I repeat now, only translating it from the language of defense into that of positive assertion— that the act of justice to loyal men stands first in rank, and that only such acts of grace to our late enemies are in order as will be consistent with the safety of the loyal people; that I will not consent to arm the late rebels with power in a manner which would enable them to deprive loyal men of their rights. By this declaration I mean to stand.

On the other hand, I am sure I express the feelings of the Radical party of Missouri when I say—and here again I am only amplifying what I stated a few days ago— that it is a sense of necessity and justice which moves us, and not rankling hate or desire for revenge. While we do not approve of the kind of forgiveness to the late enemies of the Republic which consists of forgetfulness of its friends, we mean to show that the dark fanaticism which will *never* forgive is foreign to our hearts, and that it is not our desire to humiliate but to improve and bring back to their duty those who have gone astray. I repeat again the words of General Grant: "We cannot go to them; they must come to us; but when they do come as improved men, we must not repel them." More than that, we must invite and encourage them to improve and come. Let us make them understand that they have only to do full justice to all the friends of the Union, and they may count upon full mercy to themselves; that they have only to come to us as men sincerely loyal to the new order of things and we shall meet them with the open hand of welcome. Let us convince them that although we detest treason as heartily as ever we shall hail with shouts of gladness the day when the rights of all will be safe under the custody of all and when the last of the rebels can be received back into the communion of the loyal people. Let them be convinced of this, and I am confident that, although there may be many who, with dogged infatuation, will continue to hug their old idols, yet thousands of the young and vigorous, especially those who during the conflict never swerved from the way of honorable warfare, will soon be glad to recognize the opportunity to regain their own rights by respecting the rights of others, and to serve their own interests by serving the interests of all. Let us not indiscriminately condemn the well-disposed with the incorrigible, and thus force them to remain

altogether as a class, but stimulate every germ of good
there is in them; give those who are inclined to do right
our generous encouragement; put a premium on good
conduct and pay it promptly. Every payment thus made
will prove a good investment, and as we approach the
great consummation, many, many of our enemies will
become willing to acknowledge that in being the true
friends of the country we were their true friends and that
whatever may have separated us in the past, common
interest must bind us together in the future. Such a
policy, far from endangering our ascendancy will only
strengthen our moral power. It will not be a mere favor
extended to rebels, but a service rendered to the people.
There is no way in which harmony and peace and general
prosperity can be better restored than by a policy calculated to identify the personal interests of the individual
citizen with the common welfare and to enlist the energies
of all in the common good.

My party friends, the great Republican organization
to which we belong has, by its magnificent achievements,
well deserved the power it now enjoys. But parties cannot live on reminiscences alone, however glorious. If the
Republican party wants to preserve its ascendancy it must
continue its usefulness; it cannot continue its usefulness
unless it shows that it justly appreciates the requirements
of the times and has the will and ability to provide for
them. We must not continue to fix our eyes upon the party
but turn them full upon the future. Our minds must not
be absorbed by the passions and resentments sprung from
the struggles which lie behind us, but be ready to grapple,
untrammeled in their movements, with the problems which
lie before us. These problems are manifold. We have
to set our faces like flint against the corrupt practices
which are poisoning our political life. We have to raise
the standard of political morals by putting public trust

only into the hands of the trustworthy, and being as
severe in our judgment on our party friends as we are
apt to be on our opponents.   We have to raise the public
credit by a scrupulous faithfulness to our obligations.   We
have to lighten our public burdens and develop the prosperity of the country, not merely by schemes of financial
management, but by striking out from our constitutions
and laws the trammels which clog the spirit of industrial
enterprise, by opening the resources of the land through
a network of railroad communications and by developing
the intelligence and stimulating the public spirit of our
people through an efficient system of education.

My Republican friends, we have already accomplished
so much that we shall not recoil before any task, be it ever
so great.   And we can accomplish all this, if, instead of
chaining ourselves down to the narrow gauge of party
dogmatism, we adhere to its great rule of original Republicanism, to keep the main ends to be reached firmly in
view, by admitting and encouraging in our ranks free
thought, free inquiry, free discussion as to the means by
which those ends are to be reached.   Thus we shall not
repel but attract all those whose hearts are open to the
impulse of patriotism, and whose minds are able to understand their own interests in connection with those of the
whole.   We shall make every man of intelligence and
honest aspirations feel that he belongs to us, and that
here is his place.

Indeed, whenever you cast your eyes over this great
Republic where do you find a State that opens a wider
field for a noble ambition than Missouri?   With her unbounded resources, her vast prairies still untilled by the
plow, her wooded hills, her mineral wealth still sleeping
in the mountains, her magnificent water communications,
her unparalleled geographical position, designating her as
the central thoroughfare of the greatest highway of trade

the world ever saw; her people—patriotic and highminded
—composed of the vigorous elements of all civilized nations
harmoniously blended—how can we fail to achieve a glorious future if we are only true to our great opportunities?

It is in this sense that I conceive it to be my duty to
coöperate with you in the sphere in which you have so
generously placed me.   Let us unite then, with a common
will and an honest purpose; with confidence in one another;
with malice toward none, with charity for all; with in-
flexible firmness for the right—to heal the wounds of the
past, to contribute our share to the glory of the Republic,
and to make this great commonwealth in the fullest sense
of the term what we are already proud of calling her—
Free Missouri—the pioneer of liberal and progressive
ideas, the empire State of the Mississippi valley, the heart
of the American Union.

FROM C. D. DRAKE

WASHINGTON, D. C., Jan. 21, 1869.

Notwithstanding our recent antagonism, I deem it only due
to myself to say to you that no personal feeling abides with
me in that connection.

Aside from the objections of a public character urged by
me to your election to the Senate,—which you will remember
were accompanied with a denial of personal unkindness,—I
have not had, have not now, any reason for withholding from
you an expression of congratulation upon your success.

Much less have I occasion for desiring any other relations
between us as colleagues than those of respect, good-will and
cordial coöperation.   I hope to find those feelings reciprocated
by you in our future intercourse.

When the news of your election was received here, I selected
for you the best unappropriated seat in the Senate Chamber,
and hope you will, on your arrival, be pleased with it.

TO C. D. DRAKE

St. Louis, Jan. 28, 1869.

I thank you for the congratulation you offer me on my election to the Senate and for the friendly feelings you express in your letter of the 21st inst. You know well that our antagonism with regard to that matter was not of my seeking, and I may assure you that my conduct as a Senator from Missouri will be governed entirely by considerations of public interest without any ingredient of personal resentment. I certainly do not desire "any other relations between us, as colleagues, than those of respect, good-will and cordial coöperation." I thank you sincerely for your kindness in selecting a good seat for me.

TO W. M. GROSVENOR[1]

Washington, March 29, 1869.

I wrote you yesterday before I had your letter, which arrived this morning. I am surprised you did "not understand" my speech.[2] Everybody here understood it. It is certain—at any rate it is clear to everybody here— that civil service reform measures have little if any chance of success in Congress, unless we manage to produce a pressure. And there is nothing so available and so easy within reach as this law, of which everybody knows that it will have to be amended. If we succeed in keeping the necessity of doing something in this matter alive, we have a splendid chance to make a regular reform campaign next winter. But if the matter is now finally disposed of, as it would be by a repeal, the probability is that we shall have to struggle hard to bring the reform bill properly before the two houses, with chances rather against us.

[1] At this time editor of the St. Louis *Democrat*.
[2] On the repeal of the tenure of office act.

31

I have talked with the most prominent friends of reform, and they are entirely of my opinion. They considered my speech, as to its immediate effect upon the question, the most judicious that has been made.

This is one point. Another is that there is one feature in the tenure of office law which, although obnoxious in its connection with the present system of appointments, will be of value connected with the reforms proposed.

The third point, already hinted at in my letter of yesterday is this. The growing tendency of flinging down legislative powers at the feet of "personal government," when that "personal government" is carried on by one who starts on [with] a certain capital of popularity, is rather too much for my republican blood. If done at all, it ought to be done with decency. The agencies and men principally at work for repeal are of such a character as to repel my instinct. Nothing could be better for Grant, just now, than to learn, that the Legislative power is, as such, independent and somewhat animated by an independent spirit. While suspension is calculated to convey that impression to him and accomplishes all the objects above alluded to, it gives him at the same time all the liberty of action he wants and anybody can reasonably ask for. Then we would, pressed by the existence of the law, and the necessity of remodeling it, take the matter of reform vigorously in hand next winter. There now!

I shall send you the *Globe*. Write me more frequently, if you can, and I know you can.

TO JAMES TAUSSIG

UNITED STATES SENATE CHAMBER,
WASHINGTON, April 18, 1869.

My dear Friend: Your letter of the 9th inst. has reached me. I have certainly not forgotten Mr. Waldauer

and am doing for him the best I can.   But this is a lottery,
and heaven knows upon what mysterious theory the
distribution of prizes is made.   Whether I shall be able to
get something for Mr. Waldauer, I cannot say.   I shall,
at any rate, spare no effort.   I have worked very hard for
my friends.   In some cases I have not succeeded at all,
in others too much.   So it goes.   Some Missourians have
been favored with consulates by a providential dispensa-
tion which an ordinary understanding cannot fathom, and
which, I am sure, I did not control.

To be a United States Senator may be a very high
honor.   But so far I have found it to be the meanest
drudgery a human imagination ever conceived.   I hope
I have now seen the worst of it.   The utter absurdity of
our system of appointment to office has this time so
glaringly demonstrated itself that even the dullest patriots
begin to open their eyes to the necessity of a reform.   I
have taken a solemn vow to pitch in for it next winter to
the best of my ability.

No prospect is at this moment so pleasing to me as to
shake you by the hand again very soon at a solemn meeting
of the twentieth century.[1]

TO W. M. GROSVENOR

WASHINGTON, March 31, 1870.

I thank you for your kind letter and your approval of
my speech on the Georgia bill.[2]   I have made a much
better one since on the San Domingo treaty, and I think
that will be your judgment when the injunction of secrecy
will be removed and you see it.   In my own opinion, that

[1] The name of a coterie of political friends in St. Louis.

[2] Schurz made two speeches, March 18 and April 19, 1870, on the question
of the admission of Ga.   They can be seen in the *Congressional Globe* of
that time.

speech is the best one I ever made. Your apprehension of a breach between the Administration and myself has been verified in a less degree than I myself expected. I told General Grant my opinion about the treaty weeks ago with the utmost frankness, while, as I understand, others made him hope that they would support it and then opposed it. I am told that he speaks very highly of my candor. I have met him since I made my speech, and we met and parted very cordially.

As the matter now stands, the debate will probably be dropped, the treaty having expired on the 29th; but the treaty will probably be extended and we shall commence from the beginning again. In the meantime I hope we shall be able to carry the removal of the injunction of secrecy. The project is broached to carry the annexation scheme by joint resolution, following the example of Texas. If so, the most serious consequences are to be apprehended, and I stated my apprehensions to the President with the utmost frankness. I hope this dangerous experiment may be averted. Of course, the treaty can never be ratified in the Senate by a two-thirds majority.

. . . .[1]

ENFORCEMENT OF THE FIFTEENTH AMENDMENT[2]

MR. PRESIDENT:—As the Senate will remember, the honorable Senator from New Jersey [Mr. STOCKTON] addressed yesterday, in the course of his speech, a personal

---

[1] Four or five sentences wholly about unimportant personal matters.

[2] Speech in the United States Senate, May 19, 1870. The Senate had under consideration the bill (H. R. No. 1203) to enforce the rights of citizens of the United States to vote in the several States of this Union, who had been denied the right on account of race, color or previous condition of servitude.

appeal to me, with so much eloquent earnestness that I
am not permitted to doubt its sincerity; and I think
courtesy requires that I should respond to it in the same
spirit. He expressed his belief that I and thousands of
the children of my native land had come to these shores
for the purpose of enjoying the blessings of liberty and
self-government; and in arguing against this bill, he intimated that we would certainly consider it our duty
to do all in our power to preserve and perpetuate these
inestimable blessings. In all these suppositions he was
right; but I apprehend there may be a serious difference of opinion between the Senator from New Jersey
and myself as to what those blessings of liberty and self-
government consist in, and as to the manner in which
they can and ought to be preserved and perpetuated;
and inasmuch as he has appealed to me from his point
of view I think it is proper that I should appeal to him
and to his associates from mine.

I have listened to the arguments of Democratic Senators against this bill with mingled pleasure and pain;
pleasure, when I noticed how my honorable friend from
Ohio [Mr. Thurman], whose shrewdness on this floor
nobody is disposed to doubt, thought it proper to confine
himself to an attack on the details of this bill, instead of
launching into that general denunciation of the Constitutional amendments and the legislation based thereon with
which Democratic Senators had made us so familiar on
former occasions. I might have considered that a good
omen had not some of his associates, less discreet and
more impulsive than he, hoisted the true colors of their
party and boldly declared that they did not believe in
the validity of the fifteenth amendment, and openly
proclaimed their desire to see it overthrown. Then I
could not but remember that even the Senator from Ohio,
in the opening remarks of his speech, spoke of the fifteenth

amendment as a thing of only supposed legality, though he, as a practical man, was willing to base his argument upon that supposition, for the reason that the ruling majority of the Senate were united upon that point. Well, sir, this, it seems to me, opens to us a view rather wider than the discussion of the technical points which we have been listening to in the course of this debate.

It brings back to our memories again the fierce declamation hurled against all the Constitutional amendments by our Democratic associates in this body; the bitter opposition raised against all legislation designed to enforce them; the vehement appeals in the name of liberty, of self-government, of State-rights and of all that is great and good, to leave the rights of the newly-enfranchised class to the legislative action of the States exclusively; the acrimonious charge that we were a revolutionary party; that we had already revolutionized the Constitution of the United States, and that we were about to subvert the whole system of self-government and all the political institutions to which this country owes so many of its blessings.

Now, sir, in responding to the appeal of the Senator from New Jersey, and desiring to say to him what I conceive to be the blessings of liberty and self-government, and the manner in which they ought to be sustained, preserved and perpetuated, I beg him to review with me the field covered by the bill before us. We are charged with having revolutionized the Constitution of the country by the amendments recently ratified; and that charge is reiterated so often that we have reason to suppose our opponents must consider it a crushing argument. Well, sir, I do not deem it necessary to enter a plea of "not guilty." On the contrary, I acknowledge the fact, and I suppose the Republican party is by no means ashamed of it. Yes, sir, this Republic has passed through a revolutionary process of tremendous significance. Yes, the Constitution of the United States has been changed in some most essential points; that change does amount to a great revolution, and this bill is one of its legitimate children. Let us look those facts in the face, and I think we may derive from them some conclusions which may be of service in the discussion of the provisions of this bill. What was that Constitutional revolution which the Democrats denounce as so fearful an outrage? In order to understand it fully, we must cast a look back and see what the Constitutional polity of the United States was before the civil war, according to the Democratic interpretation of the Constitution then prevailing.

Constitutions and constitutional constructions do not spring from a mere process of philosophical speculation and reasoning. They grow out of conditions, circumstances, events, sympathies, prevailing interests. We all remember that the most powerful political interest in this country for a long period previous to the war was that of slavery. We remember also that the slave-power, finding itself at war with the conscience of mankind, condemned by the enlightened spirit of this age, menaced by adverse interests growing stronger and stronger every day, sought safety behind the bulwark of what they euphoniously called local self-government and intrenched itself in the doctrine of State sovereignty. To be sure, it made, from that defensive position, offensive sallies encroaching on the rights of the non-slaveholding States, as for instance in the case of the notorious fugitive-slave law and the attempt to take possession of the whole territorial domain of this Republic; but the doctrine of State sovereignty was its main citadel, its base of operations.

What was this dogma? It was asserted and accepted as a fundamental principle, as the peculiarly democratic feature of our republican system of government, that the several geographical and political subdivisions of this Republic called the States should not only have the right to govern and manage their own home affairs, independent of all interference on the part of the National authority, but also to determine for themselves whether their whole population, or only a part, and what part, should participate in the management of their common concerns, that is to say, in the functions of self-government. In other words, the doctrine was that the States had the right to subject a large portion of their people to the absolute dominion and despotic rule of another portion, and to determine at their discretion by what means that despotic rule of man over man should be set on foot and perpetuated, no matter how flagrantly hostile those means might be to the fundamental rights and liberties upon which the whole fabric of free government rests. That was the Democratic doctrine of State sovereignty. It was called the principal safeguard of popular self-government, and canonized with the name of true and genuine democracy. And now look at some of those monstrous political fallacies in which that doctrine of true self-government and genuine democracy resulted; and when I have stated them you will at once discern their consanguinity with the very arguments which have been urged upon this floor against our Constitutional amendments and that legislation which is necessary to enforce them.

It was held that true liberty implied the right of one man to hold another man as his slave. It was held and believed that the United States could not be a truly republican organization unless the several States had the power to maintain and perpetuate undemocratic institutions. It was held that true self-government consisted in the very fact that the several States of this Union should have the power to exclude any number, however large, of their population from the exercise of all the functions

of self-government.   In other words, you, my Democratic
friends, in the name of liberty asserted the right of one
man, under State law, to deprive another man of his
freedom; in the name of democracy you asserted the
right of one class of people under State law to rule des-
potically over another class; in the name of self-government you asserted the right of the States to exclude a
large portion, sometimes even amounting to a majority
of their population, from all participation in self-government.   Now, my friend from New Jersey will permit
me to say that I, and those who like me left their old
homes, did by no means come to this country for the
purpose of maintaining and perpetuating such blessings
of liberty and self-government.

Sir, you would search the history of the aberrations of
the human mind in vain for an array of logical contradictions more glaring and monstrous, for a structure of
political fallacies more bare-faced, more audacious, more
wicked and more mischievous.   There never was a
more transparent attempt to hide the most odious and
arbitrary despotism under the guise of democratic professions; and it is indeed surprising how such a tissue of
false pretenses could ever have survived a moment's
unprejudiced scrutiny; but more surprising still it is that
even at this day something akin to it should find a voice
on the floor of the American Senate.

Finally that structure of fallacies, still so overshadowing
but ten short years ago, tumbled down.   It fell after
having heaped outrage after outrage upon the dignity of
human nature; after having for generations befogged the
minds, corrupted the logic and debauched the moral
sense of the American people; after having well-nigh
poisoned our whole political life; after having involved
this country in the most irrepressible of conflicts.   It
fell after having arrayed man against man in bloody

struggle; after having devoured five hundred thousand of the children of this Republic and untold millions of our treasure. It was finally overthrown by the shock of the great revolution. And what did that revolution put in its place? It gave us three great amendments to the National Constitution. The first ordains that no State shall henceforth have the power to introduce or maintain slavery or involuntary servitude. The second ordains that all persons born or naturalized in the United States are citizens of the United States and of the States in which they reside and that no State shall henceforth have the power to make or enforce any law abridging the privileges and immunities of citizens of the Republic. The third ordains that no State shall abridge the right of suffrage of any citizen on account of race, color or previous condition of servitude. And all three empower Congress to pass appropriate legislation for their enforcement.

That is the result of the great Constitutional revolution. What does this result signify? The war grew out of the systematic violation of individual rights by State authority. The war ended with the vindication of individual rights by the National power. The revolution found the rights of the individual at the mercy of the States; it rescued them from their arbitrary discretion, and placed them under the shield of National protection. It made the liberty and rights of every citizen in every State a matter of National concern. Out of a Republic of arbitrary local organizations it made a Republic of equal citizens—citizens exercising the right of self-government under and through the States, but as to their rights as citizens not subject to the arbitrary will of the States. It grafted upon the Constitution of the United States the guarantee of National citizenship; and it empowered Congress, as the organ of the National will, to enforce that guarantee by National legislation. That is the meaning of that great revolution; and if Democratic Senators denounce the bill at present before us as its offspring they are welcome. I accept the name.

Now, sir, what is the scope and purpose of this bill? It provides that no State shall enforce a law with regard to elections, or the processes preliminary to elections, in which in any way, either directly or indirectly, discrimination is made against any citizen on account of race, color or previous condition; and when any citizen is hindered in the exercise of the right of suffrage by means of fraud, intimidation or violence, or misuse of official power, the offender shall be brought to trial and punishment by a court of the United States. And for this the bill provides the necessary machinery. In other words, neither a State nor an individual shall deprive any citizen of the United States, on account of race or color, of the free exercise of his right to participate in the functions of self-government; and the National Government assumes the duty to prevent the commission of the crime, and to correct its consequences when committed. That is all.

If we were to judge the character and tendency of this bill from the expressions used by our Democratic associates in denouncing it, we should think that we were about to perpetrate the most horrible crime against the rights of man and human liberty ever conceived by the human imagination. It is as if the democratic institutions of this country were about to receive their death-blow, while we contemplate nothing but to secure every citizen of the United States in the free and full enjoyment of those democratic institutions.

What are the objections? It is, I believe, not pretended that the bill in its general scope and purpose runs against the Constitution as improved by the fifteenth amend-

ment; but it is objected that the bill is uncalled for, on the
ground that nothing has been done in the different States
to show the necessity of any such legislation.   Sir, is this
true?   Can this assertion be maintained even a single
moment?   For generations the practices of slavery have
controlled the minds and moral views of the people of the
Southern States.   Popular prejudice, so long nourished
by those practices, was naturally arrayed against the
enfranchisement of the former slave, and the beneficent
agency of time has by no means been sufficient yet to
allay it, whatever improvement we may observe.   Joined
to the prejudice of race, the jealousy of political power
conspires against a fair execution of the fifteenth amendment, and in view of these opposing forces, who will deny
that this legislation to enforce it is necessary?

Nay, more than that.   The very Senators on this floor
who pretend that the passage of this bill is not called for
by circumstances go so far as to throw doubt upon the
validity of the fifteenth amendment, thus exciting the
worst passions of the disturbing element in the South
to do all within their power to defeat the purposes of
this Constitutional provision.   Is it not so?   And while
on the one hand themselves fanning the flame, they on
the other hand deny the necessity of quenching it.   Will
it be unfair to assume under such circumstances that
while denouncing this legislation as uncalled for they
merely desire to defeat the purposes of the fifteenth
amendment?

The Senator from Maryland urged another argument,
which at first sight seems to have some plausibility.   He
says that the Constitutional amendment is one of the
great prohibitory clauses, as we find them in several
places and on several subjects in the Constitution of the
United States, and that with regard to them enforcing
legislation had never been thought necessary.   Suppose

this to be so; can he tell me why it was deemed indispensable to affix to the thirteenth, fourteenth and fifteenth amendments the express provision that Congress should have the power to enforce them by appropriate legislation? The Senator from Maryland says that Congress had that power anyhow. I suppose so; but why was the power never so emphatically and expressly asserted as in these three cases? Simply because it was known that the recent three amendments had to be enforced in the States lately in armed insurrection, against the opposition of prejudice, habit and political passion. Is not the distinction obvious? Is not the intent of those who drafted the amendments and provided for the express grant of power clear as sunlight? Is not the necessity of using that grant of power equally evident?

Now, sir, I will not go into the discussion of the argument offered by Democratic Senators against the details of this bill. I know there are several provisions which are objectionable. I admit it frankly. I do think that the section which confers by implication upon the President power to surround the polls with the military forces of the United States ought not to be raised to the dignity of a permanent law. I know that such a law would be repugnant to the genius of free institutions, and that it is considered so all over the world. So it is with the other clause providing that the President shall have the power to command a judge to go here and to go there; and further, it is in my opinion of doubtful propriety to stimulate the desire of a citizen to secure his rights by the mercenary consideration of money. It does appear to me if a man has not spirit enough to do it for the sake of his rights, he ought not to be permitted to do it for the sake of so many dollars. And I here express my hope that the Senate will strike out these obnoxious provisions.

But as to the whole machinery of the bill, I think the

Senator from Ohio was not quite justified in waving off
so lightly the argument which was employed against
him by my friend from Vermont that the Democrats had
found that legal machinery not only constitutional, but
positively admirable when it was used to enforce the
fugitive-slave law, while they denounce it as destestable
and infamous now. The Senator from Ohio knows very
well that a legal machinery used for a laudable purpose
may be very praiseworthy, while it is most reprehensible
when used for evil; and so the Senator from Vermont
was certainly right when he blamed the Democrats for
calling this machinery all possible bad names when it is
to be used in the service of the constitutional rights of
freemen, while they had upheld it as most rightful and
necessary, and denounced everybody as a traitor who
would not help in executing it, when it was to serve in
the unholy work of returning fugitive slaves, who sought
their freedom, to bondage and misery.

But here is another question of interest. Does this
bill really take away from the States the power to legislate on the subject? Look at it closely. Does it? Not
at all, sir. It leaves the States just as free as they ever
were to legislate for the prompt and vigorous enforcement
of protection of the right of every voter to the free exercise of the suffrage. Does it not? In that respect it does
not impose the least restriction on the power of the States.
In that direction the States may go just as far as they
please. But the bill does provide that a State shall no
longer have the power to swindle any of its citizens out
of their rights.

A State shall have full power to do that which is right
in its own way; but it is prohibited from doing that which
is wrong in any way. It is this, I suppose, that Democrats will insist upon calling an arbitrary limitation of
State rights. Or is it true, what is asserted also, that

this legislation does not find anything analogous in the Constitution of the United States? In the Constitution, sir, we find one clause which ordains that no State shall have the power to grant titles of nobility. What does that mean? It means that no State shall elevate, by the grant of privileges, one class of its citizens above the rest. And what is contemplated by the fifteenth amendment and by the law designed to enforce it? That no State shall have the power to degrade, by the withholding of rights, any portion of its citizens below the rest. Is not the correspondence here evident? But here suddenly the indignation of our Democratic friends is aroused, and in the prohibition to degrade men they find an intolerable encroachment on State-rights and local self-government. And just there, I apprehend, is the rub. It is not so much the technicalities of the bill; it is the spirit, the purpose of the bill they oppose. It is as the Senator from Maryland has just openly and boldly proclaimed, that if the bill were ever so perfect, he would vote against it on general principles. He nods his assent; and I am sure I cannot mistake him; and the same thing we have been given to understand by every Democratic Senator who has addressed the Senate on this question.

Let us see what their complaints are, then. Strip them of all the verbiage of technical points, sift them to the bottom, and you will find there a residue of the old pro-slavery logic still. As they once asserted that true liberty implied the right of one man to hold another man as his slave, they will tell you now that they are no longer true freemen in their States because under the authority of the States they can no longer deprive other men of their rights. As they once asserted that true self-government consisted in the power of a State to exclude a large portion of its citizens from self-government, so they will say now that we strike a blow at self-government because we insist upon legislation securing every citizen of the States in the enjoyment of self-government. Is it not so?

Destruction of self-government! What a prodigious discovery our Democratic associates have made! Sir, it is not because this bill lays its hands upon self-government to destroy it, but because by the fifteenth amendment, and the legislation made in pursuance thereof, the general sway of self-government is to be for the first time established all over this country, that I am in favor of the principles of this act. What is true self-government? What does it consist in? True self-government consists in a political organization of society which secures to the generality of its members, that is to say, to the whole people, and not to a part of them only, the right and the means to coöperate in the management of their common affairs, either directly, or, where direct action is impossible, by a voluntary delegation of power. It ceases to be true self-government as soon as the powers of government are conferred as an exclusive privilege on one portion of the people and are withheld from the rest. And how is self-government exercised? By the right of suffrage. The representative system knows no other instrumentality. Suffrage is the means by which it lives and breathes.

To make self-government true, general and secure, therefore, the right of suffrage must be made secure to the generality of the citizens. You limit the right of suffrage by arbitrary exclusions, and just in that measure and to that extent will you impair the integrity of self-government. Protect every citizen in the free exercise of the right of suffrage and you do the thing best calculated to make self-government a general and living reality. I do not express any opinion here of the policy of restricting suffrage by an educational test, for it will not affect the principle.

And now the Democrats accuse us of destroying self-government by the very means which are instrumental in securing it in all the subdivisions of the Republic. I repeat, there never was a more preposterous charge. Sir, in a very large portion of this Republic that which could justly be called self-government of the people never existed. Now, at last, we are establishing it there by placing the right of suffrage on the broadest democratic basis, thus making the people of all the States, in the true sense of the term, self-governing bodies. And it is for this that we are denounced by our Democratic friends here as the sworn enemies of self-government and State-rights. Sir, I apprehend it is not for self-government and State-rights that our Democratic associates are standing up; but, drawing logical conclusions from the reasoning they have been indulging in, it is for State wrongs they contend. It is not for the liberty of all, but it is for the liberty of one to restrict and impair the liberty of another. It is not for true self-government of the people, but it is for the government of one part of the people over another part.

The time is past, sir, when the cry of State-rights will serve as a guise for such pretensions. I, too, am a friend and earnest advocate of State-rights, as far as State-rights are the embodiment of true local self-government. True, I do not cling to those traditional notions which an historical period now passed by and absolved has brought down to us. I do not cherish that sentimental—I might almost say that superstitious—reverence for individual States, which attributes to them as historical persons a sort of transcendental sanctity; but I do believe that their value can hardly be overestimated as compact political sub-organizations, through which and in which the self-government of the people is exercised, and within which it finds its most appropriate and efficient organs. I am

32

therefore in favor of leaving to the States as large a scope of independent action as may be consistent with the safety of the Republic and the rights of the citizens.

In fact, sir, in my opinion, true local self-government is the great fountain from which the popular mind draws its healthiest and most invigorating inspirations. It is not only a machinery of political action, but it is one of the most efficient educational agencies of our social system. There is nothing better calculated to make a man understand and protect his interests, nothing more inspiring and instructive to the heart and mind of man than the independent management of his own affairs, upon his own responsibility; and there is nothing more inspiring and invigorating to a community of men, than free cooperation for common ends on a common responsibility in which the interest of each individual is involved.

That, sir, is what puts men upon their own feet. When they have accustomed themselves to depend on their own wisdom or energy for success, and to blame themselves and not others for failure and mishap in individual and common concerns, then they will become truly independent beings, such as the citizens of a democratic republic ought to be. Therefore, it is of high importance that as many responsibilities as possible should be laid at the door of every citizen by local self-government.

We are apt to grow eloquent in the praise of the educational systems established in many of our States. They are, indeed, praiseworthy: and yet they are as such by no means superior to the educational systems enjoyed in some other countries.

It may be said that in some German States the system is even better developed than in the most advanced States of New England; and yet we perceive here a higher average of popular intelligence. We find that the American is generally quicker of perception, readier in the compre-

hension of the practical problems of life, more vigorous
and energetic in action, than people formed by a better
school system elsewhere. Why is this so? Not because
our babies are born smarter here; not because our boys
and girls learn to read, write and cipher better in our
schools; not because their instruction in geography and
natural science is more thorough; but the reason is, that
as soon as the young American issues from the hands of
his schoolmaster and enters the arena of practical life,
he finds in the rights and duties and responsibilities of
self-government a more powerful incentive and a larger
field for the exercise of all his faculties and for the
immediate application of all his acquirements. Thus
self-government and popular education aid, inspire and
complement one another; and hence the great results
we observe.

And now let me impress upon our Democratic friends
that for this very reason nothing is more important, nay,
more necessary, for the harmonious development of the
social forces of this Republic, as they now stand side by
side and have to work together, than that all, even the
lowliest classes of the people, should be drawn within the
circle of this beneficent combination of educational influences, and that they should be carefully protected in their
complete enjoyment. And if you study our social problems
without prejudice you will find that just this is one of the
most valuable results of that Constitutional revolution
which so sorely distresses the Democratic mind.

But for the precise reason which I have just indicated
the revolution which is to protect all American citizens
in the exercise of self-government ought not to be carried
so far as to encroach upon its legitimate scope. I am,
therefore, strenuously opposed to all unnecessary accumulation of powers in the hands of the General Government,
and especially to any undue centralization of adminis-

trative functions. In my opinion, and I say this to my
party friends, it would be well for us to bridle that tendency which we have so frequently had occasion to
observe, to thrust the hand of the National Government
into local affairs on every possible occasion, and even
to disregard and throw aside the most fundamental
safeguards of popular rights for the correction of passing
abuses.

I know it is fashionable to call that radicalism; but I
apprehend it is false radicalism in the highest degree. We
ought not to accustom ourselves, nor those who are to
follow us in these seats, to the employment of arbitrary
powers, and still less ought we to accustom the people
to look always to the National Government for redress
whenever anything goes wrong in their home concerns.
Destroy their habit of holding themselves responsible for
the management of their home affairs, deprive them of
the great lesson of failure to be corrected by themselves,
and they will soon cease to study and understand the
nature of the evils under which they labor, as well as the
remedies to be applied. Thus the educating power of
our institutions will be fatally impaired.

There can be nothing more preposterous, in my opinion,
than the system prevailing in some foreign countries,
where the people are permitted to vote upon the greatest
and most complicated questions of general policy while
they are not permitted to manage upon their own responsibility their home affairs at their own doors; the great
popular school of political knowledge and experience,
which consists in self-government, being thus closed to
them. Certainly, it is not to be wondered at if in such
countries universal suffrage becomes a mere instrument
in the hands of despotism; an instrument which, indeed,
may serve from time to time to subvert one form of despotism, but only to substitute for it another.

Therefore I am for State-rights as the embodiment of true and general self-government, and I am convinced that this is the prevailing sentiment among the American people. It would be a sad day for this Republic if it should cease to be so. It is true the exigencies of the civil war have quite naturally developed a tendency to accumulate and centralize power in the hands of the National Government, and while that accumulation was necessary to save the existence of the Republic, the people of the United States willingly and patriotically and cheerfully acquiesced in it; but as soon as the pressure of necessity ceases, as soon as it becomes apparent that the great problems for the solution of which we are struggling may be solved just as well by the simple operations of local self-government as by the interference of the National power, then the tide will just as certainly set in the opposite direction. I am sure the people of the United States will never countenance an accumulation of power merely for power's sake, and the Republican party will do well to consider whether it is not better for their usefulness and ascendancy to direct than to resist that tide.

For this reason I earnestly deprecate those hazardous interpretations which have been applied to that clause of the Constitution which makes it the duty of the United States to guarantee to every State a republican form of government. I certainly recognize that duty as a great, solemn and sacred one; but I deny that it confers upon the National Government the power to do all within the range of the human imagination. I deny that it authorizes or enables us to use the arm of the National authority for the purpose of realizing by force what conception each of us may entertain of the "ideal republic."

In whatever way political philosophers may define the term "a republican form of government," it seems to me that the Constitution of the United States in its amended, or, as our Democratic friends would have it, in its revolutionized state, has provisions which give a fair index of the powers conferred upon Congress by the guaranty clause. There we read that Congress shall see to it that no State establishes or maintains slavery or involuntary servitude; there we read that Congress shall see to it that every man born upon this soil or naturalized, and therefore a citizen of the United States, shall be protected in all the rights, privileges and immunities of citizens in every State of this Union; there we read that Congress shall see to it that every citizen of the United States shall be protected in his right to the ballot, irrespective of race or color.

But the Constitutional revolution has enlarged the powers of Congress for the purpose of establishing and securing true and general self-government in all of these States, not for the purpose of circumscribing its scope and functions within narrower limits. It has, indeed, overthrown what I call State wrongs; but it was not designed to abolish what I would call the legitimate sphere of State-rights. And I venture to say—and I cannot repeat this warning too often—the party which would attempt to carry that revolution much farther in the direction of an undue centralization of power would run against a popular instinct far stronger than party allegiance has ever proved to be.

But, sir, on the other hand, the party that would refuse to recognize and acquiesce in the great results of this beneficent revolution; the party that would attempt to subvert the institution of general self-government under National protection, as now established in the Constitution; the party that would strive to overthrow this new order of things, such a party certainly cannot fail to encounter the condemnation of the people and to meet disgrace and destruction, for such a party openly, by its

own confession, constitutes itself the enemy of the peace
and glory of this Republic.   And I would say to my friend
from New Jersey that I did not come to this country,
where I hope to enjoy the blessings of liberty and self-
government, to aid any party in designs like these.

Now, sir, permit me to address a few words to the leaders
of the Democratic organization on this floor; and they
know I speak to them as men whose character and ability
I esteem, and whose personal friendship I value.   You,
gentlemen, tell us that you are in favor of true self-government.   If you really are, look around you and see how
much you can do to contribute to its success and security.
In your party are the men who threaten and endanger
it by the most iniquitous attempts to deprive certain
classes of people of their political rights by fraud, intimidation and violence;   thus to subvert the new order of
things, throwing the country into chaos again.   Your
voices are potent with them; not ours.   If you really are
true friends to self-government, then let your voices be
heard in condemnation of the disastrous course so many
of your friends are still following.   Let them be loudly
heard in favor of the great principle of equal rights, the
only basis upon which the political future of this Republic
can develop itself.

You, gentlemen, tell us that you are opposed to an
undue assumption and exercise of power on the part of
the General Government.   If you are, see how powerfully
you can aid in preventing it by removing all those reasons
and causes and pretexts which may bring it on.   What
are those reasons and causes?   Do they not consist in
those disorders which are troubling the people of the
South as to the safety of the Unionists and the rights of
the newly-enfranchised, disorders invariably excited by
men who profess to belong to your party?   And do you
not know as well as I that as soon as the people of the

United States once apprehend that a serious reaction, with only an apparent chance of success, is set on foot against the great results of the war, the tide of public sentiment will just as surely and promptly set back in favor of a more extended and vigorous exertion of the National power, and you will be impotent to arrest it? For there are certain things in regard to which the American people will not permit themselves to be trifled with; and foremost among those things stand the great results which we have so laboriously evolved out of the civil war now behind us. There is the danger; and he who is no enemy to self-government, he who is no friend to a dangerous accumulation of power, will certainly use every endeavor to avert it. For our part we would much rather reason down the disturbers of the peace in the South than strike them down; but to our voices they will not listen; to yours they will. They are within the reach of your persuasion. There is the field where you can prove your devotion to self-government and your dislike of centralized power.

You tell us also, gentlemen, that legislation like this is odious to you. Look around you and see how much you can do to make it superfluous. We, too, should be glad never to be under the necessity of resorting to it. If you want to avoid it the means is simple. Prevail upon your friends never to threaten or trouble any class of voters in the free exercise of their rights, have those rights secured and protected by appropriate State legislation, and that State legislation respected by your friends, and such measures as this will never be practically applied. Nay, more than that, if you are really in earnest, then I would advise you to accept this measure as a gage of good faith instead of opposing it. It would be far better than your attempts to throw doubt upon the legality of the Constitutional amendments, your studious efforts to hold

out to your partisans the prospect of their overthrow, and
of the subversion of all that has been accomplished for the
final settlement of our controversies and the peace of the
country.

Yes, make up your minds, gentlemen, to the fact that
your old doctrines are exploded forever and cannot be
revived. Give up your useless and disturbing agitation
against accomplished results. Go to your Southern
friends and counsel them not to ruin themselves by vainly
resisting the inevitable. Thus you will do more for the
cause of self-government, more to prevent a dangerous
centralization of power, you will render a far higher service
to this generation and to posterity, than by indulging
in those lugubrious wails and lamentations to which you
have accustomed us on the floor of the Senate—the lamentation that we are governed by an atrocious despotism
because one man shall no longer have the right to deprive
another man of his rights; that self-government has received its death-blow because nobody shall henceforth
be excluded from its exercise, and that liberty has fled
forever from these shores because at last the Republic has
thrown her protecting shield over the rights of all, even
the lowliest of her children.

Mr. President, I do not stand here to plead the cause of
my party only. If I did so, if there were nothing nearer
and dearer to my heart than partisan success and partisan
power, I should hold very different language. I would
then say to my Democratic friends, "By all means go on
with your opposition against the results of the war; go on
with your mischievous warfare against the new order of
things; go on with vain and disturbing agitation to restore
what has ceased to be and can never again be;" for if they
do, they will only prove that they are still living in a past
which this Nation has long outgrown; that they are still
bent upon sacrificing the interests of the living generation

to idols which are dead; that they are still bound to keep open the wounds of the past, and to defeat those hopes of peace and good understanding which the country so fondly cherishes, and the realization of which depends entirely upon a final settlement of the controversies which the war has left to us.   And thus exhibiting their unwillingness to understand and appreciate the exigencies of the present, they will demonstrate even to the dullest mind their incapacity to control our future; and then the people of the United States, sagacious and prudent as they are, will appreciate the fact and treat them accordingly. Acting thus, our opponents will only condemn themselves to continued impotency.

If, therefore, I pleaded for nothing but the interest of my party I would encourage them to persevere in their course.   But I plead for the cause of our country—for its peace, its prosperity, its happiness and its good name; and I cannot permit myself to forget that the people will not be secure in the enjoyment of those blessings as long as there is a large and influential party insidiously striving to undermine the foundation upon which alone they can grow, and to plunge the country again into the confusion of endless and bitter struggles.   It is for this reason that I entreat our Democratic friends to desist from their disturbing and most mischievous agitation.

Some time ago my friend from New Jersey closed his speech on the admission of the Senator from Mississippi [Mr. REVELS], who is the first representative of the colored race on this floor, with a most eloquent and touching appeal in favor of peace, harmony and good understanding; so eloquent, indeed, as to cause the usual decorum of the Senate to be broken by demonstrations of applause.   I take that Senator at his word.   Yes, let there be peace and harmony and good understanding, and let us all unite in doing the one thing needful to bring it about.   The

Senator must instinctively feel what that one thing needful is. He cannot conceal from his own eyes that there is but one settlement of our present controversy possible; that only one can be final, permanent and conclusive; and that is, the settlement which we advocate. He must see that the black man, being once admitted to the polls, the decree cannot be reversed. He must see that those broad hints, so frequently thrown out by Democratic Senators in the course of this very debate, that the fifteenth amendment is invalid and may still at some future time be overthrown, can only serve to encourage the false hopes of the rebel element in the South, can only serve to excite the worst impulses in an unthinking multitude in the North and can result in nothing but mischief, the most wanton, the most cruel mischief.

If the honorable Senator from New Jersey is really so ardent a friend of peace, harmony and fraternal feeling, let him go among his associates and tell them,

Enough of this; it is better to be right by the light of to-day than to be consistent with the errors of yesterday. If there lingers in your hearts a doubt as to the legality of the ratification of these Constitutional amendments, in the name of all that is good and great, waive that doubt; waive it for the peace of the country; waive it for the sake of those great interests which we are all called upon to serve. Do not insist upon exciting the evil passions which with so much trouble we have at last succeeded in quieting; do not tear open the wounds of the past again; do not torment the country with new struggles about those fearful questions which have kept the people so long in restless agitation, and are now at last on the point of final settlement, if we only permit them to be settled.

In uniting his party upon such a platform, the platform of such noble and conciliatory sentiments, my friend from New Jersey, who addressed me so eloquently yesterday, would do an act worthy of himself; he would render an inestimable service to our common country; and he might then at last even stagger my conviction, a conviction I have been compelled to entertain so far, that the blessings of liberty and self-government which I came to enjoy in this country, would be very unsafe if unfortunately the party of which he is a member should again obtain possession of the powers of the National Government.

But, sir, if the leaders of the Democratic party will not listen to language like this, then I think we shall be safe in taking an appeal to the masses. The people of the United States will see, if the Democratic leaders do not, that of all the policies thought of for the settlement of pending controversies, that proposed by the Republican party, the settlement of equal rights and general self-government, is the only one which by any possibility can be final and conclusive, for it is the only one in full accordance with the genius of republican institutions. The people will see, if the Democratic leaders do not, that the highest interests of the country demand that settlement to be made promptly and without cavil; for without it we shall not obtain that peace which is necessary to enable us to devote our whole attention to those moral and material problems of the present and future which so loudly call for solution. The people will, if the Democratic leaders do not, appreciate the greatness and beneficence of the idea upon which the new order of things, the settlement we propose, rests—true and general self-government exercised in and through the States; States whose power moves independently in its appropriate sphere; potent in doing that which is right; impotent to abridge the rights of even the meanest of their people; and the protecting shield of the National authority thrown over all.

The transcendent greatness of this consummation the American people will appreciate and I trust they will take good care not to put the National power into the hands of any men or of any organization of men who still speak of overthrowing the great Constitutional amendments, the price of so much blood and anxiety and struggle, the only safe foundation for the future peace and glory of this Republic.

TO PRESIDENT GRANT

2020 F St., July 17, 1870.

Before leaving this city to take part in the political campaign, I should be happy to have a conversation with you about matters of importance to the Administration and the party to which we both belong.　Recent events,[1] which cannot fail to excite a deep and strong feeling among the German population of this country, have devolved an influence and duties and responsibilities upon me more comprehensive than any that had formerly fallen to my lot.　I have spoken about them to the Secretary of State, but I should be glad to communicate my views to you in person, for, if ever, it is desirable at this moment that there should be a fair understanding between the Administration and myself.

I am painfully sensible of the change which our personal relations have suffered in consequence of our differences on the San Domingo treaty.　I have reasons to believe that there has been much mischievous tale-bearing connected with this matter.　You have been informed as I understand, that I attacked you personally in the secret deliberations of the Senate.　Whoever may have carried that story to you, I pronounce it unqualifiedly untrue. I desire now to remove this erroneous impression, not as a man who has favors to seek, for that is not my condition— but as one who has great interests to serve.

[1] Especially the outbreak of the Franco-Prussian War.

When we had our first conversation about the San Domingo treaty, I told you frankly that I was opposed to it on conscientious grounds and would endeavor to defeat it. When the Senate had closed the first debate on the treaty, I beseeched you to drop the matter there; that advice sprang from patriotic motives, and subsequent events have demonstrated its judiciousness so clearly that I should not hesitate to repeat it. In fighting the treaty, I have used all the legitimate means of parliamentary warfare, and, looking back upon my conduct, I have nothing to conceal and nothing for which I should reproach myself. I fervently hope the question is disposed of not to arise again, for it is my sincere and earnest desire to support your Administration with what ability and influence I may possess.

This is the motive which impels me to write you this note and to ask you whether and when you will be kind enough to grant me a private interview.

May I hope for an answer at your earliest convenience? I intend to leave Washington on Tuesday, to address on Wednesday evening a large German mass-meeting at New York.[1]

ADDRESS TO THE PEOPLE OF MISSOURI[2]

Sept. 10, 1870.

In pursuance of a resolution passed at the Republican State convention, which organized at Jefferson City on the 2d of September, the undersigned submit to the voters of Missouri the following statements:

A large number of the delegates in the Radical State

---

[1] The request was promptly granted.

[2] This address of bolting Republicans appeared in full in the St. Louis *Democrat*, of Sept. 11, 1870. Schurz inclosed a clipping of it with his letter of Sept. 10, 1870, to Hamilton Fish and mentioned it in a postscript of Sept. 11th.

convention which assembled at Jefferson City on the 31st
of August, a number representing a considerable majority
of those who in 1868 voted for Grant, considered it their
duty to withdraw from that convention and to effect a
separate organization. Here are the circumstances and
reasons which compelled them to take that important step.

Every sensible man knows that the civil war is over, and
that the exigencies of a great public danger which brought
forth the necessity of exceptional measures for the salvation of the Republic and the protection of the loyal people,
have ceased to exist.

Every honest friend of republican institutions admits
that such exceptional measures as the exclusion of a large
number of citizens from the ballot-box and all participation in the functions of self-government can find justification only in the extreme case of imperative public
necessity.

Every faithful Republican will remember that the
Republican party, in its National and State platforms, has
solemnly pledged itself to remove those disqualifications
and disabilities as soon as the justification based upon
public danger should have disappeared.

We consider, and always have considered, that pledge
to be an honest pledge, and the Republican party in honor
bound to redeem it. No party can trifle with so solemn
an obligation without disgracing itself.

For a considerable time profound peace has reigned in
Missouri. The governor of the State, in his last annual
message, declared: "There is no county in the State
where organized resistance to the law exists, and where the
sheriff cannot procure a posse to aid in the execution of the
laws. The rights of person and property are as secure as
in any State of the Union." And Governor McClurg,
now the candidate of the advocates of continued proscription, cannot be suspected of any inclination to over-

state the matter. Everybody knows that the pacification of Missouri is complete. Under such circumstances, the Republican majority in the legislature resolved, by submitting to the people certain amendments to the State constitution, to give the people an opportunity to wipe out from the fundamental law of the State all proscriptive features and to make this a commonwealth of equal citizens. Those amendments are to be voted upon at the next election. Thus the issue is clearly placed before the people, demanding an answer, aye or no.

How can there be any doubt as to what that answer should be? Is the peace reigning in Missouri not an undeniable fact, as clear as sunlight? Is it not the obvious interest of all classes of society in the State that odious distinctions, calculated to keep alive the heartburnings of past conflicts, should without delay be abolished? Is it not time, at last, to open to all the prospect of a common future, so that all may devote their energies to the problems we have in common to solve? Is it not the imperative duty of all friends of Republican institutions to do away with proscriptive laws which must be condemned as unrepublican when unnecessary for the salvation of the Republic? Or can the Republican party afford to stand by without taking any position with regard to this important question? Is it not time for them to prove to the world that in establishing those disqualifications they were not actuated by feelings of hate or desires of revenge, but compelled by the necessities of the situation, and that after the cessation of those necessities, they are happy to show a spirit of peace and good-will to all men? Can the Republican party disregard its solemn pledge to that effect, as it stands recorded in its platforms, without shame and dishonor?

Indeed, it would seem under circumstances so plain, under obligations so solemn, no faithful Republican, no

good patriot could hesitate a moment to declare himself
emphatically in favor of the constitutional amendments.
What reason could there possibly be for putting off this
act of good faith, true patriotism and sound policy, to an
indefinite future, either by direct opposition or insidious
equivocation? And yet, such opposition was made and
organized by all the contrivances known to the art of
political trickery.

It is our duty to tell the plain truth. It so happens that
in some parts of the State the Radical party has fallen
under the control of politicians who desire to monopolize
the local offices, and who find themselves endangered in
the possession of the spoils by the removal of political
disabilities from those who might vote against them;
and those spoilsmen, together with a class of narrow-
minded persons, whose only political capital and wisdom
consist in the resentments and battle-cries of the past,
formed the scheme of maintaining their ascendancy at any
price. To this end the State convention of the Radical
party was to be packed and controlled, the passage of
any resolution favoring the adoption of the constitutional
amendments was to be prevented and the nomination for
the governorship of a man representing them to be secured.
And in order to pack and control that convention, means
were resorted to so outrageous as to be almost without
precedent in the history of political parties.

A basis of representation was invented dividing the
white and the colored voters into two distinct classes, and
to the colored voters, who had never exercised the right
of suffrage, a representation was given in the State convention at the rate of one delegate to ninety voters, while
the whites had to content themselves with a representation
at the rate of one delegate to one hundred and forty constituents. And measures were taken at the same time,
by all the appliances of demagogism, to unite the whole

33

colored element against the enfranchising amendments and in favor of the candidate of the proscriptionists. In vain did the chairman of the State central committee protest against this absurd and flagrantly unjust basis of representation; he was overruled.

But more than that. In thirty-four counties delegates to the State convention were surreptitiously appointed at meetings ostensibly called not for that purpose, but merely for the election of local committees, prior to any call of the State committee for the election of delegates, and thus the people of those counties were deprived of a fair expression of opinion. Finally, a number of counties were represented in the convention by proxies in the hands of single individuals, though no meetings whatever were held in such counties. And all this was done in the interest of the friends of continued proscription and of their candidate.

Those members of the convention who deemed it their duty to stand faithfully by the best interests of the State and the pledges of the Republican party—actuated by a spirit of moderation and forbearance—made several attempts to correct some of the outrages above enumerated. Twice a resolution was offered to put the representation of the colored voters upon an equal footing with that of the whites, and to secure the representation of men instead of the representation of bare acres—and twice that act of justice and fairness was denied. A fixed determination was clearly visible on the part of those who had planned and instigated those iniquities, to reap the whole benefit to be derived from them. Still we submitted.

But when finally, after a full debate, a resolution, declaring the time to have come when the solemn pledges of the Republican party should be redeemed by the adoption of the enfranchising amendments, was voted down, and a substitute was adopted, drafted and pro-

posed by the very men who openly declared their hostility
to the removal of political disabilities; and when thus the
maneuvers of the spoilsmen and proscriptionists had resulted in a decided triumph, then it was clear to us that, as
good citizens and faithful Republicans, we could no longer
sit in that convention, and that it was our solemn duty to
take our own honor and that of the Republican party into
our own hands; there was no other remedy left; for, as
Lieutenant-Governor Stanard, who after an ineffectual
attempt of his friends for reconciliation, turned away from
the rump-convention and came over to us, said with indignant emphasis: "We have worked with a determination to
create harmony, but we have failed; there was a party of
men who had such a greed for office, such a determination
to have the spoils, that they would not listen to reason."

Missourians: Having faithfully discharged our duty,
we confidently submit our conduct to the intelligent and
patriotic judgment of the people.   We are well aware that
our purposes will be unscrupulously misrepresented.   We
are already denounced as enemies of the Republican
party.   There is our platform; scrutinize it.   Is there one
iota of the great principles the Republican party fought
for given up?   Is there a single one of the great results of
the war compromised in the least?   Not one.   But we do
insist that the great pledge of the Republican party to
guarantee equal rights to all as soon as the public danger is
past must be kept sacred.   We do insist upon the honest
performance of our whole duty, while the proscriptionists
recoil from that part of it, the discharge of which may not
redound to their personal benefit.   Weigh the difference
and you will find that we are the consistent advocates of
the true Republican faith, and not they.

Look at our candidates.   Is there a single one whose
past conduct is not identified with the great achievements
of which the Republican party is so justly proud?   But,

faithful to the true Republican faith, there is not one among them who, for his personal advancement, would deprive any other human being of his rights.

Republicans, you are not exempt from the laws which govern political life. When a party once falls under the control of politicians who care more for spoils and plunder than for their plighted faith and the common good, or who are too narrow-minded to progress with the requirements of the new order of things, then it is time that such a party should pass through a process of purification. A party cannot live on the glory of its past achievements alone. It cannot quarter itself, like an idle and hungry pensioner, upon the public crib on the ground that it has once well deserved of the Republic. It must come up to the living exigencies and obligations of the present and the future, or it will go under. Every true Republican will, therefore, thank us for having been mindful of those obligations, for thus only we could save our great cause from disaster and disgrace.

We are accused of desiring the support of Democrats. We have abandoned no principle to secure it. But have not those of us who ever took an active part in political campaigns, always worked for the distinct purpose of convincing our opponents of the justice of our cause, and of inducing as many as possible of them to coöperate with us? Is not that one of the principal objects of every canvass? And if there are Democrats who now, when the whole Republican program, the establishment of the equal rights of *all*, is to be carried into effect, frankly recognize the great results of the civil war as accomplished and irreversible facts, and unite with us in promoting upon that basis the common welfare—is it not well that they should do so? Would any Republican be justified in telling them: You shall not work for the same ends with us? Nay, every sensible and patriotic man will say:

Welcome all who honestly mean to coöperate with us for the good of the country.

A word to the colored people. You have just been admitted to the exercise of political rights. It has cost a long and terrible struggle to break your chains. Your trials are not ended yet. For a long time yet you will have to contend against unjust and unreasonable, but stubborn, prejudices. And now, there are unscrupulous men who advise you, when you are to exercise the franchise for the first time, to use that franchise for the purpose of continuing the disfranchisement of others. Do you not see that such a course cannot fail to strengthen the prejudices which are still arrayed against you? If you are wise you will repel those who thus strive to seduce and make tools of you, as your most dangerous enemies, for it must be clear to every one of you that your rights can be secure only if no other class of citizens is deprived of the privileges which you enjoy. Your safety can be only in a perfect equality of rights. As your sincere and lifelong friends, we call upon you to aid in establishing it. We know that many of your race are already on our side. But if you understand your true interests you will make it manifest that the colored people *en masse, without exception*, cast their first ballots in favor of giving back the ballot to those who are now deprived of it. Only thus can you establish that fraternal feeling between you and all other classes of citizens, which is so essential to your welfare.

Fellow-citizens, in laying before you the reasons compelling us to refuse our acquiescence in the action of the convention which disregarded the great pledges of the Republican party, we do not mean to say that all those who remained in that convention were responsible for the faithlessness and trickery of the spoilsmen and proscriptionists who controlled it. We know of many well-meaning men who, although at heart convinced of the justness of our cause, permitted themselves to be kept there by the habit of party discipline. To them we would say that, if they mean to be consistent in the true sense of the term, they will take their stand with us; for the honor and the moral power and efficiency of a party go with its principles and pledges. As patriots they cannot remain neutral in this contest, and they can find no satisfaction in adhering to the mere empty shell of that organization from which the element of true moral power, the will and ability to do that which is needful for the peace and prosperity of the country, has departed.

The integrity of republican institutions is menaced by great abuses. Having in this instance the demoralizing influence of the spoils system once more clearly before our eyes, we were the first of the political organizations of this country to pronounce in favor of a thorough reform of the civil service, and we call for the support of all who desire to elevate our political life to a higher level of morality.

And now, having submitted this candid statement of our conduct and views to the people of Missouri, we appeal to their judgment and patriotism. Ours is the cause of reform, equal rights, peace and fraternal feeling, and we are confident that this cause will be triumphantly sustained by an intelligent and patriotic people.

CARL SCHURZ, Senator, and pres't of the convention.

E. O. STANARD, of St. Louis co., lieutenant-governor.

J. C. ORRICK, of St. Charles co., speaker house rep.

THOS. HARBINE, of Buchanan co., State senator.

H. G. MULLINS, member house of representatives.

TO HAMILTON FISH, SECRETARY OF STATE

ST. LOUIS, Sept. 10, 1870.

Your kind note of the 5th inst. has reached me and I thank you sincerely for it. It seems you have mis-

apprehended a little what I said of Mr. Matill [?].   The
idea was not to send him into Canada, but to employ him
in the State Department and to make it one of his duties
to carry on the confidential correspondence with parties
in Canada under your direction.   He informs me that he
has written a *mémoire* on the subject which he should be
glad to submit to you.   Will you be kind enough to permit
him to present himself to you at the Department?   You
will find in him a very able, substantial and useful man
who might be employed to advantage.

The telegraph informs us that the President has signified to the Prussian Government his willingness to serve
as a mediator between the belligerents in Europe.   Judging from the tone of the German press and all the indications which float on the surface, there seems to be
but little probability that the offer will be accepted.   I
am glad you disclaimed at the same time any intention
on the part of the United States, to take part in any
combination of neutral Powers for the purpose of bringing
about a settlement of the conflict.   From a purely American point of view I think it will be the best policy for us
to let the dénouement of that war take care of itself.
As to giving an expression to our moral sympathy with
the Republic as such—and in France it exists only in
name—Mr. Washburne has devoted himself to that in
his own way.   I fear he has created hopes which will be
doomed to disappointment; the men who have undertaken to revive the traditions of 1792—an impossible
task under existing circumstances—will be apt to catch
at straws and then abuse other people for leaving them in
the lurch, because the straws are not timbers.

One thing is settled now: Germany is destined to be
the great power of Europe, and it will be a very substantial
one.   There are no humbugs and shams about it.   It is
all solid and real from top to bottom.   And in spite of its

monarchical form of government it will also turn out to be the most progressive power, steadily progressive. And this Germany and the United States together will have to make the international law of the world. I expressed that opinion in public long before Sadowa, and now it must be apparent to every one who knows the two countries. They will find their interests to agree in all essential points, and before long they will, without pre-concert, meet in the pursuit of common objects, especially as far as the regulation of the trade of the world is con-cerned. We ought to keep this prospect in view in all our diplomatic doings.

Will you be in Washington during the latter part of this month? I may have to visit the capital on domestic business and should be very happy to have a good talk with you on a variety of subjects.

[P.S., Sept. 11th.] As to our bolt in Missouri, I send you our manifesto. It was a necessary thing.

TO MATTHEW H. CARPENTER[1]

St. Louis, Oct. 20, 1870.

I have just received your letter of the 17th inst., and sincerely regret to say that I cannot leave this State before election-day.

But your note has given me much pleasure. You do not seem to be aware that Grant has read me out of the Republican party and is vigorously at work chopping off the official heads of those who are suspected of sympathiz-ing with me. Under such circumstances I have to fight right here. Had not Grant given himself in Drake's keeping and interfered in our affairs, we "bolters" would

[1] Then Senator from Wis.

have swept almost the whole Republican party with us. But the President fighting us (and fighting against himself too), we have to work; for we not only want to carry the State, but to carry it heavily.

So you may thank Grant for it if I have no time to devote to the outside world. Oh, there is much wisdom in high places!

I send you a copy of our address and wish you would read it.

FROM B. GRATZ BROWN

St. Louis, Nov. 26, 1870.

Private.

My dear General: Mr. Preetorius showed me a letter to-day in which, after expressing some dissatisfaction with my "Serenade Speech," you intimated a desire that I would make another, addressed more especially to our Republican friends, in order to strengthen your position at Washington. This I will do most cheerfully, or anything else in my power to place you in your proper strength and attitude before the Senate. You, of course, can realize the reasons that drew forth those remarks, can understand and appreciate their full significance; but I should be very sorry to have you think that I would desire in any manner to embarrass you in the premises. So far from that, I, more perhaps than any one else, realize that in this great victory in Missouri you were the true hero, and that for our success we were more indebted to your prudence, sagacity and indomitable canvass than to all other causes combined. You led the way with skill and rare tact. And now if I can do anything to help you in the mortal duel you have in the Senate, I shall be only too glad to fulfil your wish.

Our victory was that of the right, of true Republican princi- ples [and] of nothing else, and if we in achieving it elevated the Democracy to our own platform and standpoint of equal freedom, it was so much the greater victory, and I felt disposed to compliment them [*sic*] on their elevation.   I do not know what '72 may have in store for us, but assuredly I have no intention of abandoning any of the principles of my lifetime for '72 or any other glittering prize.   Rest assured, my dear friend, that I value your coöperation and fellowship too much and appreciate your commanding talent too highly to permit anything to intervene between us that may look like an interruption of that harmony, even to yourself.   I, at least, shall be frank and square with you and put you to no disclaimers on my account.   Our fight was an open one: we know its issues; and have no reason to hide the light under a bushel.   It was for State reform, revenue reform and civil service reform, and we had the right to make those issues as Republicans.   If anybody denies it, let them try it on with you in the Senate of the United States and you will touch a responsive chord in the heart of the American people that will wake the sleepers from their apathy.   Trusting you may defeat this iniquity which has been visited upon Missouri by the Executive, I remain, Yours truly.

END OF VOLUME I